MW00831075

Mark O'Connor
Crossing Bridges

[Signed: Best wishes, Mark O'Connor]

Mark O'Connor
Crossing Bridges

*My Journey from Child Prodigy to
Fiddler Who Dared the World*

Mark O'Connor Musik International
P.O. Box 39470
Charlotte, NC 28278

The first Mark O'Connor Musik International hardcover and paperback editions published in 2023

Designed by Doug Regen

Portrait of the white-painted fiddle on the back cover is by Maggie O'Connor

Manufactured and printed in the United States of America

The Library of Congress has cataloged the hardcover and paperback editions as follows:

O'Connor, Mark, 1961— author
Crossing Bridges, My Journey from Child Prodigy to Fiddler
Who Dared the World / Mark O'Connor
Library of Congress Control Number: 2021921345

ISBN-978-1-7374500-1-6
ISBN-978-1-7374500-4-7

www.markoconnor.com

In memory of my mother Marty

"She was singing as sweet as a mockingbird in that Ford Econoline"

— Nanci Griffith

CONTENTS

PREFACE

Celebrating my 50th anniversary as a musical performer, composer, re-cording artist, competition-winner, sideman, session player, bandleader, educator and author, I have decided to tell the story of my life in music as a child—a unique American musical journey. There is much to say about the procession that brought me from touring child musician to having a relevant solo voice in contemporary music.

Although there are artists today who have used my example in music as their guide, I embarked on an odyssey as a child musician and went where few, if any, had gone before. From my start in the early 1970s, I had a propensity to go against the grain of conventional thinking—the heart and instincts of a musical rebel were there from the first notes I ever played on the fiddle. In my musical journey I have crossed bridges from old-time to rock, country to jazz, and bluegrass to classical, sometimes solely on the strength of my own willpower to assert my voice as a solo artist who was hearing something no one else had heard yet—on an instrument 400 years old and the most exalted of them all: the violin—the fiddle.

With extensive archives, some excellent record keeping beginning with my family's efforts, as well as a good memory for all things musical, I was able to articulate my history faithfully and authentically from my child-hood years. The tunes I learned and the pieces I composed, the musical styles and genres I helped to develop, and the projects I created with sig-nificant musical artists are at the heart of my story. The challenges of being on the road as a child, oftentimes on my own, and the dynamics of a dys-functional family attempting to manage a young musician's career, are the rest of that story.

My mother Marty O'Connor's splendid photography along with dates and descriptions of important events proved invaluable for fully disclosing my early years in music. From my childhood musical exploits throughout my professional career, extensive archival and audio field recordings were researched and digitized. A multifaceted collection of video and television footage, concert and recording session logs from the 1970s forward, and the many feature albums prepared with liner notes, further aided me in chronicling this story. For further coincidental reference, my entire life in music was covered by the press and music journalists—a preponderance of these newspaper and magazine clippings were archived starting at age 11 in 1973, when I first took the national stage. Finally, years of personal discussions with many key musicians, the very people who are a part of my story, were invoked and thoroughly considered for this book.

I set out to write my autobiography in collaboration with David McGee initially, an accomplished music writer, biographer, and music critic. We mapped out the important parts of my musical journey with detailed outlines of the technical intricacies and artistic accomplishments, and what contributions have been made. David (who titled this book) was the ideal writer to help me shape this commentary. His expertise lands in the areas of my own musical training and career: fiddling, bluegrass, country music, jazz, rock, and classical. He has interviewed me numerous times, more than any other music critic and journalist over the past 30 years, and knows my musical output thoroughly. David is the author of three acclaimed musician biographies: *Go, Cat, Go! The Life and Times of Carl Perkins, The King of Rockabilly, B.B. King: There Is Always One More Time,* and *Steve Earle: Fearless Heart, Outlaw Poet.* In addition to writing for *Rolling Stone* magazine for 25 years (1975-2000), David has been a contributing editor at *The Absolute Sound,* served on the original curatorial staff of the Rock and Roll Hall of Fame and Museum, and was the country music editor for Barnes & Noble. Since 2008, he has served as the founder/publisher/editor of the online publication *Deep Roots,* and has written album liner notes for Dr. John as well as reissues for Steve Goodman and the Chieftains.

For a subsequent portraiture of my story in music, I worked closely with distinguished music writer Michael Nelson. We were able to focus on what of my musically technical narrative is accessible to a general audience. Together we wrote a draft of my life in music from beginning to end.

These two laborious explorations, with good and knowledgeable writers on the key elements and prevailing substance of my music and career, led to a final effort. In due course, I brought our collective work back to this highly personalized accounting here. With devoted editing and proof-reading by David McGee, Carol Wilson, and the unending inspiration and support from my talented violin-playing wife, Maggie O'Connor, who also contributed to the editing, it finally was achieved.

II

My intersections with famous and legendary musicians began when I was very young. This is where the chain of events will start to unfold from the first chapter. You will gain insight into how I learned music, and finally, my creative process. You will also hear from professional music journalists covering developments as they happened. However, the accomplishments you will read about occupy a place of importance adjacent to the very human and emotional accounts of a young artist dealing with family and school life, navigating the years of music competitions, and a childhood on the road in professional bands breaking into the music business. Conforming to the status quo was always the last thing on my mind as I bucked the system, scraping my way to the top.

Beyond it, there is no embellishment to my story within these pages. No need to trim nor overstate. Given all of the many vicissitudes you will soon encounter, the narrative is entertaining, even thought-provoking, in its verity. There will be moments you'll likely find hilarious, other times doleful or troubling, some of the bits even shocking, but most of all, it is about a young musician who mines the will to succeed repeatedly, never taking no for an answer when it comes to the music—a road map to artistic inspiration.

This book represents the unvarnished truth of an American musical artist, and my struggle to find an acceptable place in a world full of orthodoxy and the matter-of-course in traditional music and the violin, at a time when those paradigms were ready to be put to the test. You will feel the sense of rapture in a young musician absorbing the devoted lessons from the musical legends, and the uncommon contempt by others throwing up all of the roadblocks they could, just to slow the kid down. You will come to know the gameness and the downright absurdities encountered as I took the fiddle all the way to the top of the music world.

*All persons named in the book are recognized by their real names. Those individuals who may not be public figures are referenced only by their first names.

CHAPTER ONE

THE GREAT TEACHER

I WAS A MERE BEGINNER BACK IN 1973, when the legendary Texas fiddler, Benny Thomasson, stopped to listen to me in the hallway of an Oregon schoolhouse as I warmed up on my tunes with an elderly blind guitarist from the area. At these local fiddle contests, Marshall Jackson enjoyed accompanying most anyone who asked. I glanced up to see Benny Thomasson coming down the long corridor, making his way toward us. I was practicing my contest round of three tunes: a hoedown, a waltz, and my tune of choice.

My first entrance in a fiddle contest was just a month earlier at the gold standard—the famed National Oldtime Fiddlers' Contest in Weiser, Idaho. My instructor, Barbara Lamb, a talented 14-year-old fiddler who was also living in Seattle, was teaching me very well and charging just $4 a lesson. Barbara was preparing me for the little kids division at Weiser: the "Junior-Juniors." This new division got going because a few youngsters in the Pacific Northwest wanted to fiddle. None of them, however, could be accomplished enough to compete against the older fiddlers. Barbara assured my mother that I could win one of the three prizes offered, but only if I practiced my rounds just as she was teaching me. Only three kids had entered the year before.

To aid in our collective effort, my mother, Marty, snuck my guitar away when I was at school. She learned to play rhythm guitar with a flat-pick all on her own, just so I could get better timing on the fiddle tunes I was learning. I was benefitting from the harmony and the counterpoint we created between the two instruments played together—a wise musical portrait to learn the violin. I could even find my pitches better when Mom added her chord changes. Mom had no experience playing instruments other than a couple years of piano lessons as a girl. She became quite good at guitar backup, even within a few weeks. Mom kept pace with me for a while, until she figured I was speeding on past her. Like lightning.

Barbara was right. At Weiser, I came out of there with a 2nd place trophy and $15. Most of all, we met a lot of wonderful people who would become our new friends in music. Folks there informed us about other Northwest fiddle contests we should go to that summer. We stumbled into a new world teeming with old-time fiddlers.

WHEN I WAS EIGHT, I saw Cajun fiddler Doug Kershaw on television: *The Johnny Cash Show*. That was in 1969. I was so excited by it that I begged for a fiddle for three whole years before I finally got one. My parents couldn't afford another instrument, they always told me. Disheartened, I attempted to make a fiddle out of cardboard, using crayons to color it brown. I used more colors for the inlays. My effort folded up on me when I tried to use my guitar strings on it. By age 11, Mom finally gave in and got me a $50 fiddle from Al Sanderson, an old fiddler from Sweden we discovered lived nearby. For the next couple of weeks, I fiddled Kershaw's "Louisiana Man" on just one string—pretty much non-stop. I played it with all four fingers, sliding up and down the neck in various positions to find the pitches. I could relate it to guitar fingering. As soon as we found a teacher, though, I started real lessons—with Barbara Lamb on October 28th, 1972. I was filled with so much joy and wonder over the fiddle.

Benny Thomasson's favorite fiddle student in Washington state was Loretta Brank. Just one year older than me, she was winning the little kids divisions in the area handily. She repeated her 1st place standing in the Junior-Juniors at Weiser the very first year I entered. Loretta had been playing a few more years than my seven months, and it showed. Her father Kenneth, originally from North Carolina, was an old-time fiddler himself. He was responsible for making sure there was at least a little bit of prize money for his daughter and the other kiddies at Weiser. The money could provide some good incentive for those little ones to practice, he rightly expected.

Well, in a flash I was in love. Loretta was so very pretty. I did admire how good she could play at her age, too. I think I looked forward to seeing Loretta at those first summer fiddle contests more than entering them. But I thought I was too young for her, and probably not good enough on the fiddle yet. After all, she was 12, and I was still 11.

I was also going through one of the many awkward phases I faced as a child. I had a very gentle look about me, with full lips. I wore braces, too.

That year, more than a few people mistook me for a girl, including some of the new kids at school. When the old-timers would approach my mother though, I cringed as they asked her, "How long has your little girl been playing the fiddle?" I had longish hair that Mom liked on me. For some quirky reason, she wanted my hair on the sides to be parted by my ears. That meant a whole chunk of hair in front of the ears. It was just so *dumb looking,* I thought. I argued with her about it, too, but she insisted; "Your ears should show."

That was such a wacky thing with her, and I absolutely hated it. But I was plagued by my own wacko things, like this odd phobia, an undiagnosed paranoia called *koumpounophobia*—the fear of buttons. In practical terms, this meant that I would not go near anything with buttons, such as button-down shirts. The jeans had to have a snap button. So, what I wore during those years were mostly turtlenecks and pullover zipper tops. I loved those zipper tops because the turtlenecks always made my neck feel scratchy in the summer. At the time, my mother refused to allow me to wear T-shirts or sweatshirts on stage or at school. None of this helped people figure out if I was a little boy or a little girl.

I have that same button phobia even today, as I write this at 61, although it is easily manageable now. I still think about it every time I button up, though—never feeling very comfortable with the act of buttoning shirts. Despite it, I eventually learned to associate buttons with getting dressed up for musical performances—something I love to do and needed to do. I still mostly wear T-shirts when I want to feel pleasant, but as a kid anything with buttons was 100 percent a no-go.

Another remnant I carry to this day is that I never go anywhere without a handkerchief. That all started back then too. I had severe summertime hay fever in the Northwest. My Mom actually wondered if I was simply *allergic* to Seattle… and I may have been allergic to it, as it turns out. Just when I wanted to say something to Loretta at a fiddle contest, I usually had to sneeze and blow my nose first.

I had so many social oddities, I spent most of that whole year turning red in the face from embarrassment—triggered by most anything you could imagine. Even my ears would turn bright red, especially when they were "showing." If someone looked my way, my entire face turned crimson, as if on cue.

m like the most promising child to take on a life in the en-
eld. I did wonder if I could ever get to a confidence level
w...   t turn red.

Meanwhile, my Dad was a raging, abusive alcoholic at home—so in truth, my button aversion, my appearance, and my blushing were the least of my problems.

Times were very tough financially for my family, and we had to watch every penny. My Dad was back home working at the lumber yard while we were at those fiddle events. My mother, Marty (she much preferred this nickname over her given name, Martha), my younger sister Michelle (by three-and-a-half years) and I, slept in the back of our old, black 1959 Chevrolet station wagon. There were no motels for us. Not ever.

With the same three kids from Weiser entered in the Oregon fiddle contest, even the $10 prize for 3rd place would more than pay for the tank of gas we used coming from our Mountlake Terrace home in Seattle's northern suburb.

There I was, warming up on my contest round of tunes Barbara had taught me. She had me playing real old-time tunes, too—hoedowns like "Boil 'em Cabbage Down," "Wake Up Susan," "Cripple Creek," "June Apple," and "Whiskey Before Breakfast." We coaxed her into teaching me "Jole Blon," the first Cajun song I heard Doug Kershaw play on the Johnny Cash show. Barbara was quite creative as a young fiddler, and came up with her own version of it for me to learn. Moreover, I was particularly drawn to the blues on the fiddle. In my rounds, I played the blues tunes she taught me for my *tunes of choice*—"Florida Blues," "Carroll County Blues," "East Tennessee Blues." Some of the older fiddlers remarked, "How did this young *gal* get the *blues* like that?" Yeah, right.

I KNEW WHAT BENNY THOMASSON looked like, though, and there was no mistaking him either. We had just seen him compete in the Open division at Weiser, and we saw him up close at a jam session one night at the Junior High "campground." At Weiser's main event, he was playing against several master fiddlers for the national championships, particularly a couple of previous winners, Herman Johnson and Dick Barrett. Their names were all brand new to us as we were immersing ourselves into this fiddling world. My heart skipped a beat when I saw Benny Thomasson

4

now standing just a few feet away, listening to *me*. I kept my head down and played my little tunes as best I could.

At age 64, Benny was slight in stature, and at 5' 2", no taller than my mother. Even so, his authority was one of a granite *monument*. We had been listening to him a lot, both on the Weiser jam tape I recorded on our new cassette machine, and from a couple of LPs of his we picked up at the contest. I just kept playing my tunes and tried not to look up for fear of making eye contact with him. Yes, I was painfully shy.

Benny began speaking to my mother about me as I continued playing. Mom knew what a legend he was, too, and she was aware that he had recently relocated to Washington state from his native Texas. After the conclusion of the fiddle contest in Cottage Grove, Oregon that evening, my mother recounted the conversation she had with the fiddling luminary:

"How long has he been playing?" Thomasson asked my Mom.

"For eight months," she replied.

Mr. Thomasson had only listened to me for a few minutes.

"I would like to teach him," Thomasson said.

"We are certain we couldn't afford your teaching fees," my mother responded. She added, "We just started lessons with John Burke in Seattle."

"That won't be a problem, I'll teach him for free," Benny declared.

Mom saw I was growing nervous about the exchange, but she promised me that she was very gracious to him. I was thankful at least that he didn't mistake me for a girl, like some of the old-time fiddlers did. "No, don't worry about that," Mom said. "We had a good conversation," she assured me.

With the fiddler, John Burke, taking over as my principal teacher, Mom didn't want to get too far ahead of ourselves as John was a local music celebrity in his own right. He specifically was working with me on *creativity* and *improvisation* already—how to improvise on tunes for both old-time and bluegrass music. It was, quite honestly, way over my head, but John saw a lot of potential in me for this direction. He was not at all into fiddle contests, though.

Mom was a realist, and she warned me, as her practical side materialized. "Mark, Mr. Thomasson lives way down near the Oregon border!", she pointed out. Mom continued retelling her earlier conversation with Benny Thomasson.

"That is so very kind of you Mr. Thomasson, but we can't really afford the gas for the three-hour drive to your home each week. Unfortunately, it is just too far away for us," Mom determined.

She continued;

"The only way we could attend this weekend's contest is that Mark here had a good chance at the 2nd place in the Junior-Junior division, since there were only three kids entered…" Mom finished justifying her assertion.

The Texas fiddle master paused for a moment, realizing the predicament he faced against someone who, unbowed by his stature, stood her ground. So Benny Thomasson put it on the line for her:

"If you can bring him to me in Kalama, there, where I live, you see, I'll teach the boy all day long."

Looking back to that day, it is simply unimaginable that Benny Thomasson saw so much in me already. Although I had five years of guitar—classical, flamenco, and folk—behind me, I was only eight months into learning fiddle. I was nowhere close to the skill level of his number one pupil, the young fiddler Loretta.

Maybe Thomasson detected a potentially creative attribute in a very young student as well? To offer us this chance of a lifetime, based on his singular foresight, was extraordinary to us.

In retrospect, Benny Thomasson did have a sixth sense about me, and this proclivity would continue to play out over time.

To study regularly for long hours with one of the greatest and most iconic fiddlers in the country was beyond our wildest dreams. Even at my young age, I was able to appreciate the magnitude of it. Mom continued to talk it over with me that evening on the drive back home.

"It would require a major commitment, Mark," she cautioned me.

"I know, I want to do this" I assured her.

MY LESSONS BEGAN RIGHT AWAY, structured for every other weekend as a way to budget both driving time and gas money. Mom, my sister Michelle, and I loaded up the black station wagon on that first Saturday and took off for the Oregon border.

Benny Thomasson's home was hard to find—a ways off the main road in Cowlitz County, Washington, surrounded by dark evergreen trees, and with the typical overcast dampness in the air. His trailer home was situated right on the Kalama River, with its occasional rapids flowing into the great Columbia. We suspected this was the small river rumored to be the main reason why Thomasson stayed in Washington—his fishing refuge was literally *the river out back.*

Mom nervously knocked on the door of the trailer house. We were about to see the legendary fiddler and his wife Bea in the comfort of their own home.

"Why don't you folks come on in," as Thomasson squinted towards the three of us from out the top of his bifocal glasses. I was surprised by his very thick and distinct southern drawl. Mom had not mentioned that part to me. Having never been to the South, I had never heard anybody speak like him before. I could barely make out some of his words. Mr. Thomasson asked us to just call him Benny— *"Benny's just fine, there."*

Benny and Bea had four grown children, along with many grandchildren, all living in the Arlington and Dallas area. Dale, their eldest, had moved to Washington state for a job in logging. After visiting their son in the Great Northwest, Benny liked both the weather and the fishing, so much so that they decided to put down some roots up there. As a consequence, though, Benny believed his days of playing the fiddle were mostly over.

Washington wasn't known as any hotbed of fiddling—not up until that point, at least. Certainly, there was a bit of an amateur scene that we were just learning about ourselves—through Barbara and through John. The local scene mostly consisted of the various state organizations and chapters of the old-time fiddlers, along with small fiddle contests around the Northwest, as well as "fiddle shows." Those fiddle shows were concerts where most any fiddler could sign up to play a couple of tunes. Anybody was welcome to it, even if you could barely play. So, I gained a lot of experience at the fiddle shows early on. Even Benny played at a few of them.

Benny received a lot more attention once the word got out there was a world champion fiddler living in the Northwest.

BENNY WAS POOR. From what it looked like, just as poor as us. For him to teach me for free, when he could be earning money teaching maybe several people during those multiple hours spent with me on Saturdays, was a bit mystifying. It seemed like such a sacrifice for him to take up all his time with an 11-year-old beginner, sometimes dedicating the entire weekend to me. But there we were, and Benny seemed happy. Bea was so very sweet to us, too.

Still, I was nothing to write home about on the fiddle at that juncture. I couldn't help but wonder what Bea was *really* thinking about all of this as she occasionally walked through the living area during our lesson.

Always sitting right there with us, Mom and Michelle watched the lessons. I think Mom was fairly entertained, because she could actually see me improve almost by the hour. As the months went by, I noticed that Bea came in from the other room more often, and would watch the lessons for stretches of time. She usually made fried chicken during our stay—an early Saturday dinner that was enjoyed by my family with great appreciation.

Principally, my fiddle lessons were on the Texas-style breakdowns for which he was known—the repertoire that made Benny Thomasson a fiddling legend. Obviously, we began with some of his easier repertoire, but I improved rapidly to catch up. We worked on many Texas fiddle tunes: "Leather Britches," "Apple Blossom," "Little Joe," "I Don't Love Nobody" (in the key of A). "Tennessee Wagoner," "Tug Boat," "Hell Amongst the Yearlings," "Wainsboro Reel," "Smith's Reel," "Clarinet Polka" (in G). "Cuckoo's Nest," "Snow Shoes," "Lost Indian," "Sally Growler," "Jack of Diamonds," "Ace of Spades."

My lessons started off lasting three or four hours—or about as long as an 11-, and soon after, 12-year-old had the attention span for. It was awe-inspiring just to watch Benny play, too.

Right off the bat, I wanted to have a bow arm like Benny's. His right-hand wrist was like liquid—it flowed so smoothly as he guided the bow over the strings, back and forth. He described his right-hand wrist as "pivoting" the bow. Benny said of his dexterous wrist, "It allows you to go on out, as you are coming back." He added, "It makes your timing better, too."

Technically, Benny was as good as any fiddler we had ever seen in person. Although his execution had slipped a bit as he aged, and especially, as a consequence of the hard life he'd lived—it all was still magnificent. Additionally, he had hearing problems. Benny blamed it on the years of pounding metal at his auto body shop in Texas. During our lessons, Bea wanted him to wear his hearing aid so he could hear my soft voice. But he really didn't want to use it. He didn't take to that hearing aid—no sir. He didn't like what it did to the sound of the fiddles. "Mark, speak up so he can hear you, dear," Bea occasionally suggested to me. I just had to learn to speak a little louder when I talked to Benny.

Once in a while, Benny would misstep and play with a collapsed left wrist, but he might catch himself, too, and remind me to keep the nice left-hand setup Barbara gave me. Be that as it may, I wanted the *right-hand* of his—*that* bow arm. I did about everything I could think of to emulate it.

I thought up an exercise drill I did back at home. My neck and shoulder held the fiddle up in the air, just like they should. As I bowed the fiddle, playing string-crosses back and forth, my left-hand comes around to grab my right forearm, holding it as still as I could. I tried not to allow the arm to move at all, held it real tight. While I continued to bow the various strings of the fiddle, this made the right-hand wrist work much harder in positioning the bow to play all of the strings. This exercise built up the muscle strength and flexibility of my bowing hand and bow grip. *The things that kids come up with…* but in no time, it worked. Given proximity to him, Benny had the best bow arm of any fiddler. It was hypnotic. I got to focus on it all of those hours, each lesson, every other weekend.

It was Benny's Texas-style fiddle breakdowns that the lessons were really about, however. Those tunes were longer-formed musical pieces that he created from two-part hoedowns, or just little toss-away ditties. He taught me by ear. *Call and response.* Benny played the first phrase slowed way down, and I would observe what he was doing and do my best to emulate it and play it back to him, usually with his preferred bowings, if he could choose one to go with, as there was much variation in them. If it was a more technically difficult section, or a musical idea that wasn't at all similar to anything we had covered before, maybe it would be just four or five notes, deconstructing it, where I could study and replicate it on the spot.

Once through an "A" part of a tune, typically the first eight measures, we would reexamine it phrase by phrase. Any bowing patterns might become more obvious, but his unique and unusual bowings could remain a big challenge to assimilate. Then we reviewed it in longer chunks—until we had the whole part in a slow tempo, gradually putting it together bit by bit. Once I had the notes more comfortably under my fingers, then we could put it closer to tempo, and get into the musical expression and rhythm feel of the music—where to accent and how to shape the phrases. As importantly, this exercise of acquiring techniques, along with the notes, was made to be a creative process as well. I was learning how Benny constructed the music by his own course of self-editing in real time. He distilled the phrases for me to learn from the several options he could have given me. Benny oftentimes demonstrated a few possibilities before he chose the one for us to work on.

His was extraordinary music, and most anybody who heard him play it understood that. I always assumed that *breakdown* simply meant a hoedown, but with much more development. *(I still believe it to be the case)*. The power of Benny's breakdowns resonated to every other fiddler, even if those fiddlers could not begin to approach this style of playing. Benny's Texas-style fiddling is a distinctive musical form, and in the early '70s, it was not widely known outside of Texas—not nearly as much as other popular styles of fiddling—old-time, bluegrass, country, and even Canadian.

I was desperately trying to get good enough to dive into the longer breakdowns, too—his tunes with several parts to them. More development—the little masterpieces. As the lessons continued, it was going to be all about the breakdowns; however, there were other, more straightforward Texas tunes I needed to learn first. Simpler two-part hoedowns and other various old dance styles: "Wild John," "Speed The Plow," "Cattle in the Cane," "Shuckin' the Bush," "Paddy on the Turnpike," "Brownskin Gal," "Twinkle, Twinkle Little Stars" (the old show tune, originally a Schottische). There were ragtime tunes and polkas: "Black and White Rag," "Cotton Patch Rag," "Allentown Polka," "Jessie Polka (a well-known Mexican tune)." The hornpipes, too: "Fishers," "Herman's," "Golden Eagle," "Durange's," "Liverpool," "Nimrod's," "Ostinelli's."

I didn't learn more than a couple of waltzes from Benny in all—"Kelly Waltz" was one, although he knew many, and had great renditions of them. I learned waltzes on my own, mostly from recordings on the turntable back at home. They were easier to pick off the tape by ear.

There was a very real outlet for this kind of music I was learning—at the fiddle shows, the fiddle jam sessions we attended, and most importantly, the place where it all came together—the fiddle contests.

One day, Benny grabbed a dusty old reel-to-reel tape machine from the closet, and he threaded a reel of tape across the open player head. We were about to hear a recording of Benny from the early 1950s. He wanted us to hear him in his prime—his best playing was never fully documented on a professionally released LP. The tape recording we listened to was made at an old Texas fiddle contest.

The first thing heard on the tape was the announcer bringing Benny onto the stage. As Benny began to play, you could tell right away that his fiddling was plain out of this world. It was powerful, fast and clean, with clear tone and intonation. His renditions of those Texas breakdowns just soared.

All the ruckus from the emcee, Benny explained, was about performing "Sally Goodin'"so smoothly. With such resonance and ease, it sounded like he was playing the previously cross-tuned (re-tuned) version by Eck Robertson, Benny's teacher. But Benny had it in standard tuning all along. Cross-tuning the fiddle was barred in the contests.

Finally, my next lesson was on "Sally Goodin'." It was very difficult for my left hand to make all of the fingerings, so much so that I felt like my fourth finger was going to go dead and fall off. It was one of the few times when I challenged Benny over why I had to learn something of his. I tried to demonstrate that I could just play it on a single string without the unison double-stop, and still play all of the pitched notes required. Benny responded emphatically, "Mark, you want to pull that tension right into the pitch there to make an expression, you see. It puts a highpoint in it."

Speaking in the vernacular, Benny carefully guided me into being an authentic fiddler tune by tune. I was learning about musical expression and musical language from the master fiddler.

Unfortunately, I never got to hear that tape again. But I remember distinctly the emcee yelling into the microphone loudly while Benny was playing in the contest—

"He's too good!"

"Get him off the stage!"
"Nobody can play like that…!"
—and indeed nobody can.

Liner Notes Adapted from the Album *Heroes* (1993) by Mark O'Connor

"In 1909, Benny Thomasson was born fourth or so in line of thirteen children in Winters, Texas, just south of Abilene. Both his grandfather and father were contest fiddlers in the 1800s. When Benny was five, his father, Luke, let him pull his good fiddle out and rest the scroll on the edge of the bed while he figured out how to play it. A talent scout saw nine-year-old Benny and wanted to take him back East for formal training, but Benny was needed too badly on the farm.

At 19, thinking he was playing the fiddle pretty darn well, Benny entered a big contest against hundreds of Texas fiddlers. He was perplexed when he came out somewhere near 60th place. He thought technically he was playing fairly accurate, so he decided the old tunes needed to be "rounded out and smoothed up." This marks the onset of the most significant contribution to American fiddling. He took old, simplistic fiddle tunes with two parts termed sectional binary forms, and reconstructed them into musical masterpieces. He did this on his own, being almost completely self-taught.

Benny composed variations of traditional tunes, sometimes even adding additional parts, utilizing virtuosic displays. At the same time, he furthered greatly the intellectual content of the music. He did this with tune after tune. As the development of Benny's fiddle tunes became more and more intricate, a brand new style was created. It was called "Texas-style fiddling."

Benny met a gal named Bea in Sisco, who he married in 1928 when she was just 14. She was enamored with Benny's talent and went everywhere with him. He mostly played at weekend dances, and for a while did a Saturday morning radio show in Dublin, Texas, with the Star Tire Boys. Benny and Bea waited seven years to have their first of four children. Dale was born in 1935, Jerry came along in 1940, Eddy in 1944, and Connie in 1947.

Benny started winning the state championships every year, taking home the top prize about 15 times. From 1955-57 he became the World Champion by winning three years in a row in Crockett, Texas. News of his immense talent spread. The biggest Western Swing bandleaders, Bob Wills and Spade Cooley, both offered him permanent positions, and Columbia Records wanted to record him. Hollywood even wanted him to appear in the movies with Gene Autry, but he turned it all down. His reasons were simple. He thought that his kids "wouldn't have been worth killin'" if he'd left home to go on the road.

During all those years, Benny worked in an auto body shop. Around 1956, he traded a paint job for a Gibson tenor guitar and gave it to his son, Jerry. He and his oldest brother, Dale, along with Benny's young protégé, Texas

Shorty, usually played rhythm accompaniment for Benny at the contests. But by the 1960s he was playing less and less. His hearing started to go and the hard work at the body shop along with his drinking, began to take its toll. County Records recorded and released a couple of albums on him in the late 60s, but it was well past his prime as far as technical precision was concerned. To hear him at his best, one would have to listen to home recordings made during the 1950s, when the fiddle playing really was quite beyond belief."

ME BEING SO YOUNG for the rigors of multiple hours of intense, expert instruction, Benny thought we should break it up a little by going outside for *his* favorite pastime — fishing in the river out back of his trailer. After several occasions at the river with Benny, you could say I was not the young fisherman-type that he hoped I'd be. I truly didn't want to disappoint him, though. Once, when I wasn't getting any bites at all, and incessantly fussing over my tackle, Benny reckoned what might be going on. "I suppose you want to head back in and work on those breakdowns some more, don't you son?" Benny looked over at me as he sized up the situation. I smiled and nodded "yes." "Okay. Let's finish up here and get back inside."

It became obvious to Mom and me over the next few months that Benny created the majority of the Texas-style fiddle repertoire. We knew he was a legend, but it was reinforced by his own creative contributions to fiddling. As each tune unfolded, Benny showed me how he crafted his version from the original two-part phrases, then how he used these sturdy foundations as the base for his own intricate constructions. This was *his* Texas-style. He more than helped create this genre in the 1930s and 40s, with very few exceptions, Benny *owned* it. Creatively, he was a Bach-like force in American fiddle music. I was soaking it all up like a sponge — as his new protégé.

My lessons were far different than the lessons Loretta was getting. With her, they largely remained a conventional length. To varying degrees, Benny created intermediate versions of his tunes for a few of his other students to learn, and in turn, they replicated them in the contests and fiddle shows. For me, our lessons proceeded to be more about musical invention. He was challenging me to be a young innovator.

Benny was insistent on this uncustomary approach for a music lesson, even if I was a beginner, or by this time, an intermediate. He was pushing me to be creative, like how he saw himself. Benny wanted me to come up with my own versions of those breakdowns he was showing me.

The conversation at the outset between Benny and my previous teacher, John Burke, may have promoted this idea as well. Now that I was taking lessons from such a legendary player, notwithstanding his predisposition for this fresh approach, I didn't care as much about the improvisation part of it anymore. I just wanted to play the fiddle tunes as Benny played them. I couldn't imagine them any better than that.

Nevertheless, Benny would not allow me to play his own renditions of the breakdowns exclusively. With each tune, the process was learning the way *he* played it first, immediately followed by him challenging me to "make it better," as he put it. He didn't mean for me to improvise on those as much as me forming my own variations and developing my own renditions. I never fully embraced his "making it better" petitions, but I did end up making the tunes different, at least. He seemed to really enjoy having me arrange the variations on my own, too—like homework. For a good portion of my next lesson, Benny analyzed what I came up with, and he "smoothed up" (his term) the musical ideas with me.

Benny's approach was ostensibly the genius of his plan from start to finish. He must have liked this kind of work, and looked for a likely candidate to carry out his exercise. As time would tell, I was able to answer the call. He taught me his tunes; I brought him materials I generated from them, and then he showed me why some of it worked, and how others could be improved upon. In no time, *musical creativity* was our master plan together.

CHAPTER TWO

MUSICAL INSTRUMENTS EVERYWHERE

IF MUSICAL CREATIVITY INCLUDED playing a bunch of instruments, I was all in. By age 11, I had turned in my classical guitar for a Yamaha Hummingbird steel-string guitar to play bluegrass on, ultimately taking lessons from the best bluegrass guitarist in the Northwest, Tacoma's Dudley Hill. An enchanting and winsome man of 25, with shoulder-length hair, Dudley accompanied Benny at Weiser that year—the combination of them playing together was electrifying, both musically and visually.

As if I didn't have enough going on, I began to take both old-time and bluegrass banjo from Seattle's Craig Keene, a young boho who dressed like he was from the hills of Tennessee. Yes, for a few months, we were caught up in the "which one is better" argument: bluegrass three-finger banjo or old-time clawhammer banjo? So I learned to do both at the same time, splitting those lessons in two. We found a Japanese model Ventura banjo with a removeable resonator to turn it into an open-back. This way I could handle both styles with one banjo.

We even found an old 1920s dobro that was repainted all black. The dobro was how my mother became good friends with a local music shop owner, Sue Blood. Sue was also a dobroist just starting out, but she spoke in lofty ways—effusive about the future of bluegrass music in our area. She was excited to meet a kid dobro enthusiast and young bluegrass student like me, even if it was for her own self-devotion and favor. She set up a bluegrass jam date for me with another youngster, Dick Ahrens, a Mexican-American student from nearby Shorecrest High School, who had been to the music shop recently. In no time, Dick and I became nearly inseparable as a duo—my guitar and his banjo. Such a fun-loving guy, as sweet a young fellow as I could ever come across. We picked together in most any setting you could dream up, from jamming around our homes and learning tunes off LPs together, to playing at local jam sessions, fiddle shows, trying to impress shoppers at the local mall for tips, to playing at my Grandma's Amaranth Club. Our highlight that year was getting scheduled on a small outdoor bluegrass stage at the Seattle Center Folk Life Festival, which we considered the big time. We always had a ball. Dick was 17 and I was still 11.

During that same time period, I began playing guitar in a Carter Family-inspired duo with an older man, autoharpist Dick Dice. He was a schoolmarmish devotee of all things A.P. Carter, as well as old-time music from the early 20th century. Dice lined up a series of Seattle libraries for us to play shows, sponsored by the King County Arts Commission. Quite a serious person, he was ambitious with this project. Dice wanted to cover at least 90 minutes' worth of Carter Family songs. Each library would pay us $25 each. He insisted that we earn the same amount of money. I learned many of the songs directly from him, while others I picked up on my own off Carter Family recordings from the 1920s and '30s. I was steeped in this kind of old-time country music at an early age. I played Mother Maybelle's style with a thumb on the low strings of the guitar, and used my first finger to strum down and up on my nylon-string, before I moved to steel-string.

On August 24th – 26th of 1973, Sue Blood proved herself pre-eminently ambitious herself, by any measure. She was to spend all of her money — and then some — producing the first bluegrass festival in the Northwest. The very first bluegrass festival in the U.S. had taken place just eight years earlier in Fincastle, Virginia. Sue's Northwest version was going to be held in a dome-shaped, 2,000-seat arena in Woodinville, Washington. Even though she was looking at the summer months for this event, Sue knew she couldn't fend off the untiring Seattle rain for an entire weekend. The festival spot was located just 15 minutes from our house in Mountlake Terrace.

Bluegrass stars, who happened to be among my new favorite musicians on LPs, were booked at this festival. Some of them were performing in the Northwest for the first time. The lineup included a man who was already well-documented in our growing record collection — my new fiddle hero Vassar Clements. Likewise, another musical hero, my favorite guitar flat-picker Norman Blake, and dobroist Tut Taylor. Sue made sure she had a major dobro player on the roster. Also scheduled were banjoist Butch Robbins, who was soon to take a job with Bill Monroe, but currently was the bassist with Newgrass Revival, and mandolinist Buck White and the Down

Home Folks. All of these professional bluegrass musicians would come to have a far-reaching impact on my musical life very soon.

The Gold Creek Bluegrass Festival in Woodinville also staged competitions in various bluegrass instrument categories. There weren't any kid's divisions like they had at Weiser, so Sue insisted that my Mom enter me in the adult competitions. Sue's headlining artists from Nashville were among the assemblage of judges for the various categories. I signed up to enter on three instruments: fiddle, guitar and banjo.

To our astonishment, I did incredibly well in the contests. It was impossible to conceive of my success in reaching the finals at this festival, and at this stage of my development in bluegrass music. I barely knew enough banjo tunes to play the two rounds in the competition. One of my banjo tunes was "John Hardy," another was "Rueben." Of course, after taking five years of classical/flamenco/folk guitar, I could plainly move my right-hand fingers back and forth across some strings. It had to have helped me.

Before all the fiddle and bluegrass music came along, my mother entered me in the Metro Music Contest at the University of Washington's classical guitar competition when I was 10. There weren't any little kids in this competition either, so I was up against the college students. I won a gold plaque and a silver plaque—the only double entry for the day. The gold plaque was for the folk guitar category, where I played some Johnny Cash to win. To get the silver, I didn't even play the classical piece I learned from my wonderful and brainy classical guitar teacher Calvin Crist, the first person to graduate from this very same university with a degree in guitar. Instead, I played Flamenco in the classical guitar division—rasqeados and golpes (strums and finger tap). It was a piece I learned from my exciting Flamenco guitar teacher, Normando Brenis, who grew up in Peru and came from a big Latin music family. A delighter and executant himself, Normando taught me by ear. Folk music. Some of my most cherished memories from pre-bluegrass times are the guitar duos that Normando and I played at my lessons when I was nine: "Farruca," "Alegrias," "Tanguillo," "Sevillanas."

In all those years of classical guitar lessons with Calvin Crist, the one thing that sticks out the most to me was when I brought my Johnny Cash album to my lesson, hoping to have Mr. Crist listen to a small section of one of the songs. I wanted him to tell me what instrument it was, first of all. I believed it was a guitar, but he said it was really a banjo I was hearing. By then, I was singing and playing lots of Cash songs: "Folsom Prison Blues," "Hey Porter," "Pickin' Time," "I Walk The Line" (boy, I wanted a lower voice for that one), and even "Sunday Morning Coming Down." Mom helped me transcribe those lyrics. When I asked her what "stoned" meant, (a lyric of the song), she answered, "Being drunk."

Mr. Crist placed the LP on the turntable in his teaching studio, then I showed him where to set the needle down to find the little solo I liked. When he listened to it, a smile came across his face, because he knew it was something I really wanted to learn. He offered to transcribe those few measures for me right there on the spot. He said it would just take him five minutes. Watching him do that, I was in awe. He reset the needle a few times until he had it and handed me the piece of sheet music to take home.

It was so empowering that I had an *idea* about something to do with music, and that my teacher *wanted* to hear me out on it. I remember this moment like it was yesterday. To think how many times I was about to set that phonograph needle down on LPs in the very same way, learning and transcribing music… That number would probably boggle the mind.

Playing Flamenco ("Farruca") in the classical division? Well, I was hatched a musical rebel from the start. This was becoming obvious. And yes, the college kids were a little taken aback by it all. For the folk category, I sang and fingerpicked… and ran away with it: "The One on the Right, is on the Left."

At the Woodinville festival competitions, I captured 1st place in the guitar division, 3rd place in the fiddle category, and for the head-snapper of the day – 2nd place in banjo. Mom and I were truly in disbelief. All of those adult bluegrass musicians from around the Northwest were bested by a kid barely 12, who had been playing this kind of music for under a year.

Those extraordinary results earned me the Festival's Grand Prize. That meant an A-model Givens mandolin which Tut Taylor presented to me onstage. As he handed me the mandolin, Tut grabbed his own mandolin and we played a tune together for the crowd on, "Oh Them Golden Slippers." I barely got through it, as I didn't know how to play mandolin at all. Goodness gracious, did I ever ascend with "them golden slippers" anyway.

Both Sue and Mom were ecstatic over my successes. We just couldn't fully comprehend the weight of what happened to a little boy that weekend.

I now had a mandolin to add to my collection of bluegrass instruments. Mandolins seemed to be the most expensive of all, for some reason.

Yes, it would be hard to top that in the life of a child musician.

IT'S A GOOD THING THERE were more "good weekends" coming, because we had a sizeable issue unfolding with our family, and it very much threatened my budding musical progress. My dad, Larry, (he also answered to Lawrence), worked two labor jobs to make ends meet that year, yet he still struggled to pay the bills. One of his jobs was at a lumber yard, punching out at four o'clock each afternoon. His second was repairing old house foundations until dinnertime. Without any daylight, a lone light bulb attached at the end of a long electrical cord empowered him to work up until eight o'clock at night during winter months, and he did. As I turned 12, the little bit of money I picked up from playing with Dick Dice at the libraries, the busking we did with Dick Ahrens, and entering a few small contests, all paid for my music lessons and for my inexpensive $50 instruments. But it wasn't helping out with the household bills.

My Dad worked very hard. His work ethic was rather merciless, something quite apart from his being a difficult man in the grip of raging, unchecked alcoholism. Coming from the hard life of ranching in Montana at the age of five, as he describes it, his first job was "picking rocks" for his own dad and his older brothers who mistreated him. The stories of what happened to his family back on the ranch were quite dreadful, and what happened to him as young boy in some of those stories was far worse. By the time *he* was 12, Dad had dropped out of school, taking along with him a 7th grade education. While shown the door to the family house where his many sisters and mother remained, he continued to work on the family ranch. Dad lived with the older ranch hands as a little kid. He was the 12th out of 14 children.

Not fully appreciating the difference of a generation gone by, and especially, the appalling conditions of his own childhood, Dad confirmed that I should get ready to work labor with him after school as soon as I turned 12. He thought it was the age when I would have the right muscle development needed to assist him in his labor.

Dad was certainly impressed with my musical development. Although, he had not met Benny personally, he seemed happy with that developing relationship. Practicing for the Woodinville music competitions bought me a couple of weeks of time as my birthday came around, and by his standards, ready for his proposed plans for me.

Lawrence O'Connor wasn't free from his own artistic pursuits, either. Once upon a time, he started his adult life by being a pretty good dancer. In the 1950s, he taught ballroom dance at Arthur Murray's alongside my mother. The dance floor is where they met, and I daresay he swept Mom off her feet. That's what folks told me, I think, or at least my Dad told me. The rock 'n' roll generation of Elvis Presley and Chuck Berry steamrolling in, however, was about the worst thing that could happen to any ballroom dancing class enrollment.

Unable to sustain their positions, Lawrence and Marty left the well-known chain of dance studios to run their own in San Rafael, California. They specialized in West Coast Swing, Mambo, Cha Cha… but customers were still hard to come by. Soon, both of their aspirations for a life in the dance world sadly fizzled out. Mom always claimed that the "dancing part" for her, was ancient history. However, their misstep in the dance profession left my father heartbroken and bitter.

So, he went to work in lumber yards, and Mom, after giving birth to me in 1961, became a homemaker, as she identified herself. In his most reasoned composure, Dad could tell us about Mom being the best dancer he had ever seen. Occasionally, he tried to get her to dance with him in the ensuing years, but she never did—she refused to do it. Dancing was the only reason they were ever attracted to each other in the first place, but in the end, *never* dancing again was what drove an implacable wedge between them.

Mom wanted her kids to do all the dancing instead. Michelle and I were enrolled in ballet class at an early age. After complaining about being the only boy in the entire class, Mom transferred me to a Balkan dance program called Koleda. I would dance to a fiddler playing Balkan tunes for performances.

We had big fuzzy hats and wore sashes around our waist so the kids could hang on to each other with our arms interlocked—creating a "chain" or line formation across the dance floor. I was the second smallest, so my place in the line was second from the end. My little blonde-headed buddy was positioned at the very end of our snake-like whips which the bigger kids directed from the front of the line. Consequently, we were slung so swiftly back and forth, I could barely hold onto his sash and keep him from flying across the dance floor. Led by our teacher Dennis Boxell, we got to perform at the Seattle Opera House alongside the adult troupe. I was called on to perform the Slavic "squat-and-kick" dances with some other boys.

While Michelle remained in her ballet classes, I abandoned dance altogether when fiddling and bluegrass came along. My little friend who was the smallest kid at the end of the whip was named Mark, too. He went on to be one of the most recognized dance choreographers in the world: Mark Morris of the Mark Morris Dance Group.

Mom confronted my Dad about the fact that if I was working labor with him for three or four hours after school each day, "there would be no time for practicing the instruments!" But Dad would hear nothing of it. I was cheap labor for him. Or more explicitly, free *child labor.* My mother was very worried, and confessed to me that she didn't know if she could stop this from happening. I had nightmares about it, too. Dad often came back home at night telling stories of crawling under houses in the dark with the rats and the snakes.

When I won the mandolin Grand Prize at Woodinville, I think it actually bought my freedom—I believe it really did—at least for a while. The $75 cash meant I made as much money as my father that weekend. I had plenty of incentive to get good enough to win more music contests after that, and start winning them right away. I was already practicing five instruments for up to ten hours a day on the weekends—four or five hours on school days when I could. I had to prove to Dad that I needed to practice all those hours after school so I could enter more competitions, and *steer clear of the rats and snakes.* Things began to transform in my new little music world—rather dramatically.

THINGS ALSO BEGAN TO CHANGE dramatically at school, and not for the best. I was in my first year at Mountlake Terrace Junior High as a 7th grader. Terrace was a rough school, mostly all white kids with just a few Eskimo students and even less black and Hispanic students.

The angry, unhappy white adolescents were the central problem, with fist-fights breaking out everywhere. The memory of walking into the cafeteria for lunch with non-ending food fights wherever you looked, will always stay with me. I was so confused by how much food was knowingly wasted each day—all over the floor. At home, I was told to lick my plate clean. Dad would demand it. "We don't want to waste a single crumb," he scolded. It is why I can't stand tomato juice and dill pickles to this day. He made me finish consuming both after I had started eating, and after I realized I didn't like the taste of either. After that, my dislike was permanent. To go from my newfound, blissful music world to a marginal public school atmosphere with all the little heathen schoolmates was soul crushing.

There was a specific place for organized after-school fistfights. Most all of them took place down the overgrown grassy ravine by the side of the school, and just before you get to the tree line. It seemed like it was conceived as some sort of outdoor Greek amphitheater years before, maybe for an acoustic assembly of some kind. The shape of the ravine was uniform—the flat area down at the bottom where the fights took place was perfectly molded for a platform and stage. Rumor was there used to be actual music concerts held there, in a previous time. Acoustic concerts? The ravine had an eerie quality about it, a remnant of my home town from before. Nevertheless, the slopes of the gorge provided a decent vantage point to take in the fight action.

I was lured into one or two fistfights myself at the ravine. Luckily, mine didn't escalate very far—they were usually against fellow dorks, and were considered a big disappointment, although schoolmates were egging us on for more. Some school kids talked to me afterwards, specifically about carrying a switchblade so I could protect myself better. They offered their own demonstrations of how to handle one.

My Dad was a real tough guy, though. During that same time span, he carried a big, heavy log chain across his shoulder, even while inside the house. When he sat down at the kitchen table with his pad and pencil to figure job bids and supplies, he would finally take the log chain from his shoulder and place it on the chair next to him. He didn't want to talk much about it, only that he feared a knock on the door from a man he had a run-in with at work. "If he comes to the door, are you actually going to take this guy on with that log chain?" I exclaimed. "What if he has a gun?" "Don't be stupid," Dad replied. "He won't have a gun."

There were fights in that ravine nearly every day. Sometimes the boys would get their Dads angry enough at their schoolmate foes so they might attend the fights to cheer from the sidelines. One day, there was a double fight, if you will—two kids and their two Dads going at it. I definitely couldn't stomach that one, and nervously moseyed on past to go home. As I walked away from the school ravine that day, I looked up to the gray Seattle sky, and *prayed* I could find a way out of there, a big duck-shove out of this Hell—an escape from these contemptible circumstances I was forced to live in.

I got kicked out of physical education that year. I was not able to perform the *ten* revolutions of "fingertip pushups" which were mandatory in our daily calisthenics routine. I thought my long, slender, music-playing fingers were literally going to break in two. I couldn't even get through the first pushup. Mom tried to talk to Mr. Mann about it—that I was a child musician and was performing shows already… he could have cared less. So I was expelled from PE.

While I had played a couple of music shows at school assemblies in elementary (I screamed that train sound like Johnny Cash did in "Folsom Prison Blues," prompting the kids to mimic me while I was trying to finish the song, and it didn't help things much when I covered his "A Boy Named Sue" next), I made up my mind I would never play music at school again, especially not at the junior high. I never took an instrument to school a single time, out of my own resentment and because I truly didn't believe I would survive the resentment of others—from both the school kids *and* the teachers.

SITTING IN WITH A FEW local county and western bands in private clubs was where I played instead. I remember Them Cotton Pickin' Ridge Runners at one club were great old guys and very supportive of me and Mom. Other situations were more dubious; for example, the real hard-core country bar bands playing gigs at places like the Moose Lodge and the Elks Lodge. One of my Dad's work friends belonged to a lodge, and arranged for me to play a few tunes with the country band in for that week. It was exciting, playing with a full country and western band, with steel guitar and drums. Being the little boy fiddler, I got a lot of attention from the clientele that night.

A man began to talk with my parents about me while I was still playing up on stage. He professed himself to be a pop singer and entertainer with a record deal in Los Angeles. He had a recent hit on the radio—top 20, he told us. It had crossed over to country. This pop entertainer decided he wanted me to play on his next recording in Hollywood. It set in motion a series of phone calls between the pop entertainer and me, mostly talking about music and what we would do together at his recording session. I had never stepped foot inside a recording studio, so I suppose Mom and I had stars in our eyes. Could this be our big break?

He called a few more times, telling me how he planned to arrange for Mom and me to fly down to Los Angeles for his recording. We were trying to figure out what we were going to do with my little sister if that were to happen. Surely he wouldn't fly all three of us down? In the meantime, the pop entertainer was trying to line up a rehearsal. He asked me where I usually liked to rehearse. I told him I mainly rehearsed either at my house or in other musician's houses.

Our very small living room was fairly cramped for rehearsing, but we managed. We had a couch against the front window, a small black and white TV set, a phonograph console, and Dad's big black leather chair. The chair took up about a third of the living room. Dad was never home until later at night, so the big black leather chair is where I usually hung out. This is where I talked on the phone, too—our white rotary dial telephone was placed on the gold-colored shag carpet right between the big chair and the couch. Then the call came to put all of his plans in motion:

"Can we rehearse together after you get out of school this week," the pop entertainer asked.

"Sure," I answered.

"Good, I can pick you up at your school and bring you to my rehearsal studio then. I have amps and equipment there to use."

"Well, I don't know. I would have to come back home to get my fiddle anyway."

"Can you bring your fiddle to school, so we can go to our rehearsal from there?"

"Well, actually I don't take my fiddle to school. I never take it to school. Besides, I have to come home to get a snack first, because I'm really hungry after school. I usually have a peanut butter and jelly sandwich and two glasses of milk."

He liked that. Chuckling, he said, "I can have a fiddle here for you to use, an electric one, whatever you like. We can stop at a burger place on the way and I'll get you all the sandwiches and milk you want. How does that sound?"

"Well, I like to play my own fiddle. It's sitting right here. I don't see why I can't use it for the rehearsal... and my Mom will want to go to the rehearsal anyway, so we would have to come and get her."

"But I was hoping that we could rehearse without your Mom along, Mark. Just us getting into the music without any distractions."

"My mom never gets in the way," I said. "She is really good at just hanging out and watching. She doesn't interfere or anything like that."

At that moment, my mother entered the living room from the hallway. With the most serious look on her face I had ever seen, she mouthed the words, *"Hang up the phone, NOW!"* I covered the mouthpiece and in a whispered voice asked, "WHY?" *"Just do what I tell you, right now!"* She mouthed the words again, demanding I do this.

"I'm sorry, but I have to go now," I told the pop entertainer.
I placed the handset on the receiver.

Mom told me there might be a problem and not to bother her while she makes a few calls. She began with the Elks Lodge, as well as the leader of that country band who seemed to know the pop entertainer. She found out that this man was going by a stage name. After another few calls to his place of work, his real name was finally discovered. A few more calls produced what Mom had feared. He was a felon who had gone to prison for child sexual assault and pedophilia. I was being *groomed* right under Mom's nose.

Mom explained to me what this was all about. I was horrified. Had I not insisted on needing my fiddle with me, I don't know what would've happened. My Mom may not have caught it in time. I fully realized that my precious fiddle was everything good in my life, especially in those moments. My fiddle probably saved my life already. I hung onto this very sentiment more and more: the *fiddle* was going to rescue me from this albatross I called home.

The Enterprise Newspaper, Everett, Washington, Sept. 5, 1973
"Mark O'Connor likes to fiddle. He also frets, strums, picks and plays.

The 12-year old Mountlake Terrace youth does all of these things in the musical sense. And he does them well. The youngster, son of Mr. and Mrs. Lawrence O'Connor of 23207 52nd Avenue W., has become highly proficient on five different stringed instruments. Up until one year ago, he played only one.

If that sounds like a lot of musical accomplishment for a 12-year old, Mark seems unimpressed. 'It's just fun...I like to play,' the Mountlake Terrace Junior High seventh grader says.

Judging by the "string" of awards the youth won this past summer, others enjoy listening to him. His most recent award came at an event billed as "The First Annual Bluegrass and Old-Time Music Festival"...Mark won a $650 mandolin, placed first in the Open-Junior competition and first in the flat-pick guitar division; took a second in the banjo division and a third in the old-time fiddle competition. Total prize money for Mark was $75.

Mark started his musical training at age [six] with lessons on the classical guitar. Mark says he [didn't] enjoy the music very much and thus didn't like to practice.

In 1969, he saw Johnny Cash and the country western singing star became an instant idol. Mark decided he wanted a fiddle, but didn't get one until October last year.

He started taking lessons then and eight months later took second in the national fiddler's contest [Junior-Junior Division] in Idaho.

Fiddling led to bluegrass music and bluegrass instruments. Mark got a banjo last December and [started] taking lessons. In January he obtained a steel-stringed guitar and started playing flat-pick style (as opposed to using the fingers in classical style) and after two months of that he entered the folk guitar division of the annual Metro Music Solo and Ensemble contest at the University of Washington. Mark was one of seven of 250 contestants to win an award.

In February he met a [17]-year old banjo player, Dick Ahrens, of Shorecrest High School, and the two have been performing as a duo at schools, festivals and other events.

One other instrument Mark plays is the dobro, a guitar-like instrument with a resonator which is played with a steel instead of the fingers, It is a forerunner to the electric guitar.

Mark says he doesn't really have a favorite instrument, but likes them all. One advantage of the fiddle over classical guitar is its flexibility. 'In classical

26

you can't jam,' Mark says, referring to a jazz musician's favorite term for playing impromptu. 'It's fun to practice now,' he adds.

Mark says he really likes bluegrass music because 'it came from down [to] earth people, from the hills.'

Mark's not much of a rock-n-roll buff, however, like his friends at school. And he says his music doesn't really leave him much time for other school activities.

He is looking forward to entering more competitions next year and would like to visit Nashville next summer to take in some of the bluegrass festivals and fiddling contests in the area."

GETTING THE GRAND PRIZE in Woodinville and being written up in the local newspaper was good for my reputation as a boy musician in the Seattle area, but it was not without some drawbacks. Certainly, it wasn't a very good prospect for life at my particular school.

One of my teachers took this newspaper article about me, and posted it right up on the hallway bulletin board. After seeing that my photo was being used as a bullseye for dart throwers, I began to worry. The nicknames and teasing came quickly: "fiddle faddle from the fiddle farm," "you look like a girl," "fat lips" and of course, the all-too-descriptive "fiddle boy" were all hurled my way.

Each day like clockwork, a few older kids from 9th grade began waiting for me outside my final class period. They followed me down the hallway, taunting and calling me names as I ducked in and around the other kids to get ahead of them. Once I was out of the school building, the chase was on. I needed to outrun them past that ravine, just to make it home. On several occasions, I was able to anticipate the final bell, running towards the exit door to get a head start, only to see my hopes dashed with them waiting for me again.

Luckily, I could run very fast.

I did the five blocks home in nothing flat. I was always the first or second fastest runner at Forest Crest Elementary School the year before. The agility came in handy back then too.

A different kid altogether, a bully who was a recent transfer to the elementary school, was held back a year. He made me a target, and in short order was chasing me home each day from the top of the hill. Once we were out of sight from the crossing guard, it was off to the races.

The special attention given me was not so much about my music, although I am sure it didn't help. For that bully, it was mostly about me looking like a girl—my full lips I very much detested by now. His nickname for me was "sissy girl." There was a girl at school who came off as kind of an odd duck to most of the classmates, named Connie. It made way for another nickname for me—"O'Connie."

Unfortunately, most everyone in my class lived in the opposite direction of the elementary school, including my best friends, Ricky and Rodney. I wasn't living on the "other side of the tracks," since there wasn't a railroad right there, it was the *other* side of the elementary school. Mom tried to arrange play dates with them as often as she could, so we could walk to my house together from school, or go to their homes after school. That kept the bully away. Rodney always said he could "take him." Rodney had an odd way of punching, where his fists would come in from the sides. He swung in—claimed it would work well on the bully.

We loved building tree forts in my backyard—the "jungle" we used to call it—consisting of three trees—two firs, and another leafy one. We also loved digging holes and building underground forts in my backyard. My parents didn't care about our yard—we could dig the whole thing up if we wanted to. Both of my friends, Rodney and Rick, had thinner lips—features I was quite envious of. Renee, the pretty Polynesian girl I had a crush on, also lived over on the good side of the elementary. She had thin lips, I suppose you could say, I don't know... I had such a crush on Renee, I didn't know what to do about it—so at lunch I thew my empty cartons of milk at her. Things got even more awkward when I was the only kid in school to get braces. I had to have four teeth pulled, the braces immediately to follow. The trauma of all of this dental work pushed my already full lips even further outward, followed by more jokes at my expense.

All of those days walking home from the elementary school alone gave me the feeling of desolation. Our side of town was where you could find all the cinderblock government housing—a post WWII suburban project for the poverty class. There wasn't any insulation in the walls of our house, just the bare block, painted barn red on the outside and white on the inside. With the constant Seattle rain, a persistent dampness and mold grew on the white-painted cinderblock which was plenty visible inside our bedroom. Probably why I was so sickly as a child, constantly sneezing, seemingly allergic to nearly everything around me. It should be no wonder why I had to carry a handkerchief.

As the elementary school let out, my mother usually stood in the front doorway of our house. She could keep an eye on our chase down the hill. She knew of my bully problem and that I was plenty scared. Standing in the doorway like that, watching me run towards home, was her attempt to unnerve that bully—to push him back, keep him from running so hard at me.

One day when there was quite a bit of snow on the ground, I wondered if he would take a break from me… maybe *enjoy* the newly fallen snow perhaps? But the chase was back on. Having difficulty running fast, we ended up throwing snowballs at one another. As we closed in, I rushed towards him with an amount of anger resulting from everything this kid had put me through—I even surprised myself. I shoved all kinds of snow in his bad face until he cried, "quit." At which point the taunting and bullying of the last few months all came to a screeching halt.

But that didn't mean things were any better in the neighborhood.

The single mother and three daughters who lived across the street from us—ran a neighborhood brothel. The mother was the Madam employing her 13-year-old daughter as lead hooker—the main attraction. She was a pretty girl, and had recently dropped out of school. One of Mom's practices was to peek through our front curtains and count how many men would visit in a given night, guessing which female they were seeing—the mom or the daughter. They did have a brand new car across the street which we admired. We still had the old Chevy beater.

Michelle played with the younger sister during the day, but a couple of times, I even hung out with the oldest daughter—in the *dog house.* For a short period of time, the young teen hooker wanted to hug me and kiss on me a little. She was a couple of years older, and it was confusing behavior. I was too young to know what prostitution really meant, or even what sex was, but I remember Mom saying that she felt sorry for her. It made her seem to me, like she was a good girl. Still, she was "off limits" for me to play with, though, which is why we sneaked off into the dog house together.

Yes, the dog house... I made a habit of heading there a lot with my Shetland sheepdog, Frisky. I would crawl in the narrow opening and stay in that little dark cranny with him for hours. Sometimes it felt like no one could find me there, and I liked it that way. I loved my dog and felt sorry for him, too. The family who shared our back fence were drug dealers. Frisky would bark through the fence at their Doberman so often that one time he jumped the fence into our yard. They sicked their dog on Frisky. We watched in horror as he clenched Frisky by the throat and flung him around in circles before finally dropping him, when they whistled their Doberman to come back. We thought Frisky wouldn't make it, but somehow he did. They wielded hand guns and rifles in their yard, and sometimes my sister and I would peek through the fence to "spy" on them when they did. It was a game for us, but sometimes they would see us and point their guns at us.

The house to the left of us, well they had a really weird older kid—you could easily say *disturbed.* He grabbed our cat who strolled into their yard one time, and placed him on their wooden bench. He took a hand saw to him, cut right through him, alive. We saw it all happen through the holes in the fence, but we were so traumatized and scared that we couldn't mutter a word to stop the older teen. Afterwards, we asked Mom if we could get another kitty, that ours wouldn't be coming back home. Mom said that sometimes cats will wander off. So we got a new cat and kept him inside.

When that family thankfully moved out, a Black family moved in. I remember Dad saying, "There goes the property value." Our house was worth nearly nothing to begin with. But they were nice to us, and we were to them. They seemed as nervous as we were about the rest of our white neighbors.

THE MORE SIZEABLE GANG of 9th graders at the junior high, posed a greater critical threat than what I encountered before. Up until the most recent runs for home, they couldn't catch the fleet-footed fiddle-kid out on the open road. I was pretty well satisfied with it, and so thankful for my long legs. It was the one strategy I had to head them off—until that day would finally come, when they got discouraged and lost interest in me.

No matter what, though, it went on for weeks. As I ran for home, I imagined a different life for myself one day soon, and, I found ways to mentally *transport* myself to this other musical place I wished to go. Most certainly, not this place here where I lived. My heart was beating so fast—they were always just on my heals—but I always gained ground on them. So often, I had to run for my life. I came to understand that psychological state of mind I entered. For me, it was all about running for *freedom*. The freedom from these cretins, the aberrations—harsh kids who had little compassion or fellowship. I was running for freedom to get out of this hell hole. I was racing to find a way to become a real musician one day. I *daydreamed* about getting out of that junior high school, out of my neighborhood—everything. I visualized running so fast and getting past my front door to that safe place where all my musical instruments were awaiting me—the only safe place I knew about in the entire world. That 400 square-foot block house each afternoon was a place of transfiguration, and of passage. I felt that. I could sense it through the music I *dreamed* about, and played on the family stereo. I didn't know what was next, nor how long I had to wait, but I knew how to get to where I called home, at least for now.

Without fail, the final buzzer rang at school on a fateful day. The older 9th graders were waiting for me again, and I was gearing up for our chase.

I've always loved playing music really fast. I really craved it, actually. As a child, I desired and worshiped that nimbleness, the swiftness in the music. I associated speed with *freedom,* the way I saw it. I could play much faster than most any other young fiddler, too, and most any other young guitar player... the speed made me feel *liberated.*

On this day however, I didn't have a chance to play fast, nor run fast. Instead, I had to change course. My regular route out of the school building was blocked off by a couple of additional 9th graders waiting for me at the exit. Panicked, I found myself heading down another hallway. When walking briskly through the empty cafeteria, I found an exit door, but it was locked from the outside. With the 9th graders in hot pursuit, I turned left into the only place left to go, the weight room. But once I was in there, I had to stop. Stop cold. There was no way out. My back was against the wall. I faced towards them as they entered. I was cornered. Trapped in.

The group of five or six drew closer. They taunted me for a minute and then one slugged me in my stomach so hard I fell to the ground. I gasped for my breath—could hardly breathe. I was defenseless with no one around to help. As I was down on the floor and trying to protect my head, my ears, I was getting violently worked over. They began taking turns kicking my body. Decisively, one of them kicked me as hard as he could, landing a walloping blow squarely on my right kneecap. I laid motionless after that. I couldn't do anything except *imagine* another life for me one day— a crossroad sometime in the future when I could go to those musical places I could only dream of. I trusted that the radiant light I saw in those moments was that of *my* music, and that it would pull me in, pull me through... that this light was my real purpose and it would find me laying there in need. I hoped that music could shine brightly for me, still. A young life as an artist would be my reckoning.

What I remembered next was a few teachers calling for the ambulance—to come for me. After being released from the hospital, I had to wear a cast on my right leg for two months. The doctors told us that I nearly lost the use of my leg in the attack. The rest of my injuries were bruises which would soon disappear. Those little thugs permanently damaged the growth center of my leg muscles with that kick to the kneecap. To this day, I have a prominent and sensitive bump on my right knee to remind me of the beating I took long ago.

Given the dire circumstance I found myself in that day, I was ultimately spared of something far worse. Instead of my right knee, it could've been my right elbow—my bowing arm.

During the days of my recovery, I couldn't help but think of a different sequence of events. Without the violin in my arms, I was defenseless against their physical attack. But what if I had held a musical instrument in those moments? What would've happened if I was able to play music for them, instead of becoming their abused victim? Could they have had another reaction towards me?

That experience reinforced the idea of believing music itself was a survival mechanism. When I was down on the ground, it was the music that could save me. I came to this belief wholeheartedly as a child. When in trouble, I prayed that I would still be able to play *my* music again. Increasingly, my musical instruments felt like they became appendages to my own body. The fiddle was as *innate* to me as my arms themselves. With time, my musical instruments became an extension of who I was more than anything else. My music took over *from* me. The fiddle itself was continuing to save me from crises.

As a young child, this meant I was losing myself in music, yes... but I *wanted* to be lost in it. I didn't like myself otherwise, maybe I feared hating what I'd always been. It was plain to me that some people disliked me and wanted me hurt. But at the same time, there also was something hopeful taking shape in my arable mind—something beautifully affirmative and pervasive. This idea was going to rescue me even from my own demons. What began to unfold was an extraordinary ability to *imagine*. Especially to imagine music.

As far as the question I rhetorically posed to myself, the one regarding what might have happened in the weight room that horrible day—if I had an instrument in my hands? I eventually brought musical instruments to my school—years later. The same gang of kids who worked me over sat against the back wall just to observe me playing my music. No, they weren't supposed to be in there at all, but I didn't have the heart to ask them to leave. They loved the music I was playing, writing, and improvising, and it seemed to bring them so much joy now. You could see it on their faces, and through their smiles. It would've been too harmful to bring up the incident. They didn't say anything to me about it, and I didn't as well. Now that we were in the same room again, it seemed that my musical ability healed this pain we had shared. I sensed the power of its healing— the act of playing music for people. I considered *my* music a gift to others. Music was a far better gift than anything else I had to offer as a person. This much I knew.

DAD WARNED ME TO never rat on anybody. The retribution could even be worse. He said to me, "You don't want them coming to our front door, do you?" I couldn't help but think about his own tight spot with the log chain. The gang of 9th graders went without expulsion. I stayed home from school for the next couple of months recuperating, with my right leg aimed straight out in front of me—stiff like a board.

My mother didn't feel good about me just sitting around at home doing nothing except practicing. She told me, "Since you were given all of this musical talent, I think it's time for you to give back." As word got out that I charged $4 per lesson myself, in short order I had a studio of 15 music students coming to our house each week. At 12, I was teaching kids my age, like John and Pitt Calvert's kids, Wade and Kathy; there was Amar Singh and his younger sister; the Carter cousins, Tim and Cindy. I had lots of adult students too, like Jeff Gouph, and there were adult female students, too. I taught students tunes such as, "Golden Slippers," "Red Wing," "Old Joe Clark," "Liberty," and of course for the beginners, "Boil 'em Cabbage Down." I also taught some guitar and banjo, along with the many fiddle students.

During those couple of months, I had any number of instruments in my hands pretty much all day long, which turned out to be a silver lining in this whole chapter. I detested school at that point anyway, and was uneasy about my neighborhood—so there I was, staying home from school and hardly leaving my living room. I got much better at the fiddle, that I can tell you—adding up to ten hours of practicing each day... and on school days too. Any sign of working Dad's labor jobs was thankfully out of the picture, at least for now—I could hold him off until summer.

My lessons with Benny continued. We just couldn't divulge to him how I ended up with a cast on my leg. Sharing any details of that day would have been more traumatic for me than anything. With Benny, though, it would have been needlessly upsetting to him. We went ahead and told folks it was some kind of accident already. It seemed like the rest of my life was most any kind of accident. Benny and our new world of fiddling was a pristine beautiful world away from any reality.

With so much confusion over how cruel people could really be in this world, Mom often read the Bible to me and my sister. My parents were not church-going folks. Dad professed his atheism, even though his favorite song of all time was "How Great Thou Art..." and he loved the Black gospel singers we saw on TV—he'd go on and on about how *they* are the best singers in the world. Mom believed in God and she loved Jesus Christ. She was always greatly moved by Martin Luther King's speeches and his mission and struggle for justice in America, especially for the Black race. The MLK assassination was as devastating to her as her beloved JFK's. I was a boy seeing how traumatic those tragedies made my mother feel. Of course, she cried for days. For both men.

Mom particularly liked the bluegrass gospel songs on the recordings we had; "Little White Church," "Life's Railway To Heaven." and this was partly how she came to embrace the bluegrass genre herself. She was a classical music aficionado previously, so this all was quite a leap. She always loved Johnny Cash, though. Had a crush on him, and Leonard Bernstein — Doug Kershaw, too. Mom came to love traditional bluegrass songs about Jesus and family, especially for me. She thought that bluegrass was going to be *good* for me — wholesome, moral substance through-and-through.

With the loss of two grandparents when I was just a toddler, I knew my maternal Grandmother during the course of my childhood rather well. Originally from Memphis, born there in 1892, Granny presently lived just a couple of miles away in Lynnwood. Her parents homesteaded there during WWI. Granny was nearly a life-long devout Christian Scientist. Never allowing Mom to see a doctor as a little girl helped to turn my mother against organized religions, across the board. However, Mom wanted Michelle and I to be guided by the Bible's teachings.

We discovered that Benny's religion was Jehovah's Witnesses. Members of his family likely held much more strict to the doctrine than Benny, so it seemed. It turned out that moving to Washington was virtuous for Benny in another unsuspecting way. The Texas fiddlers insisted that Benny drink with them as he battled his own alcoholism incessantly. Hanging out with a 12-year-old late into a Saturday night, giving him fiddle lessons, may have helped Benny almost as much as it helped me.

Throughout his life, Benny's religion ostensibly prevented him from becoming a professional musician, as we discovered. These two pillars of his life (music and religion) proved a bit antithetical within the Thomasson family. Despite being offered band positions with Bob Wills and the Texas Playboys and joining Tex Ritter in some Hollywood movies, this kind of lifestyle allied too closely with the religion's strictures: *music, dancing* and *drinking.* Luckily for Benny, fiddle contests, however, remained *holy ground.*

Nearing the time for my leg cast to be removed, I was concerned about returning to school. The idea of enrolling in maybe some kind of private school or even religious school was not in the cards, financially or otherwise. Junior high was five blocks from my house and I could easily walk it — or run it — well, maybe after a few months I could. There was no other school choice for me, and *that* was the end of the discussion.

AT HOME I FELT SAFER with all my nice musical instruments, and relished the sensitivity of holding them and playing them all I could. I loved music so much, especially all the LPs of fiddling and bluegrass music I received as gifts from Mom.

My mother ordered albums through the County Records mail order catalog. LPs by the bluegrass traditionalists were some of our favorites:

Bill Monroe and the Bluegrass Boys, Flatt and Scruggs and the Foggy Mountain Boys, The Stanley Brothers. The Country Gentleman, Larry Sparks and the Lonesome Ramblers, Doc and Merle Watson, The Dillards. The Osborne Brothers, The Greenbriar Boys, Seldom Scene, Jim & Jesse and the Virginia Boys...

Several of the LPs were gospel albums too.

The great bluegrass and old-time fiddlers were also on our family stereo constantly:

Kenny Baker, Clark Kessinger, Byron Berline, Vassar Clements, Benny Martin, Howdy Forrester. Johnny Gimble, Georgia "Slim" Rutland, Buddy Pendleton, Chubby Wise, Buddy Spicher...

Sometimes I had to wait for a whole month to receive an LP through the mail order catalog. Other times, I waited two or three months. If the record album arrived in the fall, they could be held for presents under the Christmas tree. A little barren at times, the LPs wrapped as presents were a good way to fill under the tree. During Christmas break, local music friends might drop by for a little jam session. I began to make a connection between celebrating the birthday of Jesus and playing good ol' American music around the holidays. Fiddle tunes *and* Christmas carols. Whether it was the growing LP collection or the impromptu amateur jam sessions at the house, it kept me dreaming and imagining about truly better days.

One evening, as my family gathered around our black and white TV, we turned to the *PBS* network, the fourth of only four channels. Bill Monroe and the Bluegrass Boys were scheduled to perform. There was a very short announcement at the beginning of the hour, but what we saw next were all of these hippies on stage with really long curly hair. They were playing bluegrass instruments, just like the hippies we saw out at Woodinville. My mother was not a huge fan of the hippie movement, as she associated flower children with "free sex and drugs." She was mostly nervous about hippies for my sake, being her young impressionable boy. Several times we were stopped on the Seattle freeway by hippies demonstrating. One time, they banged on the roof of our car and said to turn the engine off. They were protesting the Vietnam War. She was scared each time it happened—but Mom loved the liberals, though. Nevertheless, she wanted a little less Jesus Freak and more family Southern Gospel.

As those hippie musicians began to play an instrumental by Stephen Foster called "New Camptown Races," I soon recognized that this was some of the best instrumental music I had ever heard. I remember glancing towards my mother during the first tune, and then looking at her again during the second one—a vocal song, "Dark Hollow." I was searching for her approval of these musicians on the television set, hoping she would like it, because I was really loving it. She ultimately nodded in approval with her genuine cheek-to-cheek Duchenne smile. I was fixated on the TV for the rest of the show. We just could not believe our eyes and our ears. We came to know this music as "progressive bluegrass."

This last-minute replacement for The Bluegrass Boys emerged as an album band called Muleskinner. The group featured the rising stars of the progressive bluegrass movement: Clarence White on guitar, David Grisman on mandolin, Richard Greene on fiddle, Peter Rowan vocals, and Bill Keith on banjo.

Interestingly, most all of them had played with the Bluegrass Boys in Nashville. After their crew cut hair days with Bill Monroe, they all amounted to California hippies within just a few years. I was fascinated by this whole new acoustic music world, a subset of bluegrass we had not discovered through the ultra-traditional County Records catalog via Floyd County, Virginia. I would always remember that PBS show precisely the way I first experienced it—a great new inspirational sensation.

Within a few short years, a significant musical relationship with nearly everyone on that TV show was heading my way. I could imagine it too. I *dreamed* about the day when I could play music like that with them.

CHAPTER THREE

THE SUMMER OF *FIDDLING* LOVE

A S WE DREW CLOSER to the summer months of 1974, my mother wondered what it would take for me to become a *traveling* child musician at age 12. She was contemplating a tutoring program which we couldn't afford, and, I was hopeful for most anything to get me beyond that godforsaken junior high. Graduating with a high school diploma under any circumstances remained her highest priority for me. In the meantime, Mom wanted to be a music manager and see what we could make of it. Yes, she thought I was getting pretty good.

Assessing our prospects, Mom often recognized how the older musicians and music teachers were greatly impressed with my talent, like Dick Dice, John Burke, and Craig Keene. She saw how Butch Robbins willingly corresponded with me from Nashville, writing me letters about cluing in his bandmate, Sam Bush, there was this little banjo kid from the Northwest. Sam Bush initially knew about me as a banjo player. Then of course Benny's unremitting involvement through my wonderful fiddle lessons, giving me everything he had, and all day long at that. Mom was thinking she needed to get me around some of these nationally-known musicians up close—the very folks we were listening to on recordings. Maybe this was a way for me to succeed as a child musician, and in the process, improve our family's woeful tribulations.

With my reputation rising at home, coupled with Dad's sympathy over the mishap at school, Mom convinced him that we needed to get a van for our great undertaking of a summer tour back East. If we were going to enter me in the bigger contests and bluegrass festivals around the country, the old station wagon was surely going to fall apart on the way. There were holes in the floorboard to such dimensions that we could watch the pavement go by as Mom drove. Being near the salt water rusted out those old cars. Dad said we could just barely afford one, but it would have to be a hollowed out van—an empty shell.

Dad sprang for a clutch and a V-4 engine. That way, we would never have to worry about getting pulled over for speeding on the open highway.

We picked out a yellow-tan Ford Econoline van. It would soon be recognized among music friends as a salutation of the O'Connors on the road.

Dad happily built the wooden cabinets inside the new van for us. He was always pretty good at working with wood. Dad constructed the sleeping area in the back for my Mom and Michelle. There was storage underneath it, with access from both the inside and from out the back doors. He put together the icebox cabinet, and a small sink with a pump handle that worked if we were hooked up to water through a garden hose. On top of the cabinets was a space for a thin sheet of foam rubber. It was to be used for my sleeping area on the floor aisle. Near the driver's seat was to be the instrument closet. My dad really wanted me to succeed in music now.

"Do you need room for all your instruments?" Dad asked me.

"Just three Dad, I'm quitting the banjo and the dobro. They are my least favorite."

"Bruzz," as he sometimes called me when he was in a good mood, "playing your banjo helped get you the grand prize, didn't it?"

"I know, Dad," I replied as I tried to evade the topic.

Dad really liked Roy Clark playing banjo on the *Hee Haw* television show. He liked all the crazy faces Clark made when he played.

"Mark, you should make those faces when you play like the fabulous Roy Clark. The audience would know how difficult it is to play these instruments like you do," Dad repeated this idea, often.

Anyway, I just felt the banjo didn't have that extra something for me, like the guitar and the fiddle did.

"It's going to be the fiddle and the guitar from here on out," I told him.

Dad built the closet to hold three instruments—the fiddle, guitar and my new grand prize mandolin.

After many months of lessons with Benny, from late summer 1973 to mid-1974, it was time to head to Weiser in June. It was also time for the maiden voyage in our new Ford Econoline. The headway I made with the fiddle that year was incalculable. We had a strong Northwest wind at our back, and the new van felt like our big tour bus. Well… it did not have air conditioning, and we were heading into the South during the summer months. Yet another way "to cut costs," Dad reasoned with us. I had never been to the South before, and evidently neither had my father.

No matter what, I was learning what winning contests had to offer me. If I could get good enough, it would be my ticket out of that school, out of my neighborhood, and out of the double-life existence I was navigating. We looked forward to meeting up with Benny and Bea in Weiser at the National Oldtime Fiddlers' Contest.

WEISER, IDAHO, WAS A LITTLE, DUSTY TOWN, resting along the winding Snake River about an hour outside of Boise. It was just a ten-hour drive for my Mom, Michelle and me, as it was for Benny and Bea, coming from the west coast of Washington state.

Weiser had to be *the* most unlikely place for the national fiddle competition. By 1974, the contest had been held there for a good 30 years, drawing fiddle champions from all over America. Well-known bluegrass stars Byron Berline and Sam Bush were among the impressive list of recent national and junior champions. For the fiddlers and fans in attendance, Weiser was the most special week of the year. For Benny Thomasson, it was Mecca. Some of that *holy ground.*

Benny was the most well-loved fiddler at Weiser, a bona fide fiddling star, and everyone's favorite personality. He was very kind to everyone in the variety of social settings around the fiddle contest environment. I really wanted to emulate his kindness as much as I possibly could.

Sometimes when I played through my tunes in the warm-up room, people offered their comments on how good I was for a kid… they were often met in return with my uneasy frown. I even argued with them to the contrary, habitually stewing over mistakes I had made—even a little bobble that I simply could not ignore. I was put out that they somehow missed it—my mistakes. After witnessing these curious exchanges, my mother asked me to adjust my attitude.

"I was not happy with my playing when they complimented me like that, Mom."

"It doesn't matter, a simple thank you will suffice," she rebuffed.

"Anytime someone pays you a compliment, that's all you have to say – thank you."

"Yes Mom," I noted.

Benny said thank you to anyone who might compliment him on his playing. No matter what, he said "thank you." Benny was gracious to everyone and I really wished to be like that, too. I was so proud for him to be my teacher. Benny often introduced me to people as "my student."

I entered the 12-and-under Junior-Junior division again. Loretta had moved on to the Juniors at age 13. As most of them expected, I won my kiddos division. I placed 2nd the year before, in the very first fiddle contest I had ever entered. That little kids' division grew dramatically in numbers, too. 21 tykes were 12-and-under and fiddling now. I received $25 and a little trophy.

Almost everyone we knew there, was eagerly anticipating my entrance into that big kids' division, the Junior Division. Since the category was age 17 and under, I obviously qualified, but no one had seen many 12-year-olds in that division for a few years.

As I warmed up on my rounds and jammed with guitar accompanists in the high school cafeteria practice room, the old-timers increasingly gathered around me in a circle to listen. They were so full of joy and laughter, seeing a little kid play their favorite old-time fiddle tunes as well as I did.

Greatly impressed, many vowed to my mother that if I kept going like I was, I could "save old-time fiddling from dying out."

This notion of old-time fiddling *dying* out was a very real concern with the older fiddlers in Weiser. They were viewing me as a kind of "pied piper," leading more kids to the fiddle. Every so often, Benny joined the others in listening to me warm up. It seemed that this part—the checking out of players going through their tunes along with the jamming backstage, was just as entertaining and important to folks as the performances in the actual competition taking place in the auditorium.

I assumed there was very little chance of getting into the top five of the Juniors. There were several older teens who had been entering the contest for years, and some were quite good. I thought Loretta was one of the best of the lot, as well. As Benny's *other* favorite student, she had improved a great deal during the year on her own volition. Since we last saw each other, Loretta noticed the difference in my playing, too. Sensing that from her was a big shot in the arm. I still looked up to her a lot.

I could feel that I was turning into a *real* fiddler at this point. I was excited about playing the tunes that Benny taught me—big breakdowns like "Sally Johnson," "Say Old Man Can You Play The Fiddle," "Dusty Miller." Rag tunes like, "Dill Pickle," but as he insisted, I applied my own renditions and style to all of them. I had something to offer. Benny and other fiddlers were recognizing it even with just these 18 months of playing the fiddle behind me.

AS THE JUNIOR DIVISON got under way, I needed three rounds of tunes ready to go. None of the previous competitions I'd entered required as many. There were 30 Juniors signed up—thus a considerably bigger field than folks had seen before. My guitar accompanists included fiddler Aaron Lowe of Spokane. I had to share him with Loretta. Sharing accompanists was commonplace, as there were far more fiddlers than accompanists. Contestants were typically not allowed more than two. For my other rhythm player, Benny made sure his son, Jerry Thomasson, played tenor guitar with me in the Junior division. At the local Bellevue, Washington, contest a couple of months before, I was lucky to have Jerry back me up there. Remarkably, I won the Open division in Bellevue. For Mom, the result oiled the works for a trip back East.

My first round in the national junior division was good. Good enough to make the first cut.

At Weiser, the judge's scoring for each round is cumulative. Some of the older fiddlers began to advocate for me as I started to gain some traction in the big kid's division. Old-timers like Garland Cunningham from eastern Washington, was giving my Mom pep talks through the whole course of it.

"Playing a clean round like Mark did will add to his overall score, now!" Garland and the others reminded us.

"Keep it going, you're doing good," as Garland smiled at me a lot and patted me on the back wishing me luck.

I felt like everybody's favorite grandson all of the sudden. No mistaking me for a girl this year—thank goodness for that, I thought. What a difference a year makes, in more ways than one.

The five impaneled judges listened to the contestants from a remote room, with the music piped in through speakers. One of the judges was

Vivian Williams, Seattle's best fiddler and Barbara Lamb's former teacher. I had beaten Vivian Williams in that Bellevue contest. But none of them knew who was playing, adding some impartiality.

The four categories for adjudication were:

Rhythm - Tone - Intonation - Old-Time Fiddling Ability.

Not knowing exactly what the fourth category meant entirely, even with some official explanations, we figured that "old-time fiddling ability," included musical creativity. I knew that I could score high in that category, because Benny required me to come up with my own renditions of tunes. I didn't remotely sound like anyone else there, that was evident. I didn't even sound like my teacher, Benny, although I was still working on *his* bow arm.

The highest and lowest scores were thrown out, leaving the middle three scores to tally up.

AFTER HEARING THAT I HAD won the small tykes the day before, and that I was heading into the Junior division, my Dad drove over to see me compete. He didn't attend the bluegrass festival competitions I entered in Woodinville, as he needed to work a full weekend. Dad was greatly impressed with that Grand Prize win, though. With Dad at Weiser, Idaho, I had an unexpected new cheerleader. I was not used to seeing that.

With so many people pulling for me, mostly because of my young age and the fact that I was Benny's new protégé, I was causing quite a stir with the audience as I performed my second round. I was playing to get into the top five. With electricity in the air like I had never felt in my life, I played in a free and flowing manner, and it was nearly mistake-free, too. I made the final five.

I had three more tunes to play for Wednesday night's final. Loretta made it into the top five, as well. We were not really making much eye contact at this point. She became much more serious. I was unworried— live-and-let-live, up until that instant, at least. The old-timers advised Mom that I could win it, if I stayed focused. I began to feel the pressure and the weight of any fiddle contest for the very first time. Loretta and I were the two young ones, the others in the top five were 16 and 17.

Many sensed the excitement in the Weiser High School auditorium. It was as electric as the Open division on a Saturday night. People were keen to see the "little kid" go up against the older kids. Despite the increased attention towards me, it still seemed rather effortless as I played my final round. It was all such a new experience; I took it all in stride and enjoyed these surprising new circumstances I found myself in. I got down from the stage and made my way back to the cafeteria, where I found my fiddle case. Several onlookers followed me right out of the auditorium, wanting to talk to me. Those folks thought I deserved to win the contest. We awaited the results together.

I won it!

The new *"National Junior Fiddle Champion!"*

Loretta came in 4th, 16-year-old Connie Bonar from Spokane placed 3rd, and 17-year-old Ron Waldbauer of Yakima came in 2nd.

On June 19th, 1974, I became the youngest ever to win the *National Junior Oldtime Fiddlers' Contest.* I broke a couple of records with that victory—the youngest to ever win the Juniors and the first person to win more than one category in the same year.

The Idaho Statesman – Thursday, June 20, 1974, Page 1

"WEISER — A Washington state youth, who has been fiddling only 18 months, added the first place junior division trophy to his collection Wednesday at Weiser's National Oldtime Fiddlers Contest and Festival.

Mark O'Connor captured the judges' hearts with renditions of a waltz, a hoedown and a tune of his choice, while being accompanied by Aaron Lowe and Jerry Thomasson.

More young people each year are coming to Weiser's fiddling festival to exhibit fiddling skills and compete for top honors. And those who have been fiddling for years often listen in amazement as a youngster in his teens or even younger tunes up and starts playing.

Coupled with their young skill is fresh enthusiasm for an oldtime art that dates back to early days in America and back to the hornpipes and bagpipes of early Ireland and England. Those hornpipe and bagpipe tunes were converted to the fiddle in America's pioneer days. And since then a host of new tunes have been added in the fiddling world, all of them following the tradition and special feeling of oldtime fiddling.

That tradition was threatened with the advent of bluegrass music after World War II. Bluegrass is not considered oldtime fiddling, the difference being a much faster beat for bluegrass in comparison to oldtime fiddling's slower, danceable beat. Oldtime fiddling is not written. It must be handed down from one fiddler to another. Otherwise it faced extinction.

The junior junior division was necessitated by an increasing number of fiddlers in that age bracket, some of whom perform at the age of six and even earlier. This year that division grew by one-third over last year, with 21 entering. The junior division for all fiddlers 18 and under has shown signs of growing, too, with 29 registered this year.

Secondly, classical violin is quite frankly 'boring' for some young people who find the lively oldtime fiddle music more in tune with their tempo of life.

One of the top 15 junior finalists is Roberta Whiting, 16...in her words she simply 'got tired of being a violinist.' So she took up fiddling a year and a half ago and has entered the Weiser festival for the second year in a row. Paul Jeff Pritchard felt much the same way when he made the conversion from violin to fiddle about four years ago. The youth who is 16, says, 'I got tired of playing classical violin.' Unlike many contestants however, he is the first in his family, he says, to take up fiddling."

Dad was truly speechless, and Mom was absolutely beside herself. We were all elated. There were camera flashes going off towards me. From every angle. I never posed for so many pictures with strangers in my life. I suppose if I kept this music thing going, they would eventually be called *fans*, not strangers.

I caught a glimpse of being that child musician in the bright lights, maybe like Mom was talking about, and was hoping for. It would be impossible to know what my mother was feeling after all the music lessons and guiding me through all of this for years—those six-hour round-trip drives for fiddle lessons with Benny, for starters. For what seemed like hours in the cafeteria greeting well-wishers, she just kept looking at me from several feet away with a mother's proud and sweet smile.

Maybe she was just making sure I was saying, "thank you," to all of the fiddlers and fiddle fans coming up to congratulate me? I made sure I was.

WE STAYED FOR THE REST of the week to watch the Open division, as we did the year before. A top-ten Open division fiddler, John Francis from Spokane, was so impressed with my performance that week he asked me to accompany him on guitar for his potential six rounds in the contest. He offered to pay me another $35 if I helped him make the top five.

We parked the new yellow van in a makeshift slot on the treed grounds of the junior high school. Functionally, it was referred to as the "junior high campground." Ironically located just five blocks from the fiddle contest site at the high school—just a quick foot race to some musical freedom.

Occupying this "campground" was quite the alternative counterculture of personalities, music styles, and jamming. There were the *bikers.* Then there were *streakers,* and a lot of hippies, too. My Mom didn't like some of this—or actually most of it—but we were able to park for free and there was still lots of fiddling going on. Many musicians we met at the campground never even made their way up to the contest the entire week. There was such a difference from this campground to the stricter and conservative nature of the fiddle competition five blocks down the road.

In any respect, over the next few days, it was so much fun for me celebrating my success at Weiser and palling around with Loretta, Ron Waldbauer, and others in and around the campsites. Ron, who hailed from eastern Washington himself, became a good friend to me right away. We were the exact age difference as me and my banjo-playing-buddy Dick Ahrens. Narrowly losing to a kid five years his junior didn't really faze Ron at all. He was a very sweet guy. Together, we were bound and determined to learn those longer breakdowns the way Benny, Herman Johnson, and Dick Barrett played them.

Dad hit it off with the old-time fiddlers. He was just laying it on thick with them, raving about *his* boy… ahem. This was new behavior from Dad that I was not used to seeing. They all seemed to take to him well, including Dick Barrett of Texas. Barrett was taking note of my playing during the Juniors and wanted to steal me away from Benny to be *his* student, so he told Dad. Those two Texans were rivals in every possible way, unapologetically. Barrett was attempting to buddy up with my Dad, because he had raked me over the coals the year before—in front of Mom. My mother remembered it very well. So did I. Barrett thought he would have a better chance with Dad in trying to snag me. But at the very least, Barrett and some of the other fiddlers knew where they could sneak a cold beer during the day, too—my Dad's ice cooler was inescapably attached to his old work truck he drove over to Weiser.

Dad seemed happier than I'd seen him before. Pleased that the van cabinets were working out, he had just a little more work to do on them once we returned home. Dad couldn't stay the whole week, though, and took off back to Seattle for work at the lumber yard.

Benny was registered in the Open again, but at 65 now, this year he was eligible for the Senior division, too. Benny's competition rounds took place over Thursday, Friday, and Saturday. Those two divisions were enormous in size—over 200 registered for the Seniors and Open combined. Benny came through in the Seniors and won against my favorite Canadian fiddler, someone who occasionally showed me lots of tunes that year, Joe Pancerzewski. But Benny didn't stop there. Accompanied by his son Jerry on tenor, his well-played six rounds led to a 1st place finish. Benny was the new National Oldtime Fiddle Champion—he won this title for the first time. As for John Francis, along with his mother playing accordion, we made the top five. He told me that he was aided by my able guitar accompaniment.

It sure was one exciting Saturday night with a packed gymnasium full of spectators, and with so many pulling for the grand gentleman of the fiddle. Benny won two categories just like I did. He grabbed me for a photo while he was still on stage holding his very large trophy—about half the size of Benny himself:

"Between the two of us, we won practically everything here!" Benny said. I was on cloud nine.

BACK HOME, MOM AND I mapped out the rest of our summer tour in the new yellow Ford Econoline. It was to be two-and-a-half months of bluegrass festivals and fiddle conventions. We chose bluegrass festivals that featured competitions in fiddle, guitar, and mandolin—or at least the fiddle. The itinerary included the *Cinderella City* fiddler's contest in Englewood, Colorado; Bill Monroe's *Rocky Mountain Bluegrass Festival* in Henderson, Colorado; Byron Berline's *Powderhorn Bluegrass Festival and Fiddle Contest* in Langley, Oklahoma; the Murfreesboro, Tennessee, bluegrass contest; the *World Championship Bluegrass Festival* at Lakeland, Tennessee; the *Galax Old Fiddlers Convention* in Virginia, and the *National Flat-picking Guitar Championships* and festival in Winfield, Kansas.

A church in Edmonds, Washington, sponsored a benefit featuring all of our Seattle music friends. Money was raised to help us with our travel expenses. The show was billed *Old-Time Music and Fiddle Show* and it was emceed by my former teacher, John Burke. Them Cotton Pickin' Ridge Runners kicked off the show, followed by my guitar teacher Dudley Hill, Ed Stoker on harmonica; Hank and Harley: The Tennesseans; Canadian fiddle champion, Joe Pancerzewski. Dick Dice played Carter Family songs with me, and rounding out the evening was John Burke and his Old Hat Band. More old-timers played, too—fiddler Lyman Rogers, and the Tarheel banjo player Roy Caudill, who was over 80-years-old—they both joined in for my sendoff.

The Enterprise, Wed., June 5, 1974

"When young Mark O'Connor of Mountlake Terrace was ten years old he was asked by a reporter, then doing a story on Mark's amazing guitar playing ability, what he would most like to do.

Mark replied that he would like to learn to play the fiddle...So far this year Mark has won the Open and Junior Divisions of the Puget Sound Fiddle Contest in Bellevue, and first in the Open Division of the recent Folk Lore contest in Seattle.

On Saturday, June 9, a group of Bluegrass musicians who know of Mark and his extraordinary talent will perform at a benefit for him at the Edmonds Seventh Day Adventist Church. The benefit will help enable Mark to tour many of the Western states and into the Southeast, where he plans on participating in a number of Bluegrass festivals and competitions. When asked about the upcoming return to the National Old Time Fiddle Contest his proud mother answered with a smile, 'He's better this year. A lot better.'"

Our friends from Spokane, Washington, Custer's Grass Band, wished to give us a big sendoff, too. A progressive bluegrass group featuring Bob Asbury on banjo, Les Panther on guitar, Tony D'Pietro on mandolin, and Dave Hackwith on upright bass, often put together shows to perform around the area, and I loved sitting in with them. As we headed east, they wanted us to swing by Spokane and play with them at the Expo. Because I was the brand-new Junior champion, they also lined up a recording session to produce my first album, a recording studio affiliated with Eastern Washington University in Cheney. Because Dave taught there, we got the day for free. The band accompanied me while I put down a dozen fiddle tunes on tape.

Unfortunately, the recording engineer insisted on placing the microphone *behind* my fiddle—quite literally underneath it. He talked like he knew what he was doing, too, explaining that the tone *we* want to pick up for the recording comes off the back of the instrument. "Right out the soundpost" he added. I was impressed he knew what a soundpost was (the small quarter-inch wooden dowel that keeps the top of the violin from caving in under the weight of the strings). But I couldn't impress upon him that when I play on stage, the mic is right over *here* (in *front* of the fiddle).

We did the entire recording the way *he* wanted to. As we headed out for our next stop in Colorado, we listened to the recording on our cassette tape deck. The fiddle sounded muffled alright. Of course, he put a microphone in *front* of every other instrument in the group. Their instruments sounded good by comparison. We thought we had a gift of a free recording session, but we were not going to be able to use it. My recording career was not off to a flying start.

We arrived at the Englewood competition taking place in the Cinderella City Mall. The big fiddle champions, Dick Barrett and Herman Johnson, were registered in the Open division. There were nearly no guitar accompanists attending this contest, so after my good job of backing up John Francis, both of them asked me to accompany them here. It was a thrill for me to do it, and back up such great championship fiddling. I won my division and placed 3rd right behind them in the Open—Barrett 1st, and, Johnson 2nd. We all had a great time together at the contest. Both of them asked me to visit them for a lesson when we made it further south to Oklahoma and Texas. Mom said we would do everything we could to try to make it.

A Western Sun Edition, Thursday, July 18, 1974

"ENGLEWOOD, COLO. — Mark O'Connor, the musical prodigy from Mountlake Terrace, has won another national contest in a summer tour. The 12-year-old musician won first place in the junior division yesterday of the Rocky Mountain Oldtime Fiddlers Contest in Englewood, Colo. The junior division is for fiddlers 25 years-old and under.

O'Connor is going now with his mother and sister to Nashville, Tenn. [He's] in preparation for a trip to a four-day contest at Galax, Va. On Aug. 8.

'It's unbelievable, I just can't believe it is happening,' said Mark's father, Lawrence O'Connor, who is a lumber yard worker."

A S WE HEADED TO OKLAHOMA for fiddling star Byron Berline's festival, we could not believe the intensely humid heat of early July in the South. We had no air conditioning in the van, and my Mom had never felt temperatures like that in her life, having resided only in Seattle and San Francisco. My sister and I tried sticking our heads out the windows on occasion, but likewise, we'd never experienced so many flying bugs such as in a southern summer. We experimented by taking wet rags and placing them across our faces—then holding our heads out the window. Mom made the better choice to do most of our driving after sundown. We found city parks during the days which had water fountains for us kids, while Mom tried to catch up on her sleep under a shade tree.

Having left plenty of time to get all the way to Langley, we showed up a day early. With our first taste of southern hospitality, the folks at the gate let us in early for a camping spot on the festival grounds. There weren't but a few people there yet, so we settled in and waited for the festival to begin. It was exciting to see all the people pull in one by one, as the easygoing jam sessions began to pop up throughout the beautiful wooded Powerderhorn Park grounds. It sounded like a symphony of bluegrass reverberations. A little like the Weiser Junior High campground, only five times as big—it was our first real southern bluegrass festival.

We didn't know anyone there, so we mostly watched folks jam, and simply waited for the fiddle contest to begin the following morning. Just as the case with Cinderella City, there weren't a lot of guitar accompanists around for the contest that we could see. As we approached the backstage area behind the outdoor stage, there were just two musicians standing there. We heard a good fiddle and guitar warming up for the contest. We got a little closer to recognize the back-up guitarist—Byron Berline himself. He had on sunglasses, so we weren't quite sure at first. My Mom, Michelle and I stood there listening to the tune they were playing. When they finished, Mr. Berline introduced himself and welcomed us to his festival. He introduced us to his brother, Leonard Berline. He was entering his brother's fiddle contest.

It was exciting to meet Byron Berline, and of course we had many of his recordings that I admired so much, like the one with The Dillards: *Pickin' and Fiddlin'.* I was also anxious about my very first appearance in a southern fiddle contest. I was wondering where all the contestants were, and more importantly, where all of the guitar accompanists were. The fiddle contest was supposed to get under way in a couple of hours.

I turned to my mother: "Where are we going to find a guitar player?" She leaned over and whispered, "Why don't you ask Mr. Berline if he could accompany you in the contest?" So, I walked up a little closer to him. "Mr. Berline, would you play guitar for me in the contest?" Catching him by surprise, I certainly had him in a tough place to wiggle out of, since he was already committed to accompany his brother. Mr. Berline nervously strummed a chord or two on his guitar, and said;

"Why sure—why don't you play me a tune? Let me see what you're going to play."

I got my fiddle out of the case and began playing a breakdown right there as I stood. Berline immediately joined in with some guitar accompaniment. Once through the first part of the tune, he took note that I was playing the Texas-style that he knew well, so he began to play closed chords that changed every beat—the guitar approach characteristic of this style. When I was finished with the tune, I had a pretty good idea he was going to accompany me in the contest when he blurted out, "Well I'll be darned," and began chuckling. He looked over at his brother, Leonard, and he as well was shaking his head and grinning. They seemed to be truly surprised by what they heard. I didn't know if there were many young fiddlers in Oklahoma, or the rest of the country for that matter—kids who could play the finer fiddle tunes like I had learned. I came to find out there was nearly no one.

We were finally in the *South*—the home of American fiddling and bluegrass music—performed mostly by adults. Several minutes later, the Broughtons from right here in Oklahoma showed up. We just saw them at Weiser. I asked J.C. Broughton's son, Larry, to join me on the second guitar accompaniment.

I won the Langley fiddle contest that day on July 5th, 1974. It was the Open division, too. They only had one division at the festival, no juniors. Clinching the fiddle contest prize as a 12-year-old against the adults, became the talk of the festival.

The Enterprise, Wed., July 10, 1974

"Twelve-year-old Mark O'Connor, son of Mr. and Mrs. Lawrence O'Connor of Mountlake Terrace, WA added another victory to his slate of them in winning the open division of the Byron Berline Fiddlers contest in Langley, Okla., last weekend.

Mark took first place over the other notables in the contest which included fiddlers up to age 47."

Many of the bluegrass entertainers were informed through various means, and rumors were going around that there was a young boy from Seattle who won the fiddle contest—*and Berline played backup guitar for him.* So, I got to meet or even jam with just about every professional bluegrass act there over the next few days.

One of our favorite groups, Jim & Jesse and the Virginia Boys, performed their set at the Langley festival and we immediately fell in love with them, even more so than their recordings. For us, seeing them perform was like seeing Elvis, or something. A polished bluegrass band with smooth brother harmony singing, their two-brother vocal blend was one of the most alluring sounds we heard in bluegrass music that whole summer. I particularly liked them singing their classic songs "Cotton Mill Man" and "I Wish I Knew."

Joined by some solid bluegrass fiddling from Joe Meadows, Jesse McReynolds' mandolin playing was also impressive. The bluegrass patriarch spent some time with me just outside their tour bus. He gave me several mandolin tips. Jesse let me play his mandolin and showed me his brand of "cross-picking." The effect was thrilling when he used it across his entire mandolin break in one of their sterling bluegrass vocal songs. Cross-picking is alternating between three strings with a flat-pick.

He took an immediate liking to me, and hoped he would see me soon. "I guess we'll be seeing you around at more festivals, eh?" After all the instruments and merchandise were packed up, and they finished greeting their fans, I watched Jesse board their huge coach to join his brother and his bandmates. The bus had the band logo on the side of it and everything. I couldn't help but daydream a little about being a Virginia Boy pulling up to summer festivals in that bus.

Another favorite band on the Langley roster was the Newgrass Revival. The opposite side of the spectrum from the McReynoldses stylistically, they did a mind-blowing late-night set—jamming and rocking out on songs for what seemed like 15 minutes before finally winding them down. On bluegrass instruments they covered rock songs like "Great Balls of Fire" and Leon Russell's "Prince of Peace." Butch Robbins, our banjo-playing acquaintance from Woodinville, was still playing electric bass with the band. The group leader, Sam Bush, with his long, frizzy hair flyin' all over the place, was flying with the mandolin and the fiddle, too. Playing a little guitar as well—Sam Bush played all three of the instruments I wanted to concentrate on myself. To us, their set came off more like "rock-grass" than "new-grass," but the official name for their music was *Newgrass*.

Butch had already introduced me to Sam earlier that day, soon after they arrived on the festival grounds. Sam had his long hair in a pony tail and he was wearing shades;

"Byron Berline came up to me and said you have to hear this young kid from Seattle who won the fiddle contest yesterday. So is that you?" Sam asked.

"I think so, yes," I replied.

"Butch Robbins told me about a young banjo player in Seattle that he was all excited over—I suppose that is you, too?"

"I think so."

"Well, nice to meet you, I'm Sam Bush."

HEADLINING THE FESTIVAL was the event's master of ceremonies, Byron Berline. He played with his group, Country Gazette. Berline is very tall, a physically imposing man who played football at the University of Oklahoma, and graduated with a teaching degree in physical education. Berline was drafted into the Army during Vietnam, after he had played on the road for a few months with Bill Monroe. His large physical presence seemed to dwarf his fiddle on stage—it seemed like he could even physically crush the fiddle if he wasn't careful. He did play triple-stops (three notes at once) on occasion.

In nothing flat, Byron Berline became a key musical figure to me. He straddled the two music worlds I was learning how to grapple with myself—the Texas-style fiddle tunes, including similar renditions of "Sally Goodin'" that we shared, and then the world of bluegrass music. Musically, he landed right down in the middle of these polarities more than any other musician we would discover. Berline wrote great fiddle tunes, too, like "Gold Rush"—the one he co-wrote with Bill Monroe while he was a Bluegrass Boy in 1967. Then his more recent "Huckleberry Hornpipe," recorded with the Gazette. I had recently learned both off his recordings.

During his career, Berline was a top recording session player in Los Angeles. He played on the *Let It Bleed* album by the Rolling Stones, and filmed a segment for a *Star Trek* television episode.

Our conversations about Benny Thomasson that weekend kick-started the idea for Benny to join him on the new Arnold Schwarzenegger movie, *Stay Hungry*. Byron was in charge of some of the film's music. It was exciting to imagine, Benny eventually on the big screen with a small acting role, portraying the fiddling mentor to Schwarzenegger's character. Berline was the body double for "Mr. Universe" when he played the fiddle on screen. I couldn't help but be inspired by the great fiddling career that Byron Berline created for himself.

Byron Berline (album notes to *Soppin' The Gravy*)
  "I met Mark O'Connor at a fiddle contest in Oklahoma in 1974; I hadn't heard of him until that day... I was backstage playing guitar for some of the other fiddlers, when this young fellow with braces on his teeth and a little taller than five feet asked, 'Mr. Berline, would you back me up on a tune?' I told him I'd be glad to, and this kid took his fiddle and began to play 'Grey Eagle.' My ears couldn't believe what was happening! I couldn't imagine a 12-year-old having learned so fast and so well. As I listened, I was able to detect the influence of a great fiddler and friend of mine, Benny Thomasson."

I also met a few teenaged musicians at Langley, each of them quite talented at bluegrass music, one especially so. Five kids from Oklahoma put together an all-teen band called the Bluegrass Revue. It featured Bobby Clark on mandolin, Bill Perry on banjo, and his younger brother Mike on bass. Jimmy Gyles played the very three instruments I played — guitar, mandolin, and fiddle. He had just won the National Flat-pick Guitar Championships in Winfield, Kansas. Their fifth member wasn't your average Okie, either. The 16-year-old guitarist and lead singer was the future bluegrass and country music superstar, Vince Gill. His silky tenor voice had been long-established.

The Bluegrass Revue asked me to sit in on their mainstage show early in the afternoon — they didn't have a principal fiddler. After the set, several of us ended back up at Byron Berline's campsite on the festival grounds to jam with him some more. In a quiet moment, I got to talk a little more to Bryon about my teacher Benny. Byron just loved Benny so much. Byron's father, Lue Berline, a contest fiddler in the 1950s, took his young son along to the big fiddle contest in Truth or Consequences, New Mexico. That was when Byron first met Benny. That afternoon we played more Benny tunes we had learned from him including "Limerock," Benny's master-piece, as well as a Berline showstopper, "Snowflake Reel," which goes from "D" to "B^b" chords, and "Done Gone." That one being in the key of "B^b."

Our first festival in the South was quite an introduction into the world of great bluegrass musicians, most all of them emanating from musical families. Save for a few transplanted Tar Heels, the Northwest bluegrass-ers were mostly first-generation players, a lot of them getting into the acoustic music scene because of the 1960s folk music revival. The Bob Dylan, Joan Baez, Pete Seeger folk music influence did quite a lot of good for spreading old-time and bluegrass music beyond its southern home. You could count my family among the recipients of this broadening appeal. But in the South, you had to admire their tradition of old-time country music ingrained in families, sometimes for generations.

KNOCKING OUT GOOD CONTEST results all summer long, it was as if all the bowling pins were set up for me to just knock 'em down. We attended ten national competitions around the country in the summer of '74—the vast majority having only the Open divisions available for contestants. But it didn't even matter. I was still getting 1st places most of the time. Many of the festivals and conventions had multiple instrument categories just like Woodinville did, so I could try to win on all of the in-struments. At the fiddle and mandolin contest in Murfreesboro, Tennes-see, that summer, I won both of them. I got 2nd in guitar and 3rd in fiddle at the Lakeland World Bluegrass Competitions in Memphis, and 1st in the fiddle and 2nd in the guitar at Winfield, Kansas, for the National Flat-pick Guitar Championships. This festival in particular, represented a story un-folding that was just getting underway. It was going to boom.

That same summer, I did very well at Bill Monroe's Rocky Mountain Bluegrass Festival in Henderson, Colorado. The legend himself stood on stage, giving out the prizes each time I got up to receive mine. He had that look on his face — *didn't I just see you up here?* Monroe paid out cash each time my name was called: 2nd place in fiddle, and 3rd in guitar. It was the first time I met the Father of Bluegrass Music. Monroe counted out the

$20 bills as I came up to collect the awards—a time when "cash prizes" actually meant *cash,* not a check.

Playing with Bill Monroe and the Bluegrass Boys at the Colorado festival was one of the best bluegrass fiddlers of all time, Kenny Baker. As long as he was on stage, my eyes were glued to him. He had the polish of a fine contest fiddler, but in this setting he was weaving in and out of a full bluegrass band—playing off the vocal and filling in around the other instruments. When he came roaring in with tasty and refined fiddle breaks, it was some of the best I could hope to hear. Baker played with solid timing, a command of the beat, all highlighted with good intonation and tone. His featured solos on Monroe's sped-up version of "Mule Skinner Blues" were some of his most classic. He first recorded the song with Monroe in 1961, the year I was born. It was a masterclass to watch him live—the notes he played each and every time, well, you could etch them right into stone.

Kenny Baker was also a very creative fiddler, writing several well-known fiddle tunes that became bluegrass fiddle standards: "Washington County," "Indian Ridge," "Big Sandy River," "Doc Harris the Fisherman." He and Monroe had just written a tune that featured quite a new sound for the traditional Bluegrass Boys—a fiddle instrumental called "Jerusalem Ridge." It was riveting to watch Baker play the tune on stage that summer. Just like Byron Berline's bluegrass fiddling, and Benny's fiddling in the Texas-style, those fiddle men created the mold. By now, I was witnessing firsthand the best players who had ever picked up a fiddle.

It was at that same Bill Monroe festival where we got to see the great bluegrass legend Ralph Stanley and his Clinch Mountain Boys, for the first time. My mother was a big fan of the Stanley Brothers albums. We might have had 20 or 30. A few of them were gospel albums. Their "Rank Strangers To Me" was rapturous—with Stanley's distinctive tenor voice, and its raspy mountain quality. Ralph was on his own now. Brother Carter had passed back in '66.

Over at Stanley's merchandise table, their fiddler, Curly Ray Cline, was peddling his keychains adorned with his own likeness. He had his own table to sell stuff. After spotting me carrying my fiddle case, he motioned for us to come over. He insisted that I take one, so I had a Curly Ray Cline keychain—one that I used for many years. Cline played bluegrass in a mountainy old-time style, a little more scratchy than I usually liked it. I was impressed by the clean and smooth playing the most.

Appearing at that same Monroe festival was the bluegrass legend Lester Flatt and the Nashville Grass. Flatt was the lead singer who I had been listening to on Flatt and Scruggs LPs all year, mainly for Earl Scruggs' banjo playing. When I was learning banjo the year before, Earl Scruggs was a mighty influence, as I'm quite certain he was for any banjo picker who ever put on two metal finger-picks and a plastic thumb-pick.

Scruggs broke off the unprecedented successful partnership because he wanted to start up with his own family band featuring his three grown sons: Gary, Randy and Steve. The Earl Scruggs Revue played electric bluegrass with a progressive country-rock sound, while Flatt kept the traditional bluegrass going himself. This band provided the better fit for traditional bluegrass fiddler Paul Warren, who helped Flatt form the Nashville Grass. Paul was one of the most listened to bluegrass fiddlers of all time—the rosin dust was flying when Warren took his exciting breaks.

There was another, younger member of the Nashville Grass who piqued our interest even more. Marty Stuart was just 15—a kid playing up on the main stage with a bluegrass icon. He's playing the exact same three instruments as I was, too. Focusing mostly on the mandolin, Stuart doubled on guitar, and he played one quick fiddle ride, but he was all about that stage—singing with Flatt, all dressed up to the nines. With Flatt's troupe, that meant a full plaid suit, a felt cowboy hat, and a smart, shiny neck scarf tie. It provided an unusual discordance to an audience full of Colorado hippies. All the same, my mother, Marty, thought the "younger Marty" was cute as a newt.

We waited outside their tour bus to meet Marty Stuart. He didn't hear me play that weekend, but we were still able to ask him a few questions about what it was like to tour with a famous bluegrass band as a youngster. Marty underscored that he was always learning from the older musicians in the band. He added that he tried to hang around his boss's old pals at the bluegrass festivals, seeing what he could pick up. "There was always something more to learn," Marty Stuart told us.

Just two years earlier, fate had placed Stuart, a youngster, right into the middle of bluegrass royalty—a fortuity reserved for only him, as far as we could tell. We didn't see anything comparable across the entire summer.

There was no doubt about it, on this scale I was just another lucky specta-tor to the giants of bluegrass. And yet at age 12, I was just beginning to *feel* the music flow out of my instruments—uninhibited and unencumbered. By midsummer, it was inexplicable as to how far I came on the fiddle in such a short time. Especially with the successes I was having in the Open divisions against the adults all around the country. I was inspired by the music I heard around me, and yes, *there was always something more to learn.*

But it wasn't just the contests and the festivals that Mom had on her mind right now. She wanted to see what Music City was all about. We drove into Nashville, Tennessee, in July of 1974.

WEISER, IDAHO, WAS MY coming out party. I had won the Junior division the month before, and every other person in the little town seemed to be offering their congratulations. Many were curious about my future plans. One such person was Tut Taylor. Sue Blood invited Tut to venture back up to the Northwest to camp out during the Weiser contest— to take in some good old-time fiddle music. Tut saw how many people at Weiser were all ears as to what I was going to do next with my music.

Mom and Tut talked about our planned trip back East that summer— attending several bluegrass festivals and fiddle conventions.

"Y'all are coming to Nashville, right?" Tut asked my mother.

"Well, I hope so, but Mark is really wanting to go to as many festivals and fiddle contests as we can fit into the trip," my mother replied.

"You have to come to Nashville though," Tut urged.

"What would he do there? He really wants to play and enter the con-tests. We're choosing bluegrass festivals where they have the various in-struments he can enter," she added.

"I think you should still bring him to Nashville, even for a few days. I could arrange for him to play someplace. When you get into town, just give me a call, okay?" offered Tut.

After a couple of bluegrass festivals the summer of 1974, I was having such a wonderful experience. I fell in love with bluegrass festivals—the *perfect* place for a small kid. It would be hard to get into trouble at those, and Mom felt the same way. As we worked our way over to Nashville, I was a little disappointed that we even had to go there at all. Nashville, to me, meant neither a bluegrass festival nor a fiddle contest—not in July at least, and those things were my only two interests anymore. I tried to talk my mother out of it. "Why, do we have to go, Mom?" I asked her. She said that she had our one *contact,* and if that didn't pan out, we wouldn't have to stay, and instead could make our way to another festival or fiddlers convention.

We arrived at the outskirts of Nashville on Wednesday afternoon July 24th, 1974. It more or less looked like any other city, it seemed to me. We exited off Interstate 40 to find a convenience store. Mom made her way over to the payphone booth. While my sister and I chased each other around the parking lot, Mom was on the phone with Tut Taylor, ringing him up at his music shop just south of town.

"Your timing is perfect," Taylor suggested to Mom on the phone. Every Wednesday night, Charlie Collins and 'Bashful Brother' Oswald who play with Roy Acuff and the Smokey Mountain Boys on the Grand Ole Opry, perform as a duo. They'll be in downtown Nashville at the Old-Time Pickin' Parlor.

"Go down to the Pickin' Parlor on Second Avenue at 8 p.m. tonight. I'll make sure you're on the guest list. I'm going to put a call into Charlie and Oswald right now and I'll ask them to have Mark play a tune in their show," Tut told Mom.

Then Mom had to yell at me to straighten up and to not tease Michelle; *"Cut it out right now… you're going to play on stage tonight!"* Tut Taylor continued;

"Everybody who plays acoustic music in town knows the place well. Make sure you park on the street. It's right off Broadway, but there's not much else down there, so lock the car doors."

Downtown Nashville was a little like a ghost town. Parts of the city center almost seemed abandoned, the exact opposite of downtown Seattle, I noted. Whole blocks of battened down buildings made for very seedy surroundings. Yes, it was kind of hard to believe this was really Nashville, the place on TV. Driving down Broadway, Mom said, "I think we just passed the Ryman Auditorium there off to the side." The Grand Ole Opry: it was all boarded up and abandoned.

We entered the Old-Time Pickin' Parlor through the music store on Second Avenue at the designated time. The shop owner, Randy Wood, recognized us as the family of three Taylor had called him about. He gestured for us to go on into the small music hall located through the shop's side door. The music was about to start.

We were a few minutes too late to get acquainted with anyone. I could tell my mother was frustrated with herself that we didn't allow more time to get ourselves down there sooner. We found a seat easily, as there couldn't have been more than a dozen people watching the start of the Charlie and Oswald show that night. Once seated, Mom and I looked at each other wondering how famous professional musicians in Nashville could be playing to such a small audience. Even at my age, I was trying to think if I had ever played to a smaller audience back home. *Nashville must be one tough place to get noticed, I thought to myself.*

Our table wasn't too far from the stage. I tucked my fiddle case in-between the table legs and looked for a soda machine. Mom allowed me to go get my favorite drink of the summer—Orange Fanta.

As Charlie and Oswald got their set going, they were playing mostly old-time songs I was familiar with by now. I'd heard many of them from the old-time musicians in Seattle, and of course, from the recordings we had. Charlie played mostly the guitar, but also a little fiddle and mandolin, while "Bashful Brother Oswald" Pete Kirby (his real and stage names put together), played the dobro, old-time banjo, and sang. He sang songs like "Good Old Mountain Dew" and "Way Down in Columbus Georgia," while frailing the banjo like his Grand Ole Opry colleague, Uncle Dave Macon. Oswald told several jokes and tall tales, finishing up with his catchline: *"Now that's the truth if I've ever told it!"*

Oswald, born Beecher Ray Kirby, also known as Pete Kirby, dates back to the time when Roy Acuff first began playing on the Grand Ole Opry. In Knoxville, he had subbed into Acuff and his Crazy Tennesseans a couple of years before. By 1939, Roy Acuff wanted him on the *Opry* as a permanent member of his new Smokey Mountain Boys, and gave him his stage name, "Bashful Brother Oswald." Acuff had to manage an issue developing within their touring ensemble and was looking for a remedy. Rachel Veach, who played banjo in the group, was unmarried. At that time, it was highly controversial for a single lady to be out on the road with a music group full of men. Roy asked Oswald to playact as her brother and chaperone in the band—therefore, he became her Brother Oswald. Charlie joined the band a couple of decades later.

When Brother Oswald went to play his dobro during the set, his music took on a much more serious tone. Oswald played instrumental hits that he made famous with the Smokey Mountain Boys, "Steel Guitar Chimes" from 1940, and his own composition, a ballad called "The End of the World." I was very familiar with Oswald's ballad, because he recorded it on my favorite bluegrass album of all time, the Nitty Gritty Dirt Band's historic two-album set released the year before— *Will The Circle Be Unbroken.* The West Coast country-rock band with some popular radio hits including "Mr. Bojangles" had sincere interest in bluegrass music. Originally, they were a jug band from the 1960s. By way of one of their founding members, John McEuen, the band's banjoist and multi-instrumentalist, together with John's brother and the album's producer, Bill McEuen, they gathered together many of my very favorite musicians in Nashville for their great recording.

"The Circle" album featured "Mother" Maybelle Carter. I had studied both her family's songs and her guitar-playing. Earl Scruggs was on the album, too. When I was learning banjo the year before, I had my *Earl Scruggs and the 5-String Banjo* book of tablature, where I beheld the *forward, backward,* and *alternating* finger rolls. One of my guitar heroes, Doc Watson, was on the album, and I loved his tracks like "Tennessee Stud." My absolute favorite guitar player, Norman Blake, was on there, too. Exaltedly, one of the album's most respected fiddlers, Vassar Clements, was featured on nearly every song. I was able to meet him briefly in Woodinville just about a year earlier—I played a little backup guitar with him along with a whole group of people at his workshop. He didn't see me play the fiddle or anything. I wasn't very good yet, anyway. The landmark two-album set from the Dirt Band featured Oswald, as well as his boss, "The King of Country Music," Roy Acuff.

I loved the album packaging with all the photos from the recording sessions, so much so that I kept the album cover with me when I went to sleep at night.

There was another recording that I loved Vassar Clement's fiddling on—a track from dobro player Mike Auldridge, "House of the Rising

Sun." The ballad goes back centuries. It's also a song that Roy Acuff recorded in 1938, making his version the first well-known recording. Later, it
was again popularized by the rock band The Animals. But it was how
Clements played the fiddle on that bluesy rendition with Auldridge, that's
what really blew me over. When Vassar Clements was left to improvise by
himself at the end—on the fade-out, it was the first time I understood the
emotional power that a fiddle could unearth. It was a distinct, haunting,
bluesy-sound, and an approach to playing the instrument which really had
a profound impact on me. After that, I just *had* to play blues songs for my
tunes of choice.

T HEY WERE ABOUT 45 minutes into their set by now. We figured
we would speak to Charlie and Oswald during the break, when Charlie began to announce something from the stage.

"We haven't played with this young boy, but in this business, when
somebody calls you, and he's a musician, and he says somebody else is
a musician, you can generally take their word for it. That person called
me tonight and told me that Mark O'Connor, a young boy from Seattle,
Washington, will be here, and he can play fiddle and guitar."
Charlie looked out into the audience to find me:

"If it won't embarrass you, would you like to come up?"

I exchanged glances with Mom as I reached for my case from underneath the table. I headed towards the stage.

"What do you want to play for us?" Charlie asked.

"How about, 'Bill Cheatham'?" I replied.

So we kicked off "Bill Cheatham." It went pretty well. They wanted
another, so I lit into "Sally Goodin'," and after that "Faded Love." Everyone was full of appreciation for how I was playing. Charlie was on the
mandolin, Oswald playing the guitar. Oswald leaned over and asked me if
I had entered the Grand Masters Fiddle Championship in Nashville last
year. I nodded, no. Then he spoke on mic,

"The only reason why he didn't win the fiddlin' contest *here* is because
he didn't enter." ...and so the evening went.

Charlie and Oswald kept me on stage for another half hour. They didn't
take their break like they said they were going to, but instead, they kept

requesting me to play tune after tune: "Sally Johnson," "Jack of Dia-monds," "Wednesday Night Waltz," "Tom and Jerry." Ultimately, their reaction to my playing was unlike any Mom and I had ever witnessed—even at Weiser. I dare say it, but they seemed to be floored by the whole thing. I was fresh off jamming for an entire month at these contests and festivals, and I was inspired by the summer developing as it was. It probably meant that I was getting better on the fiddle... likely by the day.

When Charlie and Oswald finally wound down the set, we figured that was probably it for the evening. As I walked back to the table where Mom and Michelle were seated, there were a few more people in the audience than when it began. Many more. Suddenly, we were engulfed by them. Those audience members formed a tight circle around our table, just wanting to say hello—and to ask us all kinds of questions.

As the greetings and introductions continued, we noticed that still more people were coming into the Pickin' Parlor. Charlie was on the phone, asking for folks to come down to see me play. Charlie's handiwork was apart from the store owner himself, Randy Wood, who was doing his own enterprising, too. He had been calling well-known musicians to come down to see this for the last 30 minutes.

It was far more of a reaction than we expected in Music City, the home of the world's professional fiddlers. A person named Perry Harris walked in. He was the coordinator of the biggest fiddle contest in the country, the Grand Masters Fiddle Championship in Nashville, Tennessee. That was the contest Oswald asked me about on stage. Right after Perry Harris, two big-time bluegrass musicians from the Woodinville bluegrass festival came in through the front door—mandolinist Buck White, and none other than the fiddling god himself, Vassar Clements.

As more musicians filed in through the front door, Clements took the stage to play his own versions of "Bill Cheatham," and then "Katy Hill-Sally Johnson," the two tunes I had just played, but he didn't know that. He played them with a banjo player—and at really fast bluegrass tempos. Charlie gave me his mandolin and I played along with Vassar Clements. I even got to take a couple of mandolin rides. It was exhilarating, to say the least. After the two tunes, Clements announced that it was enough of him, he wanted to hear *me* play the fiddle now. Perry Harris did too. They all wanted to hear me play more fiddle tunes. Charlie grabbed his guitar and we sat right down on the little stage, just the two of us this time. Oswald elected to watch from the audience. I began to play fiddle tune after fiddle tune—request after request. Luckily, Benny had taught me so many tunes over the last nine months, I had enough repertoire just to keep on playing—at least for a good while. I played another hour for everyone; "Billy in the Low Ground," "Dusty Miller," "I Don't Love Nobody," "Apple Blossom."

Charlie kept asking me what I wanted to play next. They just wouldn't let me quit. The reaction in the room was one of joyousness, and an unfamiliar jubilance. They were enamored that I could play the fiddle as I did while being so young. Charlie spoke into the microphone;

"Doc Harris said *he* had an invitation to the Grand Masters championship of fiddlin' next year."

Charlie looked over at me, "Did you hear that?"

It all felt like a celebration to me. I was heartened that I could make *them* so happy. Charlie saw that I was also getting tired after so much playing. He announced to the audience that maybe they could ask me to play just one more. I suggested "Soppin' the Gravy."

"He's only 12 and he plays the tar out of the fiddle. He beats all I've ever seen. Beautiful. The finest I ever heard," Charlie said over the microphone.

The audience reacted to Charlie's comment with another round of applause. After playing my final tune, Perry Harris was right there at the front of the stage to greet me.

"I want to shake your hand. That's some of the finest fiddling I ever heard."

"Thank you."

"Would you like to come to the contest next year?"

"Yeah, I would."

"I am going to extend you an invitation now. Give me your name and address. Do you have something you can write it on?"

"Do you know when it's going to be next year?" I asked.

"It will be the 15th of June."

Harris met my mother as she approached us.

"I'm Dr. Harris and I want to make sure we have him on the invited fiddlers list. An 18-year-old won 2nd place this time, Terry Morris. How long have you been playing the fiddle?" Harris asked me.

"About a year and nine months," I said, keeping good track of my progress.

"I don't see how you did it so quickly," Dr. Harris repeated.

The folks there that night at the Pickin' Parlor were thoroughly roused by the fiddling. All those old-time fiddle tunes were familiar, but my approach to them was different at the same time. I suppose it was hard for many of them to trace what I was playing—to identify the source of it. A more common reaction would be to notice where a new fiddler on the scene got a lick: *oh that's Baker, that's Clements, ah... you got that from Berline.* Of course, some of what I was doing was created during lessons with Benny Thomasson. Harris made that connection. He asked me, "Have you ever met Benny Thomasson?" But a lot of it already was just me—my own variations and renditions of the tunes. I was even improvising on these tunes for the performance.

What was most unusual for the folks listening, though, was that I didn't hail from a southern state such as Tennessee, a place where this kind of fiddling was prevalent. Equally, they were bewildered that I didn't come from a family tradition of musicians playing this kind of music. Most of them who played it were born into it. My biography was entirely new for them. Even though my mother and I couldn't have known just how much of a rarity it was to see a kid fiddler in the South, which became absolutely clear over the course of the evening, if not the entire summer of 1974. I brought with me a completely different set of life circumstances and experiences which led me to my own brand of American fiddling. All of them were responding to this.

The matter of my having played fiddle for just over a year-and-a-half did not make itself scarce either. That little tidbit bolted through the assemblage like a scalded cat. Despite such little time on the instrument, I was being *transported* here just like I had dreamed about.

Amid all the commotion, there were moments where my mind wandered off—times where I was doing some heart-searching of my own. I had to pinch myself—was this really me—right here, right now? The boy who these professional musicians were praising up and down..., is this the same awkward kid who was the laughing stock at school just a few months ago? The effigy bullseye for all their flung-away darts? The object of constant and inexorable bullying? Was I the same boy who was just one fiddle contest away from working child labor for my Dad every day after school—under the houses with the "rats and the snakes?" Instead of getting to practice? The kind of practice that got me to this very night?

On this night, there was an intangibility about it all.

I was asked about all these things from the very nice people—things they wondered about, like my life back home. Sometimes I just stood there in place—listening to them pay me compliments, but I'd zone out on them... I didn't really focus in on what they were saying to me at times. Couldn't they tell that we were *nobodies?* Or worse... that we were poor misfits? While all these people praised my musical abilities, I was flashing back, remembering how I was in so much danger that year. So many times there was such danger—because people really disliked me in my neighborhood, at my school. Part of me hurt so much to think about what my *actual* life was like. Was it possible for the summer of *fiddling love* to become of *this* world?

AFTER CONFIRMING WITH MY MOTHER that I had just won the Juniors in Weiser, Doc Harris' invitation for next summer's Grand Masters in Nashville seemed to be set in stone. The person who had hosted the greatest contest fiddlers in North America wanted me to join in.

While Harris was speaking to Mom a few feet away, I started to chat it up with the likes of Vassar Clements and Buck White. I wasn't doing any zoning out around them; however—I was wide awake. Their incredible stature in music felt enormous up that close, and I was affected by how sweet they were to me. Just like those delightful fiddlers from Idaho and eastern Washington. These men here, however, were greatly accomplished in music—seasoned professionals out there on the never-ending highways performing show after show.

As the evening drew to a close, folks began to disperse, and people started to head home. A smaller group of us remained in the shop with Randy Wood. We kept talking from one end to the other about fiddle music, stories of my teacher Benny, and what they all reckoned was a wonderful and surprising evening. Charlie and Oswald conveyed what a fiddle enthusiast the "King of Country Music" was: the fiddler, singer, and their "boss man" of the Grand Ole Opry, Roy Acuff.

"Doc, don't you believe that Mr. Roy needs to hear this boy play?" Charlie asserted.

"Absolutely, Roy needs to hear him," Harris adds.

"We should bring him down to the Opry Friday night and have him play his fiddle for Roy," said Oswald.

I really had no conception of what it meant—or how big of a deal this might be. But it was a chance to play more fiddle, and that was good with me.

"Could you folks come to the Opry on Friday? I'll make sure your names are on the backstage list and everything. Will you bring him to play for Mr. Roy?" Charlie asked Mom.

Among the few people who were in attendance when we first arrived at the club was a young couple—Bill and Bonnie Smith. They turned out to be about the kindest people you could ever hope to meet. They weren't musicians at all, but they were big fans of Charlie and Oswald and attended their shows often.

Bill Smith, a medical doctor just like Doc Harris, was curious to know where we were staying that night, likely noticing we weren't dressed at all upscale. By that point, my straw cowboy hat had a big tear in the side of it. And the leather sandals I wore… they were pretty shabby and falling apart. When Mom told the Smiths we were staying at the KOA Campground in our van, they offered to have us stay at their home for the next several days while we were in Nashville;

"If you're going to the Opry to meet Roy Acuff, which it sounds like you are, you should have a nice place to eat and relax!" they offered.

I saw my mother telling them yes, although it was not like her to consider such an offer, especially if they were strangers, and not even fiddlers. But that notion was about to change. I think Mom was so worn out from the relentless heat of the southern summer, with no air conditioning anywhere, except for going into a grocery store once in a while, or the club that night—she threw all caution aside: "Yes, thank you!" The Smiths saw that Mom was on her own with two young children on the road. Bill said to her;

"Bonnie is a great cook. Come over for dinner tomorrow night. If you feel comfortable, stay as long as you like. You'll have your own corner of the house and your own bathroom where our guests stay. We have two little girls, Kathy and Laura, who wouldn't mind having a couple of kids around to play with for a few days."

The following day we returned to the Pickin' Parlor for some more jamming. I met even more Nashville musicians there on Thursday. That evening we drove out to Bill and Bonnie's Maple Creek Farm in Goodlettsville for some dandy southern home-cooking and a wonderful air-conditioned night's sleep. I was happy that my fiddle playing *earned* my family this marvelous place to stay.

Bluegrass Unlimited Magazine – Article by Bonnie Smith

"The O'Connors arrived in Nashville on a Wednesday in July 1974, and called Tut Taylor, one of the few people they knew in town. Tut told them where they could hear music that evening and advised Mark to take his fiddle along, just in case.

The first time I ever heard Mark perform is an experience most vivid in my mind, and one which I'll never forget. It was that evening at the 'Old Time Pickin' Parlor' in Nashville where Brother Oswald and Charlie Collins were performing. We arrived a moment before the show began and ran into Charlie Collins, tuning his instruments in the foyer. He commented: 'Boy, I don't know what our show is going to be like tonight. See that kid with the hat on sitting in there? Well, I got a call from Tut this afternoon saying we should let him play. Tut says he's good, and I suppose for 12 years old he probably isn't bad. But I think we'll do most of the set before we call him up.'

After Brother Oswald had performed on his Dobro and banjo, and Charlie on his fiddle, guitar, and mandolin, Mark was called up to join them on stage. He was asked what he would like to play, and his response was 'Bill Cheatham'. Charlie said, 'Well, at least this boy knows how to pick the songs!' After a couple of licks, Oswald and Charlie about fell off their chairs and everyone in the whole 'Pickin' Parlor' was giving each other glances of disbelief. Someone got on the phone, and within 20 minutes, many new faces began showing up in the audience, including Vassar Clements and Dr. Perry Harris."

WE DROVE UP TO THE BACKSTAGE entrance of the brand new Grand Ole Opry House at Opryland. It was Friday night, July 26th, 1974—two days after our meaningful Pickin' Parlor evening. They had just opened the new Opry house a few months before. Our names were on the list at the gate just as Charlie promised they would be. Bill and

Bonnie stayed home because they observed the sabbath as Seventh-day Adventists—resting from sundown Friday to sundown Saturday. They were a little disappointed that I couldn't play for Roy Acuff the following night on Saturday when they could've been along to enjoy it. The Smiths had been to the Opry several times:

"Backstage at the Opry is not like anything you have ever experienced before," they told us.

After being directed to our parking slot, we walked into the backstage area and came to a second security station, where a veteran guard named "Mr. Bell" seemed to be in charge of anybody coming or going. As he was searching for our names on some of his lists, Charlie was called to come and greet us there. He welcomed my Mom, Michelle and me, and asked us to follow him down the hallway and past several dressing rooms. We took a right turn and walked past even more dressing rooms to finally arrive at a dressing room marked #1. The door had been left wide open. It was quite crowded inside.

As we were held up just beyond the doorway, we saw the legendary man seated just across the room about ten feet away: the "King of Country Music," Roy Acuff. The 70-year-old country music legend immediately rose from his chair to waive us in. He took a few steps towards the center of his small dressing room to greet me there. Roy Acuff looked me over for a few seconds before he spoke:

"Well, I've heard a lot about ya, young man. The boys have been telling me about your fiddling and all. We want to hear ya. Will you play something for us?" Mr. Acuff asked me.

As I glanced around, I saw that Doc Harris had already arrived. Standing next to him was the great fiddler, "Big Howdy" Forrester, an illustrious player who worked in Bill Monroe's band in 1940 before joining up with the Acuff band in the '50s. I had a few Howdy Forrester albums at home. In addition to the many fiddle tunes Forrester made famous, he wrote some of my all-time favorites, "Wild Fiddler's Rag" and "Memory Waltz,"—tunes I was just beginning to learn. He also wrote "Doc Harris Hornpipe." With the linkage to Kenny Baker's "Doc Harris the Fisherman," I learned who these tunes were being named for. Doc seemed to be synonymous with the great fiddlers of Nashville.

"I know you've met Doc Harris here. I want you to meet the fiddler who plays with me, Howard Forrester," as Mr. Acuff introduced me to the Nashville fiddling big-hitter.

Howdy couldn't have had a more ebullient smile on his face as he and all the others welcomed me and my family into the dressing room. All the seats had been taken by the time we walked in, but folks made room so that my Mom could sit down. She took one of the chairs and Michelle sat on her lap. Charlie grabbed his guitar and we stood right there, readying ourselves to play for the country music icon in the middle of his dressing room.

As I was adjusting the fine tuners on my fiddle—plucking the strings with the fourth finger of my left-hand to get it perfectly in tune and set to go—Charlie asked me what I wanted to play. By then, I was getting pretty familiar with him asking me that. I responded with "Sally Johnson."

Just uttering the name of the tune drew a good-humored chuckle from Mr. Acuff.

"Hell, I can't even play 'Sally Johnson,'" as Roy Acuff looked over at Forrester. "Of course Howard plays it. Well let's see what he can do with it," Mr. Acuff observed.
He got set to listen attentively.

I was not even through the "A" part of "Sally Johnson" before there were audible responses and outbursts to my fiddling. Roy Acuff was fairly subdued for a bit—he chose to really get an earful, I could tell. I looked up just a few times and saw Charlie smile at me while he strummed his guitar. I saw Doc Harris, his broad grin fixated on Roy Acuff, watching for any reaction the "King of Country Music" might give.

It reminded me of playing in the practice room at Weiser—all of these older gentlemen gathered around me listening intently to every single note. Except these people here were at the top of Nashville's country music world. I just kept on playing. I knew I had an audience at least for the next minute or two, until the fiddle tune I was playing headed towards its natural conclusion.

ROY ACUFF'S DRESSING ROOM door remained open as I played. The room marked #1 was the final door before the Opry artists entered the wings of the prestigious stage itself. As I played the fiddle, Opry artists, one after another, stuck their heads in through the door to see what all the fuss and bother was about. Some of the stars listened for a minute in the doorway and moved on to the stage for their slot on the show. Still others, who had more time, came all the way into the now-crammed room for a closer listen. As Roy Acuff yelled out — "play another one," some of the stars, with their guitars already strapped around their neck, joined in with Charlie to play some additional accompaniment.

Country artists who were compelled to join in with us included honky-tonk singer Charlie Walker, who sang his hit "Pick Me Up on Your Way Down," that night on stage. Another honky-tonk singer, Ernest Tubb, who sang one of his hit songs on stage, "Walking The Floor Over You," also played a little rhythm guitar while supporting us with his big toothy smile.

As Roy Acuff said "Do another," more Opry artists filed in to join us. Billy Grammer, whose big hit was "Gotta Travel On," couldn't resist the temptation to play some with the little kid. Even "Little" Jimmy Dickens ("Take a Old Cold Tater and Wait"), not being able to contain his enthusiasm, got on his tip toes pulling himself to about as short as I was. He was excited to strum along for a few chords, before he abruptly stopped playing — choosing to listen instead. Other Opry members came in to hear me for a few minutes: Hank Snow, "Jumpin'" Bill Carlisle, Dottie West, Jan Howard, the Browns, and "Whisperin'" Bill Anderson. One after another.

The Opry fiddlers started filing into Roy Acuff's dressing room to watch me play. Many of Nashville's top fiddlers were there, and they stayed in the room the longest. A fiddler sporting thick gray curly hair, Curly Fox, predated even Acuff at the Opry. One of the things Fox was known for back in the 1930s was performing in a traveling road show around the South hosting "world championship fiddle contests."

Fiddler Stoney Cooper was there listening. He performed with his wife Wilma Lee Cooper, as an Opry act. Marty Robbins' manager, fiddler Louie Dunn, was standing there the entire time I played. Fiddler Skeeter Willis, with the Opry act The Willis Brothers, was taking notice too. His three-brother act became members in 1946. Some of the older Opry stars shouted out requests for fiddle tunes they knew best, tunes common with country square dance music: "How about a little, 'Soldier's Joy,' 'Arkansas Traveler,' 'Devil's Dream,' 'Cotton Eyed Joe...'" They knew some fiddle tunes all right.

Interestingly, I hadn't the faintest idea who a lot of these people were. Out in Seattle, we couldn't get the *Grand Ole Opry* on the radio at all. Regardless, up to that point at least, my mother refused to let us kids listen to the radio whatsoever. No commercial radio played in the house. Why my mother made such a quirky distinction between commercial radio and commercial television is just one more of those intriguing mysteries of how parents come up with their own rules of the road. Mom even insisted that the Ford Econoline should *not* have a radio in it. That said, "Opry Stars" were pretty easy to spot, since they were all dressed up in rhinestone out-fits—the men all slicked out with their sprayed hairdos and standard-issue felt cowboy hats. The "big cheese" definitely stood out from the band-members. I never saw so much glitter on men in my entire life. Whatever was going on there for that hour in Roy Acuff's dressing room was one *freaky trip* for a kid.

Of all the entertainers coming into dressing room #1, the biggest thrills for me were the bluegrass Opry stars. I recognized them from our album covers at home. At one point, several legendary bluegrass fiddlers wove their way in up close and hovered over my 5 ft. frame in a tight huddle. I continued to play more fiddle tunes and taking requests like "Don't Let the Deal Go Down." One of them asked for "Cotton Patch Rag." Another wanted to hear "Beaumont Rag." The fiddlers in the crowd called out the *serious* tunes. As I played, they were leaning so far in towards me, I felt like there was hardly any more room left to bow my fiddle.

I played them tune after tune—"Billy in the Low Ground" and "Say Old Man." Kenny Baker and Tater Tate, who were both working with Bill Monroe that night, came in and stood there beside the others. Yes, the great Kenny Baker was right there listening to me play for the first time. Even Bill Monroe poked his head in from the doorway. I looked up to see him standing there.

Surrounding me, a huddle of 20 or more people packed in the small dressing room remained present, all of their faces close by mine—their smiles and jovial interruptions to my fiddle seemed to arise without fail. Their grins and revelry jutting outward—it was creating both a visual and audible counterpoint to the music I played. By their feedback and their voices, with all of the exhilaration—I played off of it and I rose up *to* it, taking their bait with my fiddle. I was *going* for things that even surprised me from time to time. Maybe it was how I placed an accent on a note or two—just a lick, a cool fiddle rhythm with the bow—then pulling it off right in front of them on the spot. At some point, it was as if everything was in slow motion. I could even feel the space between the rapid fire notes. Those interesting characters around me bent themselves forward, their heads careening over the top of me, retorting to every distinction and subtlety my fiddle provided. They all must've been reacting to what they sensed as creativity—my creativity. They were acknowledging the spontaneity of what this little *kid* was doing, for I was improvising on those fiddle tunes for them.

ABOUT AN HOUR INTO my 12-year-old fiddling display for the icons of country and bluegrass music, Roy Acuff halted the proceedings to make his pronouncement to all present in the dressing room.

"All right everyone, I'm going to bring this boy out on stage with me tonight."

Charlie looked at me and patted me on my shoulder.

"Let's let him have a little rest. He's got to get ready to go out there. We are on in 20 minutes!"

As I walked toward Mom in the corner of the room, I wasn't exactly sure what I was supposed to do, or play. I thought perhaps I was to sit in with Roy Acuff's band for a song, maybe play a short break? I'd done that kind of break before, of course. However, Mom was far more concerned about another matter. She was fretful over what I was looking like, and rightfully so. I had absolutely no stage clothes for the Grand Ole Opry.

Many of the country stars were head-to-toe in rhinestone regalia, while Acuff and his band, as well as most of the bluegrass acts, wore conventional dress clothes—suits and ties. At which point, and in direct opposition to the assembly of the fancily clad, "Bashful Brother" Oswald emerged from the changing room *ridin'* a whole other freight train. Attired in his dress shirt, tie, and slacks *before* the show, he reappeared in his actual stage outfit—faded overalls, a torn floppy hat, and oversized shoes—Oswald dressed *down* for the Opry?

As Mom persisted in looking over my own cheapjack appearance, pecking at me and tucking things in, I was looking over at Oswald's rundown getup. I was more than amused as to what ol' Os was up to. He didn't dress like that when he appeared at the Pickin' Parlor.

In time, I learned about "clowning" in the tradition of country music entertainment. It turned out there were even clown personalities in the earlier versions of the very bluegrass bands on stage that night. Clowns were usually pegged to the upright bass player, sometimes a banjoist like David "Stringbean" Akeman, a serious player who claw-hammered old-time banjo in Bill Monroe's band in the years before Earl Scruggs joined in 1945. In Flatt and Scruggs and the Foggy Mountain Boys themselves, the dobroist, "Uncle" Josh Graves, used to dress up in the clown role. Even by 1974, Acuff and a few other country stars held onto that old style of vaudeville and minstrel entertainment. As the straight man, Roy Acuff would play off "Minnie Pearl" on the Opry, the comedic character by Sarah Ophelia Colley Cannon. What a pair they were. "How-w-w DEE-E-E-E" was her signature wail along with the price tag hanging off her hat as she carried out the familiar satire of southern culture to audiences assembled from around the world. Being from a small town 50 miles outside of Nashville, her act consisted of poking fun at her own hometown folks. Acuff did some of his own hocus-pocus as well. He took the tip of his bow and threaded it through the tail piece of his fiddle, going from end to end. Then he placed the button of the bow square on his chin and balanced his promptly rigged contraption in the air.

Physical comedy = old fashioned country entertainment.

Oswald, in his baggy overalls and flappy big shoes, was the "bashful" clown personality for Roy Acuff's Smokey Mountain Boys staying around long after that female banjoist had left the band.

Mom was still worried about my squalid exterior. Let's be clear—I didn't look like any authentic country boy fresh off the back porch of a cabin in the hills. Nothing out of a clown skit either. I just looked plain bad. Trashy bad. There was the gaping hole in the straw hat, probably from being sat on and kicked around in the van. We obviously didn't care enough to replace it before meeting bluegrass stars, let alone Roy Acuff. Not owning even a pair of slacks, I had on my schoolboy black corduroys. Those were going to have to do. The foot wear—raggedy brown leather sandals, unraveled stitching, flopping around when I walked—finished off with some bluegrass festival mud and grime. The black socks showing *nicely* through.

Thank goodness I could play the fiddle well.

As my mother was coming undone over how I looked all of a sudden, I couldn't take my eyes off Oswald's getup. I whispered back to her, "Mom, maybe it's okay?"

"Mark! Straighten up, that is part of their stage act!" my mother quibbled.

Taking some inventory now—my own tattered straw hat was a dog, probably not going to make the cut. Mom insisted that it was a nonperformer at this point. I maintained that I'd been wearing it all day, and my sweaty, stringy hair was not a good look either. That angle didn't work. No one in the Acuff band wore hats for me to borrow, and we were too unnerved to go hat-borrowing backstage… but given that I was a shrimp at 5' 2", none of them would have fit anyway. Maybe Little Jimmy Dickens' would have… My first big appearance in music was to be hatless.

Roy Acuff and Charlie approached us, asking me what I wanted to play. My reaction to that question—was—well… I couldn't quite *believe* my ears actually. They were asking *me* what to play? I just figured I would sit in on one of their songs. Maybe their standby "Wabash Cannonball." Just play along, with Howdy Forrester perhaps? I didn't know… It all happened so fast. I mean that would have been a thrill, just to do that—take a solo break on something. Instead, they were going to have me play one of my fiddle tunes. At this celebrated place among all the men wearing rhinestone jackets and rhinestone pants, I was going to get a solo spot.

"Pick a good one because there are over 4,000 folks out there who will enjoy ya, and another million or two listening in on the radio."

Roy Acuff made sure I was good and ready all right. He made sure that I snapped to.

But just for a moment, I couldn't help but flash back to *Terrace,* back to life at school—in that other world of mine where no one cared much about me or my fiddle.

Charlie got my attention again. He suggested that Gene, their other guitarist, should join us.

"It'll be more *full* for you, Mark. It's a big stage."

I must've nodded yes as I lost my train of thought yet again. I thought about the dark crawl spaces—repairing rotting foundations with my Dad every day after school. But it *must* have been destiny that I got to practice instead. The kind of all-day practicing that got me here to this very place. It was such a very close call, which could have changed everything.

I didn't know who or what I was in those moments, because I felt different than even a month before. Roy Acuff was the *King.* He summoned the Opry manager Hal Durham and told him I was going to be featured on a solo tune. Just like that, no questions. Snapped his fingers. The Opry manager nodded yes. My playing back stage in Acuff's dressing room won me this spot on the Opry.

"Play one of those breakdowns you do so well, Mark. I hope you'll play one of those. They're dynamite boy, they are somethin' else,"
Charlie urged me, as I needed to choose a tune. We had ten minutes now.

I was asking myself this question: Could tonight change my life from all that hurt back home, all of that bullying, and runnin' for safety, day in and day out? Just being scared out of my wits most of the time? How would tonight impact my poor family?

I was predisposed back home to be fearful of most things. It turned out that music allowed me to not be frightened. It was a revelation that my life could change in this way. Stage fright wasn't even a thing to me. I was not scared about anything to do with music, not in the way that most everything else had been. Was I frightened by being at the Grand Ole Opry? No sir. I was very brave. I wasn't any wimp—no "wuss" like they called me back at school. I didn't intimidate easily around any musicians, no matter how good or famous they were. It didn't rattle me—not in the least. What frightened me was having to go back home. That was the terrifying part. As long as I was here at the Opry—I was safe. The fiddle made me feel all grown up. It was rescuing me. It allowed me to get away and escape.

"Mark, I know you're going to do a good job. I'm going to introduce you, so wait to the side until I call for you to come out, ya hear?"
Roy Acuff gave me my last instruction before his portion of the show began.

Then it crossed my mind, right then and there. What I really needed to do was to pretend this performance was just like a fiddle contest, because I knew I could do that. I was going to *play to win* out there, just like my teacher Benny taught me. This wasn't just for 1ˢᵗ place in the Junior division at Weiser, or even 1ˢᵗ in the Open at Langley… this one here was for all the marbles.

"Charlie, how about 'Dusty Miller'?" I suggested.

"All right, that's a good one! Let's get after it, son!"

They fetched me out of dressing room #1 and brought me into the wings of the Opry stage. When we made our way beyond the backdrop curtains, I finally saw the huge stage. This whole time we'd been in Acuff's dressing room, and I hadn't even seen the actual stage yet—all of the hub-bub going on, all kinds of people roaming around right in front of the audience. They told me I would be standing on a circle of wood flooring from the old Ryman Auditorium—where Hank Williams once stood, they repeated to me. All the greats stood there: where Johnny Cash filmed his television show… There were so many people just wandering on and off stage as the country artists performed—I was fascinated by that. Part stage show and part radio show. The flash bulbs from the audience were blinding as Roy Acuff went out there. There were 4,400 people in the audience tonight, every last seat was filled. It's the largest audience I'll have played for, and they're going to be listening to me play the fiddle.

ROY ACUFF'S INTRODUCTION OF MARK O'CONNOR TO THE AUDIENCE AT THE GRAND OLE OPRY
Friday Night, 7-26-74
Nashville, Tennessee

"We've got a fine young guest for you this evening that I think you'll enjoy, since this is the Grand Ole Opry – and especially to know that Grand Ole Opry back in 1925 was started by the solemn Judge George D. Hayes and one old-time fiddler whose name was Uncle Jimmy Thompson. And the fiddle has always played a great part in country music – the fiddle, the guitar, the banjo and the mandolin – other instruments have been added through the time, but as long as Grand Ole Opry stays Grand Ole Opry I think that the fiddle will play a very important part in it. And we are having some fiddler's contests all around over the country and different people go to them. And some of our very finest fiddlers go to these fiddler's contests. I'll tell you more about that after this boy gets through – about our contest that we have here. But I want you to meet this young gentleman and let him play for you.

I can only say that he is very outstanding. I heard him back here in these dressing rooms a while ago, and two of the boys that work with me all the time – he came to visit them and to play downtown at the Pickin' Parlor the other night, and they said he is a genius. The word 'genius' is about the only way that I know that could fit a person that is 12 years old that can play a fiddle as this boy can play it. And I'd like you to meet him right now and I know you'll enjoy him. He is from [Seattle], Washington. He's come a long ways here. His mama and his little sister are back there with him. His name is Mark O'Connor. Would you make Mark welcome?

Come over, Mark, come over and get yourself all adjusted here to the sound of this big auditorium. You're going to be playing to a lot of people listening in out on the air waves, but you're accustomed to all this. And I want to tell you now that we're glad to have you visiting here at the Opry and I think it's a privilege for me to have the pleasure to introduce a young boy that I feel has the ability that you've got. I notice that you've got a couple of my boys out here with you – Charlie Collins and Gene Martin. They're going to help you out. Is that all you want to use – just the two guitars?

All right, what are you going to play for us, Mark? Get right up here to the microphone and let's get into it professional style. What do you want to play?"

"O.K., I'm going to play 'Dusty Miller'"

"You're going to play 'Dusty Miller?' I've been playing for 35 years and I can't play half of it.

[After "Dusty Miller" - applause and curtain call]

Mark, you do a beautiful job and the folks enjoyed it, and I know they are making you feel at home. And maybe you'll someday come down to Tennessee and make your home down here and be one of our regular visitors on the Opry. You know, Joe Edwards, back here – Joe plays a fine guitar and fiddle – this boy, back here – he expressed it about as good as anybody could, I guess. He said: 'You know, seeing and hearing him play makes me believe more in reincarnation than anything.' He said: 'He'd of had to have been here some time before.' The reason he said that – now let me explain this (I could stay here a long time with this young fellow) – he's only been playing, so his mother and they all say, a year and a half. Maybe old Joe's right. Maybe he has been here before and come back.

You do such a fine job. I really think that if you feel like it – and I know you don't have to rehearse – do you want to play a little bit of another one just for an encore?

Well, while he's studying what he wants to play – you know we have the fiddler's contest here. It's in conjunction with the Fan Fair – the Fan Fair is always about the second week in June – and it's called the [Grand] Master Fiddler's Contest. Anyone who can play a fiddle equal to what this boy can play is eligible to enter this contest. You have to be pretty good to enter, I tell you that. Anyway, Vernon Solomon, down in Texas, won the first one the first year. Dick Barrett, out in Texas, won it the second year. And then last year Herman Johnson, from Oklahoma, took the nice trophy. And they're all fine fiddlers. But remember one thing, those of you that are listening in tonight, this boy has nearly another year to the fiddler's contest! I don't see how you

– as far as I'm concerned, you better stay in Texas, I'll tell you, or Oklahoma, or wherever you come from. It looks like Oregon is movin' in on you."

[after encore – "Faded Love"] "I have to say that for 12 years old I don't believe I've ever heard anything that can equal him in any way."

After several country stars and their bandmembers congratulated me backstage, Skeeter Willis of the Willis Brothers beckoned me from the hallway traffic and into their dressing room. As Skeeter grabbed his fiddle, he reminded me that I had just played "Faded Love" on the world-famous Grand Ole Opry, but he said that I played it *wrong*. He wanted to make sure I knew how Bob Wills, who wrote the tune, wanted it played.

"You're throwing other things in there that's not supposed to be in there," he said.

Skeeter was referring to a little variation in the melody that I had made up for the final phrase of the song. This was the kind of thing that Benny encouraged me to do, across the board. It didn't matter if someone wrote the tune 300 years ago or 30 years ago. Because of Skeeter accosting me like he did—still riding high from my big performance minutes before—I wanted to create an entirely new variation of the song for my fiddle, in-spired by ol' Skeeter. I made sure I always included my own variation in performances of "Faded Love."

It was plainly apparent that not everyone was going to take to the young kid from Seattle doing so well on the fiddle. Skeeter wasn't the best of the Nashville fiddlers. Howdy and Kenny Baker weren't rushing in to correct me just minutes after I got off the stage, but Skeeter would not be my last vocal critic when I was a youngster, not by a long shot—and I should get used to it. At age 12, my honeymoon on the national stage (all few hours of it), already started to rub some folks the wrong way.

ON THE OTHER HAND and apart from Skeeter, I may have just become one of Roy Acuff's favorite fiddlers ever—nearly up there with Howdy himself, so it would appear. Roy asked my mother if I could play for him in his dressing room any time we were to visit Nashville. He promised to put us on the backstage list, and I could play fiddle for him for a while, get complimentary seats to watch the Opry, wander out to the amusement rides in Opryland Park for free—whatever I wished to do Roy said.

At 70 years-old, Roy Acuff loved the fiddle, I believe, more than about anything else in the world. He loved me playing the fiddle for him about as much as anything, too—as I would come to know. Roy was captivated by great American fiddle tunes. As I played them, Roy would sit very close to me, observing my fingering hand and sizing up my bowing arm, all with so much sincerity, joy, and adoration. What I could do on the instrument in the way of those old fiddle tunes, infused with my own increasingly progressive approach to them, simply brought him even more jubilation and contentment as the years went on. This fact would be hard to overstate. It didn't matter how different or wild I got with the tunes, Roy loved how I could improvise on the melody, he just ate it all up—the more the better. In response to it, he'd chuckle and nod his head in approval as he reacted to all the new things he heard in my renditions each time.

Roy Acuff's entire life was considerable, which makes his connection to my fiddling all the more fascinating. He was an extremely accomplished person throughout his life. In the 1920s, he was so good in baseball's minor leagues, the New York Yankees considered him. But by 1929, a sunstroke confined him to bed for nearly two years. During his lengthy recovery, Acuff practiced his fiddle instead, and started to sing. Eight years after joining the Grand Ole Opry, Acuff put his hat into the ring in 1944 and ran for Governor of Tennessee—as a Republican against the Dixiecrats. However, in replacing Uncle Dave Macon as the most successful artist on the Opry, Roy reclaimed his focus. By then, Acuff's many hit songs were popular the world over: "Wreck on the Highway," "Fireball Mail," and "The Great Speckled Bird." There was "Precious Jewel," "Pins and Needles," "Night Train to Memphis," and one of his signatures, "Wabash Cannonball." It added up to 30 million record sales.

Acuff was good at the business of music—terrifically difficult to do in the early days of the Nashville music industry. In 1942, he teamed up with songwriter Fred Rose, who wrote songs for Acuff's recordings, such as "Blue Eyes Cryin' in the Rain." Together, they began one of the most successful publishing companies in Nashville's history: Acuff-Rose Publishing. Hank Williams was one of their biggest signings.

The strength of Acuff's music career became synonymous with American life, so much so that during WWII, Japanese troops yelled out *two* battle cries over their radios. As the Japanese let rockets fly on allied targets, and as they banzai-charged Okinawa, one of their rallying calls was "Long live His Majesty the Emperor." The other: "To hell with Roosevelt, to hell with Babe Ruth, to hell with Roy Acuff."

I thought that it might wear off, eventually—Roy Acuff wanting me to come backstage to his dressing room and play for him—but it never did. He became another grandfather figure to me, along with Benny. I always made a point to play for him, when I could—right up to the end of his life.

TUT TAYLOR CALLED US the following Monday at Bill and Bonnie's house:

"Well Mark, it seems you are the talk of the town! Roy Acuff putting you on the Opry for a feature performance? How about that! So, how does a record contract from Rounder Records sound to you?" Tut dropped the stunner over the phone.

"Umm… Tut, could you repeat that one more time?" I motioned for my mother to come over to the phone and listen.

"Do you want to go into the studio and cut a fiddle album next week here in Nashville? Rounder will pay for everything."

"Well, yes, yes… yes of course!" I responded to Tut as my mother grabbed the phone from me.

Tut had recorded a solo Dobro album for Rounder Records two years before, *Friar Tut.* We had *Friar Tut* at home—it featured Norman Blake. We had about everything we could find with Norman Blake's guitar playing on it that year. Tut had a good relationship there at Rounder Records, so he called them about me that morning.

Regarding our summer schedule of events, we had already planned on leaving Nashville the next weekend to attend another festival. We also didn't want to overstay our welcome at Bill and Bonnie's, but their house was so very comfortable—they had a backyard pool—it was living in luxury. Mom let me have the phone back.

"I guess we were planning on leaving Nashville next weekend, but maybe we don't have to?" I said.

"Good. My big question for you, Mark—who do you want to have play on your album? You can have anyone in Nashville you want," said Tut.

"Any musician in Nashville?" I needed clarification.

Mom confirmed it as she pulled the phone back and got it closer to her ear.

"This is a legitimate record label, so yes—anyone in Nashville," Tut replied.

I took back the phone.

"Wow… well I definitely want Charlie."

"Okay. That's good—and how about a second musician?" asked Tut.

(I was thinking big, why not?) "Umm… Does Norman Blake live in Nashville?" I asked.

"Yes he does. I will call him to see if he's around," said Tut.

Mom and I recognized that my hope to record a professional album as a 12-year-old musician was evidently becoming a reality. I decided to re-record most all the tunes I had done up in Spokane a month earlier. I was so excited—I couldn't believe it.

In a few days, Tut let us know that Norman was on for the recording. He wanted us to drop by his music shop near Murfreesboro at a time when Norman could come over to play a few tunes—to get to know each other a little. Tut was truly becoming an angel for us in Nashville.

Named Robert Arthur Taylor, "Tut" was born in 1923 in Milledgeville, Georgia. Starting out on mandolin and banjo, he began dobro when he was 14, using a flat-pick instead of the usual finger picks. During the '60s, Tut played with the Folkswingers, Dixie Gentlemen, and John Hartford's Aereo-plain band, and he became a trusted recording partner of both Norman and Vassar Clements. After he left his owner's share of the Pickin' Parlor to co-owner Randy Wood, Tut opened the GTR Music Shop, where he made the Givens mandolins, one of which served as the grand prize at Woodinville. He also made miniature mountain dulcimers with three strings. He called them "Plickets."

I got to jam with Norman and Tut for the first time at GTR. Charlie met us there, too. The front room was lit warmly by the sun peering through the sheer draping, and Norman was silhouetted in front of the windowpane. That afternoon, he mostly played the mandolin. Norman was very much the multi-instrumentalist like I was hoping to be. He could play guitar, mandolin, fiddle, and even dobro. He probably even played the banjo—all the instruments I played. That day, Tut went through several of his dobro instrumentals before Norman introduced us to some very intriguing mandolin pieces. I decided to play mostly guitar that day, and not much fiddle. Norman was my guitar hero, and Mom of course knew that. Norman was just 37, not as old as all of the men I had been playing for over the last week in Nashville.

As we played together, sometimes I looked up to see Norman shaking his head back and forth. A little like he was telling someone, *no*. As his head swayed, his expression seemed to occasionally reflect a bit of wonder before blurting out something like "mighty fine," or "well how 'bout that?" Then he kicked off a little "Blackberry Blossom" on the mandolin. Norman took a couple of choruses and then let me have it on guitar. I was playing smooth with some intricate phrasing. I had it all right in time, right with the beat. In the middle of one of my guitar solos, Norman bellows out, "All right, boy!" Then he took the lead back and ended the tune.

"Boy, just play that guitar, just don't ever put it down."
Norman rocked his head again to and fro with approval. I was so happy to have Norman help me on my first record. It was really going to happen.

Norman Blake came out of north Georgia, growing up around the Tennessee border city of Chattanooga. He had his own guest spots on the Grand Ole Opry very early in his development—as a duo with his banjo-playing partner. By 1969, he was playing in Johnny Cash's band and was on the weekly national television show that inspired me to play the fiddle in the first place. He was a key musician on Bob Dylan's *Nashville Skyline* album, toured and played with Kris Kristofferson, played mandolin on Joan Baez's hit song "The Night They Drove Old Dixie Down," and of course my favorite—Norman guested on the Nitty Gritty Dirt Band's "Will the Circle be Unbroken." I was also a big fan of his new solo guitar album, his very first one: *Home in Sulphur Springs*. I had been listening to that guitar album and picking tunes off it all year. There was nothing else like it.

Norman Blake was easily my favorite guitar player in 1974. He had the unusual combination of being an old-time/bluegrass musician, but also a progressive musician who wrote intricate extended solo compositions for the flat-pick guitar. He was playing a lot of solo unaccompanied concerts, just like he brought to Woodinville.

The collaborations that Norman had with Tut, Vassar Clements, and John Hartford, including Hartford's *Aereo-plain* album produced by David Bromberg just a year or two earlier, was the first recognition of "Newgrass music." I noticed a similar musical approach with California's Muleskinner and Old & In the Way.

THE RECORDING STUDIO was booked for Monday, August 4th, 1974—the Hounds Ear in Nashville, Tennessee. Claude Hill was the engineer, and Tut Taylor the producer. Still 12-years-old by a day, I was ready to make my first album. Norman Blake and Charlie Collins arrived soon after we did. Norman asked me to start showing him my tunes so he could look at the guitar chords.

I began to show both musicians my fiddle tunes that I selected for the session. I definitely wanted to go over the Texas-style fiddle chord progressions for some of the breakdowns—an approach using more chords and walking bass lines on the guitar. One of the breakdowns "Say Old Man, Can You Play the Fiddle," deserved a discussion on what specific chords to use. Howdy Forrester had recorded it with parts in both E major and E minor, but in the Texas-style, as I clued them in, we stay in E major all the way through it. "The *minor* notes become blues notes in the major key," I described. The tack was a little surprising to Norman, but he liked it. He nodded his head back and forth again as he played the chords over the melody. "Okay," he voiced.

There were waltzes I needed to show them the chords to. I hadn't played that many waltzes during the last week of jams. They learned the chords to both "Dreamers" and "Kelly"—those were going to be pretty easy for them to pick up—we had just a three-hour session to get everything perfected and recorded. It was really the *feel* of the faster breakdowns that we needed to rehearse, because the Texas-style approach was not as familiar to them. At Weiser the month before, I had played with Jerry Thomasson, so I had the rhythmic feel I was shooting for in mind.

We were going straight to two-track tape. That meant no re-mixing. I had to get each tune in a single take. With both Norman and Charlie on guitars, we tried out "Dusty Miller." Claude positioned the mics and got the sound together. After a couple times through, surprisingly the two guitars together weren't feeling quite right. I played guitar well enough to understand that they were playing in two different musical *grooves* from one another. Tut heard it, too. He recommended for Charlie to go to mandolin, that it might clear up the issue. After more run-throughs, it still hadn't gelled, and we had 13 tunes to cut in just over two hours left. We really needed to get going. After yet another test pass through a breakdown, Tut pressed the talk-back button again to try one final combination: "Why don't we have Norman and Charlie switch instruments?" I was sad to lose Norman from the guitar position, but Charlie had been playing guitar with me all week and was more familiar with my fiddle style by now. Norman moved to mandolin. Both of them were just going to play rhythm for me anyway—no guitar or mandolin solos. This was a solo fiddle album all the way.

The new combination clicked. Norman on mandolin complemented and even energized Charlie's guitar rhythm. Together, they established the temperament for this kind of fiddle music, and unlocked the particular drive that my fiddle tunes needed. It was magic, a singularly unique sound all of us created that day in the recording session together. Now, that we had taken up over an hour of the session, we were assured by Tut and Claude that we could go into overtime by 30 minutes, if we needed it.

As we recorded tune by tune, I went over the chord changes for each one as they came up. I had my Yamaha guitar right there lying beside me on the studio floor. I picked it up as we were to start the next tune—running through the chord sequences for Norman and Charlie. As I played, they observed my left-hand inversions on the guitar neck, while absorbing the particular rhythmic approach from my right hand strum that matched the temperament of each tune. After these brief demonstrations, I swapped my guitar for the fiddle, placing my guitar back on the floor beside my chair. I fiddled the tune through, with them accompanying me in the same manner. Often the case, we'd be halfway into a practice warmup when Tut pressed the talk-back: "It's sounding good! We could be getting this on tape and we are missing out on it!" Tut was mindfully watching the clock.

From this first experience recording, I learned that you have such a small amount of time to get your tune down in the studio—you better be ready to execute. So, in that light, I rose to the occasion that day and I proved my worth. I wanted everybody to know they had not wasted their investment in me: I did not miss a lick for the rest of the session. Essentially, a lot of first takes were keepers.

I was wholly grateful for this recording. This remarkable idea that somebody out there who I'd never met, specifically the people at Rounder Records—Ken Irwin, Bill Nowlin, and Marian Leighton—were paying for these noteworthy men: Norman, Charlie, Tut, and Claude, as well as the studio costs, just for me to record the fiddle how I play it… well it was unheard of. At age 12, I became the youngest artist to have a recording contract on Rounder Records, and one of the youngest artists to ever have a solo label deal anywhere. It was a triumph for me and for my family.

When you add up each of the events which took place inside those two weeks in Nashville the summer of 1974, the very place we were planning to skip over when Tut insisted we stop by to play a tune: the Pickin' Parlor, the invitation to the Grand Masters Fiddle Championship, debuting at the Grand Ole Opry hosted by Roy Acuff, receiving a recording contract from Rounder Records, and the sessions for my first album with Norman Blake and Charlie Collins—the entirety amounts to one of the most significant two weeks a young musician could experience. The impact it had on my future in music can't be underscored enough. We decided to call the album, *National Junior Fiddle Champion.* It was released on Rounder Records as a Long Play album (LP) catalog #0046.

Side One: Dusty Miller, Kelly Waltz, Cuckoo's Nest, Don't Let The Deal Go Down, Dreamer's Waltz, Sally Johnson
Side Two: Billy in the Low Ground, Festival Waltz, Brilliancy, I Don't Love Nobody, Roxanna Waltz, Say Old Man.

Bluegrass Unlimited - by Bonnie Smith

"Wherever Mark performs, many in the audience are skeptical of a young city boy trying to play Texas and bluegrass style, but he quickly makes believers out of all who hear. Mark is not an imitator. He greatly admires Benny Thomasson, Byron Berline, Vassar Clements, and many other outstanding fiddlers, and of course he has been influenced to some degree by each, but his style is all his own. One of his personal goals is to try to learn something new each day.

"Before leaving Nashville that August in 1974, Tut Taylor arranged a recording session for Mark with Norman Blake backing him on mandolin and

Charlie Collins on guitar. Mark calmly performed each of the Texas-style fiddle tunes with perfection, the only need for retakes being for Charlie and Norman who were unaccustomed to the Texas-style backup chords."

National Junior Fiddle Champion – Album Notes by John Burke

"...Most of us who have had the pleasure of following his development over the past couple of years have long since realized that Mark is not just another "kid" with a gift for music, but rather a gifted musician who just happens to be young. He has had help, especially from a very understanding family, and there have been some fortuitous circumstances which have accelerated his attainment of musical maturity, but by and large his achievements are the result of the energy, curiosity and determination of just one person: Mark himself.

"Mark had no trouble learning tunes and his exceptional manual dexterity and metronomic timing were easily sufficient for eventual mastery of the technical aspects of fiddling as well as all the other instruments he was learning to play. Like most youngsters, he had an uncanny ability to mimic the playing of other people, but by the time I started working with him, he had already become dissatisfied with copying other people's music. Mark is shy, but very direct and forthright. He has strong feelings, and he knew that this type of music was an excellent way to express them...

"...he was too young to drive and there were no other people his age in his area who shared his interest in this music. So Mark had a problem, but he wasn't one to wait around and wait for the problem to solve itself. In a manner reminiscent of his attempt to make his own [carboard] fiddle, he began to provide himself with his own "musical family," a group consisting of: Mark the fiddler, Mark the guitarist, Mark the banjo-picker, Mark the mandolinist and Mark the dobro-player. His apparent skipping around from one instrument to another was very different from the normal childhood inability to maintain interest in a thing long enough to master it. By working on the special qualities of each of the instruments, he was able to give himself a sense of perspective about the one thing they all had in common: the music he wanted to play.

"His music will doubtlessly change over the years, become more personalized and reflect the different feelings and perspectives acquired through life. But as long as he retains the ability to share his feelings through his music, and as long as he enjoys doing so, it will always be a pleasure to hear."

-John Burke (Seattle, January 1975)

CHAPTER FOUR

STIFFER COMPETITION

W E ALREADY ROLLED INTO a lot of old-time and bluegrass contests during the summer of 1974, but now it was time for the grand-daddy old-time fiddle convention of the Southeast: the 39th annual Galax Old Fiddlers' Convention.

My mother thought that getting to Galax was important, although we didn't put too much thought into its official designation: *Old Fiddlers* contest. As opposed to; "Old-Time" fiddlers contest... surely they didn't mean you had to be *old* to win.

Mom and I were big fans of the great West Virginia fiddler Clark Kessinger. Galax was Kessinger country indeed. He won untold numbers of fiddle contests between Galax, Virginia, and the fiddlers convention an hour away in Union Grove, North Carolina. To absorb a little bit of some Galax magic dust, I was able to meet with Mr. Kessinger on the way up to the Virginia mountains. He had heard of my Grand Ole Opry performance and decided to receive us, even though he was restrained by the full effects of a devastating stroke that halted his fiddle playing. He was in a care facility by this time. Clark Kessinger was very nice to me and so very encouraging. When I told him that my teacher was Benny Thomasson he smiled. Kessinger was just one of a few great fiddlers I had met who were born in the previous century. Having just celebrated his 79th birthday, it made his birth year 1896. He thanked me for visiting with him and wished me well in Galax.

Clark Kessinger was beloved all through the country for his old-time fiddling. Because of his training and skill level, he wasn't scratchy with the "jiggy-jiggy" simplified bowing that so many of the local mountain fiddlers used. Kessinger's was a huge and pure tone, big luscious vibrato on the waltzes, and he played with lots of dynamics, driving rhythmic accents and color—and a healthy dose of showmanship. One of the reasons why Mom and I loved Clark Kessinger's playing so much was that he was an old-time musician with influences from the classical violin greats—Fritz Kreisler, Jascha Heifetz, and Joseph Szigeti. Those three violinists were among

Mom's favorites, along with Yehudi Menuhin. I grew up listening to them on the family turntable.

Mom surely loved Clark Kessinger about as much as she could love any old-time fiddler. I wanted to emulate his technical command of the fiddle, too, and energetic play—it was hugely impressive. He was quite a bit older than my teacher, who I viewed as pretty old indeed. Benny looked up to Clark as his own fiddle hero, in fact. I couldn't wait to tell Benny once we were back home, that I got to speak with Clark Kessinger for a while.

Clark Kessinger died within a year's time.

We pulled up our Ford Econoline close to the registration area on August 8th, just four days after recording my first album. The scenic view of the Old Fiddlers' Convention grounds in Galax looked like a set design in a cinematic movie. It was so different than Weiser. This contest was taking place outdoors on a ball field nestled in a large basin.

The town of Galax itself was a gateway to the Blue Ridge Mountains. The visible horizon was opulent green, even by late summer. The welcome tent was positioned at the top of the natural ravine, and from there you could take in all the musical gaiety befalling visitors as they entered the grounds. There was the small wooden stage at the end of the ravine as fiddlers dotted the landscape throughout the gulch—warming up—playing through tunes. Many of them were accompanied by buck dancers and cloggers, each of them kicking up their heels just a couple feet away from their favored fiddler, likely getting ready for the buck dancing contest.

When Clark Kessinger played, he would just haul off and do some clogging himself, right in the middle of his own fiddle tune. I was so thrilled to be here, so far away from home. The carefreeness of the fiddling and the dancing all looked so pleasing and fun. Folks didn't buck dance much at Texas fiddle contests that I ever saw. Maybe it was time for our family of dancers to strike up a few steps in Galax?

MY MOTHER AND I TOOK our place in the short line, signing me up for the contest. The registration table was positioned at the front edge of a large canopy tent. When it came our turn, Mom told the man sitting at the table that she would like to register me for the fiddle contest. The man asked us if we had been to the Galax convention before. We answered, "No, we haven't." Mom added, "We came all the way from Seattle, Washington!" The man observed me standing there holding my fiddle case. "If you would excuse me for a moment…"

The man went back into the tent area about 20 feet or so and began speaking to another man. Both of them gave my 5' 2" presentation a few once-overs as they glanced our way. A couple of minutes went by before the second man approached the table.

"Can I help you ma'am?" the man addressed my Mom.

"Yes, I just want to register my son in the fiddle contest."

"We don't have fiddle contests for kids here. Where're you from again?"

"Seattle, Washington. We already understood there weren't any kids divisions here. I've been entering him in the open and adult divisions all summer," Mom informed him.

"Well, if you knew there weren't divisions for kids here, then you would've known that you have to pre-register for this contest."

"No, we didn't know that. It wasn't printed in any of the magazine advertisement that we saw. We haven't run into that before. Usually fiddlers can register when they arrive," Mom asserted.

The man turned around to grab a flier. He showed the piece of colored paper to her as he pointed to the line that stressed pre-registering.

"Sir, we drove 400 miles from Nashville yesterday to come here," my mother was pleading.

This second man asked us to give him another minute as he turned back into the tent area. He gathered up a couple of other men to talk with. They stood in a taut huddle for what seemed like several more minutes. More peering across the way at me, *more* stalling—he finally came back to the registration table.

"Nashville, eh? Yes, we've heard about him," as he looked down at me again. "Look, ma'am, I'm sorry you had to make the trip, but we can't break the rules. I'm sure the boy is talented—that's what they say back there—but this contest is not for kids. This is a contest for old-timers. The fiddlers who win this convention are old men with long beards. Do you understand that?"

"But I drove all this way for him to be here, can't you please make an exception? There seems to be young adult fiddlers registering for the contest here. My son wants to participate in the contest. He won the National Junior Fiddle Champion in Weiser this summer."

"Oh, I know about Weiser, Idaho. But this is different here. I just talked to our judges back over there. This boy's reputation precedes him," as he looked my way again. "If we let him enter this contest—and if he wins it...

There could be a riot!"

MY MOM WAS STUNNED by what the man had to say, and of course, she felt greatly dejected. This was the famed contest she had dreamed about ever since we decided to make the trip to the Southeast. After gathering herself, realizing we were running out of avenues to rationalize with them, she gave in;

"Then I'll just purchase three admission tickets for my family to enjoy the contest as spectators. I don't want to deprive him the opportunity to see the world-famous Galax fiddle convention."

The man paused for a moment, measuring what he was about to say next.

"Ma'am, I'm not going to allow you to stay on the grounds. If word gets out that this boy was prevented from entering the fiddle contest—well, that is yet another controversy we don't need around here. We don't want any trouble. I am politely asking you to leave."

I didn't see my mother bristle too much. Up until that moment, she was having the time of her life all summer long. But with this matter here, she was indeed offended. As we looked all around us, we didn't see just old men with long beards and fiddle cases—we saw hippies with long beards and fiddle cases, too. It seemed patently unfair to Mom.

The Journal of American Folklore (Vol. 99, No. 393, Sep.,1986)
"In 1974, before an audience of 30,000, the 39th Galax convention gave five prizes each for flatfoot dance, clawhammer banjo, bluegrass banjo, dulcimer, guitar, bluegrass fiddle, mandolin, and folksong: and eight prizes each for bluegrass band and old time band."

"Don't I have every right to buy a ticket of admission as a spectator, just like anyone else here?" Mom insisted.

"If you don't leave now, I will have our security folks show you out."

CROSSING BRIDGES

Washington Old-Time Fiddlers Newsletter, August 1974, VOL. 10, No. 8
"The Galax Fiddle convention in Virginia. We are sorry to say that Mark couldn't enter it because he wasn't pre-registered. A real shame to have driven 3,000 miles and then not be able to play."

I COULDN'T HELP BUT *imagine* if only... I was a foot taller. To be bigger like my Dad was. They wouldn't have looked down on me like I was some freak object. Maybe they wouldn't have treated my mother so badly, either—and I could've stood up to them to defend her. She was so worn out from driving me around the country, through the middle of the night, and, in that relentless southern summer heat. It was really getting to Mom—she needed to lay down during the day more and more.

My mother seemed to be getting more sickly. She suffered migraines, and she was losing strength. If there was anything heavy to lift, I had to do all of that for her. She was a cancer survivor and I feared she was hiding something from me. She blamed what she was feeling on her menopause.

I couldn't help but think that if only I was older, and taller, I *would* have been more imposing to them, and, they would've let me enter alongside those hippies. I supposed they figured none of the hippies could win their fiddlers' convention, but they thought I had a chance to.

As we got back into the van, we remembered that one of our other favorite southeastern fiddlers, Buddy Pendleton, won the Galax convention several times while in his 30s. This wasn't just about *old men* with beards, the problem was *kids*. Something against young kids who played fiddle. In the early 1970s, it was almost unheard of to see a child fiddler anywhere across the Southeast, at least one who could play well and stand toe-to-toe with the top old-timers.

In time, the unfair and coarse people who were afraid of a talented child from Seattle winning their fiddlers' convention would be lost to history. Fiddle kids would soon populate these grounds at Galax one day, and yet it is a stark reminder that I drew my breath in uncharted musical times and territories.

Mom had a trouble-making son—a young kid who could cause a crowd to "riot" just by taking the bow to his fiddle. So they said.

MANY ELEMENTS OF my musical journey were going to be congenial and encouraging, such as my early interactions with Acuff,

Blake, Clements, Collins, Oswald, and Taylor in Nashville—all of those men, let us not forget, were southern *old-time* musicians, like the men in Galax. But on occasion, things were going to wind their way towards further confusion and adversity—some of it contemptibly insulting, other times threatening, and even dangerous. This certainly wouldn't be the last time I confronted challenges within the music scene as a traveling child musician, only to find a way around and navigate forward again. Heck, I was just getting started. The difference being, I wasn't going to stay a five-foot tall child forever, and I'd find a way to get the last word in—at least some of the time.

Eventually, I unraveled some remarkable ways to wade through the muck and find what I was looking for. The heart of the matter being musical artistry—the way I envisioned it for me. The music itself should always win in the end.

For the time being, any kind of conflict meant I was walking away with a big, fat zero for it. In time, I would learn how to assert myself as a young musician and skillfully plow and till the ground ahead.

We backed out of our parking space by the check-in tent and headed out of Galax. As my Mom shifted gears on our "three on the tree" stick shift, revving the engine just a taste while releasing the clutch, I looked back at that beautiful vista one more time, the same one that I gazed at when we arrived just 20 minutes earlier. The lush green enclave with all those fiddlers speckled across the embankments, accompanied by buck dancers and cloggers—it was so perfectly enchanting. In my mind, I turned the scene into an *Americana symphony.*

No matter the contest itself, it was still one of my favorite visualizations and musings in my young and impressionable mind—a spectacle I couldn't enjoy beyond the few minutes we were allowed to stay.

I never returned.

NOW THAT WE WERE NEARING the end of summer, it meant heading back home—3,000 miles west in the Ford Econoline. We planned for a few final stops on the way. We made it down to Dick Barrett's place in Pottsboro, Texas, for that fiddle lesson. Dick had won the 1973 Grand Masters, and for the two prior years, the Nationals at Weiser. He was going to show me some things.

Despite what happened in Galax, contests were going to be my saving grace as a very young fiddler whose family aspired for him to be on the national scene. As exciting as Nashville was the week before, none of it paid for a single gallon of gas in the tank. That's not to say it all wasn't a giant investment into the future—of course it was. But what do we do now with an empty pocketbook? Mom and I knew that I had a knack for winning contests—if I was allowed to enter them. It could only improve with some more experience, and maybe some further imparted wisdom. Buddying up alongside the greatest fiddle champions of the era wasn't going to hurt.

Being one of the most colorful, and I suppose, *saucy* fiddlers you could ever run into, Dick Barrett, in his late 50s, made entering fiddle contests his full-time occupation. He worked some construction here and there, too, but fiddle repairing—trading and hustling fiddles at the contests, where each deal afforded him the upper hand—was his main gig. With his hornswoggles and outwits, Dick Barrett was one of the most prolific fiddle contest winners in history.

Barrett's foremost criticism of me was that I was playing everything "too fast" and was sticking too much improvisation into my breakdowns, already—and getting too far from the melody. He very much disliked bluegrass music and he felt that all bluegrass fiddlers played too fast and improvised too much. There you go. He believed the proper place for improvising on the fiddle was the swing style, which he was also an expert in. Barrett admonished me that bluegrass was going to "ruin my fiddling." He wasn't alone, with similar warnings from at least *some* old-time fiddlers.

The 1970s were a time when there were still substantial divisions between some of these American traditional musical worlds, the very places I was continuing to immerse myself in simultaneously. I was intently focused on cross-pollinating all of it instead of any further isolation. The old-time and bluegrass segregation was significantly pronounced. I viewed it as a wall to tear down, even as a young kid.

When I met Byron Berline the month before, I asked him what his time was like back when he won at the national contest in Weiser. Byron told me it was a great experience. Then he paused for a second, "Except for Dick Barrett," he added. "I suppose you've run into him?" Byron asked me as he scrunched up his face. Byron still harbored quite a grudge against

Barrett. As he described it to me, in 1970 Dick Barrett tried to get the officials at Weiser to disqualify Byron from the contest for playing bluegrass in his rounds. Byron showed his appreciation for Barrett's gesture of kindness by beating him, and winning his second national championship. After that, Bryon retired from entering contests altogether.

As gamey as Dick Barrett was the years I knew him, he had experienced quite a noteworthy early life. As one of eight children picking cotton, he lived through the Great Depression and Dust Bowl of the Southwest. Barrett was drafted into WWII and was decorated in the U.S. Army with medals for Valor and Extreme Bravery in a Combat Zone while he fought in the Philippines.

After the war, he earned musical pedigrees that ranged between Country music and Western Swing. It included touring with *The Sons of the Pioneers,* "T" Texas Tyler, Tex Ritter, and Rex Allen. He ran his own Texas dance band nightclub during the 1950s with engagements up in Eugene, Oregon, and even in Seattle.

But in the fiddle contest scene, Dick Barrett became known as quite an intimidating force of nature, who demanded to win every contest he entered. His hardline demeanor was offset by his constant roar of laughter. He would be amused by the things people did, or played, or by what he would say in response to what he heard. On more than one occasion, Benny told me that when Barrett came up short, he grabbed the winner's trophy away and tossed it into the dirt. Then he went ahead and stomped on it while it laid there (sometimes in mud), for good measure. In my own young life, my personal introduction to him was an unpleasant run-in.

Just a little over a year earlier when I was 11, we were attending a little dinky fiddle contest in Longview, Washington. It was just a couple of weeks before the contest in Oregon where we met Benny for the first time. Mom had just gotten a portable tape recorder with a hand-held mic so I could tape fiddlers and learn more tunes for fiddle contests. I had taped a lot of jam sessions at Weiser a few weeks before. We spotted Dick Barrett warming up and jamming with a couple guitar players in the school lobby in Longview. Mom encouraged me to get up closer to the jam session to record a few tunes on our new cassette recorder.

As soon as I got up close enough to turn on my tape, Barrett abruptly stopped playing. He looked straight down at me and bellowed;

"I didn't give you permission to record me, did I?"

"No," I nodded.

"Have you bought all of my record albums?" Barrett grilled.

"No," I responded.

He was castigating me in front of eight or ten people standing around taking all this in. He obviously considered me a nobody kid—inconsequential. As I stood motionless, turning every bright shade of red from being humiliated, he glanced over at his LPs for sale—at the lobby merchandise table:

"Go on over there and buy my albums first, and then you can record me, okay?" Barrett railed, as he started up his next tune.

More than a little embarrassed, I was somewhat traumatized by him over it. My mother was upset at herself for sending me into the shark's mouth. She wasn't very impressed with Mr. Barrett's behavior towards children, to say the least. It was yet another reason why I just couldn't wait to get taller, and get a little older... so I was more evenly-matched with the older men—at least for those moments when I didn't have a fiddle under my chin.

Now, one year later, and very much still a half-pint, Barrett was trying to make it up to me; that is, once he heard me play at Weiser and realized I was going to be *a somebody* in fiddling. He told us that he would spend the rest of his life apologizing for what had happened at that little Longview contest between us. He also fleshed out something else. His behavior was brought on by his alcoholism. At which point, that very incident caused him to quit drinking. It made him re-think how he was going to treat little kids who played fiddle. Heretofore, kid fiddlers were mostly just a nuisance to him. Dick eventually became a fiddle teacher to many children and turned over a new leaf.

Having been the cause for and a witness to at least some of his redemption, I saw that Dick Barrett still remained quite a gamer in and around the fiddle contest scene. Now that I was on his heels in the Open divisions, he wanted me to be a little closer to him, most likely so he could get in my head some. He maintained that Benny was not a good teacher for me, himself being much better—attempting to steal me away from his fiddle contest nemesis. So for now, Barrett remained rough around the edges and even pretty grim—with or without alcohol. If he was prepping himself to be around fiddling pubescents, he was still at the very lowest point of his transformation. Barrett was still that foul-mouthed, slippery, fiddle-trading hustler who managed to show up at every major fiddle contest—except for bluegrass fiddle contests in the Southeast. He was unsympathetic about my Galax debacle. He would not have attended, he told us.

Back at the house, Barrett was impressing me with all kinds of fiddles and bows. For us it was pretty straightforward—we had absolutely no money to buy anything. Dick gave me one of his trademark handmade chin rests with a kind of scalloping carved in the wood underneath. The chin rests were quite large, nice-looking and remarkable in a kind of odd way. As he fit the chin rest onto my fiddle, he seemed to slide my old chin rest into his *keep* pile. When I noticed it, the thought crossed my mind that I'd like to hang onto that one—just in case. I didn't say anything. Barrett's chin rest was tooled with a particularly fine edge. I thought it was unusual that he made them that way. He could have rounded the edges and it wouldn't have lost its general appearance.

When we got back home for my first fiddle lesson of the school season with Benny, he recognized the Barrett chin rest on my fiddle right away. Bea asked me, "Do you find it comfortable, because Ben can't use the one he gave us." I remarked that it was a little sharp along the perimeter, especially the edge that presses up against your neck. Benny drew up in his chair and peered at me through the top of his bifocals to offer his hypothesis: "Well that's what I thought about his chin rests too, Mark. It's like ol' Dick wants to cut our throats!"

The more Dick dogged me about my bluegrass and having the wrong Texas-style fiddle teacher, I must confess that I wanted to win fiddle contests just to prove him wrong. Dick was trying to splash some cold water on my fiddling, which he viewed was within an inch of catching fire. He began to see me as a future threat to his dominance on the circuit. As long as I continued to take contests seriously and figured out how to get to the biggest ones by the next fiddle contest season, Dick reckoned he had something to worry about.

I understood the adjustments I had to make in general, though, and his advice was not entirely off base. I was going to have to slow the tempos down in the big fiddle championships, and calibrate my variations and renditions so the judges could hear every note and intricacy of my performance. I was also going to have to take a few less chances hunting around for hot licks through improvisation.

I was already working on this idea of what I began to call "controlled improvisation." Benny was a master of this naturally, and I was doing it some in those jams at the Pickin Parlor and backstage for Roy Acuff. Controlled improvisation is where I could still improvise on a fiddle tune, but do so in a way that closely adhered to the melodic line, as opposed to the "take off" and swing-style improvising that Barrett and others played separate from the contest rounds. I was still two years away from getting into playing swing violin modeled after the greatest jazz violinists—Stephane Grappelli, Eddie South, and Joe Venuti. I loved the albums I had of those players, but in my own methodology, I wasn't *there* yet. In the meantime, I would not have to sacrifice my creativity regarding fiddle music. The improvisational nature of my fiddling provided a real edge of excitement to the old tunes.

I wouldn't have to wait long to take some hard runs at Dick Barrett. By the end of our visit, I accepted that the old weathered veteran and the little boy had really only one thing in common: *Fiddle contests.* He won the big ones, and I wanted to. My mother and I both understood that winning contests, coupled with the prize money the pre-eminent contests bestowed, was the one way I could get ahead—to finance my own trips out of Seattle.

We could see it was imperative for me to continue to be around the best players in traditional acoustic music, and to develop as a young musician. Since I didn't live in the South where the best players were, I would have to travel across the country to get there, and often. Mom saw how well I responded to the professional musicians all summer, and it lifted me to another level. If I wanted to stay clear of crawl spaces under rotting houses, I would have to pay for this music *habit* (as my Dad sometimes referred to it). Contests were the only way we could see it happening. To start winning major fiddle championships, I had to get through Dick Barrett first. I reminded my Mom: *"Let's be real... I just turned 13."*

MY NEXT FIDDLE LESSON stopover that summer was with Herman Johnson of Shawnee, Oklahoma. Herman was the current

Grand Masters Fiddle Champion, and he had already won a few national titles at Weiser—1968, '69, and the year I first attended in '73.

Herman played his breakdowns as smooth as silk, and played them just a bit faster than Barrett, which I loved. At age 54, Herman Johnson was one of the most successful competition fiddlers of all time. While Dick Barrett demanded that he win every time, Herman Johnson was more calculating in an interesting, contrastive way. Herman only attended fiddle contests where he thought he had a good chance of winning—carefully assessing the panel of judges in advance before he ever cranked up the engine to his little camper truck. He had his own strategic reconnaissance. When Johnson lost to Barrett at Cinderella City earlier that summer, it wasn't the best day Herman ever had.

I witnessed Herman Johnson arriving at a big regional contest in Omaha, Nebraska. He sized up everything at the welcome table, and said hello to me, Benny, and a few others. He noticed Barrett there across the lobby, laughing out loud and carrying on like he usually does. Then Herman turned around and stoically walked out the front door. He drove on home and we didn't seem him again—seven-hours each way. His strategy for entering the fiddle contests where he knew he could do well (and ignoring the rest) worked quite well for him.

Herman didn't attend Weiser every year, judiciously spacing out his visits; skipping a year or two to let others have some limelight. Once hooked on Weiser, most players went every year until they either burned out from entering, or their welcome was well worn. I wasn't going to have the luxury of passing up events on that basis. As a kid, a year gone by was an eternity. So I played for antagonistic judges, because even 2nd and 3rd place finishes paid enough money to make the trip worthwhile. Herman had a job as a business man and didn't need to enter contests to get ahead financially. His day job accounted for his sharp, "executioner styled" suit and tie attire at fiddle competitions.

As much as they were night and day from each other in temperament, Herman's earlier life was nearly identical to Dick Barrett's. Johnson came from a long line of fiddlers in the family, one of 14 siblings (the same number as my Dad's). He was largely self-taught, but he had a little help from *his* father and his uncles. He was drawn to Country music and especially the music of Bob Wills and Western Swing. After serving in the armed forces in Germany during WWII, often performing for his fellow troops stationed in Europe, Herman came back after the war to enter the music profession for a while. He played all around Oklahoma and Texas, mostly leading his own groups.

During our visit with him, Herman taught me a few tunes, including his own "Herman's Rag." He showed me a little swing too, which he loved to play. All of the contest fiddlers as well as bluegrass fiddlers like Kenny Baker, Chubby Wise, Vassar Clements, and Byron Berline, liked to play the swing style.

Herman's waltzes were very nice. His version of "Wednesday Night Waltz" had double stops moving in and out of third position—crisp slides, with glissando sweeps right into pitch. Like Barrett, Herman's tone was fine, his intonation was spot on, and he played with a tasty amount of vibrato—just right for fiddling. His renditions of tunes were always crafted with consummate taste. He was like the Texas-style version of Kenny Baker playing "Muleskinner Blues" or "Jerusalem Ridge." Just slaying it.

Herman had us stay overnight. He and his wife were so kind to this scraggly kid from Seattle… and like Bill and Bonnie's, his air-conditioned house felt like heaven to us after a summer of hot southern weather with no a/c. Herman told us stories about first meeting Benny in the 1950s, when he was just getting started in fiddle contests in Texas. He loved Benny and reinforced the fact that I *did* have a great teacher in him.

I could sense that Herman knew I was going to get much better soon, tangential to his giving me tips on how to move up in future fiddle contests. Sitting directly across to learn from him, this mental picture made the lesson feel extraordinary. He was flattered that I loved his playing and wanted to learn his own tune "Herman's Rag," but at the same time, I had my own designs on his tune, too. I wanted to create a different rendition of it, using my own variations that I was already thinking about—doubtlessly purposed for pitting me against him in fiddle contests.

Indeed, "Herman's Rag" would become one of my fiddle contest standbys later that year. Eventually, I developed a few moves in it that wowed the judges nearly every time I played the tune. On the "A" part variation, I came up with figurations that moved between first and third position on every single beat, rapidly, attempting to not lose any pitch or ragtime swing. It was some wild fingering technique, not the kind of thing that Dick and Herman were doing. I had a sense it would work in contests. I guess time would tell.

Despite the competitive nature of fiddle contests, and how I was bound and determined to close in on the top cash prizes and play alongside the masters, I really liked Herman as a person as well as a player. It was my one and only lesson from the great champion. It was off to the races after that. The following day, we set out for Seattle—the glumness and exigency awaiting me back home. My adrenaline-charged, two-and-a-half month summer of fiddling sweated out in our Ford Econoline had come to a close.

DURING THE FOLLOWING school year I was now 13, and miraculously, I found a way to grow a foot. It was positively divine intervention—sprouting up a good six inches above the rest of 8th grade. I no longer was a twerp. The extra inches were really going to help me, even if I was a bit asymmetrical—my youthful face on a 6' 2" body, but I'd take it. My oldest half brother, Tim, was 6' 6", so height on my Dad's side was in the family. I had two older half brothers and a half sister: Tim, Larry, and June. All were adults (and tall) living elsewhere by the time I had started in music.

While I devised some future action plans for fiddle contests, for now I had to come up with a few tactics for my own middle school survival. The last thing I wanted was another school gang coming for me because I played fiddle in Nashville. While I didn't look much like a girl anymore, I feared that I still stood out, enough so that I would draw too much attention—teasing, bullying, and worse. Thank God my mother didn't make me wear the head gear for my braces to school like she did in the beginning. I was afraid of some kid grabbing and pulling at it. Wearing it just at nighttime, I was going to have my braces on for quite a bit longer—three years, as it turned out. Preening for the stage was not my priority anyway.

Dick and Herman had their great fiddle contest strategies; I had the summer to think about my own resilience strategy for 8th grade. And did I ever have it all figured out. Beginning with my face, I worked on tightening my lips during the school day—pursing them, scrunching, whatever it took. Another good idea of mine was to never fully comb my longish hair. My made-for-rough-school matted mess of hair, caused my appearance to

101

be impressively more menacing, I thought, and more ghastly. I had tangled knots in my hair for days at a time, if not quite a bit longer.

The big arrow in my quiver towards looking truly rough was wearing my padded school parka all day during class — never taking it off for anyone to see my long skinny arms, no matter what. The parka made me look bulkier, more formidable. While the other stocky boys were stripping down to their shirtsleeves in class, I was just trying to look *bad* enough to stay alive. No matter how warm it got in the classrooms, I kept the jacket on. With my new school makeover this year, kids actually left me alone for the most part. It was going to work.

However, my parents were not as excited about my new growth spurt. In addition to buying me all new clothes for school, they also believed I would get far less attention as a child musician with that extra foot of height on me. They feared the additional inches would cost me in terms of publicity, audience interest, and therefore, dollars. No more little-boy fiddle champion angle to sell to the public. I wasn't concerned about it.

I had last year's well-worn, rust-colored parka jacket and was all prepared to wear it for school. It still looked good and bulky on top, albeit a little short. Surprise — my mother came home with a new puffy parka a couple of sizes up. Good, I thought. On opening the shopping bag, I discovered the most calamitous, awful color of clothing I could have ever envisioned. To my dismay, the hue she chose for my school jacket was "baby blue." I was just putting the final touches on my offensive, ungroomed schoolboy look, and now this.

"Oh Mom, really! "How could you…baby blue?"

"Too bad," she said. "You can learn to like it. It's gloomy all year in Seattle, and this is a bright color for you."

Yeah, bright all right…

On my way back from school that first day, I took the familiar slog through the swamp in the woods, just this side of the ravine. This time I waded in chest deep. The mud stains and grime made the brand new jacket look a little better, I reckoned. The new baby blue parka remained sullied throughout the entire school year.

Yo-yo also became popular that year at school. Not the cello-playing Yo-Yo Ma, but yo-yo tricks. Glenn Godsey, one of Byron Berline's friends, was a yo-yo expert. A professor of art at the University of Tulsa, and a blue-grass guitarist, he edited a manual for Duncan yo-yoing and taught me tricks when I stayed over at his house during my visit to Langley. Far beyond "rock the baby" and "walking the dog," I returned to school with moves like the "braintwister." I even used the yo-yo on stage that year. Did the gag with Oswald where he came out with his large yo-yo made of two frisbees. Just as he did with Roy Acuff who played the yo-yo on stage at the Grand Ole Opry.

No matter how many newspaper write-ups about the "National Junior Fiddle Champion," this magnificent growth spurt, and a new gross appearance at school along with "lindy loops" and "flying trapezes" kept me on solid ground.

The 9th grade gang had moved on to high school anyway.

MEANWHILE, IN THE ABSURD double life I was leading, fiddle lessons with Benny took on more significant dimensions. Benny and Bea relocated to another trailer home about a half-hour closer to us, in Toutle, Washington. We apprised them of the master stroke of a summer of good fortunes. Since we last saw him, Benny observed how much I had grown, in every way. He also saw how serious I was about getting better at contest fiddling. Picking up where we left off with the schedule of lessons every other Saturday, our work on the breakdowns began to last well into the wee hours of the night.

We insisted that Benny take at least some money for the long lessons. I was winning more local contests now, and had quite a few shows lined up with Seattle-area bluegrass bands. With my mother's help, I was able to join up with several adult musicians wanting to play with me during the 1974-'75 school year. My stock had risen considerably in the bluegrass scene around the Northwest, given my Woodinville, Weiser, and summer tour exploits. Mom was able to book me at most every kind of place you could hope for—local fairs, senior citizen centers, street festivals, store openings, flea markets, school gym assemblies. Hospitals and convalescent homes... and a political rally for Mayor Wes Uhlman. A couple of events downtown at Pike Place Market. Wherever one could get on a stage. Anyplace except bars and clubs—where it was against the law for minors in the state of Washington. There were a couple taverns I played bluegrass at, though. They brought the mic stand over where I stood in the doorway to play the set. They passed my hat afterwards and I took home nearly 50 bucks at those.

One of the local Seattle groups I joined up with was the Curly Creek String Band, consisting of Roger and Janice Maddy playing mandolin, guitar, and singing harmony vocals. Larry Edwards played the upright bass. All three were in their early 20s. Both Roger and Larry played a little fiddle so they had a good appreciation for how I could blend my fiddling in with their vocals already.

Another collaboration was with a duo dubbed "The Tennesseans"— traditional bluegrass pickers hailing from Tennessee relocated to the Northwest. Hank English played guitar and sang, and Harley Worthington played banjo. They were a bit older than Curly Creek, in their late 30s. My little sister strummed the Givens mandolin in the group, too. Mark O'Connor and the Tennesseans started playing quite a few bluegrass music shows around the Seattle area. We landed a weekly gig at Dan and Jo's Restaurant on Thursdays, a place that took dinner reservations on the evenings we performed. The eatery was located right in my little hometown of Mountlake Terrace.

Benny often refused to take any money for the long lessons that year, but once in a while he might accept a $10 bill. Usually, he would have nothing of it. If she was in the room at the time, Bea might persuade him to "just go on and accept their money," as she rocked back in her chair with a look of slight frustration at her husband's genteelness.

During the increased lesson hours with Benny, lasting well into Sunday afternoons nearly every time now, I was learning new breakdowns as well as recalibrating those I already knew. No matter what, he always steered me towards innovation. The old-time fiddle tunes that Benny had crafted into his own finished versions were subjects for me to develop my own variations on. Benny challenged me to return for the next lesson with new variations of tunes to play for him. He insisted that I could come up with something better than where he had them. Of course, I never believed this to be the case for a second. His renditions were absolute perfection to my ears. But it was clear that we were doing something else.

Benny's doggedness over this steadfast idea of *creativity* caused me to start *believing* and *imagining* music even more than I ever had before.

I HAD MORE THAN OUTGROWN my more recent $200 fiddle and needed a better one to keep up with my progress. My fiddle was on the smallish side—shorter by just about a half inch in length, but it's remarkable how much difference that can make when you are holding it under your chin. It was time to upgrade, considering my new height, especially.

During the following weekend down at Benny's, my mother stated that it was time for a new fiddle. Benny was a little bit of a fiddle trader and repairman himself. Not nearly as bellicose as Dick Barrett, granted, but Benny did have all kinds of old fiddles he picked up and traded for at the local contests—and they were all over his trailer home. Fiddles were spilling out of his front room closet, from under the couch, out from under the bed… and a few of them hanging right there on his trailer wall.

Suspended from Benny's living room wall was a new edition to his collection—an outlandish looking violin by any description. It easily caught my eye—you couldn't avoid it. I was gawking at an unsightly white-painted fiddle, perhaps even more soiled than my baby blue jacket.

"What is that?" I asked Benny.

"I believe you might like that old fiddle, Mark," Benny grinned.

"Why don't you take it down there and give it a try."

Instantly, I fell in love with the old white fiddle. I could not put it down. A big-sized fiddle, it was much louder than mine. It rang out with enormous overtones that I had not experienced before.

"Where did this white fiddle come from?" I asked. We took a seat while Benny told us the whole story.

Benny had been fishing with a neighbor earlier that week. When they returned to his acquaintance's barn to clean their fish and tackle, Benny spotted a white-painted fiddle hanging on the barn wall. It had neither strings nor pegs, neither a bridge nor tailpiece. It was merely a barn decoration. But Benny could tell right away that it was very much a *real* instrument. Benny queried his neighbor about it: "What would you take for that old white fiddle hanging up there?" Benny thought he could use it for parts. Maybe the neck or the back could help him repair fiddles he was working on. His neighbor began eyeing one of Benny's fishing rods. "Give me that one right there," he said, "and you can take that fiddle with you."

Once back at the trailer, Benny started to look this old white fiddle over more carefully. The top had some small cracks, so that part was probably unusable for another fiddle. But the neck looked good and the back was in fine shape. He suspected it was a 19th century instrument, and was leaning towards it being German or Czech. It didn't have a label. But of course, the paint job scraped away any real value an original instrument would otherwise have.

As he was about to strip the paint off and dismantle the white fiddle entirely, he thought better of it. Benny glued up the top, found some pegs that fit, and with the care of a dutiful craftsman, prudently cut a soundpost and bridge for it. Finally, he strung up the fiddle. Benny went to all those lengths, just in case the white fiddle sounded much better than it looked.

Well, it certainly did. Benny unearthed a *cannon* of an instrument, one that possessed a massive and resonant sound. He was well satisfied. He tried to clean it up a bit more, and got it ready for my next visit.

A fiddle that had hung outdoors for years, in a damp, cold barn… and painted with an enamel coating for a barn decoration, became my principal instrument. Benny gave this magical white fiddle to me without a second thought. From that point on, fiddlers could always tell when the kid from Seattle arrived at a fiddle contest. The sound of the white fiddle carried so very far. Folks could hear me play it from clear across the field.

The old white fiddle could also cut through a stage mic like nothing else, too. With the commonplace Shure PA systems found at most fiddle contests of the day, I was now twice as loud as the old-timers. That was disconcerting for them. I was ready to be just *bigger*—in every way. I didn't care about the whippersnapper that Mom and Dad were sad to see disappear. Since I was jamming and performing with adults anyway, I wanted to be at their level—a big kid, a big repertoire, and a big fiddle with a huge sound. I had never felt better about my future more than I did on the day I got ahold of that old white fiddle.

Armed with my new eyesore, an instrument that could make the least unsuspecting person turn away from it at first sight, the fiddle allowed me to *believe* and to *imagine* that I could get ahead of Dick Barrett and Herman Johnson. My playing skyrocketed during my school year of 1974-'75.

"Mark is becoming the best fiddler in the country," Benny told my mother.

"He's going to win every fiddle contest in the country on this white fiddle right here."

As I readjusted to the winter season, my lessons continued with Benny. We worked together to create new variations and renditions: "College Hornpipe," "Martha Campbell," "Forked Deer," "New Broom," "Black Mountain Rag," "Draggin' the Bow." They were all lesson tunes, as Benny challenged me to create new variations for them. Mostly, we continued to work on the great Texas-style fiddle breakdowns. By this time I knew them all. I won at Weiser and other places with them. But we still worked on them—Benny's masterpieces: "Sally Goodin'," "Tom and Jerry," "Grey Eagle," "Say Old Man." Then "Billy In The Low Ground," "Sally Johnson," "Dusty Miller." All the while, I continued to work on the "controlled improvisation" practice, and employed this concept in playing my new variations.

Benny's contest strategy for me going forward was to not bother using the more obscure tunes in the rounds. We were just going to stick with the celebrated warhorses, and "just play them better than anybody else," Benny surmised. As he pushed me to rework our lesson tunes, this creative work ended up becoming established versions that fiddlers played around the country.

B ENNY TOLD US about a young boy from Texas when we were down to his place for a lesson. Terry Morris was a new fiddler on the scene and was all the rage. Benny heard him during a recent family visit to Dallas.

"They're all talkin' about this boy down there... Norman Solomon and some of those ol' boys are all sayin' it," Benny related. "He's better than all of us who've come along from our generation down there."

Benny was marveling over the young phenom, Terry Morris. I sat there, taking it all in as he continued to speak about him. We didn't run into a single teenager all summer long who played the fiddle at the level of a champion or professional.

"He's just 18 years old, Mark," after a brief pause. Then Benny looked directly at me and said:

"He is great. But he's not better than you."

Benny was fashioning me into his fiddle champion protégé. I had not seen such a competitive side to Benny before. But I suppose you don't become the undefeated Texas State Fiddle Champion 15 years in a row, playing against the likes of his own teacher, the historic Eck Robertson, and not be more than a little determined. It seemed that his quest these days was more about his student, rather than himself. Benny further advised:

"Mark, you will beat Terry in all of the fiddle contests around the country—except in Texas. They will never let you win in Texas."

Benny stressed, "They're jealous of what we're doing up here. Word has traveled."

So it turns out there was already a bit of a rivalry before I ever signed up for one. Most of this cageyness was coming from Benny's old mates. They felt that Benny should be down in Texas helping out and even teaching Morris, a once in a generation Texas fiddler, rather than "wasting his time" in the state of Washington.

The first time we heard a little about Terry Morris was about his 2nd place finish to Herman Johnson in Nashville, and that he nearly beat Dick Barrett in Truth or Consequences, New Mexico that year. He was right on their heels, a place where I hoped to be soon.

Stakes got a little higher from the older fiddlers in Texas, chatting up the two young'uns all the time—rumors abound. Everything seemed to point to next summer's fiddle contest season. I didn't know if a 13-year-old could ever be expected to go up against those big-time adult fiddlers, but I did sense I was getting better and better—and by the day. I knew a lot more tunes this year as well. Benny made sure of that.

Late one night, Benny elaborated on some of his own contest exploits from the 1930s and '40s, especially the stories about his chief rival, Major Franklin.

"Me and ol' Major, we were neck and neck in some of those contests, down there in Texas," Benny told us.

"Them judges, well they tied us again and again for 1st place, you see. It was always nip-and-tuck."

Benny talked about the legendary play-offs that are today's fiddling folklore. One time, Major Franklin was listening to Benny's round from afar and heard him play "Sally Goodin'." He went up to the judges and accused Benny of cheating. His charge was that Benny was playing the fiddle cross-tuned in the contest again. Benny argued that he wasn't re-tuned at all. Fiddlers believe that it's easier to play some of the tunes on a re-tuned fiddle; therefore, *scordatura* was outlawed. Franklin demanded Benny produce his instrument at once so he could thump the strings for all to hear. Sure enough, Benny's fiddle was in the standard tuning. He just *sounded* like it was played retuned.

Benny eventually broke most of his tiebreakers with Major Franklin, he told us, because Benny knew more tunes and had better renditions of them. My teacher made sure that the quantity of my own repertoire was sufficient for anything which might come my way on the contest circuit that summer.

Collectively, I learned more than 200 fiddle tunes from Benny Thomasson over the course of the few years I took lessons from him. This didn't include all of the tunes I was learning from others, or picking off tapes and albums on my own. I had the entire amount of repertoire memorized, and could recall them to perform at any time—without any sheet music to refer to, whatsoever.

Benny told us another story. It was about the time that two great fiddling stars, "Big Howdy" Forrester and Robert "Georgia Slim" Rutland, knocked on his front door in Arlington, Texas. Hearing this particular story tickled me, since I got to hang around Howdy in Nashville. Forrester and Rutland were playing twin fiddles on KRLD's Texas *Roundup Show* in Dallas during the late 1940s. They thought they should pay the undefeated world fiddle champion a visit.

"Hello there," Benny said. "What can I do for you gentlemen?"

"We came to hear what the best fiddler in the world sounds like!" Howdy and "Georgia Slim" remarked.

"Well, come on in then," Benny chuckled to himself.

Benny picked up his fiddle and began to play right there in the living room, as Benny explained it to us.

"Ol' Georgia Slim, he plum got down there on the floor and began to cry, you see." Bea nodded, yes.

B ENNY THOMASSON, THE LEGEND, was instilling in me the glory of being a great fiddle champion. While Benny did not have any financial means, he undoubtedly had his music, and his considerable reputation of being one of the greatest fiddlers in the world. It was interesting to compare the great professional fiddlers who I met the summer before to

Benny. My teacher never put together a career in music, but he "made it" with his years of fiddle competitions. As far as we could see, only Byron Berline was able to be both a great fiddle champion as well as a solo artist on the professional circuit around the country.

I wanted to accomplish both of those things like Berline, if I could—contest winner, and a recording artist and soloist. But there wasn't any other way for me to make an impact in music as a kid, for now, other than competitions. Winning the major competitions could put me on the map—Benny knew that as well as my mother and father did. Perhaps there was the remote possibility I could get picked up by a nationally-known band, like what happened to Marty Stuart at the age of 13, but it wouldn't be something I could determine on my own. I would have to be invited, and those music leaders would have to practically parent me on the road.

By late September, my mother fully embraced the idea of a child musician career based on winning competitions. She made the calculated risk of sending me on my first solo plane trip to Winfield, Kansas. I stayed with Jeff Pritchard and his parents, a family who we had met at Weiser. Jeff picked me up at the Wichita airport and we drove into Winfield together. I won the fiddle contest there, and I came out with a 2nd place finish in the National Flat-pick Guitar Championships. I accomplished this feat on the cheap Yamaha Hummingbird imitation, no less. Guitar-playing would continue to be a major factor in competitions and in my musical life.

Emboldened by the success in Winfield, Kansas, and especially seeing how I dealt with that kind of pressure on my own, even away from her care, my mother instinctively understood that the bit of nation-wide attention I was garnering could not be any fluke. She continued to survey the national music scene for any professional kid fiddlers or bluegrass players.

Marty Stuart started touring with The Sullivan Family in 1971 as a 12-year-old, and followed them with Lester Flatt and the Nashville Grass at 13. Other than Stuart, there were the 16-year-olds, Keith Whitley and Ricky Skaggs, who began singing with Ralph Stanley and the Clinch Mountain Boys in the summers, beginning in 1970. They went on the road full time with Stanley once out of high school. The two young singers were able to use their voices to mimic the style and sound of Carter and Ralph Stanley together. Ralph heard them as his impromptu opening act one night and wanted to feature them on his shows in a tribute to his late brother, Carter. According to Skaggs, Stanley paid the two youngsters $25 a piece per show. At that rate, they would've had to work an entire summer on the road with Ralph Stanley in order to equal a single fiddle contest win at the Grand Masters Fiddle Championship, paying out $1,000 for 1st place.

As far as the profession of bluegrass music for kids was concerned, this was the entire kit and caboodle. Since neither Stuart, Whitley, nor Skaggs entered national music competitions, and they were singing on stage when I wasn't, there were no road maps leading me to where I was going—or where I *must* go. There were no fully-made role models here—neither a precedent nor a framework for what I was attempting to do as a child musician. The path I was on was one of the narrowest of all pathways that any young musician could travel. But my teacher Benny believed in me and my set of talents—and my Mom believed in me, too. We weren't heading towards a child music career just for my own sake, we were heading there as a family.

A S WE BEGAN TO TALK ABOUT moving south, it was evident that Benny was not in the best of health—he was missing his family more and more. Benny's son, Jerry, and his Mexican wife, Sandra, had seven children who all loved their "Gramps." A few of them, including the oldest girl, Terry, were all young friends of mine. There were no fiddlers among them, but they all sang family harmony. The Thomasson clan was a fixture at many of those early contests I attended. They always honored a request to sing the final song at the end of an evening's fiddle jam (no matter how late the hour), accompanied by Jerry's beautiful tenor guitar.

After Benny learned that we were looking seriously at moving to Nashville and starting a new life there in music, he made plans to move back to Texas that December. It was difficult to know how to react to the news of him departing the Northwest. The sense of loss I felt right away was emotionally devastating. With a jolt to my heart, I sat there in his little trailer in Toutle, Washington, one last time, my face all flushed—seated across from my teacher Benny.

My mind was cycling back and forth, thinking about all the lessons I had and how much he believed in me. I didn't know what it all meant. Texas is a very long way from where we lived in Mountlake Terrace, and it was a very long way from Nashville, too. Benny assured me that Nashville was at least closer than Seattle was—and that we could see each other more often than I was fearing.

On the drive back from my final lesson near the Oregon border, the feelings came barreling in. He was more than my fiddle teacher, he was my mentor, and the grandfather figure I never had. I came to love him as much as folks in my own family, probably more so—the older man with his healing spirit in my intricate life. He was the most sweet and stabilizing influence for me in a music world which was becoming increasingly dynamic. There was so much achievement, balanced by so much uncertainty and confusion, stress, and loneliness. He was an angel, my angel.

Benny Thomasson left the state of Washington, and we never envisioned that happening. He was supposed to retire there. Instead, Benny taught me to be in his image as the great champion fiddler that he was.

I spent the rest of the day trying to make sense of what I was recognizing. Was Benny staying in Washington just for me? Because we decided to leave, he was going to leave as well?

For the first time in my life, I was going to be fully self-taught. Who could possibly follow Benny as my principal teacher in Seattle—if we stayed up here? I was going to pick up things from the musicians I played with—that was already evident. I was bound and determined to do everything I could this year to continue to make Benny proud. Mom said that we should be grateful he stayed in Washington state as long as he did.

I TOOK STOCK OF WHAT I had at my fingertips, those being the talents I possessed by age 13. I was playing the fiddle much better this year. I was playing the guitar much better, too. Incredibly, I had a record deal with Rounder. No other kid in fiddle or bluegrass music had a record deal and an opportunity to record feature albums on any kind of frequent basis. Starting that year, my Rounder recordings were supported by album budgets just as large as the major bluegrass stars, and with equal international distribution and marketing.

Then there was my own musical creativity. Not just in arranging traditional tunes and improvising on them, but, beginning in 1975, writing music. The National Junior Fiddle Champion album release was getting positive reviews and receiving wider circulation, more than we ever expected. Rounder Records wanted me to record a second album, so I worked on two original tunes for it—one for the fiddle named "Mark's Waltz," and my first one for the guitar—"Pickin' in the Wind."

I was fixated on coming up with some melody lines and chord progressions which were unique from anything I was learning or playing at the time. Most every tune I knew, in those days at least, ended the final phrase with a "5 to 1" chord progression: "5" being the fifth degree of the scale (a *dominant* chord), and "1" chord being the home key. For "Mark's Waltz," I created an end-phrase that sidestepped the common "5" chord anticipation of the home key, and instead used a "4 to 4-minor to 1" harmonic sequence.

When I ferreted out this idea for my new tune, I asked Mom if she had heard anything like it before. Seeking to be gentle, and maybe dodging the question oh just a weensy bit, she responded: "I'm not sure that I have, honey, that sounds beautiful!" It was an unusual chord sequence for a fiddle waltz at least, but of course it is very difficult to be the first one to come up with anything new in music. But still, I was bound and determined to do just that. I was attempting to, even with my first composition. Regardless of whether "Mark's Waltz" represented any musical breakthrough, it turned out to be a fairly substantial waltz, something that I could easily play in fiddle contests and do all right with amid the classics—"Festival Waltz," "Forty-Year Ago Waltz," "Lucinda Waltz," "Westphalia Waltz," "Ookpik Waltz." Importantly, though, it was an original tune for the next album.

For my first guitar composition, "Pickin' in the Wind," I enlisted some Major-7th chords, not at all common in bluegrass music. It was evident that I was already thinking outside the box in every way that I had the capacity to. This tune featured a slow cross-picking intro alternating between three strings using both a C Major-7th chord and an F-minor chord in the sequence—also, not many F-minor chords in bluegrass guitar. For the body of the tune, I *reoriented* the slow intro idea, and changed the characteristics to up-tempo bluegrass. Like my other original song, I felt like I was exploring. I was on a journey to find something new in music.

Coloring outside the lines might as well have been a *commandment.* I knew I was barking up a far different tree when I could not get my own band, The Tennesseans, to learn my new tunes for our shows. It was so frustrating, too—Hank and Harley simply couldn't learn the chord sequences. I finally gave up on them ever getting it. When I got down to Nashville for the recording sessions, I'd never given "Pickin' in the Wind" a test run. I had to *imagine* and *trust* that the new music was going to work.

W ITHIN THE REALMS of all possibility regarding my first attempt at the Grand Masters Fiddle Championship in Nashville, if there was any way to make the top ten, it could put me on a trajectory for having a child music career. That's what my Mom was saying, at least. A music career that could create an income for my mother and my family so we could set out on our own, and away from Dad.

A music career such as this would be enough to get me out of my junky neighborhood, escape that detestable school with all the bullies, slip out from under Dad's rotting structures, and pull me out of *our* current household—one that was increasingly more threatening and abusive, as a raging alcoholic father ruled over it. On a daily basis, my mother evaluated and brooded over how I could make enough money as a kid in music. She kept notebooks of my small amount of earnings with multiplication and division tables in the margins—reams of calculations.

One time I asked her about going on welfare: "Why not welfare?" I was old enough to have at least heard about it. In contempt of any acknowledged rationale, Mom swore that if we were on welfare, we "couldn't do the music"—not on any national scale that we longed for. The significancy of her position was simple. I would not be able to travel to music events with my family in tow, "Not on welfare."

Whether it was an accurate assessment of our plight or not, it is what she believed our rather unique case to be. With a two-year degree from the University of Washington and being as studious and resourceful as Mom was, one would have to believe that if there was any way to receive funding for her talented kid, she would've been filling out the proper paperwork. But as she explained it, the academic side of this "was not going to pan out." She surmised: "There were no scholarships or grants for a talented child playing fiddle music—not in 1974." But in spite of that, I was getting some more gigs, and drawing a bit more attention.

I was invited to perform on Channel 9, the local PBS station, KCTS-TV. It was a double bill with the longtime concertmaster of the Seattle Symphony, Henry Siegl. Mr. Siegl was readily impressed with what he heard from me, so he told my mother. He himself had learned from Hungarian Gypsy violinists in his neighborhood as a boy, so that made for an interesting connection he reflected. But he also said it wouldn't hurt to augment my training with some top classical violin lessons.

Mom, being a big classical music fan going back to before I was born (if it were not for her love of the legendary classical guitarist Andrés Segovia, I wouldn't have begun classical guitar lessons), she took Siegl's interest in me, and his comments, quite seriously. We contemplated adjunct lessons with Mr. Siegl to fill in any gaps in technique I might have. Mr. Siegl didn't take young students at that time, but he wanted to recommend us to a man he described as the "best classical violin instructor in Seattle," Ted Dragoo. An initial lesson was set up for me at his violin studio—and at a bit of a price-thumping at that: the lesson fee was $45 an hour.

So there I was walking into Mr. Dragoo's violin studio with the old white fiddle. Yes, it was awkward and I was very much aware of that. As I brought it out of the case, just the sight of it made Mr. Dragoo nearly pass out, I swear. The fiddle lived up to its eyesore billing. To Mr. Dragoo, my white painted fiddle was a wicked abomination—evil, probably. So the first box was decidedly check-marked on his pad of paper: *Needs to replace his current instrument.*

"You come highly recommended by Mr. Siegl. Play me something," Mr. Dragoo requested. I played him a little "Limerock."

"You have some facility young man, but what is with that bow grip, eh? That grip has to go."

"Well, my teacher Benny Thomasson... that's the grip he uses, and I like it a lot," I responded

"If you are going to take lessons from me, the grip has to go."

I might've been interested in changing my bow grip again, but I'd already changed it from the traditional grip I started with from Barbara, to Benny's grip. In order to bow like Benny does, while using the traditional grip, I had developed a painful corn on the side of my first-finger—a raised bump with painful inflammation. It sidelined me for a few weeks. I just couldn't put any more pressure on it. However, if I held the bow with my thumb under the frog like Benny did, the clasp of the bow grip rested comfortably in the crevice of my first finger (the *PIP* joint), and avoided that nasty corn.

"You might have to give me a few months with it. I'm aiming to compete in the Grand Masters Fiddle Championship in Nashville, Tennessee, and I wouldn't want to suddenly change my bow hold right before the competition. Right?"

"Maybe you didn't understand what I was saying, young man. We are not proceeding with the lesson one minute more today, until you change your grip," Dragoo put his foot down. Or, more like he shoved his foot right in my face.

I can't tell you how good it felt to be Dragoo's height, though, and look straight across at the man. I'm glad he couldn't look down at that shrimp I was the year before, humiliated by those older men who belittled me and made me turn red. I was proud that I finally had some confidence, some backbone. I stood my ground, because what I offered him about the matter I thought was reasonable. It was another insult to my teacher Benny, which I didn't appreciate. My mother was sitting in the corner watching all this go down—not saying *a word*. She was going to let me fly solo with this thing, or get buried alive. Mom allowed me to dig my own hole if I had to.

Dragoo and I stood toe to toe. We paid—or I should say, "I" paid for the full 60 minutes and he wasn't offering any refunds. So we just kept standing there for a few minutes more. It was uncomfortable for me, so I tried to make it uncomfortable for him as well. I just continued fingering my fiddle in a guitar-playing position, to some tune in my head. Nothing much audible, just the sound of my fingers tapping against the fingerboard in his quiet violin studio. It had to have annoyed him. He finally broke the stalemate.

"Well since you are here, I might as well teach you something for your money. Whadya say?"

I agreed.

"I will teach you 'Pop Goes the Weasel.' You familiar with that one?" Dragoo continued. "So, we are going to learn the tune in A-major. And, we are holding the bow halfway up the stick. This will help get your thumb off that frog. When we get to the lyric "pop," we pluck the open

"E" string with our left-hand ring finger, then we'll twirl the bow around and play the repeat of the tune with the frog side of the bow up in the air, like this"—he demonstrated quickly. "You can use this for your fiddle shows—*your* audience will love it."

We drug out learning "Pop Goes the Weasel" for the remaining 45 minutes of my $45 classical violin lesson—or as I dubbed it, my "musical torture chamber" lesson. It was one of the longest 45 minutes of music I'd ever spent. After the annihilation, my mother gave up on finding any scholarship or grants through established academic and classical music circles, for good. I was on a different planet: *planet fiddle.* Whether my wandering star had an atmosphere that maintained any oxygen remained to be seen.

Mom and I got back into the van to head home after my lesson, neither of us saying much of anything for a while. Then I looked over to her to say "At least I made him teach me something for the money we paid him." Despite the confrontation, I continued to play with exactly the same bow grip that I first entered Dragoo's studio with.

ON NOVEMBER 23rd, 1974, we took a little weekend expedition southbound, this time down to California. We drove the 900-mile distance all the way to Madera, California, for the Western Regional Fiddle Championships. By contrast, a bit of fortune did follow us there, indeed. I won the Regular division, and was voted "most popular fiddler." At this contest, the "Regular" division was beneath the "Open." That division was taken by the reliable regional fiddle champion from Spokane, John Francis. No matter what, though, my prize was worth $300 for my win that weekend, well worth the drive in the trusty Ford Econoline. The trip was a good morale boost, too, especially being voted most popular fiddler. I didn't even have to play "Pop Goes the Weasel" to earn it. Tis Mr. Dragoo.

As we waited until summer's contest circuit to start up, there was another early indication of just how a young fiddle champion would do in terms of audience interest. When any monetary earnings were obtainable for the "boy champion fiddler," the usually overly-protective mother did not balk at putting me on a plane by myself—this time for a concert in Columbus, Montana. It was several years before the "unaccompanied minor program" was instituted by the airlines.

I was on my own for those assignments at 13. Mom arranged for my stay with a local fiddler, Montana state fiddle champion Bill Long. We didn't know him well, but we did meet him at Weiser briefly. Mom trusted the fiddle community by this time—she had to if we were going to get where we wanted to go.

Old Time Festival Of Strings
Sat., April 19, 1975. 7:00 p.m. – High School Gym
Sponsored by the Montana Fiddlers Association-District No. 4

Featured Artist
Mark O'Connor - Youngest National Junior Champion - Star of Grand Ole
Opry - Prize winner on mandolin, guitar and fiddle

Bill Long lined up a local guitarist and bassist to accompany me for a set of fiddle tunes and a couple of guitar tunes thrown in. My appearance fee was $400. I made half that amount again selling my brand new LP hot off the press. Just released, we had ordered several boxes of them to resell. By the side of the stage, I doled them out from the cardboard shipping box at $4 apiece. As I was making change, I had dollar bills spilling out of all four of my pants pockets, as well as both cowboy shirt pockets. *If only Mom could see me now, I kept thinking.* Amidst all of the Montana state champion fiddlers on the show bill, I was *the* hit at this well-attended concert of 600 fiddling enthusiasts.

Maybe Mom was right. Perhaps her idea for my being a child performer was possible as a fiddler. This was Mom's plan: move us to Nashville and make enough money in music as a 13-year-old to take care of my mother and sister there. The pressure of that prospect was greater than any I felt entering fiddle contests. Put them together, well—this is a different conversation about *strength of mind*—whether that was mother's mind, or my own. I needed to do well at the Grand Masters—that was our consequential big picture plan. With Benny's guidance, I practiced, I prepared, I created, and I *imagined.*

Our sights were set on Nashville, June 15th, 1975.

STIFFER COMPETITION

The Seattle Times, Sunday January 12th, 1975
"MARK BEGAN playing the classical guitar when he was 6 years old, and switched to the violin only two years ago. He caught the 'fiddling' bug... Although Mark can read music, he plays country music mainly by ear, picking out the themes by hearing them on recordings or broadcasts. He adds his own embellishments to a basic melody.

An eighth-grader at Mountlake Terrace Junior High School, Mark doesn't have time to play in school music groups and he isn't interested in performing symphonic music anyway.

MARK'S MOTHER says the family may consider moving to some Southern city, where country music is more fashionable than it is here, if this will help Mark make faster progress in a musical career."

CHAPTER FIVE

THE BOY CHAMPION FIDDLER

MY FIRST ALBUM FOR Rounder Records did well enough that it led to a recording budget increase for a second album, considerably so. The additional funding would accommodate a full studio band for one day of recording, plus an additional day for overdubbing and remixing, all taking place in a Nashville recording studio. Even I was thinking: *Not bad for 13!*

Bill and Bonnie Smith took more of an active role in lining up some good musical opportunities for our trip back east the summer of 1975. They were big Jim & Jesse and the Virginia Boys fans, just like we were, but recently Bill and Bonnie had been given a role in their fan club. This led to an invitation for me to play a fiddle tune on their Fan Fair banquet show, part of a country music festival in Nashville. Jesse McReynolds kindly remembered me from the Langley festival.

Bill and Bonnie had been communicating with Rounder Records during the year as well, offering their help in coordinating the production for my next Nashville recording. I was closing in on the list of tunes I wanted to record—a mixture of Texas-style tunes and bluegrass tunes. Even though there was a constant drumbeat I heard all year that these two styles were incompatible and should always be segregated, here I was, bound and determined to include both styles on the same album. I was preparing music such as "Dixie Hoedown," written by Jesse McReynolds, and "Lonesome Fiddle Blues," by Vassar Clements, as well as fiddle contest tunes like "Grey Eagle" that I had been working on with Benny. And oh yes—"Herman's Rag."

Bill and Bonnie asked me who I wanted to play on album #2? For sure, I hoped to have Norman Blake and Charlie Collins again. "Good. Who else? You can have a full bluegrass band this time," they told me. My favorite young mandolin player was Sam Bush, who lived in Kentucky. "Would he consider being on my album?" Bill and Bonnie would inquire.

"How about an upright bass?" I was enamored with Junior Huskey from the *Will the Circle be Unbroken* album. He would certainly be the perfect bass player to get. Bill and Bonnie informed us that Junior had tragically died of cancer just a couple years before at such a young age. They discovered that he had an 18-year-old son, and word had it that he played the bass just like his father. We were able to schedule Roy Huskey Jr. for the recording—a fellow teenager.

After Sam Bush was confirmed, an incredible five-piece band was assembled for my recording sessions. I was absolutely fired up over the album now. This time, I planned on featuring a few tunes on my guitar and mandolin as well. My guitar and mandolin playing up to that point was largely unfamiliar to Bill and Bonnie, and to Rounder Records. So I was just looking to sneak in a couple of those tunes. This album was going to remain mostly about the fiddle.

Bill and Bonnie rang us up in Seattle to give us an update on how things were coming together. They confirmed that all of the musicians were in place for the sessions on June 11th and 12th, and that the rehearsal would take place at their home the day before, on the 10th. The recording sessions were booked at Johnny Cash's studio in Hendersonville, The House of Cash, the engineer (Johnny Cash's engineer) was to be Charlie Bragg. There was an additional item they wanted to discuss with us.

Bill and Bonnie said they had a most unusual offer. Banjoist, guitarist, fiddler, singer-songwriter and originator of Newgrass music, John Hartford, called Rounder from his home in Hollywood, California. Hartford asked the folks at Rounder if he could play on *my* album. They tossed the inquiry over to Bill and Bonnie to field. A subsequent phone conversation with John Hartford ensued. They had to tell John Hartford that we had all of the musicians already booked for the album and we had no budget left to fly him in from Los Angeles anyway.

"I tell you what, don't worry about paying me a thing, I'll just fly myself to Nashville and I'll be at your service, how about that? I want to be on this young boy's record, I'm a big fan of his."

My mother and I were blown away by hearing this. We just couldn't fathom why he would not only shell out a plane fare, but devote so much of his time for my album from clear across the country. John Hartford was a big star, too. We saw him nearly weekly on Glenn Campbell's *Goodtime Hour* television show. We also saw him on the Johnny Cash television show. The man who wrote "Gentle On My Mind" wants to play on my record. For free.

By now, I was so inspired with anticipation for the recording with all those great acoustic musicians, I worked even harder on my playing and on the album's repertoire. I fine-tuned my arrangements of old-time fiddle tunes, worked on solos for the bluegrass standards, and composed my first original tunes specifically for the album. I wanted to record "Faded Love" with a new variation I wrote (*inspired* by Skeeter). I was pleased to make my first recorded tribute as well. My teacher Benny told me how his father and uncle wrote the gorgeous fiddle waltz, "Midnight on the Water." He taught me how the piece was created with a unique cross-tuning of the fiddle, bringing the high string from E down to D, and the G-string all the way down to a low D. "Midnight on the Water," had become reasonably well-known by then—David Bromberg had just recorded it as the title track for his new album on Columbia Records.

Side One: Pickin' in the Wind, Midnight On The Water, Tom and Jerry, Cotton Patch Rag, Tammy's Waltz, Lonesome Fiddle Blues
Side Two: Daybreak in Dixie, Mark's Waltz, Grey Eagle, Dixie Hoedown, Goodbye Waltz, Herman's Rag, Faded Love, Dixie Breakdown

Album Notes by John Hartford, 1975 (excerpted):

"...by the time you read this, he will probably have won all the rest of the major old-time music contests in this country and who knows what else...

You can't imagine how Norman, Sam, Roy Jr., Charlie and myself "got off on" making this album with Mark... who must be too young to know anything about being nervous... he just sat in front of us in a bright orange Snoopy tee shirt and laid his whole left forearm down on his left leg and bowed a white fiddle with Benny Thomasson's autograph on the back of it in what looked like black paint. Every once in a while he might raise up just a little bit for some real high intricate lick.

Charlie once told me about the first time Mark ever came into the 'Pickin' Parlor' with his mother and Tut had called him and asked him to let Mark get up and play. It was kinda late and Charlie and Os were anxious to get home and were thinking... 'Here's another kid gonna get up and play out of tune or something.' But after Mark played his first number, Charlie said he rushed over to the telephone, called Vassar and said, 'You better get down here right away and hear this kid. I don't believe it.'

I hope he doesn't get so good that he loses the amazement of it all (if that's possible)... I'm trying to comprehend what it must be like to be that good...

it's probably so far inside his subconscious that when he reads this he'll wonder why I'm even making such a big deal out of it."

Bluegrass Unlimited, April, 1976 (Mark comments about his recording session):

"'It was really something sittin' down with all those good musicians, especially to work out my tune, 'Pickin In The Wind.' It was exciting to finally hear it with all the parts, the way I had it in my mind, how I wanted it to sound. Up in Washington, I had tried to teach it to some friends. They practiced it for two hours and by the next day had already forgotten it! But the second time around, these guys had it down! It was really neat getting to make a record with super musicians.'"

A T THIRTEEN YEARS and ten months old, I entered what was the biggest fiddle competition in the country on June 15th, 1975. Benny made it over to Nashville from Texas—he was entering the competition. This will be the first time I found myself in a fiddle contest against my teacher, Benny. *So, how does his student prepare for that?*

This 1975 Grand Masters Fiddle Championship boasted the most impressive lineup of competition fiddlers ever assembled in U.S. history. The Masters was an invitational, and I was chosen to participate as the current National Junior Fiddle Champion. If you should be lucky to be one of the 15 invited contestants, you were also given free lodging at the brand new Opryland Hotel. No sleeping in the yellow van for us this time.

The recently-turned 19-year-old Terry Morris arrived in Nashville as promised. The Texas fiddle phenom was predicted by most everyone to win it. Of course, the year before, he had placed 2nd to the fiddle contest exemplary, Herman Johnson. I met Terry on the eve of the contest during the official jam session party. It was held in the television studios backstage of the Grand Ole Opry. Several Opry stars drifted in and out during the evening to listen to the fiddle jams: notably Roy Acuff, Buck Owens, Porter Wagoner, Tennessee Ernie Ford, Marty Robbins... Upon meeting him, Terry seemed fairly nice to me. He was just brimming with confidence, too. Terry knew that Benny Thomasson was singing my praises and it put him on edge with me just a little. One look at me, though, standing there wearing my hand-embroidered cowboy shirt, plastic cowboy hat, braces on my teeth—he probably figured: *not a problem.*

Mom and I had decided to get one of those new black Sharpie pens, and have some fiddlers sign the white fiddle. We thought it would look better to go over at least some of the white paint with famous fiddlers' signatures. Benny's was first to go on. He signed his lengthwise down the back when we were still back in Washington. I asked Terry to sign it and he obliged. After getting several fiddlers to sign the fiddle that night, it became obvious that no one had ever signed their autograph on an actual fiddle before. *A new tradition?* It was going to be quite a busy weekend, just with the Sharpie.

The legends of Texas fiddling were invited to the Grand Masters in 1975. Benny's old running mates and fellow competitors in Texas, notably Major Franklin's nephew Louis Franklin, and his son Larry Franklin, were both there to compete. More Texas fiddle legends including the brothers, Norman and Vernon Solomon were there. The 1960s world champion, James "Texas Shorty" Chancellor, was there to win it. Shorty was Benny's first protégé. Other Texas fiddle contest upstarts were there, particularly Terry's brother Dale Morris, and Randy Elmore, who was one of Terry's pals. They were both fighting for high placements, if not going for the whole thing.

If those players weren't enough for the contest lineup of the century, top fiddlers in the Southeast, J.T. Perkins and Roy Crawford were there to compete. Top Canadian national champions were routinely making their way down to the Grand Masters, like Graham Townsend, Peter Dawson, and Rudy Meeks. Even young Sam Bush was intently playing for the Masters' top prize.

The judges were an impeccable collection of fiddling royalty on top of everything else. The head judge was Herman Johnson, and the Nashville recording session stalwarts Buddy Spicher and Johnny Gimble were judging, too. Recording on albums with singing stars ranging from Bob Wills to Patsy Cline, both Gimble and Spicher were considered fiddling aristocracy. And speaking of eminence, Mr. Guitar, Chet Atkins gadded about backstage as he wished.

Mom spoke to me about setting my expectations astutely, rationally... to not get lost in the hype we were hearing about me—the buzz already astir that a "13-year-old fiddle whiz from Seattle" could somehow have an outside chance. Even a year gone by, it continued to be a rarity in the South to lay eyes on a kid fiddler who could *play.*

The circumstances in the early 1970s which led to having a few more fiddle kids come out of the Western states brings to light a few observations since last summer. The proprietors of Western fiddle contests put up junior divisions for kids. This very good development promoted the idea that kids belonged at these events, too, not just the adults and the seniors. I would not have been in Nashville at all without the Junior divisions at Weiser as a pathway. For that matter, I may not have even been fiddling.

Under 18 was the age qualification for the Juniors at Weiser. On last summer's tour, it was the last time we ever saw a kids' division heading east. The Rocky Mountains must have been the cutoff for any notion that children should be in fiddle competitions. By Colorado, they said the Junior division was for ages 25 and under. The farther south we went, that age requirement kept creeping away. In most southern fiddle contests, the "Junior division," if they had one at all, was either for 35 and under, or more popular, 45 and under. Often "Juniors" meant age 55 and under—a few even 59 years and under. Climactically, I saw a contest or two where the "Junior division" was all the way up to age 65—which at the time, was just three years off the average life expectancy for a man. There, you were a Junior, up until the day you were a Senior. Then another three years, and you were gone.

In the South, young kids were not encouraged to speak to an adult unless something was wrong, and usually not even then. *"Children should be seen and not heard"* was an old English proverb perfectly adapted. This war cry could easily extend itself to the fiddling environment—enter the kid from Seattle. At fiddle contests, I didn't have many other people to talk with, except adults—therefore, the grown-ups made up my friends circle. I think they enjoyed the back-and-forths, too. Breakthroughs abound.

Old-timers at Weiser were excited that I could "save" old-time fiddling—the pied piper for more children to play fiddle. On the flipside, southerners' reactions to my 13-year-old fiddle playing weren't any less enthusiastic, but this precise sentiment was never accepted wisdom. More readily, southerners insisted on measuring my ability to play the fiddle alongside adult professionals—never other children. Just the year before, Roy Acuff's introduction of me at the *Opry* had me pitted against the likes of Vernon Solomon, Herman Johnson, and Dick Barrett—my prepubescent voice hadn't even changed yet. Their consideration wasn't about *saving* old-time fiddling, as much as it was about me stacking up with the best.

Further examination finds the Northwest with no music industry to speak of, and, certainly not an industry which included the fiddle. Many old-timers located in this region of the country viewed the future of their beloved fiddle music as solely in the hands of the young people to keep alive.

Whereas the music industry in the South most certainly included the fiddle, and they were doing the job just fine, many believed. No real fear that the fiddle would disappear from Nashville, as long as the Grand Ole Opry hired fiddlers, and as long as there were artists like Bill Monroe, Ray Price, and Mel Tillis, and their producers, hiring gobs of them. When bluegrass festivals featured fiddlers on stage day and night, why would they need to be worried about extinction? The folks at Rounder Records themselves were never anxious about having fiddlers to record; they just kept making albums of them.

At the Masters, the age difference between me and my 23 fellow (adult) competitors was impetus for a lot of fuss. While Terry Morris was indeed a teenager, the second youngest to me, our six-year age difference was considerable to all of those looking on.

My mother's goal for me that day was playing good enough to make the top ten. As out of reach as this pursuit now seemed, having a good chance to stare down the vast field of top competitors rolling out, this remained the major achievement we were angling for. The top ten was the deal— play like the dickens to get out of the first round. Once in the finals, that meant I was in the money, and all the status a whippersnapper could ever hope for. After all, it would be a long way to come only to play three tunes.

I GATHERED WHAT I BELIEVED were my very best contest tunes for the Grand Masters Fiddle Championship; tunes including: "Grey Eagle" and "Cotton Patch Rag." Tunes I had just recorded for the new album the week before.

The old white fiddle was a marvel to almost everyone who heard it that weekend. The thing just sang. An enormous sound, and looking a little better with Sharpie signatures building—although the fiddle was still quite the freak show. I was well-prepared for this contest. After playing about as well as I could play in the round of 24 (save for a few bobbles, as Mom called them), they tallied it all up: and… I made the *top ten!* The goal we set out to accomplish was achieved. Candidly, it was my mother's goal, and she believed it would make the difference in my young career. I breathed a sigh of relief after seeing the top ten list posted backstage.

All the same, I didn't seem to be terribly overwhelmed by this moment. I kept it cool. Even drawing a range of attention, I thought there might have been more nerves, but by then I was quite familiar with competing in fiddle contests and going up against the adults. Of course, this weekend was on a whole other level. I couldn't emphasize enough how recording with America's top acoustic musicians the very week before—Blake, Hartford, Bush, Collins, and Huskey, on my own feature album—afforded me a consequential self-assuredness for this major contest. A super confidence-builder by any measure. It was all going incredibly well and I was on a roll.

On closer inspection of the top ten finalists, Benny did not make the cut. My heart skipped a beat as I stared at the bulletin—I was a little shocked, and even embarrassed—it was hard to believe that I made it in and my teacher didn't. To win the nationals in Weiser the year before, Benny had played so very well, but his health was on and off again—no longer consistent with his best execution. But still, I thought it was unfortunate not to make it in. Louis Franklin and Norman Solomon failed to make it into the final round either. This was a towering field of top competitors. Mom could only shrug her shoulders and attempt to refocus me on the new task at hand. I had to prepare and warm up for the final round—it was starting up within minutes.

Benny's attention turned towards me for the finals. He was standing right there watching me go through the tunes with my guitar accompanists, Charlie Collins and Jerry Thomasson, giving me all the conviction he could muster. Folks were circled around me behind the stage and listening to me play—just as they did at Weiser. Some just wanted to see what all the hubbub was about—the young boy from Seattle in the finals. Still, others watching me warm up on my final selections claimed that if I played my round on stage like I was playing it backstage, I could win the whole thing, "take it all home." Benny echoed them—but of course he would do that.

While I paused for a minute and took a breather, I also tried to tune out some of the hullabaloo. I couldn't help but notice that across the way, Terry wasn't practicing his round at all, but taking requests from onlookers. He seemed unfazed by it all—just drinking it in. I felt like I could seize the occasion, though, and play like I've never played in a contest before. If I played my best, maybe it could make some of the others nervous, at least, and cause them to perhaps make a mistake or two? Flustering them? It was not out of the realm of possibility. I was conjuring a "competing-against-the-kid" angle. A legitimate tactic—a genuine strategy. In the back of my mind it was.

When I played the final round, it was as good as I ever performed on a stage: "Tom and Jerry," "Roxanna Waltz," and yes... my cracked open rendition of "Herman's Rag,"—one, two, three—just rolling off my bow as if I was one of those Opry stars singing his three greatest hits. These were three of the tunes I recorded just days before. Given the amount of pressure I felt from these older fiddlers, I had some kind of ice in the veins up on stage. I came off to some folks that weekend like I had no nerves at all. Some were confused by my laid-back demeanor. I was never the hyper child, just always kind of chillin' out and taking it all in.

I went over to the side of the stage to see Terry's final round. He was definitely not laid back, every time I saw him, he wasn't. Terry was *unconstrained*—the life of the party. I detected some nerves showing, though, especially with the waltz he played. When you get some nerves going, it can show up in the slow music. Maybe the moment finally added up for him, too? Despite it, Terry was incredible. I had never seen a young virtuoso play the fiddle before. I could sense right away that he was some kind of natural musical genius. A raucous "Mozart" of the Texas fiddle is how I could put it, and I was truly captivated.

As I stood alone, off to the side of the stage, some part of me doubted that I could play as good as Terry, but at the same time, I will have to admit that another part of me felt that I did. Hearing the takes back in the studio the week before, the recorded takes of these very tunes I entered the championships with, allowed me to step outside myself and analyze what I actually accomplished this last year on the fiddle. The progress made. I could quantify my growth as a player and notice these changes by the month. Even by the week. It was wild.

I SUPPOSE IT WOULD NOT SURPRISE anyone just how hard it is to express in words what being a child prodigy feels like: *a young child who can be compared to adult professionals*—for all intents and purposes. That weekend in Nashville, I was 13-years-old and had only played the instrument for two-and-a-half years, but found myself in the top ten of the Grand Masters Fiddle Championship, and going up against the very best in the world, both amateur and pro. Some of these players had been winning contests for 20, 30 and 40 years.

Professional musicians at that time maintained that I was this manner of *"prodigy."* Regardless of what I thought of it, my early musical career was essentially shaped on this widely acknowledged acceptance.

I can say that when I played the fiddle, every so often it did feel like someone was playing *through* me. I couldn't say *who*. I guess I presumed that God wanted me to play like that as a young kid. I was surely an unlikely vessel to possess this particular talent—coming from a family without a single musician in it, high to low. Then the matter of the geography: growing up in Seattle, which is a very long way from the cradle of traditional fiddle music. Maybe it was Benny *playing* through me? I sometimes wondered that, because he cared for me so much.

I seemed to be very aware and observant. I was persuasive at that age, too. I appreciated the circles of musicians I found myself in. Hanging around mostly grown-ups, and a lot of old-timers at the fiddle conventions, almost every conversation I had with anyone back then was with adults. These settings shaped my real life education. At school, I mostly kept to myself, the grimy baby blue jacket and all. But just as most of the older fiddlers were baffled by how a boy so young could play like I could, I shared in their difficulty.

I was inspired by music, that was unmistakably so. I wouldn't know how to proportion the amount of inspiration that I received compared to other children. I did work very hard. The work ethic part may have been inherited from my father. There was also some incentive to stay away from his labor sites, that I can promise. Maybe being frightened a lot of the time forged a distinction—the need for a musical restoration—away from all the rats and the snakes and the schoolyard bullying… a motivational factor? I believe there had to be one. I viewed music as a *safe harbor.*

Musical creativity was encouraged and that could have made the biggest difference for me. I was a perfectionist, too. It exacted a lot of self-reflection, if not constant analysis. Like the studio albums — I was comfortable in the recording studios. I was never nervous to record, even when studio veterans were staring at me, wondering if I could fork over — deliver. I was never obnoxious before — when I was 12 or 11, I think, at least I don't remember being that way. I always tried to be sweet to people, like Benny was. I probably learned that from him. Allowing myself to be kind and attentive to folks gave me a sense of personal responsibility.

My mother was the artsy one in my world — the eclectic eccentric. That could easily describe her. She willed me to play, perhaps to fulfill something lost inside of her that could never be fully expressed. My mother got me to the places I needed to get to, and usually on pocket change. Even willing to put me on airplanes by myself and stay with strangers, just so I could play shows and contests. For this consideration alone, it was immeasurable to my development as a young player. Perilous yes, but it may have been another turning point.

You could say that my mother was my biggest supporter, and she backed my decisions regarding where I wanted to go next with my music. She allowed me to make important choices as a child in that way, like choosing the repertoire for my two albums, and choosing the tunes for my contest rounds. This was greatly empowering to me. Mom drove me to all of the lessons of course, and thank goodness for that.

The act of playing the various instruments, the multi-instrumentalist capacity I was allowed to find, made me feel more free to dig into all the layers of the music I loved. It gave me yet more choices to make on any given day, too. The pure act of *playing* music was motivational, and it was always hopeful for me.

Beyond all this, still… music was saving my life. I associated my music with *freedom*, not something which was just merely fun, like I told all the journalists that it was. No, it was far deeper. I *imagined* and *transported* myself to places through the music. I wanted it to carry me far away from where I found myself in that little house in Mountlake Terrace. I felt it was divine providence that placed me at the knee of the greatest fiddler in the world, Benny Thomasson. How could anyone possibly replace 18-hour-long lessons over repeated weekends—my mother just sitting there witnessing it all happen? Really unfathomable. But given that circumstance, Benny ultimately saw himself in me. He recognized this *prodigy* potential, even before I could hardly play the fiddle.

Most adults encouraged me to be the best, and I felt that compassion expressly from them. So, I had many mentors really. I considered all my favorite musicians on recordings as kind of musical mentors too, even if I hadn't met them yet. Sometimes that didn't even matter, because I drew upon the art of imagination and could transport myself to them—just by *dreaming* of that better place. My youthful ascension in music was my own personal reckoning.

Unparalleled, in a most unusual way, I considered all of the adults I was beating in these fiddle contests—my teachers. They *all* were.

THE TOP TEN FINALISTS were called to the stage at Opryland's outdoor Theater by the Lake. There was a big audience for this contest, about 3,000 people in attendance. I stood off to one side of the stage and tucked myself in-between a few of the master fiddlers. Terry Morris was standing on the opposite side of the stage. I could observe him pal around and ham it up with his big brother Dale and his best friend Randy. To me, they came off as pretty full-blooded, magnanimous Texas *cool*—confident and imposing. They had a friends circle which I was not a party to, of course. To a large extent, I felt like a six-foot dork with braces, hailing from the most incorrect state of the 50 in our union. Then I snapped out of it—focusing my attention on what was happening at the front of the stage. Meanwhile, I had lost track of where my mother and sister had gone to. Didn't know where they were going to watch the awards ceremony.

As they began to announce the standings, starting with 10th place, my name was not called out. But great fiddlers' names were being called instead.

The emcee for the Grand Masters was the country music superstars Porter Wagoner and Roy Acuff, as well as veteran Opry announcers Hairl Hensley and Grant Turner. Additional entertainment had been provided by Opry members Sam and Kirk McGee and Wilma Lee and Stoney Cooper, and others. I had been concentrating on my fiddling to such an extent that I overlooked just how cool it was to have Grand Ole Opry stars be so responsive to the fiddle championships.

After a few fiddlers had accepted their award at center stage, Porter Wagoner called for the next finalist.

"Vernon Solomon gets 7th place."

Vernon won the Grand Masters the first year it was held in 1972. As far as his recordings, notably, he was featured on the 1965 *Texas Hoedown* album I had with Benny on it. Vernon was such a gracious and sweet man—he kind of reminded me of Benny himself, with his likableness. Boy did he love Benny too. It was endearing how he and his brother Norman treated Benny like he was their uncle—probably growing up around him in the Texas fiddle circles. Their father, Ervin Solomon, was one of the very first authentic Texas-style fiddlers, and running buddies with Benny. By placing over someone like Solomon, I was bustling in some untraveled terrain. I clenched my hands and tried to prepare for most anything to happen.

THE COORDINATOR OF THE CONTEST, Doc Harris, was on stage and making sure each fiddler got their plaque, and their check. The Grand Masters was Harris' brainchild. Considered by many in Nashville as the biggest fiddling fan there ever was, he didn't play a lick on the fiddle himself; however, his brother did, so his was still a musical family. Doc met Roy Acuff, Howdy, and Oswald in North Carolina while he was going to college in his home state. When he moved to Nashville to study medicine, he hung out with the Smokey Mountain Boys about every week backstage at the Opry, for several years now.

The preliminaries to the Grand Masters were held the day before at the iconic Ryman Auditorium. These were open to anyone who wanted to challenge the invited master fiddlers for all the marbles. It was the only musical event taking place in the condemned "mother church" of country music, the recent home to the Grand Ole Opry going back to 1943. God forbid any notion of a wrecking ball. Doc told my mother that he thought the preliminaries would be a good idea to prevent any controversy over inviting a young boy as a "master fiddler." The judging panel chose nine from the preliminaries at the Ryman to join the 15 invited fiddlers for Sunday's finals. I was included in that nine.

"5th place goes to James "Texas Shorty" Chancellor."

While I wasn't that nervous when I played my rounds, butterflies were starting to blow up in my stomach now. What could be happening, I thought? I played as well as I could play that final round, yes—but could it mean that I played as good as these great fiddlers? "Shorty" was my second favorite fiddler next to Benny in the Texas-style. I had all of his 45s back home. My mother and I purchased Shorty's records from his father, who had a small converted camper van covered with billboards and photos of his son. The banners affixed to the outside of the camper read "World Champion Fiddler - Texas Shorty." Mr. Chancellor drove the camper up to Weiser and opened up shop right there on the curb in front of the high school. With speaker boxes heralding the fiddling of his son for passersby to hear, he was able to sell "Texas Shorty" merchandise all week.

When we got to meet Shorty at the Masters, he was embarrassed by this story we retold. But it was *our* good fortune. Right there on the curb, we bought all of his 45s from Mr. Chancellor. I listened and studied them over and over again, they were spectacular. I loved Shorty's waltzes, too. I learned all of them from the records on the family turntable, part of those ten-hour practice days. Back on stage, I was more or less going a little numb at this point, everything started to play out in slow motion.

"3rd place goes to Sam Bush."

Together, just the week before, Sam and I had spent several days rehearsing and recording my album. I was a little surprised that he was entered in the Grand Masters, given his star status as a bluegrass festival headliner. Sam was the lead singer of the Newgrass Revival, and he was ably one of the best mandolin players in the world. I didn't remember him talking about the contest much during the week; nevertheless, he was an invited contestant and knew he had a chance to win it. He remained serious about his contest fiddle playing. A three-time National Junior Champion in Weiser, the very same title I currently held, Sam was competitive alright, and he brought professional performing experience onto the contest stage.

Sam's father, Charlie, was the shot in the arm for old-time fiddling in the Bush family—he seemed to be about as big a fiddle fan as Doc Harris. He also brought young Sam to play for Acuff as a teenage fiddler. Charlie

Bush's job at the Grand Masters was one of a volunteer, gathering up fiddle contestants and ushering them to the stage for their rounds. He got to hear some good fiddling in the course of it, too. Competing in the Grand Masters was plainly a big deal for Sam Bush, and for the Bush family.

When Porter Wagoner got ready to announce 2nd place, I went ahead and got myself all adjusted, readied myself for that walk out there to center stage and to end all the suspense—not just for my own sake but for everyone else, too. It was just Terry Morris and me left. On mic, Porter Wagoner announced.

"And 2nd place goes to…"

I was moving in Wagoner's direction to receive the 2nd place award, but taking into account the incredible luck I had on this extraordinary day. It was another unimaginable week in Nashville, just like it was exactly one year before. However, Porter Wagoner didn't call my name again.

"2nd place goes to…

Terry Morris from Decatur, Texas, give him a hand folks!"

Wagoner raised his hands with his familiar signature gesture towards the audience.

I was shocked—just absolutely stunned. Terry's mouth nearly dropped to the floor when his name was called for 2nd. He really thought he had it, but meanwhile—they awarded me with 1st place.

I became the Grand Masters Fiddle Champion, the youngest ever to do so, and a record that has never been broken, even nearly 50 years later as I write this. As one would expect, my life changed mightily that day.

I received the champion's plaque, and they put the men's blue blazer jacket on me. I'd never tried on a suit jacket before. Roy Acuff awarded me the check for a whopping $1,000. Before I even arrived in Nashville, I knew what the 1st place prize was—it was more than my Dad could make from a couple months of hard labor. My mind was racing; I could sense this championship would assure my future as a musician. While they kept listing off the prizes I was receiving, what was going through my mind instead was that I had a future in music now, for certain. Laboring with my Dad under houses, now a distant impression.

Wagoner announced additional prizes for winning the *Masters*—an appearance on the Grand Ole Opry, a feature appearance on his own show—the nationally televised *Porter Wagoner Show,* a feature appearance on the *Hee Haw* television show. All of it was broadcast over the public address system as my mind went into triple-slow motion. This day was utterly staggering. I was awe-stricken.

After a couple hours of salutations backstage and some downright fascination from new fans and spectators, Benny could not wipe the smile off of his face. I think he was a little stunned by seeing this happen to his student. But at the same time, he *did* predict this.

I could tell that my mother was shell-shocked—her mind buzzing for what all this could mean for our family. The Associated Press covered my win all over the country. My name was becoming well-known as the boy champion fiddler.

I COULDN'T WAIT to go to the jam session that finished off the weekend's festivities. Benny and most of the other fiddlers were headed there—a party at Fiddler's Barbecue. Nashville was such a remarkable city for music: a restaurant named Fiddler's Barbecue. I loved jamming on the fiddle, but on this occasion I kept my fiddle in the case and opted to play rhythm guitar accompaniment behind some of the other fiddlers. I thought it would be a good gesture on my part, maybe a way for them to *like* the kid a little more after what just happened to them? I had spent enough time under everyone's scrutiny for one day, anyway. Jerry Thomasson and I found ourselves in the kitchen area backing up Terry Morris for an hour. The owner of the restaurant, H G Roberts Sr., didn't mind at all if fiddlers were back in the kitchen, he being another huge fiddling fan.

While I had my contest rounds down pretty well, I'll give you that, Terry, on the other hand, could really jam. What I heard from him that night as I backed him up in the kitchen was some of the best breakdown fiddling I had ever heard. Terry became a new fiddle idol for me that very evening. I liked the physicality he played with, too—how his body bent forward and backward as he carved into the breakdowns. He had so much fun playing, sometimes yelling out while he's playing—a few "oooh's" thrown in for emphasis when it was feeling really good. Every now and then he seemed to surprise even himself by what was coming out of his own fiddle, and I was impressed right there along with him. There was so much inventiveness and spontaneity in his playing, but it was rooted in his own authenticity of the music—flawlessly performed with good tone and intonation. The assertiveness of his delivery captivated my attention. Together with our guitar accompaniment driving him, the jam session made a big impression on what Texas fiddling meant to me for my future. Rather than chasing the old-timers around, I could better relate to competing against an older teenager like Terry even more so.

While Terry respected that I was Benny's protégé, he was regretful that he couldn't have had a similar relationship during those crucial few years I had with him in Washington. Among most of the Texas fiddlers, Benny was known as the best teacher of fiddling, in addition to everything else he represented to this music. But it was only Benny's recordings that Terry had to learn from in his formative years—his main teacher being Norman Solomon, who entered the contest that day. But since Benny had been back in Texas since December, Terry could get together with Benny easily now, where I couldn't anymore.

Given the circumstances I was left with, and I'm sure with Terry as well, it felt like I was ready to be on my own and didn't need a fiddle teacher any longer; and I was still hoping to relocate to Nashville by that fall. I was without a fiddle teacher for six months, so winning the Grand Masters proved the theory to both my mother and me, that I had what it took to become *self-taught*.

As well, I made good decisions in selecting what to play in the contest. In the competition rounds earlier that day, Terry played additional breakdowns for his tunes of choice because breakdowns were his forte. Weiser and many of the contests out West didn't allow the fiddler to play a breakdown for a tune of choice, but in the South this was permitted. Still, I played Ragtime for a choice tune and I demonstrated my versatility as a player by doing so. In a close race, the variety of genres was going to help. I had an edge on the waltz playing as well. While Terry had the one genre down pat, I demonstrated all three more equally, and it likely swung the contest my way. Later my mother commented on how I made some "goofs" during the first round, because I was worried about the six-minute time limit imposed; however for the finals, I just let it all go. I didn't even abbreviate my waltz like I'd rehearsed. Instead, I played the whole course of it leaving my accompanists scrambling to figure out where I was going.

But I didn't miss a note of it myself, and that may have impressed the judges even more.

I felt an uncommon acquaintance to Terry Morris, and the situation we found ourselves in was truly exceptional. I could tell that Terry remained uneasy about me of course—a little cautious from the loss to a 13-year-old. It must have been a trip for the teenaged phenom that *he* was. Our individual places in this widening fiddling world, mindful of both the unsimilar geography and the big personalities and supporters around us… well, it would be a lot to withstand—if we were to be friends.

Speaking of some of those personalities and supporters: a few of the other Texans didn't take kindly to the final results of the contest that day. As it happened, they wanted to rain on my little parade some. One or two Texas fiddlers even claimed my win "was a fluke," and that "it was rigged" for me to win because I was a kid. Because I was from the Northwest (a persuasive constituency in fiddling, evidently) a couple others said "the fix was in…" and the biggest conspiracy put forward: "The jacket fit! —"

That blue blazer was swamping me, that I can promise. We spent some money to have it taken in eight-plus inches for a single photo opportunity—holding my plaque. But I still hated buttons. I never wore it again.

So in time I sent some rain back on their own promenade. Having the upper hand at the Grand Masters Fiddle Championship for years to come, I achieved additional 1st place finishes in both 1980 and '82, and 2nd place finishes in both 1978 and '79, most all of it as a teenager.

Whether we preferred it or not, a great fiddle contest rivalry was born between Terry and me. Benny got what he was hoping for.

Music City News, July, 1975
"A fitting Fan Fair finale was the Grand Masters Fiddling Contest held at the Theater By The Lake at Opryland. This year's winner was 13-year old Mark O'Connor of Mountlake Terrace, Wash. Mark took home the top prize of $1,000. Terry Joe Morris of Decatur, Tx captured second place and won $300. Sam Bush of Austin, Ky was third."

The Nashville Banner, Monday June 16, 1975
"Thirteen-year-old Mark O'Connor, of Mount Lake Terrace, Wash., is the new Grand Master Fiddling Champion…who began playing the fiddle two years ago.

Before the contest, O'Connor was munching a sandwich, sipping lemonade and talking with his [guitarist] Charlie Collins, one of Roy Acuff's Smokey Mountain Boys.

'If there's such a thing as reincarnation, he's it.' Collins said, nodding his head towards O'Connor. 'The boy's a genius.

'He's got to be the rebirth of some great musician,' he said. 'You just don't start off being a master.

'Mark can play the fiddle, guitar and mandolin, all of them almost perfectly,' he said."

Country People Magazine, July, 1975

"Throughout the United States there are many fiddlin' championship contests held, but the Grand Masters boasts of being the 'Grandaddy' of 'em all.

Top honors would be the goal of a fiddler of any age but to achieve that goal at such a young age is virtually unbelievable. In this world of wonders, the unbelievable has happened and thirteen year old Mark O'Connor of Mountlake Terrace, Washington is the 1975 Grand Master Fiddlin' Champion.

In accordance with contest rules, judges do not see the contestant, nor do they know his or her name or age. Judges are located in a remote unit several blocks from the contest site, and the only sound they hear is that of the contestant's fiddle.

In the final round of competition, Mark chose Roxanna Waltz, Tom and Jerry, and Herman's Rag. The contest rules and regulations are set up so that each fiddler will be judged on an equal basis. This speaks well for Mark's ability to win in competition with adult and long time fiddlers.

Mark has been playing the fiddle for about two years.

As for other future plans, at this point Mark isn't sure, but there may be a move to Nashville when possible. You can be sure you will be seeing more of Mark O'Connor."

The Tennessean, Monday June 16, 1975

"A crowd of 3,000 sunburnt, sometimes foot-weary fans settled into the Theater By The Lake at Opryland to watch the 24 contestants vie for the title of Grand Master Fiddler.

A strong favorite with the crowd, 13-year-old Mark O'Connor of Mountlake Terrace, Wash, walked off with the honors, plus first-prize winnings of $1,000.

'Been playin' for two years,' the youngster murmured backstage prior to his performance, where he and most of the contestants wandered back and forth between little groups of pickers jamming in the shade.

'Playing 365 days a year...well, I could have missed a day here or there,' the champion said.

This year's Grand Masters was the fourth event of its kind in a row, coordinated by Dr. Perry Harris of Nashville.

Events got under way at noon for the day. After opening remarks by Roy Acuff, premiere fiddlers Howdy Forrester and Johnny Gimble demonstrated different styles and techniques for the audience.

Emcees Grant Turner and Hairl Hensley then introduced the 24 contestants in groups of five, each group separated with a guest performance, 'Special guests' for the day included Herman Crook, Sam and [Kirk] McGee, Wilma Lee and Stoney Cooper, and Ramona Jones.

There was a mid-afternoon break after all contestants had appeared, featuring a dozen members of the Nashville Symphony Orchestra, with Bill McElhiney conducting, as accompanists to the Leah Jane Singers.

With six minutes allotted each contestant to play a waltz tune, breakdown and a 'choice,' contestants were judged on the basis of 'tone, timing, execution and overall accuracy,' according to Harris.

The Lone Star State managed to dominate a good part of the entrants' list, and almost half of the top 10 fiddlers hailed from Texas.

'They think when they come down here into the woods from out of those wide-open spaces, they're gonna get snake-bit,' jibed Acuff on stage. 'So they come good and prepared for it.'

There were other fiddlers from parts of the world as far as Stockholm, Sweden, or Japan."

CHAPTER SIX

ROUGHHOUSING WITH SUCCESS

THE GRAND MASTERS CHAMPION conquest at age 13 seemed to boomerang back in Seattle that summer of 1975. It wasn't even a week before Hank and Harley approached my mother at Weiser, informing her that they were "breaking up the band." While my success in Tennessee had to have impressed them, The Tennesseans saw some sort of problem with it. They unceremoniously told Mom it was over. Highly irked by this news, we still had a few big shows coming up in Seattle together. We were having our wonderful Weiser experience that we cherished until the timing of their bizarre announcement.

Bluegrass Unlimited Magazine interviewed Harley Worthington:
"'We could see Mark progress. When he won the Grand Masters I said, Hank, when he comes back that's the end of this. We were at Weiser and when he got back Mark showed me the thousand-dollar check that he got. Hank and I talked about it and decided that this was a good time to let go. From that time on we never played any more shows with him.'"

Otherwise, so many fiddlers at Weiser were bowled over by my win in Nashville the week before. It created quite the bruhaha in the Junior contest, namely: why was I still competing against kids? The very Junior division that had motivated me and propelled me to move forward was now holding me back. More than several veteran fiddlers were saying it out loud: "The way Mark is playing, he could challenge fiddlers like Barrett and Johnson for the top prize in Weiser as well."

I went on to win the Juniors, Loretta came in 2nd.

When we got back home, Mom confirmed with Hank and Harley that they were goners. We had a couple of nice Seattle area dates which my mother booked for Mark O'Connor and The Tennesseans that summer, one being the King County Fair, where I was picking up quite a bit of media attention with notices in the papers. Not honoring the dates they had committed to, even just a few weeks out, was genuinely unsettling. Mom and I had to scramble to figure out a replacement band to play with—a tall order in Seattle, given the very limited supply of bluegrass musicians to begin with.

While being done in by The Tennesseans, professional bluegrass musicians currently residing in Tennessee wanted me to join up with them for festival dates beginning the very next month: expressly, Jim & Jesse and the Virginia Boys, and Buck White and the Down Home Folks.

Curly Creek String Band, the other Seattle bluegrass group I played concerts with, was obviously a good choice for the fair dates coming up. I always enjoyed hanging out with Roger and Janice. A lovely girl—Janice was barely 20 herself. Like a big sister, she always enjoyed ribbing me, tickling me and, giving me a hard time about most anything in a playful sense. That was all before the Grand Masters win. Still, I played a practical joke on the phone with Janice, something pretty immature—but my hunch was that it was harmless. Just in case people forgot that I was still a stupid kid at times:

"Hello, is George there?" I said over the phone with a disguised voice.

After hearing Janice say that I had the wrong number. I called again in another unrecognizable voice;

"Hello, is George there?" I asked.

And finally the third and fateful time—and in my own voice;

"Hello, this is George. Did I get any calls?"

My mindless juvenile antic turned out to be quite the unforgivable act. Janice was upset—I mean really upset… they definitely expected more of me, she and Roger admonished. Yeah, I got the message all right. After all, I was a Grand Masters Fiddle Champ, for goodness sakes—GROW UP. Due to my self-inflicted phone *faux pas,* our fun collaboration began to unanticipatedly dwindle from there. (Caller ID could have unquestionably saved *that* band). In the meantime, Buck White was on the phone;

"As soon as you can get back down to Nashville this summer, Mark, we want you with us. We'll put you to work. How about that?"

I made a mental note: No dumb phone pranks to professional Nashville musicians. On another phone call, Jesse McReynolds was making *his* request;

"Mark, we would like to invite you out to play some festivals with us this summer."

What? I get to be a *Virginia Boy,* and wear the string ties and ride in the tour bus? The plan was for me to play twin fiddles with Joe Meadows, learn the repertoire on the job, get one feature fiddle tune each set, and ultimately step into the lead fiddle role, as Joe wanted to take some time off each summer. I reminded them: *"Remember, I am only 13!"*

There I am sitting on our big black leather chair in our tiny living room, with a makeshift concert schedule planner. I was scratching in all of the new booking info. Both Jesse and Buck were in attendance at the Grand Masters. Winning the competition was having some far-reaching repercussions.

Back on the home front, Dudley Hill felt that I didn't need any more guitar lessons from him. He was getting a new bar band going, and going electric — didn't have as much time anymore. Dudley sold us his cherished 1958 Martin D-28 for $250. Selling it was emotional for him, but he was glad it was going to me instead of someone else, he said. I definitely needed an upgrade from my cheap Yamaha for bluegrass playing.

I was squeamish by how my contest earnings allowed me to buy Dudley's old Martin guitar, while he couldn't afford to keep it himself — a grown able-bodied man in his 20s, and so very talented. He informed us he was working mainly construction jobs for income now. I had such fond memories of Dudley playing his beautiful rendition of the fiddle tune, "Bitter Creek," on that old Martin guitar. He learned it from Benny, like I did on fiddle.

Years later, Dudley formed the band called Pearl Django which finally did bring him nation-wide attention. I made sure he knew that I loved my guitar lessons with him, as I said goodbye to my bluegrass guitar teacher. I was reminded again to fully understand what was at stake when Mom talked about my abilities to win major competitions that paid *real* money. I saw the backup plan right there with Dudley Hill: giving up your favorite acoustic instrument; working construction jobs like my Dad to make ends meet; or going electric to play in bars to get any work at all as a musician.

Next, Byron Berline rang me up on the phone. He wanted to have me sit in with him in Langley, Oklahoma in a couple of weeks, if I could make it to the festival, that is. He said I was welcome to enter their contest again, too. There was no problem entering the contest and performing with him on the mainstage. "The prize money increased" — he reminded me.

Within a couple of weeks, Mom had me fly on my own to Oklahoma City. I stayed with the Broughtons overnight, and they drove me over to Langley the following day. I won in Powderhorn Park for the second year in a row. Byron let me borrow his F-5 Gibson and I sat in during his set playing mandolin. Byron had some good news to tell me about a show in Los Angeles that he wanted me to play with him. He scheduled a four-fiddle jam set featuring both him and me, along with John Hartford and Richard Greene, the progressive bluegrass fiddler I saw on television with the band Muleskinner. Our back-up band was to include mandolinist David Grisman.

I got to sit in with Jim & Jesse on their set at Langley. They invited me to ride in their tour bus back to Nashville. The thrill of riding on a real tour bus with professional musicians, joining up with one of the top bluegrass bands for festival dates that summer, was beyond my wildest dreams. They were some of the patriarchs of bluegrass music. Jesse, his wife, and their son Keith, the bassist for the band, had me stay at their house for a few days before I flew back to Seattle.

Reviewing the recent entries in my newly formed weekly planner, along with the Seattle bookings, I was going to be crisscrossing the country at quite a clip—all on flights going solo. While I was getting these big opportunities all of a sudden, I also needed to be resourceful. I had to put a band together, and lickety-split—the Seattle fair dates were booked under my own name. It was advertised all over the area papers: "Boy Champion Fiddler to Perform at King County Fair." Since I couldn't find any bluegrass players in Seattle who were friendly to us anymore, I reached out to members of the Old Hat Band. It was my former teacher John Burke's group, featuring guitarist and old-time banjoist Jeff and Ellen Thorn. Their music was exceptionally old-time—not a lick of bluegrass amongst them. There can be clear distinctions between these two styles of string band music, and they made them. Ellen played clawhammer banjo and sang old-timey songs—some of the same repertoire that Oswald was singing at the Pickin' Parlor. In spite of the exogenous bluegrass and Texas-style fiddling I insisted on, Jeff and Ellen signed up to play with me, wanting to do the best they could with my repertoire. As Mom filled them in on the reason for the last-minute replacement, they were sympathetic to the aggravation I unexpectedly found in Seattle's bluegrass scene.

Despite the dramatic ups and downs I was experiencing back home, music continued to be the *only* refuge away from my much more worrisome school life and increasingly difficult family life. But without warning, there wasn't anybody left for me to play bluegrass music with in Seattle. Dick Ahrens had joined the Navy the year before. Others seemed to push me aside, discard me. The considerable gains I had recently made in music had the opposite effect on the local musicians, the very community I hoped to find support from as a child. As I listened to Jeff, Ellen and Mom discuss what was happening to me with the Seattle bluegrass community, it all seemed to lead to one place — a local bluegrass music couple.

THERE WAS A GROUP OF bluegrass musicians who in short, ran the show in Seattle. Led by Phil and Vivian Williams, perhaps like some of the Texas fiddlers, this bunch didn't much appreciate my newfound success in Nashville. Vivian, the best fiddler in Seattle (until the day I turned 13, I suppose), did her best to keep me off the local bluegrass shows. The skullduggery likely began as soon as I beat her in a reputable Seattle fiddle contest.

I had entered the Puget Sound International Fiddle Contest back in March of 1974 when I was 12. I not only won the Juniors and placed above my former teacher Barbara Lamb, but it was one of the first times I was able to win in an Open division. Joe Pancerzewski was 2nd and Vivian Williams 3rd. Local Irish fiddle expert Frank Farrell, as well as Benny Thomasson, were two of the three judges.

Bellevue American Newspaper quoted Frank Farrell after the contest:
"'He just out-fiddled 'em all. We all knew it had to happen some time.'"

Most likely, Vivian was beginning to tire of me at this point. We had heard about how Vivian and Phil snubbed the Woodinville festival, thrown off balance that somebody else would bring Nashville bluegrass stars to Seattle and create the first bluegrass festival in the area. One of Vivian's preferred contrivances was to cite my mother as an annoying "stage mom," and that she was difficult to deal with. It was just not true — but she spread this rumor. There was no professional musician on the national scene that thought this about Mom.

Vivian and Phil, along with their "clique" of Seattle bluegrassers (Mom referred to them as "the clique"), helped to turn Hank and Harley against me. Their scheme was to embed an upright bass player named Thane Mitchell into Mark O'Connor and the Tennesseans. This was achieved by Phil and Vivian scheduling a local performance for KRAB Grass Radio with me, Hank, Harley, and Thane as a quartet. Their clear message to us was that we needed an upright bass to get on "the clique's" bigger shows around town. I thought it was cool to have a bass player, but Mom rather liked it the way it was, because—Thane was a *hippie.* Mom was afraid that the nice clean-cut and "cute look" with the two O'Connor kids would vaporize. Hank and Harley leaned on Mom to accept him into the group. Acquiescing, she tried to at least talk Thane into wearing pants without visible holes in them on our shows.

Thane was a member of "the clique," too. We weren't sure how to put our finger on the sudden attention we were getting from this bunch, but it came to mind, at least, that my recent success led to new acceptance? Maybe? But in an expedited fashion, Thane aimed to reshape Hank and Harley's affection for me, and rather dramatically. While playing in our band, Thane found opportunities to take them aside, complaining that I was getting *too* much attention, and hogging the spotlight from the other bandmembers—all that *boy champion* stuff... He cautioned that it was increasingly difficult to develop a unified "group sound" this way. A plaque from the Grand Masters was not going to help with group cohesiveness.

At the same time, "the clique" promised The Tennesseans access into their inner circle. This pseudo promotion was hinging on their own desire to lose the little kid—along with *the mother.* There were very few bluegrass musicians in Seattle to begin with, and the Vivian and Phil clique was able to round up most of them successfully. My mother was fit to be tied by all the conspiring. This turn of events bothered Mom more than any other snag we came across during my early childhood years. *How could they do this to her son?* Previously, we did have a lot of appreciation for Thane, as he showed me some bluegrass guitar licks at The Folk Store on University Way—when I first got my Yamaha. He taught me the standard bluegrass guitar (Lester Flatt) G-run for gosh sakes. Was there nothing sacred anymore?

Jeff, Ellen, and Mom talked about the fact that some musicians were going to be jealous of my abilities at music, and could simply turn against me for that reason alone. Perhaps it would have nothing to do with what I did to them personally (save for that one practical joke on the phone). I was going to have to learn how to maneuver through these kinds of exercises being a child musician—either adapt to it, or suffer more consequences like I had here in Seattle. Just as I was looking to trust people more, and to fully admire all the good musicians around me, I had to remain guarded with some increasing cynicism. If I was going to be a traveling child performer, I couldn't be gullible anymore. I was going to have to grow up to be a man at 13 and take care of myself.

Because of Vivian and Phil Williams' yucky prosecution (Phil was a lawyer by trade), I learned how damaging these kinds of factions can be in music, and especially involving talented kids. So after that, I made sure to navigate towards the sidelines of any musical clique I ran across. I developed a strident desire to just break up music cliques wherever I could: *Bring down those walls,* I always liked to say.

IN MANY WAYS I WAS OUTGROWING all of those bluegrassers in Seattle, just like *they* figured I was. Mom and I mentioned several times in the newspapers that we were wanting to move down South where there was more appreciation for someone like me. Maybe the Seattle bluegrassers were collectively thinking, *"Just move already!"* For all I know, they did me a favor; perhaps they would have held me back if I stayed around.

Before it was time to head out across the country, however, there were two more consequential seeds planted in my musical mind which would take root, several years ahead.

Mom took me to see the classical violinist, Itzhak Perlman, with the Seattle Symphony. Concertmaster Henri Siegl got us some good seats in the orchestra section about 15 rows back. I sat in exuberance, studying Mr. Perlman's performance. It was my first time to see a symphony orchestra live. It reconnected me to the years of classical guitar I took, as well as all the classical recordings I grew up listening to as a smaller child. But more importantly, I was transported to some other beautiful place that I wanted to visit in the future. By then, I understood it was probably not going to be about playing classical violin as much as musical ideas—compositional ideas. Mom used to tell folks that she did blind tests when I was age three: *"He could identify the music of Mozart from that of Beethoven's."*

We also got word that the great jazz violin legend Stephane Grappelli was to play in Vancouver, BC. We drove the couple hours north for his concert with the Diz Disley Trio. Here, I was *mind blown* as well. I remember thinking that his playing was like no other player I had ever seen. I kept trying to tie it to the Western Swing I was around a lot at the contests, but still, Grappelli's was contrastive. My takeaway was one of amazement, and, that it was going to be very difficult to ever understand how to play that kind of jazz violin. But I really wanted to try eventually. Even so, that night I started to identify with the manner of how he was embellishing melodies. Afterwards, I jumped in the autograph line and had Mr. Grappelli sign my white fiddle. All the way home I whistled one of the standards he played—"This Can't Be Love." In one fell swoop, I got to see two great living legends of the violin. The impact was immeasurable.

After attending those two exquisite palate-purging concerts, it was time to dive back into some hard bluegrass again. I had Dudley's 1958 Martin D-28 guitar now, and was absolutely enthralled with it. On the guitar top, there was an impressive amount of pick scratches dug into the face of it. In one place, a hole was nearly worn all the way through. This old Martin made me feel like I was much older than I was, like a real music veteran. I wanted to cast this presupposition. Always drawn to older instruments more than shiny new ones—to me, the roughness was fine, while there was a cheapness to the overly polished. This guitar had that cool dreadnought sound that I had heard all last summer at the festivals. At Winfield the year before, I got 2nd place on a Yamaha. With this Martin, and my increasingly fast licks, I reasoned my chances improved.

I didn't take anything for granted though; I was practicing and figuring out new arrangements of tunes, the likes not heard before on a flattop guitar yet. Each round at Winfield consisted of two selections. I thought a good strategy for me was to play one "fiddle tune," followed by one "banjo tune"—all played on the guitar of course. At this time, there were very few actual bluegrass tunes exclusive to the guitar. I composed my guitar arrangements of the banjo tunes "Bluegrass Breakdown" and "Rueben," along with the fiddle tunes "Lonesome Fiddle Blues" and "Blackberry

147

Blossom." I prepared a potential final round using the fiddle tune "Cotton Patch Rag," and finished up with my new *crazy* arrangement for the banjo tune "Dixie Breakdown."

I was particularly excited about some banjo-like chromatic runs I was adapting. They were fast, and modal, with "minor 3rd and flatted 7th" blues notes all the way through 'em. With the momentum I felt in my playing, I was psyched for this guitar contest. My overall game plan was to play non-stop hot licks from the moment I started the tune, until the tune concluded. Uncustomary to fiddle contests, I was just going to skip the melody pretty much and go for wall-to-wall licks. This was my own guitar contest line of attack—a 13-year-old's guitar assault on the field of impervious middle-aged contestants. It's what I wanted to do, and Mom let me take my own path with it. September 1975 in Winfield could not come soon enough.

MOM WAS GETTING READY TO move us to Nashville for good. She was growing weary of the pettiness in the Seattle bluegrass scene. Groups were drying up for us, along with those player friendships. She hoped that she was prescient too—thinking that my income as a child musician could support the family. Scheduled for the fall in Nashville, we already had a few major publicity appearances. The Grand Masters win earned me those television tapings. We had just added the long-running *Cas Walker* television show in Knoxville, where Dolly Parton got her start at age 10, singing old-time country songs. Jim & Jesse lined that one up for me.

Our plan by September had our Ford Econoline pulling a small U-Haul trailer to Nashville, stopping in Winfield on the way. Right up until that date, I was flying solo—back and forth to Nashville all summer. I was doing festival dates with Jim & Jesse and The Whites. Mom cycled me between the homes of Bill and Bonnie, Jesse McReynolds, and Buck White, all of them living on the north side of Nashville.

A casual glance through my summer/fall 1975 makeshift planner found the itinerary looking about as daunting as most any bluegrass musician's on the road. The Grand Masters win, as well as my first LP, had evidently worked wonders for my national reputation as a young musician.

Appearances for Mark, July – November, 1975

June 28th – Ogden Regional Fiddle Championships – Ogden, UT

July 5th – Byron Berline's Powderhorn Bluegrass Festival contest and
performance – Langley, OK

July/August – Touring with Jim & Jesse and the Virginia Boys

July/August – Touring with Buck White and the Down Home Folks

July 16th – King County Fair, Enumclaw, Washington

July 20th – Seattle Folklife Society, Seattle, WA

August – Exit Inn, Nashville with John Hartford and Norman Blake

August 2nd – Horse Pens, Steele, Alabama Bluegrass Festival contest/perf – AL

August 10th – Cowles Auditorium, Whitsworth College – Spokane, WA

August 17th – Kitsap County CK Mall Aquarium Society, Kitsap, WA

September – Getting ready for the move to Nashville

September 20th – National Flat-pick Guitar Championships – Winfield, KS

October 5th – Oklahoma State Fiddle Championships, Tulsa State Fair, OK

October 16th – "Hee Haw" T.V. Show - Nashville, TN

October 23rd – "Cas Walker" T.V. Show – Knoxville, TN

October 26th – Porter Wagoner T.V. Show – Nashville, TN

October 30th – Buck White/Down Home Folks - Recording, Nashville, TN

November 1st – "Grand Ole Opry" with Roy Acuff – Nashville, TN

November 3rd- 7th – Childe Herolde Club with Tut Taylor – Washington D.C.

November 9th – Newlife Folk Festival with Tut Taylor – Chester, PA

ONE OF MY FIRST ASSIGNMENTS in Nashville during the mid-summer of 1975 was performing with Buck White and the Down Home Folks. They took me to their family church and fed me down-home southern cooking, while we rehearsed and performed a few local Tennessee dates. Everything was according to my mother's plan — family and gospel. Wholesome songs like "Everybody Will Be Happy Over There." Buck was a wonderful musical mentor.

Hailing from Texas, Buck White began his music career just after WWII as a piano and mandolin-playing, honky-tonk musician in Texas dance halls. In 1961, he and his wife Pat began their own group in Arkansas called the Down Home Folks. Eventually their kids, Sharon and Cheryl, grew old enough to join and make it a family band. They were Nashville-bound by 1971. The range of their material went from traditional songs turned bluegrass standards, like "In the Pines" and "Salty Dog Blues," to contemporary country songs done with bluegrass instrumentation, such as Eddy Raven's "Good Morning Country Rain" and the Louvin Brothers' "If I Could Only Win Your Love."

The Down Home Folks had a bluegrass festival booking on August 2nd—Horse Pens 40 Festival in Steele, Alabama, and they asked me to play it with them. We drove down in Buck's car the night before the show. The Down Home Folks was not the top-billed headliner on the circuit that Jim & Jesse was, so things were on a fairly tight budget. Buck's wife Pat was in the front seat, their daughter Sharon Hicks, who plays guitar, was in the back seat on the driver's side. Buck's 19-year-old daughter Cheryl, who plays the upright bass, was back seat middle. Cheryl was dating Keith Whitley, who was currently on tour with Ralph Stanley's band. I was to the right of her, on the passenger side.

It was rather easy to remember this seating configuration for the Down Home Folks, because Cheryl was the prettiest girl in all of bluegrass music. Every guy on the scene knew that. During that evening's drive, she was dozing off a few times in the back seat, each time her pretty little head fell right onto my left shoulder. Her head just stayed there, too. During those moments, I did not move a muscle.

I had already seen the Horse Pens festival flier, and discovered they were hosting a guitar contest that paid $900 for 1st place. I was going to get paid a bit more for the Down Home Folks set than Ralph Stanley had paid Keith and Ricky as teens, but it wasn't a lot more. I couldn't help but think about that guitar contest—a chance at winning that 1st place prize money they advertised. I had been practicing like a maniac on Dudley's old Martin for Winfield.

After waiting to make sure that Cheryl was plenty awake—and the sound of my own voice never being the reason she would move from her previous position—I asked Buck what he thought about me entering the guitar competition. Being the judicious type, Buck, in contrast to some other bluegrass boss-men, cautioned me against it. He reminded me that I was going to be performing on the main stage with them and, "It might look bad." I let a moment go by as I thought about what he said. I reminded myself to always be respectful—but never gullible. I was learning to look out for myself. Left only to others, I was going to get dismissed and overlooked at least some of the time. I reflected on Byron Berline's *A-okay* in Langley, given exactly the same scenario a few weeks earlier. After all, my name was not being billed as a performer, just hired as a teenaged sideman. It seemed fair to me. I spoke up again about it and put it this way:

"When we get there in the morning, I can ask the folks at the registration table if I could enter. If they say yes, that would be okay with
you, right?

"Yes Mark, that would be just fine!" Buck found me in his rearview
mirror and gave me a wink.

Buck had to quickly come to his senses. The 1st place prize could increase my take-home pay from that festival ten-fold.

Well, it's a good thing I probed as I did. The contest organizers gave
me the green light, seeing nothing wrong with me playing with the Down
Home Folks and entering their guitar competition. Besides, I was just a
kid—what damage could be done?

I won it and their $900 prize. Combined with my $100 for two shows
from Buck, I came out of there with as much as the Grand Masters. Buck
and the girls were mightily impressed with my big weekend in ol' "Ala-
bam." On the drive back, all my wishes for that weekend came true.
Cheryl fell asleep on my adolescent shoulder again.

JIM & JESSE AND THE VIRGINA BOYS was *big-time* bluegrass. It was
dreamlike pulling up to a bluegrass festival in their tour bus as a Virginia
Boy. For those back-to-back summers when I was 13 and 14, touring with
one of the patriarch bands of this genre, it was dyed-in-the-wool bluegrass
heaven. Similar to Buck being all about family, Jim & Jesse represented a
similar family tradition—wholesome and gospel, too. The brother harmony on songs like "On The Wings of a Dove" was a great bluegrass
sound. The front men, of course, were the famous brothers, while Jesse's
son Keith sang baritone in the trio when they obliged him. With them, it
felt like I was a bluegrass *star*. Their fans treated me like one, too.

Jim and Jesse McReynolds began as a brother duo act near Coeburn,
Virginia in 1947. Their grandfather, Charlie McReynolds, was one of the
first musicians to record for the *Bristol* sessions, overseen by talent scout
Ralph Peer in 1927. Those sessions were regarded as the birth of modern
country music, thanks to the success of the Carter Family and Jimmie
Rodgers on The Victor Company (the first incarnation of RCA Victor).
The brothers themselves were signed to Capitol Records in 1952, affording
them their first major recording contract. In 1964, they signed on with the
Opry. Besides their striking two-brother-harmony setting off Jim's hallmark

and enhanced tenor voice, Jesse was an innovator on the mandolin, with his particular cross-picking style and a stunning split-string playing that had most every mandolin player's head spinning. Some of their most popular singles included "Diesel on My Tail" and "The Ballad of Thunder Road;" Jesse's virtuoso mandolin instrumentals included "El Cumbanchero" and "Border Ride."

Occasionally, Jim & Jesse were booked for the gospel sets at the festivals on Sundays. This is where we would light into "Jesus is the Key to the Kingdom" and "Over in the Glory Land." Mom was well-pleased about it, and the safe bet that I was finally dressing better on stage again. In a revolving door of banjoists during those couple of years—Garland Shuping, Mike Scott, Vic Jordan, Tim Ellis, Allen Shelton, and even more—it was Shelton who was tall like me; I suited up in his Virginia Boy stage clothes with ease. The scarf ties were their signature, and I had already been wearing them on shows I played back in Seattle. I was so thankful that Jim & Jesse loved me like I was their own, just like Buck White and his family did. The McReynolds brothers watched out for me, making a place for me in their band on those summer tours.

Joe Meadows, their main fiddler, would either play twin fiddles with me, or during the times he took off for a few weeks, let me have the fiddle spot all to myself. He ran his own summer festival in Virginia, so I was of some help to everyone, covering for Joe by stepping in on the festival dates.

Meadows took a strong liking to me, too. There really wasn't a hint of jealousy over the attention I was getting as a 13-year-old fiddler on stage standing next to him. When Joe was playing the shows, Jim & Jesse would usually have me join mid-set, but they still featured me on my own fiddle instrumental each time. For those features, Joe would just let me take it all, as he stood to the side of the stage. He liked watching me "do my thing" while bearing the biggest of grins. After I would finish a fiddle tune feature on stage, sometimes he'd come over to me and whisper, "I don't have the slightest idea how you do that!" Then both of us gathered around the fiddle mic to kick off the next Virginia Boys song with some twin fiddles. I never gave that stuff he said much weight, as he was a heck of a fiddle tune player himself. He was just being nice to me.

Joe took on the role as a proud mentor, and indeed he was. He showed me every fiddle ride and harmony from the records that I needed to know.

The second summer I was out with them, Joe convinced the McReynoldses not to work the same weekend as his own fiddle contest he was hosting in Virginia. He'd been bragging to me about his contest all year long, because he was offering a $1,000 1st prize. He was so proud to offer this amount of prize money at his contest—he wanted to match the Grand Masters. I can't tell you how many times he discussed it with me while on the road. He felt no one could touch me on a fiddle tune, so he made sure that I was there to enter his contest—a young "Virginia Boy" in a Virginia contest. I entered and won 1st place, just like Joe predicted. He personally awarded me the big prize on stage.

Then on top of everything, there were those gospel sets on Sundays that Mom would have loved. I wished Mom could have even seen one of the shows with the songs we did—"Family Bible," "The Family Who Prays"—but I was out there without family around, thousands of miles away from home. Mom was so happy that our dreams of me being a stage professional were coming true.

On one of the runs with Jim & Jesse, we headed north to festivals in New York and Canada. Whenever there was a fiddle or guitar contest featured at those festivals, they allowed me to enter. I always offered to check with the festival officials just as I told Buck I would. Jim and Jesse didn't care about that; they wanted to turn me lose on the field of contestants and enjoy watching what I could do against them. I asked anyway, out of courtesy, but I always got the green light—being the youngster in the band. The festival promoters thought, *"Why deny the kid?"* A full year gone by and Galax was in the rearview mirror. I had some increased credibility as well, riding in with the McReynolds bunch. This is exactly how I won the New York state fiddle competition two years in a row—walking right off the Jim & Jesse bus and onto the stage for some fiddling. No camp tent for me, I was well rested.

The bunks in the bus, however, were on the short side. When I was sleeping, my bosses would have to be careful to navigate around my legs, which were sticking out of my bunk curtain and into the aisle. The brothers thought it was kind of amusing having to maneuver around my feet and not crash into them each time.

At the New York fiddle contest hosted by the Berkshire Mountains Bluegrass Festival, there were some menacing lightning strikes on the festival grounds. It looked like the flashes were right upon us. During the actual contest, a man in the audience was struck by lightning and was sent to the hospital. The medical report described the man's pants zipper as the conductive object sending a billion bolts of electricity through his body. The officials decided that the 1st place fiddle award should be dedicated to the man struck by the lightning bolt. Such a bizarre event, it was hard to know how to process it all, including whether I should have been happy that I won.

At Jim & Jesse's repeat summer booking in the Berkshire Mountains, I entered the same fiddle contest and won it for a second time. Instead of receiving a winner's trophy, the festival had a necklace designed to commemorate the man struck by lightning. The necklace's pendant was a silver lightning bolt. After I got off stage, I showed the lightning bolt necklace award to Jesse — he was standing nearby and watching me accept the prize.

"Well, Mark, they're just not going to let you get away from that lightning, are they?"

The following day at Berkshire, I was sitting in the tour bus by myself, just chilling out while the rest of the band was out and about on the festival grounds. I liked looking out the bus window at all the festival goers, who could never be invited inside Jim & Jesse's bus, but would love the opportunity. I was startled by a knock on the bus door. They had it locked, so I wasn't worried about anyone getting on board. I drifted up to the front and had a closer look to see who it was. A guy was standing there, an older teenager. He had about the same length of hair as I had, covering his ears, and he had a banjo case with him. I yelled through the glass window: *"Jim and Jesse are not here!"* He recognized me through the window, then he raised his voice so I could hear better: "I wanted to meet you and see if you want to play a tune?"

If it was just this one older kid, I figured, maybe no one would mind if I had him come onboard. I opened the bus door to tell him that we probably don't have much time before the others return, but we at least had a few minutes. As he started up the bus steps, the kid carrying the banjo case said, "Thanks! Nice to meet you. My name is Bela Fleck."

I grabbed the guitar and we played through a few tunes like "Salt Creek." I pulled out a chord chart to something I was working on with more complicated jazz chord spellings. As he was searching around for these chords on his banjo, a few of the band members came back to the bus. I announced that we were just leaving. Bela Fleck and I decided to walk around the festival grounds together.

Bela asked me what is it like to already hit the "big time" at my age? Bela was 17 himself, and I was now 14. I told him it was always my dream to play in the biggest bluegrass bands, and now I get to. Bela asked me about my future goals. I thought about it for a minute and realized that I didn't have any goals other than to keep doing what I was doing. We both agreed that the idea of living in Nashville was a goal each of us shared — him being from New York City, and me being from across the parallel. I told him that I was moving there next month, actually. As we parted, we pledged to see each other in Nashville one day.

In the meantime, the bluegrass festivals were going strong. I got to go on and off the stage for several summers with Jim & Jesse, and adjacent to the other patriarchs of bluegrass: Monroe, Flatt, Scruggs, Stanley, the Osborne Brothers, Reno & Harrel, Jimmy Martin, Mac Wiseman, Country Gentlemen — week in and week out. Every time we played the gospel set on Sunday morning — "Wait a Little Longer Please Jesus" and "Two Thousand Years Ago," I knew that Mom would imagine me playing the music she loved from 3,000 miles away.

ANOTHER BAND I GOT TO play with during this time period was J.D. Crowe and the New South. I saw them for the first time the year before with the lineup of Tony Rice, Ricky Skaggs, Jerry Douglas, and Bobby Sloan. I got to hang out with them after their rollicking set of bluegrass quotes at the Pickin' Parlor in Nashville. They spent the entire second set spoofing Bill Monroe and Lester Flatt on stage: Skaggs inheriting Monroe and Rice singing Flatt. It was so funny, I had tears in my eyes from laughing so hard. I knew all of the inside jokes they humorously satirized. J.D. already *did* Scruggs better than anybody. He didn't have to try very hard.

The next day the New South members all came over to Buck White's house where I was staying. Pat and the girls fixed a big southern cooked meal for everyone, and Ricky was eating it up. "I only want the homemade ice cream if I can have some more of your delicious beans on top of it!" He was flirting with Sharon Hicks too, Skaggs obviously had a little crush on her.

It was great to see the incredible young guitarist, Tony Rice, especially. Overnight, he became my new bluegrass guitar hero. Tony was ten years older than I, which would make him 23. After seeing an emerging virtuoso of the bluegrass guitar, I came away armed with a few new ideas and approaches for the guitar contest at Winfield. Jerry Douglas, who played dobro in the group, was a 19-year-old phenom. What a band—likely the best band I was around in contemporary bluegrass during those years.

The boss man of the group, J.D. Crowe, was one of the best banjo players in the history of the instrument. While still in high school, James Dee Crowe began playing banjo with bluegrass heavyweights Mac Wiseman for the summer, and then joined Jimmy Martin's, the Sunny Mountain Boys, for several years. He played on Martin's albums such as *Skip Hop and Wobble* and *Good 'n Country* on Decca Records. After making quite a name for himself on the five-string, introducing banjo instrumentals "Bear Tracks" and "Crowe on the Banjo," J. D. returned home to Lexington, Kentucky, by the early 1960s. There he formed the Kentucky Mountain Boys with soon-to-be-bluegrass-legends Red Allen and Doyle Lawson. For years the band played local bars and taverns, before returning to the bluegrass festival circuit. By 1971, he formed a new band under his own name, J. D. Crowe and the New South and hired Tony Rice. In 1975, Ricky Skaggs and Jerry Douglas signed on.

He was exceedingly kind to me at the house party. Ricky and Bobby played a little fiddle in the band, but they didn't have someone to fill that role for the entire show. I don't know how I ended up with J.D.'s banjo in my hands, but I played something he wanted me to show him. I actually *taught* J.D. Crowe one of my semi-chromatic banjo licks, even though I hadn't played much banjo in a couple years. For whatever reason, my little banjo lick tickled Crowe to no end, and he simply insisted that I teach it to him. For all practical purposes, this event was where any real banjo credentials of mine began and ended.

By the following summer, J.D. invited me to join the New South on fiddle. When I joined up with them to try it out by the fall months, they were back to playing small clubs for week-long stints in Lexington and Louisville. J.D. had lost all of those great players in the lineup just months before. The outfit was still quite good, though: guitarist and lead singer Glen Lawson took Tony Rice's spot when Rice moved to San Francisco to launch the David Grisman Quintet. Mandolinist and tenor singer Jimmy Gaudreau took Ricky Skaggs' spot while he, along with Jerry Douglas, formed Boone Creek with Vince Gill. Driven by J.D., his band's bluegrass grooves were still very deep. The timing had a particular sophistication within its ensemble, and it really swung for bluegrass. It was almost addictive playing it with them, like you couldn't get enough of it.

What my mother and I were not entirely aware of was that by the mid-1970s, the bluegrass music industry was largely seasonal—even for the big bluegrass groups. After three or four months of summer festivals, it was either time off for most of the band membership to find regular nine-to-five jobs, or to stay afloat, resorting to low-paying week-long stints in bars through the winter months. Being a member of a bluegrass band that played bars was going to be nearly impossible for me to sustain as a kid. Despite the thrill of J.D.'s old boss—the "King of Bluegrass" Jimmy Martin—sitting in with us once in a while, the current conditions looked doleful for a child musician. Being far underage, I was physically limited to the dressing room or on the stage itself. Glen, Jimmy, and the other bandmates were interested in having a drink and talking to the fans during the breaks, especially the ladies. Single and in their 20s, they left me alone in the dressing room in-between sets while they *worked* the room. I loved playing the music, but those weeks were lonely during the day, and lonely even at the bars at night. At the festivals and fiddle contests, I had free rein, where I could run around and always find something to do—but not here.

J.D. was sweet to me though. After we were done each night, he tried to make it up to me. He took me to the nearest White Castle burger joint and bought me as many White Castles as I could eat—until I couldn't eat anymore. I just gorged myself at those after-midnight outings on their half-sized burgers. My record was ten down the hatch. J.D. just sat there and chuckled the whole time watching me do that. He said he was going to go broke just feeding me White Castle burgers. I don't think he ever ate a single one himself, even after three or four sets played. Whatever it took, he didn't want to lose me out of the band, especially after the loss of personnel he just incurred. Burger by burger, it was like earnest money.

But in no time, he realized the inevitable. I was never going to last the winter.

LATE SUMMER saw me flying to Los Angeles to stay with Bryon Berline for a few days. He put together a monster fiddle jam set with John Hartford, Richard Greene, and David Grisman. Our set took place on what could be termed a "rock-and-roll stage" set up in the middle of a sports field. More than 10,000 people were just standing there bobbing up and down for the entire time at Bob Baxter's Bluegrass Banjo Band Bash. A lasting image from that show was David Grisman and his long curly hippie hair, bending over at the hip sideways as he played his mandolin solos. It was cool to meet him and play with him. Tony Rice was in California as well, and just starting up the David Grisman Quintet. As a young teen, I really did relate to Grisman, too—experiencing the ground floor of progressive bluegrass music. I started to like hanging around the nonconformists and free thinkers. Another hippie on the show, John Hartford, was quite pleased that I was added to this fiddle jam. We had already recorded together. Richard Greene, the third hippie on our set, had an interesting response to me, though.

It was the first time I had met Richard Greene. I liked his playing in Muleskinner, especially on that PBS TV show they recently performed. He seemed to be a little startled by how I could play all the fiddle and bluegrass tunes so easily—all the tunes that Byron chose for the jam set. Byron and I knew most of the same ones, courtesy of Benny Thomasson. Richard had never heard of Benny.

Each time it was my turn to take a solo on the tunes, my old white fiddle seemed to really cut through the mic, much more so than Richard's violin. Anyone could hear the difference just by the sound from the PA bouncing off the distant bleachers and reflecting back to the stage. The white fiddle was coming all the way back, strong and loud, while Richard's instrument was kind of petering out. Richard started making a few quips to Byron about me, remarking that my microphone was hotter than the other fiddle mics on stage. The next thing I knew, Richard wanted to switch places and play through my mic instead. So we switched places midway through the show. After my white fiddle was kind of killing it through Richard's mic, he wanted to switch back to be next to Byron again. We traded places as he wished.

Then Richard sneered at Byron, *"What's up with the weird-looking violin?"* (the one I asked him to sign with the Sharpie earlier that day). Without warning, Richard asked me to switch instruments. I definitely didn't want to, but it would be pretty awkward for a young kid to refuse Greene's request in front of the whole world up there. So I reluctantly gave him my fiddle while I played his. The set was only 60 minutes, so I was hoping I'd have more chances to play on my own instrument before it was all over.

Richard's violin was outfitted with a shoulder rest pad of some kind, and a rubber chin rest pad — you could see rubber bands all over the fiddle. There was all kinds of gear on it that I'd never thought about. Richard was a *classical* fiddler. Most traditional fiddlers in the 1970s did not even use a shoulder rest. I didn't. It felt funny and bulky — his whole setup was difficult for me to play. While I enjoyed trying out other fiddles at the various festivals when offered, I couldn't get this one to work very well. I was hoping that I didn't have to play his fiddle for the rest of the show — but because of the way things were going, I was fearing I might have to. Richard kept the white fiddle for a couple of tunes, and then gave it back. "Hey, I can't get anything out of it," he made sure to tell me.

After our set had concluded, all four fiddlers ended up at Byron's house in Van Nuys for a late-night jam session. Richard couldn't believe how many fiddle tunes Byron knew, and therefore, how many I knew along with him. One after the other we both fell right into the tunes, while Richard was kind of left to just lightly noodle around and play a rhythmic stroke near the frog of his bow. It was all kinda blowing his mind. He'd never played tunes like "Grey Eagle" before. "Where do you guys learn these tunes?" he asked. Richard couldn't help but show his frustration over not being familiar with the American fiddle tune repertoire, but at the same time being known as one of the preeminent bluegrass fiddlers who could improvise over most anything. It was so peculiar to me that he played with Bill Monroe, but was not steeped in fiddling. Although, fiddlers like Vassar Clements and Chubby Wise were mostly swing players when they joined up with Monroe's Bluegrass Boys for the first time. Nevertheless, it made Richard's unique career seem that much more distinctive. I must admit, though, it felt good being immersed in the rich fiddling tradition that Benny gave me. We could just play tunes from memory all night long. I felt lucky to already have the pedigree I did.

I'll never forget that Muleskinner band with Richard Greene, David Grisman, Peter Rowan, Bill Keith, and Clarence White, though. Tragically, their great guitarist Clarence was hit by a drunk driver as he loaded his musical equipment into a vehicle. Not even out of his 20s, he was dead. Clarence was one of my great bluegrass guitar heroes, even though he was more known for his string-bender (B-Bender) Telecaster playing in his hit rock band, The Byrds. The Devonshire Downs festival director, Bob Baxter, was an impresario for Clarence's return to bluegrass. The festival was intended to be a vehicle to promote Clarence White's acoustic playing as part of his comeback to the scene. There would have been 10,000 music fans to cheer Clarence on, too. Grisman and Greene were booked at it, obviously sharing a band with Clarence. Byron had just played with Clarence in the Country Gazette, and, Hartford had just played with Clarence the year before on the road. His acoustic music buddies were going to be there with him, but the great Clarence White was struck down far too soon. Clarence's acoustic guitar-playing was such an inspiration to me, it seemed befitting that I ended up performing there with all of his friends.

During this Los Angeles festival weekend, I found myself in the middle of progressive acoustic music mavericks. I also met Darol Anger that night for the first time. He was an unknown player out of San Rafael who David Grisman had just picked up for his new Quintet with Tony Rice. I couldn't help but wonder if this stuff was what my future looked like, more than the family tradition—wholesome—gospel bluegrass route. I couldn't let Mom in on how much I liked those hippies. There was a headwind a blowin', "Walking My Lord Up Calvary's Hill."

ONCE BACK HOME IN SEATTLE, I regrouped with my mother as we began to pack up for our move to Nashville in September, 1975. In her mind, I could support the family out of Nashville on my music income. Mom was considerably weaker physically than the summer before. She spent half her days laying down on the living room sofa, but Mom assured me that she was ready to make the trip. We're just going to have to take longer rests along the way, she told me—so she could lay down in the back of the van and relax there. She still affirmed that her discomforts were due to menopause. Mom was 44. I was still two years from being able to drive, so I couldn't help her in that way.

We rented a small U-Haul trailer to pull, said goodbye to my Dad in a way that seemed a bit transitory, and we set out for Winfield, Kansas. Mom had to make frequent stops, more than we anticipated. She just could not drive for more than a few hours without having to lay down on the foam mattress in the back. We didn't leave much of a time cushion before we needed to be in Winfield, so at some point, she started to worry about even making it to the guitar contest.

On the third day of our journey to Kansas, Mom spotted a big empty parking lot off to the side of the highway. She pulled into it and asked me to get in the driver's seat of the van. "Mom! I can't," I implored. "Yes you have to," she insisted. "If we want to make it to this guitar contest you've worked so hard for." She simply could not drive the entire way on her own. So, Mom taught me how to drive on a roadside parking lot just west of the Rockies—"three on the tree" and popping the quick clutch of the Ford Econoline.

Just turning 14, I found myself driving the family down the highway— my sister up in the front seat watching me, while Mom laid down in the back. Boy, did she ever put a lot of trust in me. I ended up driving the majority of the time. I quickly got accustomed to highway driving, barreling down the open road, and on my way to sweet musical freedom at the Winfield festival. It was only when I had to take an exit and got into some stop-and-go traffic that I panicked just a little. But the *highway*, like nobody's business, was *my* new friend.

During the drive to the National Guitar Flat-picking Championships, there was a certain palpability which was understood inside our van. The unmistakableness was *over and above*—a conviction bolstered by a strength of will I didn't believe I had any control over. As I drove us down the highway, I realized that everything in my young life now, relied on winning this guitar contest. A new kind of *will* to win had surfaced, whether it was my mother's determination, or the manner in which I rode into town behind the steering wheel. Whether it was contending with my Dad for being the family's breadwinner, or yet again, just whipping up my own escape from reality—in my mind, everything was riding on this contest. I didn't even recognize my own particular quality from before. It was all different now, I was a young professional at 14, and it was so much more serious. Taking my turn in the driver's seat, winding our way to Winfield that September, was still another reckoning.

WE SAFELY ARRIVED IN central Kansas. Jeff Pritchard and his family welcomed us to stay with them in Wichita while we attended the Winfield festival. Mom finally had a few hours to rest in a comfortable bed. Jeff thought I was going to win the guitar prize this time, after coming in 2nd as an upset the year before.

A good violinist/fiddler, Jeff was a violin concerto competition winner in Kansas before he set his sights on championship fiddling, inspired by several recordings including my first album. I filled him in about playing with another classical violinist turned bluegrass fiddler, Richard Greene, in LA a few weeks earlier. While I had my guitar tunes well in hand and primed for the contest, I spent that night figuring out various phrases from Jeff's classical sheet music he had laying around—just seeing what of it I could throw into a fiddle tune. This was not at all a Dick Barrett-approved methodology, but neither was bluegrass music itself. Besides, it was fun to try—it gave me a couple of my own ideas. I was constantly reworking fiddle tunes, and it was a welcome distraction from the intensity building towards that guitar contest. The next morning, however, it was off to the rodeo.

The Walnut Valley Festival in Winfield takes over the rodeo and fairgrounds, where they normally have all the things you would expect: barrel racing, livestock sales, barnyard Olympics, figure-8 races, 4-H poultry, pigeons, and food auctions. But this weekend, the rodeo hosted a carnival of pickers. Straightaway, we ran into the Morton twins. We got to know them a little bit at the Lakeland competitions in Memphis the summer before. Both 19, Randall plays banjo and Greg plays the guitar—they were there to enter the contests. Greg was a good guitar player, too. Absent the year before, his presence shored up the competition. Actually, we soon discovered that the competition stiffened dramatically, with over twice the amount of entrants from the year before. Most every guitar flat-picker in the land who thought they had a chance to win was here—$1,000 in cash and prizes for 1st place.

I couldn't wait to show Greg my 1958 Martin D-28. He loved it. He agreed it was quite an upgrade from that Yamaha he saw me play in Memphis. Greg and I decided to back up each other in the contest. Both of us backed up Randall in the banjo contest, too—I switched to rhythm mandolin for that. All of the supplementary competitions were held on a stage set up in the barn that first day—banjo, fiddle, and mandolin. My circle of friends did mighty fine, too: Randall won the banjo contest; Jeff won the fiddle contest, while I got 2nd. Then I turned around to win the mandolin contest, playing my Givens A-model no less. Barnyard Olympics, yes siree. Together, we *swept* this barn plum out.

It looked like the festival was getting to be a much bigger deal by 1975. Even within a year, some of these bluegrass festivals grew dramatically from what we could see, drawing audiences and competitors from all over the world. The Winfield headliners were the three bluegrass guitar greats: Doc Watson, Norman Blake, and supersized fiddle tune flat-picker, Dan Crary. They played together on the main stage for a thrilling three-guitar jam-set. It was momentous. I tried to hang onto every guitar lick they delivered. The Winfield festival designated all three of them to be judges for the guitar competition. With all the know-how in that judges room; *there's no hiding place down here.*

FOR PLACEMENT, I DREW number 23. It was how I was identified to the audience for the duration of the competition. Similar to Weiser and the Grand Masters, the judges (Watson, Blake, and Crary) were hidden away in a trailer—the sound was piped in. The officials didn't want to take any chances with an errant mute button; the names of the contestants were never uttered. For the guitar competition on Saturday, the crowds were very large at the grandstand stage. By the finals, the grandstand was as full as it was for the headlining acts—nearly 15,000 people were there watching it all shape up.

I had been surprisingly relaxed the day before, thinking I would breeze right through my rounds with few, if any, nerves. But that changed on Saturday morning, when the weight of the moment hit me like it hadn't before. I felt a huge lump in my throat and a pit in my stomach. It was more like an impervious lead weight. Of all of the competitions I'd entered before, I never experienced my stomach actually hurting from anxiety. I felt the pressure I put on myself, and perhaps it was indirectly from Mom. I wasn't sure. I told Greg that I couldn't eat lunch—had no appetite. He told me it's going to be all right: "Let's concentrate on the pickin'," he reminded me. Greg was playing some really cool stuff on the guitar, too. We had a mutual favorite guitar player in Clarence White, and both of us liked incorporating some of his influence into our own guitar renditions. But Greg was getting into some of the brand new Tony Rice licks. I had just heard Tony a couple of months before. I told Greg about that special day at the White's home hosting the New South. We loved thinking about the great guitar players of our era, and especially those three icons sitting there in the judge's room.

Warming up backstage, all of these older guitar entrants were eyeing me—checking me out. It felt different than the fiddle contests, because here, it seemed to be more about hot licks than anything tradition-based. I hesitated to play my contest tunes in front of any of them, for fear of my licks getting lifted by a fellow competitor. It was my apprehension, at least, so I was hiding my best stuff you could say, downplaying it and *underplaying* backstage—the opposite of what I would do normally in a fiddle contest. The fiddler who's got the hot hand backstage seemed to always do well at the fiddle conventions. Sometimes the "no holds barred" fiddler in the jam sessions the night before led to a successful outcome in the contest, by way of osmosis. Not letting them see all my cards here at Winfield seemed a better strategy. I *was* saving it all for the stage.

As a kid, I probably experienced about every contest strategy known— either being on the receiving end of these devices, or trying them out for myself. At Winfield, though, my stomach still hurt and I was not playing my best backstage, even if I had wanted to. Before the final round, I didn't have dinner either—growing boy and all. Mom was worried about me not eating anything.

Winfield emcee:
"Now the last of the semi-finalists. We will call to the stage at this time, Number 23. Contestant Number 23, to the stage please."

IT ALL HIT ME LIKE a ton of bricks. I could sense my metamorphosis. This was the first major contest since Mom was moving us back East, and that move was riding on my ability to make it—the one who brings home all the bacon. Nobody around us knew about this rather pivotal demand on me. It was a prevailing family secret—ultimately, an unnatural family embarrassment. Mom didn't want this idea *out there*. Neither Jeff nor the Morton twins knew the extent of our little family plan. Me paying the bills was taboo to talk about, as my mother warned. Without any way to succeed in Seattle, and a distinct possibility of carving out a career in Nashville, this effort was for my benefit, yes… but Mom was counting on me to make it happen for our household, too.

I always felt much better about everything once I got on stage. That's what I was—the child performer. I was far more comfortable up on the stage than off. I came to understand that the audiences were always my friend. My fellow guitar competitors—well maybe not so much. Amongst all of those strangers gawking—the *backstagers* looking for something weird about me, it seemed—it was all winching up by the second round. Looking me up and down, curious as to where I came from—guessing how old I was—probably thrown off balance by how a 14-year-old face was on a now 6' 4" body… I had grown another inch or two. That I wore a dark sloppy sweatshirt, but still looked like a disheveled dork with braces, was probably not as galling as checking out my new licks, though—especially the speed at which I was attempting to play those licks on a Martin guitar. Once on stage and away from all of them, I felt free from all the issues. The stage was a place where I always wanted to be, so I could just fly. Fly far away from here again.

None of those guitar players were very nice to me at Winfield, anyway.

As I climbed the small flight of stairs onto the grandstand stage, a smattering of welcome applause broke out. Some remembered the "young boy" from the morning preliminaries who played "Lonesome Fiddle Blues" and "Bluegrass Breakdown." Greg followed me up onto the stage to accompany me for this second round. We sat in the two chairs already placed from the previous contestant. We promptly adjusted the microphones. We knew to get those mics within inches of our sound holes—to achieve the best projection from our guitars. Most all of the guitar contestants were seated on stage when playing the rounds. The fiddlers always stood.

I had some good renditions worked up to play in the final rounds: "Blackberry Blossom," "Rueben." This year I had the better guitar, and with this old axe I could put out some volume with my young hands. I played a peck louder than most of the adults in the contest. Maybe I got used to all the clanking because I had my high-decibel white fiddle in my ear all the time. Probably going to lose some hearing in my left ear from it, eventually. Playing in bluegrass bands all summer, as well, helped me play with volume. I played faster and could cross-pick up a storm by now (thank you Jesse), but with no loss in bang and boom when I lit into that manner of picking—the flat-pick going back and forth over multiple strings like a three-finger banjo roll. Shoot, when I cross-picked like that, it might've been even more brazen. I wasn't at all worried about playing nice and pretty at all, the mindset was non-ending bluegrass runs—every hot lick from the bottom of the neck to the top, and at the highest rate of speed childishly possible. I was runnin' again for safety, on my way to bringing this contest home.

With that pit in my stomach, I had trouble drawing up my "inner kid" sensitivity. Instead, it was going to be one relentless joy ride through two blistering tunes. Maybe it was similar to illegally commandeering a van through Colorado on the open road... the gas pedal pressed to the floor and maxing it out at 80mph with the V-4 engine in our Ford Econoline. I kept up with my ground plan of choosing one fiddle tune, followed by a bluegrass banjo instrumental.

I made it to the top three. Now it was time for "Cotton Patch Rag" and "Dixie Breakdown." Greg must have narrowly missed making the final round. After they posted the three contestants left standing, we looked at each other and quickly absorbed it all. He told me, "Let's get this thing, brother." I took a deep breath for the tune that could cinch it for me. I was the first guitarist to create a rendition of "Dixie Breakdown," with the stop-choruses like I had them. It worked for the banjo players, so why not with bluegrass guitar? As I was getting ready to play it, I was thinking about all those guitar players warming up backstage for most of the day now displaced and sitting out front as spectators—they probably muttered to themselves: *"I can't believe that punk thought of that."*

It was all about punching this round out—*obliterating it.* My young hands holding those metal strings down to the fret. The pick contact was crucial, too—getting those down-and-up pick strokes really even, like I wanted them... It was all merging together at another level now. I usually played with a lot of excitement, and this day was no exception. It would be hard not to be all charged up, with that big crowd on top of my every guitar line. I could feel that the audience wanted me to do well—they were pulling for me, indeed. At times, I could feel that they were even holding their collective breath as my fingers flew to match the pick strokes. As we took off, each of my high-difficultly licks began to connect. I was able to continue the musical line throughout, up and down my finger board with banjo-like tempo—the same speed that usually requires three-fingers on the right hand to accomplish. My flat-pick was alternating with up and down strokes—cross-picking on the choruses.

In fiddle contests, I was not supposed to play too fast. Here I was on breathless rapid-fire, but still, I held it and tucked it in. I never played beyond my capacity on that final round. My earlier rounds were admittedly a bit uglier, sloppier—but not on the final round. No, I was focused in on it. I got better each round, and the pit in my stomach began to disappear as the rounds reeled off. Greg was accustomed to banjo tempos from playing with his twin brother. We were right there together.

I suspected that each of my stop-choruses could elicit some hand-clapping from the crowd. But the audience was told to *"withhold your applause during the performances."* Nevertheless, I could tell that the crowd wanted to, especially the first time through the stop-chorus. But they didn't. They hung fire. The second time around the tune—same thing. They continued to hold their breath for "the kid." I could tell they were sweating it out with me.

As I rounded the third and final turn of the piece, I sensed the audience was with me all the way—and they were going to just break. They could not hold back any longer. During my highest degree of difficulty stop-chorus, I kept pressing for the wall with every bit of physicality I had in my adolescent body. Some in the audience began to cheer before I was done, while the rest of them restrained themselves in hopes I would finish strong for them. When I ripped out the final run on my instrumental tag, and pounded out the last note on the lowest string of that great old Martin guitar with the biggest tone I could make, the sound of it resonated throughout the bleachers. The place went off. I don't know how it came to me exactly, but I *imagined* that my music would take me where I had to go. I *trusted* that highway I'd been driving to find a better place for those moments on the stage. To someplace that wasn't the same old rodeo.

Winfield emcee:
"OK folks, calm down."

Old Time Music Winter 1976/77 London, England
"His guitar is excellent, and he selects numbers which to me are completely new to the guitar, including an incredible 'Dixie Breakdown'... the live cut which won him first place in the 1975 National Flat-Picking Championship."

Bluegrass Unlimited Vol. 11, No. 3 September, 1976
"His guitar playing is just as good as, if not better than, his fiddle work. Included here is a live recording of Mark's Championship performance of 'Dixie Breakdown' at last year's National Flat-picking contest and what he does is nothing short of phenomenal."

CHAPTER SEVEN

GETTING JAZZY

B Y THE TIME WE GOT OVER TO NASHVILLE, my mother was exhausted. All this traveling was taking so much out of her. Of course, we couldn't just "move in" with Bill and Bonnie Smith, so Mom had already lined up a Days Inn motel at a weekly rate—on Dickerson Pike— our new digs in Nashville.

We had a few musical opportunities all ready to go—all of them potentially very good for my young career. I was invited to perform on the Grand Ole Opry again, and, I played for Roy Acuff in dressing room #1 for most of the evening. It was such a precious time there backstage, like no other experience. Lester Flatt's fiddler, Paul Warren, spent some time there watching me play. I had to pinch myself. I always felt like I was hanging out with musical royalty in Roy's dressing room #1. But the occasion we had been anticipating the most occupied our attention: I had a feature guest spot on the national TV show, *Hee Haw*. This could very well be the biggest break of my young career.

Hee Haw was a highly-rated syndicated television show that found its way into practically every household across the country by the early 1970s. The show initially went on air in 1969 as a summertime trial run, then practically overnight, it was moved to replace the controversial primetime *The Smothers Brothers Comedy Hour* on CBS. The new country music show, created by two Canadians not well versed in the cornpone humor of the American South, quickly grabbed hold of most every parody and hillbilly mockery with their effort. Loosely based on the *Rowan & Martin's Laugh-In* format, rural buffoonery took center stage. More significantly, the series was a showcase for country music. Interestingly, CBS's lineup featured several shows with a country theme, including *The Andy Griffith Show, The Beverly Hillbillies,* even *Lassie*—all favorites for me to watch in urban Seattle. By 1971, the nicknamed "Hillbilly Network," let go of all of them in what was characterized as the "rural purge," and yet, *Hee Haw* found a way to play. Anchored by their popular country music hosts, Buck

Owens and Roy Clark, it remained a favorite of television audiences through national syndication from Los Angeles to Chicago.

It was the first time I had television "makeup" put on my face. In their makeup room, they "made me up" side by side my fellow musical guest, the guitar great, Merle Travis. He was genuinely interested in my playing, about my guitar accomplishments at Winfield a few weeks earlier—he talked to me a little bit. When the cameras were rolling, my fiddling performance of "Sally Goodin'" was staged with the entire *Hee Haw* cast seated around me and picking along. The house musicians included well-known serious banjoist Bobby Thompson, seated by their banjo-playing humorist, Grandpa Jones. Even though it was my first national television appearance, I dare say I played like a seasoned pro—I don't think I missed a thing on it.

Our hopes were dashed a little when we learned the air date for my *Hee Haw* episode was being delayed by several months; it wasn't going to help us out much for this fall in Nashville. But we had one more national TV appearance to make it happen in Music City, so we could afford to hang on— *The Porter Wagoner Show.*

With the bluegrass music scene largely dormant past October, this TV show appearance was crucial for us, and thankfully, a quick turn-around for airing. It was the last of our three big appearances by way of the Grand Masters win. Porter was perhaps our biggest chance to get noticed by the Nashville music industry before the winter months set in. By any reasoned criteria, it was the right show at the right time.

The Porter Wagoner Show was one of the longest running syndicated shows featuring country music on television. It got its launch in 1961 filmed in black and white, but we were in living color by the time I appeared in 1975. Filmed at Opryland, on a stage adjacent to the Theater by the Lake, I was about to get a rousing introduction from the country music legend, a huge supporter of fiddling and the Grand Masters contest.

Born in 1927, Porter Wagoner hailed from West Plains, Missouri. He got into performing and writing songs by the early 1950s, and scored a #1 hit in 1955 on RCA Victor called "A Satisfied Mind." This led to regular appearances on ABC's *Ozark Jubilee.* Within a couple of years, he became a member of the Grand Ole Opry. Wagoner charted over 80 singles during his career, including "Green, Green Grass of Home" and "Skid Row Joe."

170

In 1967, Porter replaced his female singer Norma Jean with an unknown 21-year-old singer from East Tennessee, Dolly Parton. The new partnership released countless duet albums, producing seven years of hits like "The Last Thing on My Mind" and "Just Someone I Used to Know." When Dolly headed out on her own, leaving Porter just a year before I appeared on his show, she wrote "I Will Always Love You" in dedication to him.

Right before I stepped out on stage for my Porter Wagoner spot, my mother took me aside and said this to me:

"If things go well, and we get a lot of attention from this appearance, the family could stay on in Nashville, without Dad—and live on the money that comes in from music."

I thought about what Mom was saying to me as I waited in the wings for Wagoner's introduction. I was wearing my new hand-embroidered cowboy shirt Mom made for me. Had a new felt cowboy hat. I was ready to play as best I could, but I was also a bit chilled—the weather had turned cold by October and there was a stiff breeze around the outdoor Opryland stage. My fingers felt a little numb. But that wasn't going to hold me back much. I was less sure of Porter's band, The Wagonmasters. I was skeptical of how they were accompanying my Texas fiddle tune after our run-through. Their musical interpretation of a fiddle breakdown was plenty chilly all on its own. I hoped it would be better when the cameras were up and rolling. I really needed a good performance to make it right for my family.

Porter Wagoner introduction:
"Now I want you to meet my special guest. Each year during the Fan Fair in Nashville where all of the country music fans from all over America come here to visit the Grand Ole Opry and everything, we have what we call the Grand Masters Fiddling Championship. And this is where fiddlers from all over the world come here to compete, a great event. Some of the greatest fiddlers in the world are here. I want you to meet now, the champion from last year. And he's a boy who is I believe only 13-years-old, and he's one of the finest fiddlers that I've ever heard in my life. I know you'll enjoy him. Give him a great welcome to our show, his name is Mark O'Connor. How about it!

Mark, we're delighted to have you on the show, and I know it is a great thrill for you to be the champion fiddle player. And uh, you ain't gonna talk a lot I'm sure, so... [laughter] What are you going to do for us on the fiddle? 'Tom and Jerry!'"

I performed "Tom and Jerry" while Porter and Mack Magaha (his "dancing fiddler") looked on. But to my sincere disappointment and frustration, The Wagonmasters were missing chord changes and flubbing bass lines. When they decided that never-ending steel guitar chimes played loudly right in my range was a good idea, I saw any serious musical aspirations as a kid *wagon wheel* right off that Nashville dirt road. I was upset when performances didn't go like I wanted them to, no matter whose fault it was. The motivation to do well, given the new-found responsibility to take care of my family's living expenses, and to somehow remain focused through the Wagonmasters' many mishaps, and those inescapable chimes rammed into my eardrums, revealed the grit I had developed as a traveling child musician. I played well, but was this great music-making? Or was my valiancy itself, enough to take on Music City?

I sat in with Charlie and Oswald each week at the KOA campground. They were hardly getting paid for it, so they couldn't afford to give me anything. We played for a few handfuls of tourists coming through. I went over to the Opry's backstage area several more times to play for Roy in his dressing room. I attended rehearsals with Jim & Jesse for a potential recording session. They were calling their former banjo player, Allen Shelton, out of retirement for it. But the recording never came off. There was that solo spot on *Cas Walker* in Knoxville that Jesse had set up for me. We had the Morton twins come over from Memphis to join me. It was good, but it didn't really move the dial much, professionally. It didn't pay anything either. Back in Nashville, there was a new group that just started up, Riders in the Sky, a trio specializing in cowboy and trail songs. Their fiddler, Woody Paul Chrisman, invited me to sit in with them a few times.

Woody, Too Slim and Ranger Doug had their western regalia on and told lots of jokes to the audience at the club. I felt a little out of place, just a kid wearing a T-shirt most of the time. In response to one of their sillier jokes, I grabbed Ranger Doug's pistol out of his holster and jokingly held it to his head. It freaked everybody out, including Doug. I definitely was not supposed to do that. Maybe it was loaded? It *was* downtown Nashville in 1975.

Otherwise, I had a lot of time off without much to do as winter grew near, so the Morton twins visited us quite a bit at the Days Inn. We ended up hanging out on the motel asphalt parking lot for days on end—just talking about everything from music to growing up as a teen. Talked about girls, some. We picked up some cheap skateboards and learned to ride them. Mom wanted peace and quiet in the motel room at all times while she laid in bed with a wet rag over her forehead. I wondered if she was ever going to get well. As the weeks went by, we realized I wasn't going to make money in Nashville that winter. Everything I did was either for free or next to it. I could still make good money entering fiddle and guitar contests, but those were going to wrap up soon until next summer.

My mother told me we couldn't hold out very much longer, "unless there are more music opportunities." "What more can I do!" I exclaimed.

The motel housekeeping came by to drop off some towels along with those plastic cups with shrink wrap stretched across the top. Trapped inside one of those cups was one gigantic cockroach. When Mom reached for a cup, she saw it and screamed—she nearly fell over, and that would have been very bad, considering her feeble condition. Mom called up housekeeping to have them drop by to see their handiwork. She announced we were going to have to find another motel with a weekly rate.

What I remember most about those motels around Nashville was all the blacktop parking lots—it all seemed to be the same—my new back yards. It's where I spent most of my time since Mom was resting in the room. A lot of that time was with the Morton twins just hanging out, messing around with those cheap skateboards.

I had a couple of engagements with Tut Taylor on the road: a club in DC for several nights and a folk festival in Pennsylvania, where I got to hang around Doc and Merle Watson a little more. I pretended I was Norman Blake on guitar for those duos with Tut. It was just him and me on those, leaving Mom and Michelle at Days Inn #2.

MOM PUT ME ON A PLANE out of the Nashville airport on October 5th. I was headed for Tulsa—the Oklahoma State Fiddle Championship. After an entire summer of playing professional bluegrass music, I swept right into the Texas-style fiddle competition and beat Dick Barrett for the first time, and on his turf, too. This contest win brought a badly needed $600 check back to our Nashville motel lifestyle. Since I wasn't attending school at this point, Mom wanted me to be curious and inquisitive, to learn things from the older fiddlers I was around—not just fiddle tunes, but to further educate myself on other things I found interesting.

At the Oklahoma fiddle contest, I met a few top Native American fiddlers from their reservation. Tulsa itself had once been part of what was known as Indian Territory, prior to Oklahoma statehood in 1907, and most of the city remains located within the Creek Nation. I was fascinated by the earlier lives of Native Americans, I *played* "bow and arrow" back home, pretending to be the "Indian." Dozens of tribal jurisdictions make up Tulsa and the surrounding area: the nations of the Choctaw, Cherokee, Muscogee (Creek), Chickasaw, Osage, Cheyenne, Kiowa-Comanche-Apache, Seminole, Citizen Potawatomi, Absentee Shawnee and more. Some of these tribal communities have fiddlers in their populations going back many years, long before the Trail of Tears—the tragic result of President Andrew Jackson's "Indian Removal Act" of 1830. A few of these "Indian fiddlers" entered the competition there at the Oklahoma state contest, including Ace Sewell.

Ace showed me a couple tunes on the fiddle that weekend, and I remembered fondly how he could play "Choctaw," a great American fiddle tune. Ace was Cherokee, and there were other prominent fiddlers who were Native American as well. Benny's close friend, Bryant Houston, who wrote "Limerock," was Cherokee. Native Americans had been playing the American fiddle for hundreds of years in the South. Being introduced to the European violin through the early colonization of the new world in the 1600s—battles, massacres, and broken treaties notwithstanding, the American violin became an important part of Native American culture, and a testament to the devotional power of the fiddle.

Dick Barrett, who's also part Native American, didn't stay around very long after they handed out the trophies. Instead, I got plenty bullyragged by another Texas fiddler's wife. Dale Morris got 3rd place, and *she* let me hear about it. *"Mark, sweetheart, you know you didn't win this here contest, don't you?"* she said to me in her steamed up Texas drawl. I didn't know what to say except to agree with her, and try to be a gracious winner. She did call me "sweetheart." *"I am glad that you know in your heart that you didn't win this contest, Mark."*

I still had the 1st place trophy (a huge silver bowl) in my hands, though, and I beat the menacing Dick Barrett for the first time. Dale's wife was tryin' all right, but that $600 was going to go a long ways for me and Mom that October, since both *Hee Haw* and Porter's TV show paid about a $100 apiece.

What a piece of work, I thought. Dale Morris' marriage to that woman didn't last much longer, anyway.

There were the other fiddle contest runouts that we hoped would keep us afloat in Nashville, such as the Kentucky State Fiddle Championship prize I won. I made a trip to Monroe, Louisiana, for their state contest, which took place at the Louisiana State Fair. I got over to Memphis and drove down with the Morton twins and their mother. The group we formed won the band competition. For the fiddle division — Benny won it this time. Barrett got 2nd. My 3rd place over Terry Morris' 4th place finish meant our rivalry of the young guns continued outside the Texas border-line. At yet another big regional contest during the same time period, one in Ogden, Utah, I beat Dick Barrett for 1st place. I was emphatically making the case for contest success.

Without much going on in Nashville, though, I began to lose interest in practicing every day like I once did. Days might go by and I might not even touch my instruments. It seemed like *being* in Music City and *not* getting to play was far less motivational than being in Seattle and *dreaming* about going to Music City one day. At least to a kid.

Exasperated by not getting any leads for performing or recording in Nashville, by late December 1975, we made the long drive back to Seattle, and for the rest of 9th grade. Mom promised that I could still travel on my own to the biggest fiddle contests around the country.

F IDDLE CONTESTS, HOWEVER, once an All-American safe haven for me, started to get a bit more unsettled by the time of America's bicentennial year of 1976. Some of the older fiddlers started to tire of "the kid" getting so much attention everywhere, during which time I was routinely beating them in the fiddle contests. For some of those fiddlers, it meant that I was going to receive some additional interest they hadn't given me before. A good case for this new attentiveness could be made in New Mexico, where I went up against another big field of competitors in the Open division. The big regional contest took place in a little town called Truth or Consequences. By '76, this contest had been going strong for years. It was the same venue where Byron, as a youngster, first met Benny in the 1950s. Now, 20 years later, at my age of 14, it would be the third time in about as many months beating both Dick Barrett and Terry Morris in a big championship. Texas fiddlers were getting irritated by their prospects anymore, what with the "boy champion" from Seattle swiping away the prize money at the biggest fiddle conventions across the South. What happened to me in Truth or Consequences was noteworthy, and it revealed signs of more prickly times ahead.

When Mom dropped me off at the airport, she trusted that the older fiddlers would watch out for me as well as they could. Fiddling friend Junior Daugherty, usually placing in the top 10 or 20 at these big contests, lived in Las Cruces, and was given the enviable task of keeping me out of trouble for the weekend. However, he couldn't watch me every minute of the day. I was particularly excited about being there because I got to play against Terry Morris again—that was exciting for me and kept me well motivated. Benny said that I was going to have the advantage against Terry in most any state other than Texas, so here we were—yet another contest outside of Texas. Terry was leaving his safe harbor to poach a few outside the line. I suppose I was sort of doing that, too. But at this stage, there was no similar sanctuary for me where I lived.

Benny's teacher and mentor, Eck Robertson, was in attendance at Truth or Consequences. He was such a genial old man to meet for the first time. Born in 1887, Robertson was just a couple years older than my grandma Helen Adriance Storm, who was raised in Memphis, near his native Arkansas. "Uncle Eck," as Benny called him, made history in 1922 by becoming the first recording artist in country music. He and his accompanist, Henry Gilliland, drove a Ford Model T from Texas all the way to New York City, just to knock on the door of the Victor Talking Machine Company. He wanted his fiddling captured on the new recording device he'd heard about. Finding this largely unknown fiddler a bit curious, if not rough around the edges, especially with the Confederate regalia worn by his much older, Civil War-era accompanist, they informed Eck that he would have to audition before anything like that were to happen. The audition was set up for the following day. Shortly after, fiddling history was made. Eck Robertson recorded tunes such as "Arkansas Traveler," "Turkey in the Straw," "Billy in the Low Ground," "Sally Johnson," "Done Gone," "Ragtime Annie" and his classic unaccompanied 13 variations of "Sallie Gooden." He blazed a trail with the Texas-style genre, handing it off to his protégé, Benny Thomasson, to blow the thing wide open.

During the contest, 89-year-old "Uncle Eck" sat near the front of the stage in his wheel chair. It was exciting to play in front of him looking on, a man who was entering fiddle contests as early as the turn of the century.

I was feeling more or less unrestricted at this contest, you could say—feeling no pain while I was at it. I thought my rounds were going well as the day went along—but this may have been a bit of a false impression, or at least a *sozzled* one. It turned out that some of the other Texas fiddlers had already been *spiking* my cups of Coca-Cola with hard booze during the day. I had wondered why my speech was slurring a little. I was already competing while rankly *compromised.*

For the contest, I chose Christie Barrett as my accompanist, Dick's daughter. She was a very good guitar accompanist, who was several years older than I was, and a lot of fun to be around, at least when her Dad wasn't right there. I had to ask Dick's permission for her to play with me, as she said it would be appropriate to do so. Dick agreed to let her accompany me, if I paid her, of course. There weren't many good guitar accompanists at this contest, so I went without any second guitar.

Christie Barrett didn't attend very many contests, but I saw her at a few here and there. I only had a small window of time with her to go through my rounds, once Dick was finally done with her. It was a little nerve wracking because she obviously knew his tunes and renditions much better than mine.

While Dick evidently quit drinking by that point, his replacement habit was chewing tobacco. Once we got into the late afternoon hours, Barrett urged me to try chewing some of his tobacco with him. *You know, like the other fiddlers did...* Why even Christie chewed some *baccy.* So, I wanted to show him that I was a big man and could do it, no problem. My spiked Cokes were causing me to take more chances. I dipped and chewed for the first time in New Mexico. As a consequence of that, I got sick and threw up right before I had to play my semi-final round.

By the time I got to the last round of the championship—competing while tipsy and recovering from barfing up tobacco chaw, it would be an understatement to say I was playing about as *wild* as I've ever played the fiddle. As I stumbled onto the stage for the awards ceremony, I ended up getting 2nd place in the Open. This time I lost to Dale Morris, but I still beat Dick, coming in at 3rd and Terry coming in 4th. I had a real chance to win this one if it were not for all of the unethical behavior going on. Mom won't be happy to learn about all the dirty tricks, so it will remain a secret. But spiking a 14-year-old's *Coke* with alcohol from their flasks, so they could beat him in the fiddle contest? Well it didn't quite work out for them, anyway. Maybe Uncle Eck, a contest fiddler who had seen plenty of high jinks in his day, saw worse. But I doubted it.

I was willing to forgive and forget the grownups. I just needed to be a little smarter next time (and put a stupid lid on my cups of Coke—*and get a straw),* but Dick Barrett wasn't quite finished with me yet. Ol' Dick was not taking the contest results well—his third straight loss to me in these big events. His little maneuver with the tobacco rub may have put me on my back for a moment, but it fell short. Most of the time, fiddlers who placed in the prize money give their accompanists $20 or $30. If the accompanists play behind several fiddlers, it adds up to something substantial and can pay their way to attend the contests, plus a little to take home. I understood the tradition well by then—I often accompanied fiddlers, too.

After the contest was over, I made sure I put my 2nd place check safely in my wallet. But Dick and *his* 3rd place check found me in the lobby and took me aside to have a little talk.

"Mark, you just gave Christie $30 to play with you."

"Yes?"

"She doesn't know I am talking to you about this, but that is not enough for what she did for you. You know that, don't you?"

"Uh...Yeah?"

"That's right, you do know that. You need to pay her more than what you paid her."

"How much do you think I should pay her then?"

"Well, how about one-third of your prize money? Don't you think that would be fair in this situation?"

"I guess so."

As I was shaken down by Dick Barrett, I wanted to pretty much say about anything to get out of the tight spot he was putting me in. And of course I needed all of that prize money to pay for my plane ticket. But I forked over every bit of cash I had on me from my record sales in the lobby. I really liked Christie, but I never asked her to back me up again in a contest. I couldn't afford her father.

This new form of psyching out the 14-year-old was becoming normalized patterns at fiddle contests: the monkey business of spiking my drinks, intimidating me into dipping snuff like the older fiddlers. Some of those grown men were feeding me beers at the late-night jam sessions. No doubt suspecting a sufficient teenage hangover during the morning contest rounds. But the business of going toe-to-toe with the legends at the notorious, after-hours Texas fiddle jams, might have been worth all the rawhiding and horsewhipping in 1976. The fiddling version of *cutting contests* was the stuff of fiddling fables.

All the mischievousness, though, was backdropped by full-throated belly laughter and great Texas-style fiddling. The late-night jams were fiddle contests in and of themselves. Everyone knew who had the edge before we ever got on stage to compete.

I AM NOT AT ALL SURE IF impropriety or puckishness ever caused me to perform *badly,* but what it did do was to send me down the path of a much more pumped and extemporal fiddle playing that was going to hurt my contest results in short order. As I got more interested in jazz and swing violin, a kind of *uncontrolled* improvisatory nature began to take over on my breakdowns and tunes of choice, and really everything I was playing. Even though I was plenty warned by the contest fiddlers who occasionally judged me, some of those who cared about me, I started to lose more and more contests, especially by the time I was 14.

The word on the circuit was; *"If only he could play like he was 13 again."*

Dale Morris finished on top in Truth or Consequences. The judges probably liked his straightforward no-nonsense approach to the tunes. I wanted to get away from Barrett after the contest as fast as I could, so I hung around with the winner, Dale. He said to me, "Help me find Terry — I don't know where he's gone off to." We looked in the motel bar where some of the other fiddlers had congregated. Not there. We went to Dale and Terry's room. Dale unlocked the door to find Terry in bed, fully clothed, the covers pulled up over him and his bull-rider cowboy hat over his face. He was crying—I couldn't imagine for how long. Dale went straight to the edge of the bed and sat down by his brother to console him. I remained standing in the doorway.

I thought at first that Terry was faking it—or something… and just pretended to be crying—maybe giving his brother a hard time for winning? But the more this went on, the more it became very clear. In a sobbing voice, Terry blurted out in his very thick Texas accent, *"These damn fiddle contests."*

I did feel badly for Terry, as I admired him, too. He took this loss extremely hard. Terry was a considerable competitor, that was for sure, and he won practically every time he ever entered a fiddle contest in his home state of Texas. They loved him and coddled him there. I was having a different experience in my home state. But he could not bring himself to be happy in the immediate moments for his big brother winning the championship.

Dale continued to show a lot of compassion for him. He wanted me to step forward and say something to Terry in their motel room that night— he wanted me to agree with him that *contests didn't really mean anything at all*—hoping it would cheer Terry up. So I did just that—I parroted Dale for their sake, even though for me, they meant the whole shooting match. In every single way. Frankly, I was proud to beat Terry in those contests as a 14-year-old. I survived all of their game-playing, head trips, intimidation, hogging of the accompanists, spiking my soda drinks, luring me into dipping snuff, shaking me down for money, getting me to drink with them late at night, not letting a young teenager get enough sleep… and then to come out near the top like I did? I was rightly pleased.

This very personal story connecting Terry to that day in Truth or Consequences is only meant to illustrate the great significance that fiddle contests had on its champions by the mid-1970s, despite what any of us said out loud about them. The *awe shucks—it's just for fun* manner of talking points… that was all for show, for the newspapers and for the fans. The fiddle champions took it as seriously as any person entered in competitive events could, easily as consequential for the younger ones as for the old-timers and gatekeepers. It was a way of life for those of us who found our-selves good enough to place in the prize money every time. It became a craving—especially when winning the kind of money that the '70s era con-tests provided—equal to a month or two months of labor back home. When you were that good, you kept showing up, and that is what we did.

But what was most revealing to me about that hobbled day was that Terry could bring himself to cry over a fiddle contest, while I could never summon that, even as a kid. I am quite sure those contests meant as much to me as they did to him, but I couldn't let myself sob over much of any-thing at age 14. I was so hardened by my family life with its abusive alco-holism, coarsened by school bullying, and castigated by my home town music circles, literally pushing me out of the music scene in Seattle. Now, I was rejected in Nashville to the point where my family had to move back to Seattle, a place where I definitely didn't want to be—a city I had already given up on for my music. I developed a fairly thick skin at that young age. It probably wasn't healthy, personally... I couldn't remember the last time I shed tears about anything. Probably when I got beaten up at school a couple years ago. I just put all of the emotions I had into the fiddle itself.

Terry, being 20, exhibited all of the Texas fiddler *machismo* qualities that I was envious of, though. But some of that, I could guess now, was just an outward appearance. Inside, he was that boy-genius fiddler, fitted into a "cowboy suit" with a bull-rider hat on. Was Terry a bull rider? Was I a bull rider? Because I wore a hat just like Terry has? In those moments, that is all I wanted to be, too—a fiddler in a cowboy suit, wearing a rodeo-style belt buckle. Just like Terry.

I related to Terry in our collective crossroads. I felt a special connec-tion, even more so now because I could see his vulnerability as a young man—of someone I looked up to. We were kindred spirits in some ways.

I started to get an idea about us recording together on that night he was suffering so. I thought this recording idea would make him happy. It was going to be with Terry, not Dale.

MOM AND I HATCHED an idea for a new recording: *A Texas Jam Session – Four World Champion Fiddlers*. The recording was to feature Benny, as well as our new friends, James "Texas Shorty" Chancel-lor, and Terry Morris. I was so excited. My third album was on its way.

In the days leading up to the recording, we saw Terry win the 1976 World Fiddling Championships in the little town of Crockett, Texas. The same place where Shorty had earned his title the decade before, and Benny the decade before him. Benny was the first to win the mandatory "three-in-a-row" to qualify as world champ, Shorty to follow. This year it was the third time's a charm for Terry. All three men had one thing in common when it came to *this* world championship: each of them were Texas born and raised nearby. Benny warned me not to attend, but what the heck, I did anyway.

Crockett, Texas, represented quintessential Texas fiddling culture. The little town was named after the American war hero and Tennessee "fiddle legend," Davy Crockett, just for the reason that he camped there overnight on his way to defend The Alamo. Davy was a hero of three wars fighting for America's freedom. He was also quite a fiddler himself, a music star, and a champion buck dancer. In yet another facet of his accomplished life, the frontiersman represented his home of "Nashboro" as Congressman—the original name for Nashville, before so many towns were renamed using the French, "ville"—a *je vous remercie beaucoup* for taking the fight to the British and all their "boros." In a contradictive balance of opposite forces, the town of Crockett was also known as a training site for the Confederate conscripts during the Civil War.

When we arrived to where the fiddle contest was staged, at a little town park, the atmosphere of fiddle enthusiasts felt quite different than Seattle, or Nashville… different than most places I'd been. But there was Terry jamming on his fiddle behind the outdoor stage. He spotted me as I approached him:

"You're a long way from home aren't ya?" Terry assessed me with a bit of apprehensiveness.

"Yeah, I sure am!"

He clearly didn't think I was going to be in his home state of Texas to challenge him for his world championship. If things worked out for him, it would be his third time to cinch it for good. We certainly did come a long way from home, driving down from Seattle… but it turned out to be worthwhile. I won my division. I became the *Junior* World Fiddle Champion in Crockett.

It wasn't one of those kids divisions, either—I was one of only a handful of teens in the entire place. The "Juniors" in Crocket was more like middle-aged and under—I mean it was up there. Regardless, they were saving Terry for the final play-off round that was afforded the defending champion. In my division, Ken Smith, a teenager from Louisiana, came in 2nd to me—he was just a few years older. He had gotten 5th place in the Juniors at Weiser to my 1st place that year. He didn't do well over in Monroe at the Louisiana State Fair either, his home-state contest. This certainly wasn't the stiff competition we expected at a place like Crockett.

It must be confessed, and despite what they've named their contest, this was rather a small-town affair. The prize money was a pittance—not much more than $200 if you won everything. The "championships" must have dwindled since its heyday, feeling more like a small shadow of the legendary competition we'd always heard about—the place where Benny and Major played repeated tie-breakers and whipped up all the mythos. The pocket-sized afternoon had an audience of a hundred or so at its peak. Most of the time we were playing to a lot less. Folks seemed to just be walking up from the town. Free to the public. None of the Texas fiddle legends attended, unlike the Grand Masters where they all seemed to come.

In spite of my good result in the "Juniors," a little later that afternoon the Crockett contest's master plan was fully revealed and my fate was sealed. In the following round to determine the "champion of the day," the Texas judges chose Ken Smith to face off with Terry Morris for the noteworthy one-on-one playoff for the world championship. *It's the darndest thing I have ever seen,"* echoed a few new supporters of mine, hoping for a showdown between the two wunderkinds of fiddling. This way, however, the Texas contest organizers could rescue that small audience from an exciting and contested final, allowing Terry a luxury cruise right on to the win.

We lingered afterwards to say goodbye to some new friends. Terry was the top dog all right and it was memorable to see him play in his absolute element—in his home state of Texas. I was glad to witness it, as it remained fixed in my mind. He was very gracious to me afterwards.

"Hey Mark, that turned out interesting, didn't it?" Terry leaned over to me, speaking in a hushed voice.

Well, yes you could say that. Yes indeed.

What a showdown that would have been though, a playoff between the two of us for the prize in Texas. They would've been talking about that for years, no matter who won. But the organizers and judges said, *"naaah."* It was much better to make me pay for that raw deal up there in Nashville where I beat Terry the first time. Why, it must have been unforgiveable to them.

As things in Crockett were winding down that day, some folks were curious why I even came. They knew we had driven a long way, farther than anyone else that day to be sure, just to be treated this way by their own fiddle contest heritage protectors.

"We never get Yankees down here entering this contest," an attendee offered up.

"So, nobody from up north ever comes to the world championships?" I asked.

A more sympathetic attendee interjected: "Your fate was sealed as soon as they heard that white fiddle from across the field."

It would be years before I returned to compete in Texas after that. Benny was portentous about me entering Texas contests, however, I did come back several years later to win the Sun Bowl Winter-National Fiddle Contest in El Paso. Unlike Crockett, the judging was handled by top men of fiddling: Benny Thomasson, Herman Johnson, and Byron Berline. I won this one—the biggest purse in Texas fiddle contest history: $1,500 for 1st place. I guess I had to prove Benny wrong at least one time.

PLANNING OUR DRIVE to Tennessee for the Grand Masters, I was going to be a judge this time, even at 14—the head judge granted me by winning the year before. Terry asked if he could hop a ride with us to Nashville. We said, "Sure, c'mon!" Despite being disappointed with my Texas fiddle contest debut, still the best way to make good friends on this circuit was to lose—and to be a judge in the next contest coming up. On the 12-hour drive over, Mom and I talked to Terry more about the recording idea with Benny and Shorty—to recreate a jam session in the studio. Mom dubbed it *A Texas Jam Session.* Terry liked what he heard. Mom also got Terry to help drive the Ford Econoline, too. It was probably good form to hide my own driving protocols.

Once at the Nashville recording session, Terry and I played rhythm guitar and mandolin for Benny and Shorty. For the tunes that involved all four of us trading off the fiddle solos, Terry played guitar on a portion of it and then grabbed the fiddle for his solo break. I did the same. On tape, we captured what it was like to be present at an authentic Texas fiddle jam, but with top studio quality sound. Mom was just having the time of her life. She was producing it and directing traffic. She asked for some of the folks in the control room looking on to stand right there in the recording room to give us the feeling of being in a jam session environment. Folks yelled out during the recording when the fiddling got hot. All of those vocal reactions became a part of the recorded performances.

Terry was an absolute ham, hollering out loud the entire session, even while he was playing the fiddle. Mom and I gave him permission to turn it on with the yaupin'. Benny followed suit. He took off on Terry's slapstick while offering his own species of shrieks and bellows throughout. I felt so happy for Benny at the recording. He was having the best time being around all his protégés, recording the renditions and styles of tunes that he put on the map: "Billy in the Low Ground," "Sally Johnson." So much joviality and ebullience.

Texas fiddler Bartow Riley, who stayed around to give Terry a ride back to Texas, added some guitar on the four-fiddler selections, and Benny's son Jerry played the tenor guitar throughout the recording. I took a couple of guitar solos on the record with Jerry accompanying me, then he, Sandra, and the kids sang a song to conclude, just as we were accustomed to by now. *A Texas Fiddle Jam* was one of my mom's crowning achievements with the fiddlers who we admired and got to know. She brainstormed it with me, along with some of the best fiddle tune players of all time.

Rounder Records released my previous two LPs, but was set aside for this one after they criticized the master tape—too many vocal interruptions. They didn't "get" the jam-session elements we strived for. Mom learned that we could release this record on our own label, one that we could create together. We named our new record label by using the first syllable of my last name and the first syllable of Mom's maiden name.

(O)'Connor and (Mac)Donald = OMAC Records.

We had our first *indie* label release in 1976.

W E WERE EXCITED by our first recording effort for OMAC Records, so we immediately planned our second one—a live concert recording with two bluegrass fiddle masters and national champions—Byron Berline and Sam Bush. The live concerts were presented in Seattle and Spokane, and taped with a friend's reel-to-reel recorder. The no-frills audio without any re-mix made it another shoo-in to release on OMAC— again a low-budget affair. The shows we hosted went so well, we figured out a way to host Charlie and Os that year too, and another concert with "Uncle" Josh Graves. If we couldn't find a way to succeed in Nashville, the Nashville musicians were coming all the way to Seattle to play with me.

The Josh Graves invitation was particularly eye-opening, though. I liked his playing on the Flatt and Scruggs records, and played with him a little on the circuit in and around Lester Flatt's Nashville Grass, but didn't know him well. We picked him up from the airport and dropped him off at a Seattle hotel. Since Mom and I were going to be involved with setting up the show, he insisted that he'd catch his own taxi down to the venue for rehearsal and soundcheck. He never showed. Mom was baffled, it was 30 minutes to showtime. We were panicking, there was no answer at his hotel room. I began to know enough about some of the bluegrass musicians by then, and told Mom that we needed to drive over to his hotel and check the bar. He might be there. She had a hard time believing that, but she had to trust me, with no other good option available. We went in, and sure enough, Uncle Josh was seated at the bar. He wasn't only sloshed, he didn't have his teeth in. The imagery he projected was the drunken smile of a clown, a vestige of the old entertainment persona he used to inhabit in Flatt and Scruggs. The concert started late.

With the two additional OMAC albums featuring great musicians playing top-notch traditional music, I doubled my sales on the road. My Dad customized "metal cam" cinching box straps, affixed with leather guitar case handles. I no longer needed both hands to carry the single heavy box of 50 LPs through airports and festival grounds. My Rounder LPs cost quite a bit more to purchase for resale—buy for $2 and sell for $4. I had much larger profit margins on the OMAC albums once our recording expenses were recouped, and those were nominal. The vinyl cost us just cents to purchase, not dollars. I launched my "indie" label long before it was fashionable.

HANGING OUT, TOOLING around at the Days Inn motel parking lot during the fall of 1976, sometimes for days at a time, gave me a chance to fully reflect on what had happened to me in professional blue-grass music that summer.

Oh yes, this was my family's second attempt in as many years to move to Nashville—we were here again. We were also waiting for a monthly apartment rental to become available. I never told my mother about half the things I encountered on the festival circuit that summer, for fear she would shut it all down and not let me go on the road again. Those top bluegrass bands didn't pay me much to play, but I was having a good time performing on the festival stages and sneaking in a few contests along the way, and I could sell my albums at the merch tables. For a 14-year-old kid, what more could you ask for?

My mother was plenty happy that I was playing with the top bluegrass bands at summer festivals. The Uncle Josh incident set aside, she believed it to be a righteous and wholesome entertainment—all about *family tradition*. This notion empowered Mom to continue having me go on tour without any parental supervision. Her theory was borne out in the gospel music sets we often played. Not many bluegrassers could ever turn away from this material: "River of Jordan," "There's a Light Guiding Me." However, that didn't mean everyone in the Virginia Boys lived a life according to the *gospel sets.*

On one particular run with the Virginia Boys, my bandmate and room-mate liked to hit the sauce pretty hard himself. When we were back in our room, perhaps it was simply out of politeness that he offered me a sip out of his hip flask practically every time he unscrewed the top. Like a good little boy, I kept saying no. Politely. *"No thanks."* In response to it, he might sling a little grin my way and predict, *"It's just a matter of time, just a matter of time,"* as he opened 'er up to take another swig. By this specific month of my 14th year, I had never willingly tasted a hard drink before, other than in my Coke which had been spiked by some contest fiddlers. Recalling what Jesse McReynolds said to me in the Berkshires—"Well

Mark, they're just not going to let you get away from that lightning, are they?"—I thought, Yeah, *"white lightning* at that."

When he got loaded, my roomie seemed like a good-naturedly happy drunk, unlike my Dad. Of course it was untoward that he could not curb the booze while rooming with the kid in the band, but this was the "big time" in bluegrass and I was not about to inconvenience any of the adults with the issue. But, oh how I wished the man's escapades could've ended there. At the bluegrass festivals, he always seemed to be on a serious prowl for women. He advised that the festivals in the "Deep South" especially, were great for picking up the ladies. I braced myself when we played blue-grass festivals in the Deep South because his chances improved mightily—according to his own tabulations. I was pulling for him to be on good be-havior, and for me to have a quiet night back at the motel room.

Many of his pursuits didn't pan out. He wasn't the most handsome guy to ever walk the face of the earth, so I was thankful for that. But once in a while his propositions delivered. He usually worked it out with me to not come back to our room until a specified time, until he was finished with his date. "You're cool?" "Yeah, I'm cool." I sometimes hung out on the bus, but they didn't keep the generator on overnight, so it was really hot in there. If the bus was parked back at the festival overnight, I just roamed around outside of the motel by myself. More asphalt parking lots—*it felt like home.* Hopefully, I might run into some festival folks who just hap-pened to be hanging outside their room at the late hour, and that way I had someone to talk with to pass the time.

The gospel sets were much more prevalent at the southern festivals than anywhere else. Several of the top bands booked them as part of their weekend package; either performing two sets on a Saturday with the third set on the Sunday, or sets on Friday and Saturday with the add-on for the "Lord's day" as some of them described it, that being the gospel set day for us. We played all of those nice songs about Jesus that Mom loved on our bluegrass recordings at home. But during this particular run with the band, I began to dread the gospel sets because it gave my bandmate an extra night to find a date. Otherwise, we would be pulling out after our Saturday night show and driving through the night. I loved that part—driving through the night. It made me feel all grown up.

At one particular festival in the Deep South, we were back at the motel after our Saturday night show. I was in the room on my bed watching TV when my bunkmate walked in. He sat down on his bed across from mine and told me he had "a young lovely" coming to our room in a few minutes. "She's just down the hall waitin' for me." He explained that she didn't have any place to sleep that night, so he invited her to spend the night with him—with us. "You mean right there?" I asked incredulously, pointing to his bed. I conveyed to him that I was kind of tired and needed to get some sleep for our gospel set in the morning. We needed to be ready for songs like "When My Savior Reached Down for Me." But he wasn't asking me to scram and find something else to do at midnight. The man was either too tight-fisted to look into renting another room, or maybe the motel was sold out because of the festival… but there seemed to be no other option for him, or for me, other than to have her stay the night. He suggested that I "stay right there, we'll turn off the lights and you'll probably be fast asleep in no time." He added, "We'll be real quiet."

Well, I did not go fast to sleep, at all. I was petrified. She was a very young girl too, under age. She said hi to me as he walked her in. The girl could not have been but a couple years older than I was. He turned out the lights and they started to make out, and I was *freaked out.* Disgusted. My voice cracked in the darkness: "Do you know how long you're going to be—before you go to sleep?" "Mark, remember she is spending the night, just ignore us and go to sleep." Not being able to wake anyone else at this late hour to help me—it would surely expose this whole situation. I didn't want to be a troublemaker kid, either. I really wanted to be treated as an adult, as much as was possible. Otherwise, I was afraid of getting booted out of the band if I didn't play along with the adult antics. My Dad told me to never rat on anyone… There'd be paybacks.

While they were going strong, I got up from the bed, pushed the top mattress off and stood it up against the wall. Then I took the box springs and stood it on end between the two beds, creating a partition. I put the mattress back on the bed frame and tried to sleep through all of the moaning after that. He blurted out, "Mark, you didn't have to go to all that trouble, we'll try to stay under the covers." I replied, "No, it will be better this way." At least I wouldn't be seeing them out of the corner of my eye.

I couldn't sleep very much. I just laid there and *dreamed* about playing my fiddle and my guitar as best as I could and just tried to tune it out like he said to. The power of mind control. I simply could not tell my mother about this, because it would surely ruin my chances of getting to play with Jim & Jesse again. It wasn't my first road secret I had to keep from her, but it was a big one. I was quite traumatized by it all, and the memory of that night haunted me for a very long time.

AFTER THE GOSPEL SET the following morning, Jim and Jesse were intending to spend the afternoon in the area and have the bus engine looked at. We had the week off until Thursday, but I wanted to get out of there. Bill Monroe's son James Monroe and his Midnight Ramblers played a gospel set that morning as well. They were heading out to Nashville in their tour bus right after the Gospel finale sing-a-long had wrapped. By then, I was friendly with some of the band members on the festival circuit, so I asked if I could hop a ride. I was staying at Bill and Bonnie's that week. "Come aboard," they said. "James won't mind." I called Mom over my new travel plan that day—catching a ride with the *son* of the "Father of Bluegrass Music." She thought it sounded exciting and a chance to enjoy the company of another big-time bluegrass band. She was glad to know they played a gospel set, too.

Mom was so single-minded on this "gospel-wholesome family tradition" stuff. Her ferocity on the subject could likely be traced to a whole other kind of family back in Seattle: The Love Family. Not too far from us in the Seattle suburbs was a hippie commune called The Love Family Ranch. Much of the commune seemed musically inclined. The musician members of this "ranch" saw me play at a local music event the year before and just fell in love with the boy fiddler. The hippie girls, especially, were fawning all over me. They were begging my mother to bring me out to the Ranch to jam with them, but she was scared witless that I would somehow get swallowed up whole, losing me to this commune. They were winning me over by promising all the homemade ice cream I could consume— and that would have meant quite a bit of ice cream. Disappointed that Mom wouldn't allow me to visit them, three of the girls in their early 20s came over to our house so they could jam with me there. Mom acquiesced. They wanted to work up the Beatles song, "Blackbird." After we had it down pretty nice, they asked if I could record it on our tape deck for them. It was my first engineering job, I guess you could say. They were impressed that I knew just where to place the two mics. The hippie girls wooed me with more promises of ice cream, jamming and fun if I could come over the following weekend. Mom said no thank you, again. Later, she told me that we could never go out to their ranch because she suspected that these girls were "married" to all of the other men in the commune. Yeah, those hippies and their over-sexed environment.

"But the homemade ice cream, Mom?"

James Monroe's tour bus was configured differently. Everybody in ours slept in the bunks, including both Jim and Jesse. For James Monroe, there was a bedroom in the back of the bus where he slept. This was called a "star bus." The band members slept in the bunks towards the front. As we took off for Nashville, I overheard that one of the bandmembers was back in the "star" room with a woman he had met at the bluegrass festival after the gospel set. There were a few snickers and snide remarks, but everyone seemed to be having a good time. We talked mostly about music.

After about an hour or so, the fellow came up from the back bedroom to sit with the rest of us. He ran his fingers through his hair and took a big stretch as he welcomed me onboard for the ride back to Nashville. That was pretty cool, I thought, everybody there kind of *knew* who I was. As he nodded towards the back of the bus, he reported to his bandmates; "She's good." She invited any member of the band to head on back for a visit. She would be willing to see the whole band by the time we made it into Nashville, he advised. The proposition was met positively.

It wasn't but five seconds before there was a taker, thanking his friend as he made his way back there. After about 20 minutes or so, that band member came back up to the front with a grin on his face: "Okay, next." One of the willing bandmates gestured for me to head back myself. The offer caused another's encouragement for me to go for it—that I'll "have a good time with her." I said, "No, that's all right." The other band member said, "Are you sure, because I'll go next if you don't want to," as he craned his head toward the back of the bus. I added, "Go right ahead, I'm okay." "You're sure?" "Yes, I'm sure." As we made it into Nashville proper, half the guys on that bus spent some time with the woman before the first guy felt like it should be his turn again. At this point, my entire view of blue-grass and its family tradition—wholesome—gospel… was utterly warped and grimly adulterated. My outlook was shaken to its core. I was learning what hypocrisy was *all* about.

BEING ON THE ROAD in bluegrass music at age 14 on my own was not everything a mother could have hoped for. I didn't have the emo-tional capacity nor mental defensiveness to know what to do in many of my awkward and even licentious encounters. At still another festival that same summer, this one on an Indian Reservation, I stayed pretty busy at the Great Northern Bluegrass Festival in Mole Lake, Wisconsin. They didn't have a contest there, but I ended up playing with several acts on stage, sometimes even for only one fiddle tune: J.D. Crowe and the New South, John Hartford… I helped Vassar Clements for the entire set on gui-tar, and, even played guitar with Benny Martin for his set—the legendary country and bluegrass fiddler whose signature "Me and My Fiddle" was one I heard often growing up. Finally, I ended up sitting in with a band that I hadn't heard of before, the Morgan Brothers.

"The Father of Bluegrass" Bill Monroe asked me to come on his bus to talk with him for a while—probably wanted to know why a kid was so "in demand" there at the festival he was headlining. Like some of the other tour busses on the grounds, Mr. Monroe's was parked a good ways back from the stage behind the audience fence line. I gladly answered the call.

I took a seat on one side of the kitchen table while Mr. Monroe sat directly across from me, and to his side, an attractive young lady. Monroe was about 65, the young lady was probably in her 20s. I wondered if she was *"like a relative."* Maybe an assistant who sold the merchandise… or something? There was just the three of us on the bus while I was there. After getting to talk music with the bluegrass legend for about 15 or 20 minutes, occasionally interspersed with some light flirting between the young lady and Mr. Monroe, he announced that they had to "take care of something" in the back of the bus. I noticed it was a "star bus" like his son traveled in. However, he told me, "Stay right here and wait for me. I want to finish speaking with you, young man—if that's all right with you?" "Sure, that's fine," I responded.

192

Both Bill Monroe and the young lady got up from the seat bench and headed to the back. I believed that the "taking care of something" was not something related to sex or anything—at least not while I was there by myself. Certainly not *like father, like son?* I hoped. As I was sitting at the kitchen table, I was left to just twiddle my thumbs. I turned around to see if I could notice anything interesting, instruments, musical equipment of any kind... Then from a complete standstill, the once motionless coach waggled a couple of times at first, then it began to gently sway—back and forth. Soon, the bus was swinging from side to side. After a while, I couldn't help but notice that all the *rolling* was at a pretty steady clip, too, the *timing* was solid. Roll on buddy. You could even say it was a little like Bill Monroe's mandolin rhythm—just driving it like a muleskinner. Like he was known for? I sat there pretending not to be affected by it too much. I shouldn't be embarrassed, no one could see me. But I was. I just waited... *and* waited longer.

I thought about exiting out of the bus, but would he ever invite me on again if I ditched our visit without saying goodbye? I didn't have the answer. So I hung on for the "Father of Bluegrass." To pass the time, I started to just roll with it. I was humming some of my favorite Monroe tunes to the rhythm of the rocking bus. In one sense, I guess you could say I was jamming to "Big Mon's" great rhythmic feel. I was harmonizing to some "Drifting Too Far from the Shore." Then after a while, I could only picture some "Raw Hide," and definitely "Big Mon."

Eventually, they did come back up to the front. Bill Monroe and the young lady seemed like they were tucking in their garments, making final adjustments to their clothing as they walked down the bus aisle. After they took their same places at the kitchen table, as if what just happened was absolutely normal, we resumed our conversation about his bluegrass music posthaste. I discovered why he wanted me to stay put. He brought his mandolin out. He wanted to show me some tunes he had just written. He loved writing *fiddle tunes* on his mandolin. Soon after, Bill Monroe finished up with me; and he wished me a good day.

I left with an irregular bluegrass music lesson and a sense that he appreciated my talent for his music. He was well impressed by how some of those festival acts were getting me on stage with them that weekend, but he wasn't entirely pleased with all of them, either. He said that a lot of it wasn't at all to his liking. He did recognize that I could play a fiddle tune really well, hence my invitation for the *ride* in his bus, but he refused to accept that "Newgrass" music was a spin-off of what he did. He told me he couldn't even call that *real* music. Depraved and dishonorable, I'm sure. Unwholesome, and even perverted.

It was... *"No part of nothin'."*

"Roll on, buddy, roll on, wouldn't roll so slow, if you knew what I know, so roll on, buddy, roll on." -Bill Monroe, James Monroe

LATER THAT NIGHT, I was hanging out with Brian Bowers of Seattle, a fine autoharpist and one of those festival acts who had me play a couple on stage with him. I couldn't speculate as to what Monroe thought of Brian Bowers; but at least it wasn't "Newgrass," I reckoned. After I sat in with the final band for the day, Brian coaxed me out onto the festival grounds to this magnificently large Sokaogon Chippewa tipi. The hippies there were hosting a communal jam session in it. Of course we were both welcome to sit in, but we decided to watch for a while. It seemed that Brian's primary motivation for attending the tipi jam was a special hot liquor homebrew that he heard was being served up for any guests who dared savor it. After some indulgence, he nodded to me, suggesting I take a sip. I passed it up. Remember, the Mole Lake Festival was located on an Indian Reservation, so most anything was possible here.

Brian liked me—two guys from Seattle, a fact he was proud of. One of my few Seattle music friends left? He was also the only other national touring act in folk and bluegrass music out of Seattle. A handsome, witty guy who could captivate an entire audience with his solo autoharp, his songs, and his story-telling. It wasn't but a few minutes before a couple of young girls were hanging out with Brian. They seemed quite friendly.

Brian said to the girls, "Meet my friend, Mark." The older of the two came towards me to talk a little. Frieda, 18, was just learning to play the fiddle. After Brian finished the drink he'd been ministering, he suggested that the four of us walk backstage, grab his rental car, and find a local diner for something to eat.

An hour of fun and laughs was punctuated by Brian's zany storytelling; something about sleeping with a man once, to which he amended that he liked women better. A pickup line? I laughed nervously, then realized maybe I shouldn't have. We headed back to the festival grounds. On the way, Brian pulled over to the side of the unlighted highway and announced, "Excuse me ladies, but nature *is* calling. Mark, need to take a leak? Why don't you join me." As we were taking a whiz into some tall grass, baring all for most any driver who passed us by, the two girls waited for us in the car. Brian turned to me and said:

"That girl wants you, Mark! She is eating you up my man! I think we've got to do something about this, right? Why don't we go back to my room and take this a little bit further. You know what I'm talkin' about?"

A huge lump came into my throat, as I could only eke out a murmured "okay," just to be agreeable. I wanted to be a grown-up like all the entertainers at bluegrass festivals, so I didn't want to always come off as a stick in the mud in most every social setting I found myself in. Brian added, "I think we should be open to seeing where this leads us." Well, if Mother found out, it could lead to whipping me into some of my own *rawhide*. But, perhaps Mr. Monroe would approve? Frieda was every bit as beautiful as Bill Monroe's girlfriend, undeniably. There was a big age difference between us, too.

Brian's room had only a single bed. Frieda and I sat on the floor at the foot of his bed as Brian flipped off the lights. It was pitch dark in there, I couldn't see a thing... but Frieda and I hugged and kissed a little. She was attractive and quite voluptuous, the kind of older girl that any young boy would ever dream about. I hadn't really kissed a girl for longer than a few seconds before that night. I was petrified that I didn't know what to do after that, though. But I received some pretty good news. She whispered that she was a virgin. To me, at least, that meant she wasn't expecting anything much. Instead, we sat there on the floor embracing, trying not to giggle while having to listen to Brian and Frieda's girlfriend canoodle all night. It started out as fun, I suppose. She definitely was impressed by my fiddling, but the longer the night wore on, the more I ended up being freaked out by the whole situation again. I couldn't leave, as it was the middle of the night and I was staying in another area motel. I didn't want to leave Frieda there alone, and she didn't want to leave her younger girlfriend alone.

As a 14-year-old, I was continually shell-shocked with all the bluegrass festival shagging. I held on, but not without after effects that would last a long time. As I grew older, there were residual effects. My mother was unfortunately wrong about many of those professional singing bluegrass entertainers being moral and righteous, singing the God songs. Not the *safe* bet.

All the monkey business began to sour me on the wholesome and traditional bluegrass-child-musician route. I was evolving—wanting to get a little more serious about music and looking for more progressive outlets to explore for my growing musical appetite. I wanted my young life to be more about musical artistry. For me now, that meant incorporating jazz and swing styles but played on bluegrass instruments. If bluegrass and country music were, as they say, "three chords and the truth," well I'll be darned.

THERE WERE MORE fiddle contests that kept us afloat financially, and afforded me a couple of new instruments I'd been lusting after. I ran into Vince Gill at a Grand Ole Opry bluegrass showcase the summer of 1976. I was playing with Jim & Jesse while 18-year-old Vince was full-time with Lonnie Peerce and The Bluegrass Alliance. I approached him to say hello. Vince was always so chill and laid-back. I gazed at his cool-looking old Martin guitar and asked, "What is that?" Vince responded by saying, *"a '42 'bone"*—acting all cool as a cucumber about it. He only owned the very best vintage Martin guitar for playing bluegrass music. Now, I wanted a WWII era Herringbone Martin D-28, just like his.

Mom permitted me to go over to Gruhn Guitars downtown and spend some of my contest money on an incredible 1945 Herringbone Martin D-28 guitar. Gruhn had let me come in and play it a few times—truly, the guitar of my dreams. The guitar model draws its name from the herringbone purfling inlaid around the edge of the guitar top. I was so thankful to get this guitar. The instrument had so many colors and layers to the sound—the dreadnought tone I was absolutely captivated by. While I was at it, I told Mom that I wanted to buy one additional instrument at Gruhn's—a Gibson 1924 mandocello. I had no real use for it, other than it made me feel happy. Mom detected my mounting distress. Those instruments were rewards for my handiwork out there on the circuit. The mandocello was a very special instrument, I could tell, and I wanted to learn how to play it. For a kid, Gruhn liked me a lot, so he gave me a good deal: $3,500 for the Martin, and $1,700 for the Gibson. I also got ahold of a 1960s era Martin tenor four-string guitar for a couple hundred dollars so I could accompany fiddlers just like Jerry Thomasson did with *his* tenor.

Exploring the pathway of Nashville's finest musicians kept leading me back to Buddy Spicher. Buddy liked my fiddling as a lad and he got together with me several times to work up his twin fiddle tune arrangements. His dream was to get his own country instrumental hit on the radio featuring fiddles. Despite our get-togethers, we never made it into the recording studio.

Not as much of a breakdown fiddler himself, Buddy was quite the *jazz* fiddler. It was when he played jazz tunes that I thought he was at his very best, and now it was what I was most interested in. But at the same time, he was easily the most versatile of all the fiddlers I knew. Being the top session choice, his adjustability was a big asset. I felt I had a similar affinity so Buddy's musical resourcefulness was tremendously inspiring. A few years earlier, on a lark, Buddy traded country for classical lessons with Stephen Clapp, the first violinist of the Blair String Quartet at Vanderbilt University in Nashville. The effort was with the sole purpose of Buddy passing the Nashville Symphony audition. He ended up playing with the orchestra for a year before he returned to full-time country session work.

Buddy hosted a substantial fiddle and bluegrass music competition out at his ranch during the summer of 1976. If I attended a contest that featured multiple instrumental divisions, per usual, I entered them. Creating the impression of being a little bored, I wanted to mix things up a little this time. For the guitar division I played my new tenor guitar instead of the standard six-string, even though I had just acquired the Herringbone. For the mandolin competition, I played the newly acquired mandocello. The Gibson, steel-stringed instrument, is tuned like a cello and requires cello fingering—a lot of use with that fourth finger on string gauges measuring .074 (piano wire). The tenor also necessitates cello fingering. At risk of boredom with old-time and bluegrass genres as a youngster now, it gave me something else to learn. No one at Buddy's ranch had ever seen such instruments. For the fiddle division, I played my *normal* white one, but I threw in all kinds of new jazz licks I'd been working on. Perhaps it delighted Buddy Spicher, but it wasn't going to impress old-time fiddle judges.

My mother warned me, "You're playing way too jazzy to win these fiddle contests now." I insisted that this was how I wanted to play anymore, but I would try to tone it down in the contest rounds. She saw that I was reexamining both my musical foundation and aspirations. I was beginning to drift further away from bluegrass music.

Immediately before the competition got underway at Spicher's ranch, Mom and I eyeballed the most unusual scene. Buddy brought a local preacher up on stage to lead the audience in a prayer specifically for the music contests he was hosting, and a beseeching of the three appointed contest judges. As we all bowed our heads, the preacher asked for God to aid our judges in choosing the best musicians in the competition—that those with the most talent and best performance of the day may win their respective instrumental divisions.

So, instead of being disqualified in the guitar and the mandolin divisions, like I was daring them to do, it turned out that I won them both.

For the fiddle contest, though, and the bigger purse, I came in 2nd to the Alabama fiddle legend and elder statesman, J.T. Perkins, somebody I had already seen at the Grand Masters the year before. J.T. had taught me some of his fine variations on "Cotton Patch Rag." Playing variations on ragtime tunes was a gateway to swing and jazz for the fiddle. Ragtime came from the original term, "ragged time"—swung 8th notes. I loved how one thing in American music always seemed connected to something else. J.T. helped me to understand that with "Cotton Patch."

Buddy, however, was dismayed by the outcome of his own contest.

"I had us pray on it and everything, Mark. If it was truly fair, you should have run away with it," Spicher insisted.

It was an interesting perspective to fully extrapolate at age 14: 1st place in guitar, 1st place in mandolin, and 2nd in fiddle, all in the Open divisions, and all on the same day—but this was a big disappointment? Nevertheless, the results didn't get me any more work in Nashville, nor did Buddy and I get into the studio to make that hit fiddle song of his. So maybe it was a big disappointment.

B Y THAT FALL, WE HAD some more time to look closely at the progress I had made so far, and what my potential was to "make it" as a child musician. As important: if I had the mental stability to "hang in there," given the *certifiable* nature of the music scene, and my own desire to do what it took to progress as a young musician. It was going to be next to impossible to make a living in Nashville as a kid in music (just as the year before).

By the fall of 1976 the festival season for bands like Lonnie Peerce and the Bluegrass Alliance had wrapped up. Rather than the Alliance waiting around to reconstitute the following summer like most bluegrass acts did, the band suffered some kind of revolt. Vince Gill and the other bandmembers left Lonnie to form a swing band on their own they called Lazy River. In support of their band name, they were playing a lot more jazz than bluegrass. Booking week-long club engagements in Kentucky and Missouri that winter, they invited me to join up for a few of them. Their banjoist Bill Millet, who was leading the charge towards more swing and jazz, knew that I was getting into playing this music more and more: standards like "Honeysuckle Rose," "Satin Doll," "Take the 'A' Train," Lady Be Good," and the old jazz classic, "Up the Lazy River." They were all on the setlist. For those longer clubs runs, the band augmented to include more players: Bob Briedenbach, Eric Weber, John Bieser, Frank Heyer, Bruce Cromer and Pat O'Conner. Mom let me go on my own. The entire band stayed in a single house; not much room for my family anyway.

By then I had heard Stephane Grappelli live and was really getting into other jazz violin greats—Stuff Smith, Joe Venuti, and Eddie South's recordings. I got to try out newly-learned swing tunes and licks I was picking off recordings and hoping to improvise more extensively on stage than I had the opportunity to do in bluegrass bands. I was looking to *stretch out.* While the bars in Missouri and Kentucky allowed under-aged kids to perform, as was the case with J.D. Crowe, I had to spend the rest of the evening in the tiny dressing rooms often by myself while the bandmembers milled about at the bar, drinking and hanging out.

Bound by the constant flow of alcoholic beverages for well over a year now, I suppose it was inevitable that on one of those runs, I was going to take my first sips of a Scotch whisky. The venerable Great Midwestern Music Hall in Louisville, Kentucky, that hosted artists from Doc and

Merle Watson to Muddy Waters, seemed like as good a place as any to take the plunge.

A kid with the *spins* believing he was going crazy or worse wasn't the manly profile I was hoping to swagger in front of my new bandmates. I didn't touch a drop of Scotch for quite a few years after that one.

Despite the more beguiling music on stage, and getting to test out my Venuti-styled improvisations on tunes like "Sweet Georgia Brown" and "Caravan," the pay for playing these bars was never enough to support a family in Nashville. My mates were mostly all single men — most of them having to just look out for themselves. Fans bought them drinks in between the sets — a conferment. At any rate, playing swing on stage was thrilling for me as I turned 15. I was catching the bug. I really went for it on every set, too. All the guys got a real charge out of my progress on jazz fiddle.

The Courier-Journal, Louisville, 1976, by Billy Reed

"Asked to talk about his talent, O'Connor is apt to do his 'Aw, shucks' number, smiling and shrugging and acting somewhat embarrassed, as 15-year-olds do sometimes.

'You just gotta have an ear for it, then train your fingers to move,' he said. 'This comes with practice. I just sit down and learn something, I guess it might be part natural ability, 'cause some people can't do it.'

The proprietor of the Great Midwestern Music Hall, Doug Grossman, regards O'Connor as one of the more remarkable fiddlers he has ever seen because 'he can pick up a song he has never heard before, in any style, and play it.'

Right now O'Connor is on his way back to Mountlake Terrace from Nashville, where he played a gig last week...Although his parents worry when he is on the road, they let him travel realizing that he has a leg up on what could be a lucrative career."

BY DECEMBER, WE COULDN'T hold out any longer in Nashville — the second try in as many years. Mom said that we were heading back to Seattle again. There was nothing else for me to do that winter in Nashville other than play in nearby taverns for small amounts of money. We had been gone for six months this time.

Mom was worried about Granny and her health, saying, "She shouldn't be left alone anymore." Mom called the Mountlake Terrace High School to enroll me for the second semester. They informed us that I was going to have to take extra classes and stay after school for an hour each day to make up the first semester. They warned us that once I was in 10th grade, I could not miss more than four days in a quarter or they'd flunk me for the entire quarter. I was hoping they weren't serious. Knowing what we already did, though, the future looked bleak for my return to Seattle.

I took out my frustrations on my sister by teasing her even more than usual. And for that, my mother struck me routinely on my arms with her favorite brass ruler. (Oh, that beast of a ruler). She didn't have it with her for measuring anything other than my arms, that I can tell you.

On the drive back across the country, we had to get through some of the worst days of winter storms we'd experienced. The snow, ice and wind nearly forced our van and small U-Haul trailer to skid off the road more than a few times. Mom had to drive that part of it all the while keeping her golden ruler handy to whack me when she had to. One time she grabbed it and I pulled back. *Thwack,* she got me on the top of my hand that time. By then I was well bruised up and down my arms. I asked her if she really wanted to damage my hands the same way—to the point where I couldn't play music? But all I had to do was "quit the teasing" and mind my mother. The whole thing was all the three of us could handle.

Once or twice, we had to wait it out on the side of the freeway, Mom cutting the engine off so we wouldn't run out of gas out in the middle of nowhere. All we could do was huddle together in the van with every blanket we had. She said we could never make this drive again in the winter. But that wasn't all. This was our last chance for moving the family to Nashville. And Mom was sure that she wouldn't be well enough to drive me much or anywhere again.

We didn't "make it" after all.

In calmer moments during our 3,000 mile journey back to our Seattle home, I reflected on my own bizarre childhood musician years thus far. I was growing a little weary of my chosen path in music. It was hard to make sense of having to make everyone around me feel better about every rough patch I crossed.

One of my most lingering memories from Nashville was all the times we went backstage at the Opry and visited dressing room #1, just so I could play fiddle tunes for Roy. As wealthy as Roy Acuff was, worth tens of millions of dollars, he never helped me out any in the way of remuneration.

One time he reached into his money clip and pulled out a 20 spot for me and shoved it into my hand. "Take Mom and sis out to a nice dinner, won't ya?" I tried not to believe that all of those tunes I played just for Acuff and his friends were worth only twenty bucks. It didn't seem altogether right. I sort of wished Roy hadn't given me that $20 bill, because I feared it may have been my true worth—in Nashville at least.

In country and bluegrass music circles, Roy Acuff and others weren't worried at all about my schooling—that crazy idea of getting through school while keeping up my music. The matter of my education was never on anyone's mind. Just so long as I could draw a bow across a fiddle, I was golden. According to them, I already had everything—I was the "privileged one." My position in the category of musical talent was "enviable." They let me know it.

What I really wanted to do now was learn and play jazz music, and try to get my mind off of other things. There was certainly no money in this kind of music for a kid musician either, but it didn't matter—I didn't have to be the "breadwinner" child musician anymore. Going back to Seattle in full retreat, I couldn't know what was ahead. But whatever was in store, the idea of learning and practicing jazz music made me feel like I was worth something after all I had been through. With the additional responsibility of being self-taught, now I wanted to regain my footing, and music still meant so much to me.

I CONTINUED TO HANG ONTO the music itself at all costs. At age 15, I still had a few avenues to play music with professional musicians. In January and February 1977, the Morgan Brothers hired me for a run of dates in the Chicago and Milwaukee area. I risked being flunked out of my sophomore year in high school over the month-long tour in the Midwest. From Wisconsin themselves, I had met up with the Morgan Brothers at the Mole Lake Bluegrass Festival, where they took a big interest in me. They came up with some bigger shows, including the illustrious University of Chicago Folk Festival on January 28th and 29th, with rising folkies David Bromberg, John Prine, and Steve Goodman on the bill. The Morgan Brothers wanted to feature me in much the same way as Lazy River did. I shared with the band my interest in all the swing tunes I was learning, and my desire to really concentrate on this kind of music now—I wanted to continue to *stretch out.* Traditional bluegrass was beginning to bore me and hold me back. Don Stiernberg, the group's mandolinist, was into the swing style and was a student of jazz mandolin legend Jethro Burns in Evansville, Illinois. Don made sure that I had the forum with his band to experiment with my new repertoire on stage—even for the bigger shows.

Chicago Tribune, Wednesday, January 12, 1977 by Jack Hurst
"'I don't sit down and practice a whole lot,' he admits. 'I just learn stuff and practice it onstage.'

There is increasing variety to the stages he plays. He spent much of last summer in Nashville, where he played on the Grand Ole Opry twice on his own and once with the Opry's bluegrass duo Jim & Jesse.

Next summer he is to become a member of banjo player J.D. Crowe's New South Band of Lexington, KY. Crowe plays bluegrass festivals throughout the U.S."

The J.D. Crowe offer wasn't going to work out. While J.D. was expanding his horizons into more contemporary music now, it was in the country and western direction with steel guitar and drums, not swing and jazz. There was little way for a 15-year-old and his mother to operationalize it—the limited amount of money offered as band salary during the year, and participating in a band full time out of Lexington while living across the country in Seattle.

The Morgan Brothers offer was just for a few weeks. The band included Don's brother John Stiernberg on banjo, Jon Parrish and Ed Biebel on guitars; they were all into jazz as well as bluegrass. I was being billed as a featured guest and getting paid well as a soloist for the tour, not just a bandmember. Don and the band booked a couple nights for us at Charlotte's Web in Rockford, Illinois, the highly-regarded coffee house/tavern music venue where even music legends like Stephane Grappelli and Joe Venuti recently performed.

While most of the Morgan Brothers took the complimentary meals at the Web, the guitarist Eddie always had his Bunsen burner with him. He made his own. Curious, I asked him what he was cooking up—I'd never seen anything like it before. Eddie got me hooked on "health food." Right off, I became a sucker for tamari brown rice, tofu, and the pineapple-co-conut juice to go with it. I came to be a life-long natural foods lover after that.

WHEN WE MADE IT down to the University of Chicago Folk Festival, some genuine serendipity came our way. Just as the band was letting me strut my new Venuti licks on stage, the spectacular jazz violin legend himself, Joe Venuti, was performing at Rick's Café Américain. We all went to see him play on our night off.

Once we arrived at the reputable Chicago jazz room, we were shown our table. The club accommodated ritzy cloth-covered tables, swanky chandeliers, and a compact dance floor nestled in front of the bandstand. It was considerably upscale from the folk music bars I was playing down in Kentucky, the kind where your shoes stick to the floor as you walk across the joint. The evening's music began in short order and Venuti, like Grappelli, blew my mind. I drank in every minute of it.

At 74, Joe Venuti was still playing really well. The father of jazz violin employed aggressive rhythmic refrains, double-stop melodies, and was most known for his trademark up-tempo "hot" jazz violin he helped to popularize.

Born in 1903 in Philadelphia, Joe Venuti's formative years in music were spent playing in the James Campbell School Orchestra string section. Venuti and a fellow violin student in the orchestra, Salvatore Massoro, began to experiment with jazz violin. By 1926, the two friends relocated to New York City, where Massoro changed his name to Eddie Lang and changed his instrument to the guitar. Together they began to make recordings as a duo, Venuti becoming a pioneer of jazz violin, and Lang one of the first single-string guitar soloists. The duo got to perform and record with other jazz greats of the day such as: Bix Beiderbecke, Frankie Trumbauer, Paul Whiteman's orchestra, Benny Goodman, Jack Teagarden, and Bing Crosby, until Lang died from a medical complication as a relatively young man in 1933. Venuti went on to lead his own big band, and by 1944 he was a full-time studio musician at the MGM radio and film studios in Los Angeles. There, he regularly appeared on Bing Crosby's radio shows. After the War, Venuti fell on hard times, suffering alcoholism. However, by the 1960s, he got back to regular touring and recorded with small jazz ensembles all over the U.S. and Europe.

For his backing ensemble that night, he used a Chicago-based jazz trio of piano, upright bass, and drums. Venuti played an acoustic violin fitted with a DeArmond pickup and ran it through a poor-sounding guitar amplifier. Although I wasn't wild about Venuti's electric sound (and neither were my bandmates), I was riveted by every note he was playing. I had my trusty cassette recorder with me and placed it right on top of the tablecloth, its auxiliary microphone propped up beside the tape deck. After the first set was over, I let Don and the guys know that I was heading over to Venuti's table where he had just taken a seat for his meal. I wanted him to sign my white fiddle. I was no longer that shy boy of a few years ago.

"Mr. Venuti, I am a big fan of yours and I was wondering if you would sign my fiddle."

Venuti looked at my white atrocity, grunted, and then motioned for me to hand it to him. Venuti signed it with my Sharpie and shoved them both back at me. That was all *he* wrote. Winding my way back to our table to have the guys see the new signature, I was over the moon. Don said, "You are a brave man to go over there and ask the legend for an autograph while he was having his dinner." Without even balking, I replied: "You only live once!"

NEAR THE BEGINNING OF Joe Venuti's second set, someone from the audience yelled out a request, "Turkey in the Straw!" It caught Venuti's attention, and he paused for a couple of seconds as if he was actually going to consider the request. He turned to his talkback mic and said to the audience;

"I don't know that one, but there's a boy in the audience who probably could play that one for you."

I raised my eyebrows. Looking over to my bandmates, *"He's not talking about me, is he?"* Most everyone nodded, yeah-huh. It was unclear if he was waiting for me to come up on stage that very minute, or not. But it seemed like Venuti was stalling—waiting for something. I asked my friends, *"Do you think this might be one of his practical jokes?"* Hesitating a few seconds before they committed to any definitive answer, a couple of them tightened their faces a little, wondering if it could be. One of them was more optimistic, and thought it might be on the up and up, but other faces morphed into full scale grimaces: "This could be embarrassing for you, Mark."

I went for my fiddle case, because *"I don't care, this is my chance to play with the great Joe Venuti!"* As I was heading to the bandstand, Venuti's ensemble kicked off "Turkey in the Straw," featuring a piano lead. Straight away, Venuti barreled in with a hoedown tune that sounded more like Roy Acuff's "Wabash Cannonball." Was I too late…did I miss the cue? Whatever… I was heading on stage with a jazz violin legend.

By the time Venuti was rounding the second chorus of "Wabash," he was playing a kind of silly little refrain and repeated it incessantly. I waited for his signal. Then he motioned me over to play through his talkback mic—it was a good ten feet down stage from the ensemble. I found it like a magnet. I knew what to do, fully knowing how to bury that thing in my f-hole to get more gain. I needed it going up against his electric setup. On the downbeat of the next chorus, Venuti's playing came to a halt, and he just let me have it.

The jazz trio, by this point, was playing the chord changes to "Ragtime Annie," in D major—Venuti had led them to the tune. So I lit into it and started improvising Texas fiddle, hot swing style—partially inspired by Venuti himself, and some of it take-off style from the Western Swing players like Gimble and Spicher. It was working well, especially since the trio was playing in a kind of "country" groove already. It was right up my alley. As I started to carve up the tune in all kinds of manners, I was winning over the crowd—fabulously. If this was a practical joke, this was not working out for Joe.

My bandmates and I had good reason to believe this might be a practical joke setup: Joe Venuti was famous for them. Most all musicians who followed string jazz had read about his pranks. I knew most of them. There was one caper he pulled, calling dozens of upright bass players from the musicians' union for a date in New York City. They showed up at the venue only to find a set of locked doors. Venuti rented out a hotel room across the street so he could watch all the musicians pile up on the corner with their double basses in tow, waiting for someone to let them in.

Another time, Venuti was playing a week-long engagement, but didn't care much for the elderly bass player hired for him. Since the fellow kept his upright bass on stage overnight, leaning up in the corner, Venuti got the idea to pour a little sand into the f-hole of the bass, causing the instrument to grow heavier with each day. By the end of the week, the poor fellow believed he was becoming so feeble he could barely lift his own bass anymore. Venuti definitely had it out for the bass men.

While I was playing the chorus on the tune, the crowd was loving it, and Joe had heard enough. Venuti came in on the downbeat swinging—playing that same dumb lick up high just to drown me out. When I hoped that this might be a legitimate invitation to trade some licks with the master, the song suddenly changed keys. I was left to find it as quickly as I could. I resumed soloing almost immediately in the modulated key and accomplished it, hardly missing a measure.

My bandmates taking in all the roguery from back at our table told me that Venuti was signaling his trio to modulate to another key while I was playing. He counted them in for the modulation on the downbeat of the next chorus. Once we were in the new key, Venuti kept on playing loud. He didn't even let an entire revolution go around this time before he led his band to a F# minor modulation—halfway through the third chorus. It surprised me, all right, but I heard what was taking place behind me as I continued to riff away on my fiddle. I found the new chord change almost as fast as the band did. I took off on it with my *wild* soloing, even throwing some fast triplets in.

The audience was getting thoroughly excited, folks who were already on the dance floor began moving closer to the bandstand to better untangle what was blowing out on stage. They were standing close to me, about three feet from the mic stand. They could feel something hair-raising going down. Any musical arranger worth his salt knows that the use of modulations are designed to build audience interest and momentum. But ol' Venuti was just trying to trip me up with the new keys.

At the beginning of the fourth chorus, Venuti pushed his electric violin volume even louder to cover me. I snuck a look over my shoulder and thought I saw him telling the trio to pick up the tempo. Ol' Joe was the speed demon—the original "wild cat." But this here was going to prove futile for him. Picking up the tempo was not going to mess me up much and would only enhance audience interest yet again. Bring that on, I was thinking. I had been playing bluegrass all summer, for goodness sakes.

But Venuti's ensemble *protected* "the kid" and wouldn't go where Joe wanted them to go anymore.

Later, my bandmates elaborated on what they had seen happening. Venuti had spun around towards his jazz trio, but this time he seemed *put out* by how things were going. He signaled for the tempo to increase immediately. After he looked around to see that I was still keeping pace, he was giving his head nod to increase tempo: *pick up that tempo!* At this point, the audience started to clap in time to the music, holding us right there as I continued to bury my f-hole into his talk mic. I learned to do that on all of the shabby sound systems I played in order to cut through. The loud white fiddle helped me some, too. But no matter what, this PA... was bad... and did it ever start howling—the feedback was *screaming.* The house soundman was trying to goose me up—he definitely wanted more of me. The audience was rooting me on for more. Why, the entire Rick's Café Américain started to erupt in applause like I was at some old-time fiddle contest.

Of course Venuti, the old hand from an earlier show business era, should have known that the act he put on that night was a real risk to him. The comedian W.C. Fields, who predates Venuti by 20-some years, once said; "Never work with children or dogs... they are scene stealing and completely unpredictable." Ol' Joe was getting snagged by a kid musician well experienced on stage. If I was the fuel for his prank, it spurted and sputtered—it backfired.

Hastily, Venuti closed it all down—like a scalded wild cat, he did. While he pounced and scratched, we lasted together, though, to the end. I just kept going for every hot lick I could think up, that I hadn't gotten off of Joe Venuti, at least. In animated fashion, Joe ambushed me with some fiddling double shuffles and we raced to the finish line.

As I left the bandstand, Venuti said, "Let's give the boy a nice round of applause out there, huh." I swung around to shake his hand, but he was already speaking through the talk mic and waived me off. Then he kicked into "Sweet Lorraine," as he got his set back in order. When I arrived back at my table, all of the bandmates were blown away at what just happened, giving me high fives, guys shaking their heads—lots of laughter. They told me all about the antics up on stage and what he was trying to do behind me the entire time to throw me off. They all said it was one of the greatest musical events they'd ever witnessed—the old violin legend and the new upstart met up in Chicago in 1977.

I never minded how Joe Venuti mucked me about that night. From what I'd already seen out there on the road as a kid, it was just different sides of the same coin. I still loved his playing, nothing changed that.

Between Venuti, Eddie South, Stephane Grappelli, and Stuff Smith, as a fiddle player, I was the one that was changed, for good.

The Beloit College Weekly, Beloit, Wisconsin, February 24, 1977, Round Table, Volume 131 Number 6

"It was sacrilegious to hear 'Take The A Train' done with a fiddle, a banjo, and a mandolin, but I loved it... It was Mark O'Connor who made the show really swing. His playing on fiddle had the same vibrancy which one only hears today on old seventy eights, and I still don't understand how he made his fiddle do what only traditional jazz instruments, such as saxophone or guitar, have done in the past. On the guitar, although he didn't have George Benson's full, luscious tones, or the incredible speed of McLaughlin, he did work himself up to the highest levels of melodic development. He used both the jazz and bluegrass cliches, but more often he built them into unending, rippling waves of sound that came from nowhere and went . . . who knows where. Plainly put, it was an evening of transcendental bluegrass... I even gave them a standing ovation. Nobody else in the crowd of some two hundred people did, though. I guess nobody appreciates genius."

Milwaukee Sentinel – Wednesday, August 10, 1977
By Dorothy Austin, Sentinel Staff Writer

"BLUE MOOD HITS FIDDLING'S GOLDEN BOY

OSKCOSH, WIS. – So young, so gifted, so glum. Mark O'Connor (15 at the time of this interview), a young man of enormous bluegrass talent.

O'Connor is 6 feet [4]...hands full of talent, head full of music and contradictions. And today is a downer, a bummer. Everything about him droops, his lanky hands, his mood, his curly brown hair.

This is the day after the Great Northern Bluegrass Festival at Mole Lake last weekend, by most accounts a highly successful event. But not to O'Connor. He talks about it glumly in the back room office of the Morgan Brothers' Music on Main St. here.

'It was like a rock festival misplaced, like a big party, like all they were listening for was heavy drums and bass, and they were mostly stoned out of their minds,' O'Connor says.

HE LOOKS DOWN AT his hands most of the time as he talks quietly of the crowds, of the marijuana smoke so thick that you couldn't see the stars of a wonderful summer night, of the "cage," the fenced-in area he and other performers played in, sometimes wandered out of and then could not return to without 'a big hassle.'

He is obviously painfully shy, and yet he has something to say and enough youthful candor to say it. 'It's hard to play for a crowd like that, because they don't come to hear the music, and they don't appreciate what you're trying to do with the music.' And as for the playing, 'it wasn't really that great.'

...The weekend, which apparently still rankles, even though he (and everyone else) was summoned for encores: 'I really don't play what audiences want to hear. I suppose I could have gotten up and played 'Foggy Mountain Breakdown' like everyone else. But I am really into playing music more than entertaining.

'Some people are happy with what they're doing. But I am never really happy with what I'm doing.' ...This is the youth with many friends in musical circles and a growing number of fans, the youth some colleagues call 'the best there is.' So why isn't he happy?

WELL, SOMETIMES HE wonders what it would be like to play 'really good.' He doesn't feel good about his playing...He knows he will have to finish high school. Everybody says so, including his mother and his musical colleagues who have been through all that. And it is a boring prospect.

'I don't like the atmosphere. They (other high school students) are like infants.' This from the vantage point of one who has spent most of his young life with adults. He will be on tour, off and on, and will have to come back and catch up on his studies. The best grade point average he ever achieved was in ninth grade, a 3.83, which would have been a 4 if it had not been for his grade in chorus. Since then, the grade point has been going down.

He enjoys playing bluegrass with Jim & Jesse, with whom he will appear Thursday at the Wisconsin State Fair. But he knows now that he will not be able to play bluegrass all his life. All his life is a long time, and he already feels that he has been playing bluegrass a long time. 'Bluegrass is too limiting,' he says. 'You can only go so far with bluegrass, and if you try to go farther, it turns into something else which is not really bluegrass.'

Now he thinks many bluegrass musicians are naïve. 'They think bluegrass is all there is,' he says. There are times when he thinks, 'Here comes another song in G.' Lately he's been listening to jazz a lot. 'I like every instrument,' he says. He could listen to jazz piano for hours.

FOR THE NEAR FUTURE, he'd like to spend a year with a bluegrass group to get recognition.

Doesn't he have enough recognition? He smiles meagerly.

'I'm known as some kid,' he says.

'You can get a name in bluegrass, and then play some jazz,' he says. Sure, he could be worse off, he knows. Many good jazz musicians go hungry. 'You have to be Oscar Peterson,' he says."

ANOTHER BIG FIDDLE CONTEST took place during the summer of 1977. The bedlam went down in the midwestern city of Omaha, Nebraska. I really wanted to win this one, too—they were offering a whopping 1ˢᵗ place prize of $1,500—the biggest fiddle contest prize yet. At age 15, most fiddlers thought I was far too jazzy to win an old-time fiddle contest anymore. I could always find my way back to the discipline of a 13-year-old—but I was unpredictable in those days. I suppose it all depended on if everything went smoothly and if I could stay out of trouble. Therefore, I always had a chance at least. Benny was expected to attend, Dick Barrett, Herman Johnson, Terry Morris... It looked like the big guns were having a showdown on the prairie. As usual, I came solo.

My mother contacted the contest director asking if there was anyone I could stay with. They told her about the competition's sponsor, a wealthy man named Dick Bishop who lived in a large mansion. When Mom rang him up, she was met by this verbal obeisance on the other end of the line; "House of Bishop, can I help you?" Once Dick Bishop was summoned, he told my mother to send me on down to Omaha, he had plenty of room and I would get picked up at the airport in a classic Rolls-Royce. It turned out to be a Porsche instead, with the *Rolls* in need of a repair. After arriving at the mansion, I was taken to my room downstairs near the back entrance. The outdoor patio and swimming pool were just outside my window. My bathroom was just across the hallway. I would likely meet Mr. Bishop and some of the others guys living there the following day. My bed was a lavish king-size monstrosity; I had never slept in a bed as soft and as large. My bedroom was bigger than most people's apartments.

The following morning, the same guy was designated to drive me over to the fiddle contest. I had a little breakfast cereal in the kitchen while meeting a few more young men living there. I put my fiddle and guitar in the Porsche's back seat, along with my box of records with the guitar handle strap, and we took off for the civic center with the top down. I glanced over to the floorboard as he revved up the gas pedal. I observed that he was wearing shorts. Then I noticed that his legs were completely shaven.

"Bishop will take care of you after it wraps up this afternoon. He'll drive you back over to the mansion to join the rest of us buckaroos. We'll figure out something exciting to do."

"Okay then, thanks for the ride," I replied.

In the lobby of the civic center, I started to see all of the familiar faces. Fiddlers were coming in from everywhere for the biggest prize money ever offered at a fiddle contest. Contestants came from the East, from the South, the West, from Canada... Benny, Terry, Jeff Pritchard, Dick and Herman were there. A bunch of Texans came up for this, a few Terry's age, like Wade Stockton. Even Loretta came in from Washington state. Why not? Most anything could happen and this contest paid very well through 5th place. A younger friend of Loretta's, Jeanette Beyer from Redding, California, came along with her. Jeanette was talented and very pretty. At 14, she was one-year younger than I.

All of the fiddlers ended up staying at this one local motel. It sounded like a lot more fun than being stuck overnight with several strangers who weren't fiddlers. If I went over to the motel to jam, I would need someone to drive me back out to the mansion, maybe late at night. I didn't have a house key and they might be asleep by then. I wasn't even sure of who all lived there yet—I only saw several stylishly dressed young men wearing what looked like designer shorts that morning in the kitchen. Wishing I was at the motel with all of the fiddlers, now, I couldn't bring myself to tell the contest officials that I no longer was interested in staying at Mr. Bishop's mansion—the main sponsor of the championships. It risked me coming off as just another problem child. After all, what would be my excuse? *They promised me a Rolls, but I only got the Porsche?*

In the lobby of the civic center I met Dick Bishop, a man in his mid-50s. An interior decorator by trade, Bishop was wearing a polished calf leather cowboy suit, leather pants, finished out with an abundance of fringe, and a cute matching leather cowboy hat. He asked me how I liked his outfit as he welcomed me and all the fiddle players to Omaha. I suppose you could say that Dick Bishop had on his "fiddle suit," sort of like the rest of us. He spoke to me with an accent that sounded like Liberace's. The pianist. I saw Liberace a few times on the *Johnny Carson Show*. There weren't many "out of the closet" gays by the mid '70s.

Given my childish ingenuity, I hatched quite a master plan. I systematically apprehended most all of the fiddlers throughout the day. I made sure they knew to attend the "pool party-potluck and fiddle jam" at the big mansion tonight. It was a two-day contest and nothing much was going on that first evening other than fiddlers looking to play a little. The mansion was an intimidating place to stay by myself (thanks a lot, Mom)—so my idea was "strength in numbers." Of course, I had no permission whatsoever to throw a party at the mansion. But I made sure all of the fiddlers had the correct street address.

After the day's contest rounds had concluded, I drove back over to the mansion with Jeff. Loretta and Jeanette came along with us. I noticed that Loretta and Jeff were starting to like each other, and I again noticed how cute Jeanette was. Things were getting interesting.

The four of us took a seat by the pool, waiting to see how many of the fiddlers would come to my party... and did they ever come. Camper pickups and camper vans, on top of camper trailers began to pull up out on the street in front of the mansion. The scene looked flat-out *hilarious*— some kind of Beverly Hillbillies going on. It had a strange congruity to Venuti's prank with the upright bass players all called to the same venue. Fiddlers by the droves were walking onto the property and heading around to the backyard pool, just like my instructions said for them to do. Benny came, Jerry Thomasson was there with Sandra, Terry Morris and his whole camper full of Texas fiddlers. There must have been 30 or 40 of us in no time.

A couple of the wives approached me to ask about the potluck part. Did I need help with the food? Ahem...yes. I had nothing in the way of food. Taking note of my guestlist arriving, some of the women came to my rescue and hastily went to the grocery. Some of the other fiddlers went for beer and returned with multiple cases. People could already sense that tonight might be a sparky one. Before too long, we had quite a spread going on. Bishop and any inhabitants of the mansion were nowhere to be seen.

After eating and socializing, fiddles and guitars started coming out of their cases. The jamming began right there on the cement deck around the pool. As night fell, most everyone was feeling roused and rosy. I turned out to be quite the hit of the weekend. People couldn't believe how I had credibly administered a shindig of these proportions and commandeered a mansion for the party all by myself. I truly soaked up their adulation. In no time, some of the fiddlers were hitting the beer pretty hard and folks began to act a little crazy around the pool.

While the outdoor lights were fully illuminated by now, the pool lights themselves were off. Some of the young Texas fiddlers thought it might be a good idea to jump into the pool with nothing on but their drawers. There were dares by others to skinny dip, too, but nobody was taking it to the next level, thank goodness. Benny and Bea were sitting right there by the poolside, smiling nervously. The drinking escalated and fiddlers seemed to be sufficiently losing their minds.

Without warning, Terry Morris stripped down to his skivvies and jumped in. Everyone began to whoop and holler as he was urging his friends to jump in, too. In short order, the moment got to her I guess and Jeanette jumped in with her sundress on. People were howling. Terry took over as the gagman and life of the party. Everything he said from the middle of the pool was side-splitting to all the fiddlers. Some dared him to take it all off: *"Skinny dip, Terry, take 'em off!"*

No one could see anything below the surface of the water, the pool was dark. Terry pulled his underwear off while in the deep end and tossed them up onto the pool deck. The fiddlers went bonkers. Terry was hamming it up alright, drawing attention towards his haywire antics and banter. It was both funny and shocking to me at the same time.

Out of the blue, the pool lights were switched on. Oh my gosh. Terry started squalling for help, holding his hand over his groin while grabbing onto the pool coping to keep himself afloat. Many of us yelled out, "Turn the pool lights back off!" A few of Terry's friends screamed, "Keep the lights on!" Terry grabbed Jeanette and held her in front of him to block people from seeing him in the water. She was shouting, "I'll protect you, Terry, don't worry!" But there were plenty of times they separated in the water during their struggle to hang on.

As I looked over to the far end of the pool, I recognized some of the young men who were hanging out at the House of Bishop earlier that day. A couple of them knelt down to grab some photos of the fiddle jam session taking place in their backyard pool. Finally, after an excruciating five minutes of dumbfounding hysteria and future fiddle contest lore, the pool went dark again and Jeanette no longer had to be Terry's human shield.

214

After that little number, most everyone dilly-dallied towards the exit, observing that it was *"quite an exciting evening, wasn't it?"* They all cleared out after that. Except for Terry and his three Texan friends. They stayed a bit to have a few more beers and dry off from the night. I found them towels in the closet outside the bedroom.

"You know who put those lights on in the pool? The guys who hang out here, and, I think they're all homosexuals," I said. Since it was late and they were really drunk, the Texans had asked about crashing at the mansion. One was sleeping in the camper, anyway, but that little item certainly threw cold water on their idea. They decided to scram and risk it behind the steering wheel, instead.

"Wait a minute," I said, "you can't leave me here all by myself!"

I looked at Terry.

"It was your bright idea to go skinny dipping in their pool, and now they have photographs!" I added.

"What do we do?" one of them asked.

"Look," I emphasized, "the bedroom where they have me staying is right there," as I pointed to it.

"It's huge—two couches in there, and the carpet is softer than any of the beds at that motel." I continued,

"There's a lot of places to sleep in there and then we can confront them about those photographs in the morning."

They were much too drunk to drive anyway.

Me and the four Texas fiddlers headed inside for the guest bedroom. We snickered about what the other guys in the mansion must be thinking about us right about now. The good news was that the bedroom door locked from the inside. The bad news is that the bathroom was across the hallway. About every 20 minutes, at least one of us had to take a leak. So, when that fiddler was trying to get back into the room, the other fiddlers kept the door closed and locked just a little longer than required. Just to optimize any fear component. I was plenty nervous; I didn't have permission to have done any of this.

After things quieted down and we started dozing off from our various deployments around the room, we awoke to a knock on the bedroom door. We all sprung up—and panicked all over again. All five of us were accounted for. It must be someone else on the other side of the locked door.

After that number, the five of us ended up on the big bed—no one wanted to be left by themselves on the other side of the room. We all agreed: *"Gotta get some sleep. The second round comes pretty early in the morning."* One of us whispered, *"They probably think we're having too much fun in here.* Another snickered, *"Maybe they feel left out?"* As everyone tried their best to hold back their gibes, this was all plainly ridiculous, and quite hilarious. While I was 15, they were grown-up men. I had to laugh at how I roped them into protecting *the kid* at the mansion, the young fiddler they never cared to help out much because I always beat them in the contests. It wasn't but a year ago that some of these guys were spiking my Cokes after all.

With a near sleepless night, all of us had headaches or some manner of hangovers by morning. We needed to get to the contest for the finals, as the biggest prize in fiddle contest history was on the line. I packed my bags and squeezed into their small camper, knowing I wasn't returning that night to stay. I had a great excuse now: my fiddle party just got *way* out of hand and I wore out my welcome. Since we were in danger of missing the fiddle playoffs, and a little nervous about confronting anyone about the photographs, we disappeared out the back door. It was a shame, because they had some nice breakfast items laid right out there on the kitchen counter again and I was starving. With just enough of a window to get to the civic center, Terry's wisdom was drinking warm cans of leftover beer for breakfast. He argued it was the best way to handle our hangovers. When we arrived at the fiddle contest, I tried to disappear amongst the throngs of fiddlers, and did the best I could to evade any contest officials. Compromised again, my hopes for winning this contest also evaporated.

The fiddlers who made it a much shorter night at the mansion placed higher in the contest. Herman Johnson wisely declared the weekend "unpredictable" and he had gone home, as he was known to do once in a while.

Pritchard 1st, Barrett 2nd, I got 3rd and Terry Morris 4th.

I was getting way too jazzy for fiddle contests anyway.

Omaha was the last time I went head to head with Terry Morris in a fiddle competition. Our contest rivalry had come to a natural conclusion.

Several years later at age 32, the great Terry Morris tragically drowned in a swimming pool. His untimely death occurred at a pool party.

CHAPTER EIGHT

BOARDING THE BLUES AWAY

NO WAGE EARNER HERE, nevertheless I wasn't done being our family's caregiver. While Dad's workload and finances increased enough where he could manage the household bills, he took out his resentment and anger on my sickly mother. There were more than a few times when he threatened her physically while he cornered her in the kitchen. Sometimes she pulled open the kitchen drawer to grab the butcher knife—Dad's choice steak knife he sharpened on his whetstone once every week. Well, she was wielding it at him again. If I was there in the house, she would call out for me to rescue her. I was able to grab Dad and physically pull him back out of there. I was now 6' 4", and a lanky 165 pounds. He was a big man of 6' 2" and 225 pounds. I was still 15, and he was a raging alcoholic.

My Dad hit my mother a few times, as Mom described it to me. I didn't see any of those incidents actually take place. Mom felt she had some hearing loss from his hand slap once. Dad also was aggressive with my sister, as she told me. She often defended Mom when I wasn't there, and one time he pushed her out the front screen door. He was drunk during those tirades, so I never doubted the possible consequences of his aggression and malevolence. When this behavior escalated, and it often did in the evenings, one of my tactics was to taunt him and steer his ire towards me: smart-mouthing the barbarian during his overconsumption. I lured him away from the females in the family like a big ogre in a late night scary Vincent Price movie. In the course of it, there was the time he got so mad at me, he chased me out the front door welding one of the kitchen chairs as a weapon. I assumed he intended to crack it across my back, but he was unable to catch me on the open road. When coolheaded, he swore up and down that he would never hurt me badly, though. Not my hands, especially. Many nights, the three of us had to run out the back door to get away from Dad. We headed for the Ford Econoline and drove a few blocks down the street to sleep the rest of the night there—while he slept it off back at the house.

One of those nights when we were parked down the block, Mom had an unusually sobering talk with me inside the van about her endangerment and its worsening by the day. She felt that I was going to have to physically protect her from him if it got bad enough. I fully understood my changing role within our family structure, insisting that I was already taking this very approach: from breadwinner to physical security. My *modus operandi* was to get in between them, shifting his anger towards me in those instances by distracting him, creating an opportunity for her to move to a safer place. My mother admitted that I was "good" with the execution of my plan, and it saved several powder-keg moments from exploding. However, she warned me that it could get even worse.

It seemed like Dad didn't have the kind of animosity towards me as he did for Mom and Michelle. Likely, he thought I was a potential big-time musician who could bring the kind of credibility to him that he always desired in his life. This, in addition to his sexist belief system devaluing the females in the family. He always wanted to be a "big shot," and he thought I was close to becoming a big shot in music—maybe for *his* benefit. Having no concern over my sanity, however, his terrifying cussing fits and physical threats continued—night after night. My plan of action pressed forward: diffusing the hostilities and making him mad at me instead of Mom. I always evaded any physical threats he posed to me in the process.

Most mornings when I got up for school, he forgave me for deriding and challenging him the night before. Oftentimes, he wouldn't even remember that I did what I had to. Even in my mid-teens, Dad still came upstairs in the morning to wake me up for school. He rubbed me on my back or on my legs, sometimes for a few minutes, until I was fully awake.

After which my day's unceasing cycle would play itself out again.

It was a gruesome way to live, and I believe that my mother did fear for her life. But if Mom wasn't going to have us call the police and have Dad charged with domestic abuse and violence, what was the alternative? After two failed attempts in Nashville, she refused to leave our home again, and *he* wasn't going anywhere. Neither of them were interested in a separation or divorce. Still, my mother advised that *my* strategy, keeping them apart in the house, was not going to hold out. She wanted me to be prepared to grab that same butcher knife out of the kitchen drawer myself, like she had to do when she felt threatened. I told her that I couldn't do that, "not against my Dad. It's not in me to do that." Mom disagreed. She felt that if her life was in danger, I was old enough and big enough to stop him. I argued that what I already was doing was sufficient. Mom went further:

"You might have to be ready to kill him."

"Woah, wait a minute here… I am not going to do that, no way!"

"Do you want to see me killed instead?"

"Of course not, no… but it's unfair to ask me to challenge my Dad with a knife. There has to be a better way. I'm not going to do that."

We never had a gun in the house when I was a kid. If Dad had access to one in any of those moments, or my mother for that matter… I shiver today to think what could have transpired.

From that moment on, I fended off both of their actions in the home, because I didn't trust either to do the right thing. I finally discovered that Mom was holding something back this whole time—the reason why she was gravely concerned about our finances more than I ever knew: her cancer had returned. The real reason she required so much bedrest wasn't menopause after all. We had no health insurance, and she didn't want to drain what money I had in the bank from my music earnings over this. It explains another layer of urgency for me to hit the "big-time" as a child musician.

To cope with even more difficult-to-understand dynamics, Dad had already known about her cancer returning, but he still behaved so ugly and violent towards her. Every day, I found an endless and perplexing nightmare unfolding. My difficult challenge was to try to figure it all out, to take care of everything I could and to keep people safe. To keep all of us alive.

A few years earlier, my Dad built an upstairs addition to the house for Michelle's and my bedrooms. I was so appreciative for my new room because I could get farther away from all of them, and away from the mold and mildew in the downstairs bedroom that I shared with my sister. But I couldn't enjoy it much after all—I had to be the watchdog. Michelle's new bedroom on the second floor became Mom's place to rest and to sleep.

I organized my day around the predictable madness, as if the daily ritual was all spelled out on cue cards. He always hit the beer on the drive home from work, and was plenty charged up by the time he arrived at the house. The window of our vulnerability to his attacks was between eight and 11 o'clock, before he would finally pass out. As soon as we could hear Dad pull into the driveway, I got busy. I ushered Mom upstairs to the bedroom—no *ifs ands* or *buts*. She was not to come downstairs for the remainder of the evening unless she needed to use the one bathroom we had. For those slogs downstairs, I shielded her from him back and forth, his growls and expletives flung her way as she limped along and bent over at the hip—increasingly in horrendous pain.

Prayers were answered that contained Dad to the downstairs floor in the evening tirades. After our new living arrangement, he didn't come up the stairs looking for her—never took his rage past the threshold of the downstairs doorway. Otherwise, it was like dealing with some wild animal caged in. He yelled and cussed up the staircase sometimes for an hour or more straight. The delirium was always quite frightening, but this became a routine—predictable. The three of us stayed disciplined under my guidance and didn't respond to him during those nightly histrionics. Eventually each night, he would wear himself out with the yelling, his voice itself giving out. When I finally had mastered the nature of his drunken routine, I could put on my headphones and listen to jazz-rock music loud enough to drown out his threatening language towards my mother, while she herself listened to his every word and was made to swallow it. It was all quite merciless—as if Dad already was spending every last penny on her future cancer treatment. Without health insurance, there was little doubt what was ahead.

During those years, it seemed that we could barely get through this unending praxis. I never had to threaten my Dad's life with a weapon, though, as Mom insisted I should be prepared to do.

*M*ARK, *"YOU HAVE NOT touched your instruments in months,"* mother scolded.

"Yeah, well I don't feel like it. I just wanna *board*," I replied defiantly.

"After all you have done with your music, the least you could do is practice once in a while," Mom reminded me.

But something even haughtier was stewing inside me. At this point, all I was doing was skateboarding and listening to jazz records. These were my two escapes at age 15. I was taking in everything from traditional jazz — Stephane Grappelli, Django Reinhardt and the Hot Club of France, Joe

Venuti and Eddie Lang, Charlie Christian, Wes Montgomery, Joe Pass, Pat Martino, Oscar Peterson, Miles Davis, Dizzy Gillespie—all the way to contemporary jazz-rock artists: Jean-Luc Ponty, John McLaughlin and the Mahavishnu Orchestra, Wayne Shorter, Jaco Pastorius and Weather Report, Chick Corea, Al Di Meola, Stanley Clarke and Return to Forever, Pat Metheny and, Steve Morse with the Dixie Dregs.

For contemporary acoustic music that year, I was particularly into Shakti with John McLaughlin on his scalloped fret guitar and the East Indian violinist L. Shankar, as well as the new David Grisman Quintet album with Tony Rice on it, the tape fresh off-the-rack and into my new headphones. When I let Dad try my pair of phones, he couldn't believe it. He was bewildered by this technology, the look of bafflement on his face over where the music was coming from around his head, was pretty funny. It was a feast for my ears, too. I was approaching music my own way and on my own terms—getting plenty of musical nourishment by listening to my jazz records.

How I went from Texas fiddle contests and bluegrass festivals to a broad array of jazz music as a kid could be considered somewhat remarkable. I was passionately developing a taste for a broader range of musical genres. I wasn't about to leave my prior music behind completely. It has always been second nature for me to *compartmentalize*. My instinct for keeping track of instruments, styles, and musical language was synchronal—I looked at all of it within the bounds of possibility. Once I could obtain something musically, it went straight into my repository. The split personality indications of my real life existence just to make it through the day, easily carried through to music. Even as a younger child, I relied on it— given school, and given my home life. Not many people around me understood what I was doing at age 15, but not many people ever did before. Now that the pressure was off with regards to making a living as a kid musician and moving my family to Nashville, I felt like I could do whatever I wanted to. That was, other than being our home's night watchman. 1977 was a musically *freeing* year, even if I wasn't touching the instruments with my own hands, as Mom demurred.

And the skateboard? Well, my boards became the very essence of my own animating spirit. Skateboarding the streets of the suburbs in Seattle was going to save this kid's heart and mind. As a child performer I had

221

already been through more than a family could bargain for. I already dealt with a lot of dysfunctional domestic abuse, the problems at school, and some bizarre behavior on the road. I demanded some independence and extrication from the recent responsibilities. I was skateboarding and listening to music non-stop.

"Rounder Records called again and they want a new album from you. This is the third time they have called. What do you want me to tell them?" Mom asked earnestly.

"Tell them that I don't *feel* like making an album!"

In a nutshell, it was pretty much all I did anymore: skateboard after school until dark, and then lay on my bed with my new gigantic set of headphones and listen to jazz, tuning out Dad *and* Mom. Tuning out the rest of the world.

That year, I came to a full understanding that this particular activity — skateboarding — was perfectly suited for my railing against the establishment and the status quo confines. So, to say that boarding was my hobby, would be a gross cheapening of the daily *quest*. Skating was my *new* way of life. I breathed it, thirsted over it, and would do about anything to skateboard every day. I was so disheartened each time the rain came, putting a stop to riding my board. In Seattle, dampness was unfortunately typical. Boarding had become my way of life and key to my mental survival — as long as the ground was dry, that is. It also helped me outmaneuver that childhood musician life I felt was hopefully in the past. I was needing to do most anything to get past it.

I began to see everything like a skateboarder might view the world — a rebel who was misunderstood by elders, and misunderstood by most other kids, which of course aligned with my narrative of the "child musician." In the mid-70s, skateboarding was not at all popular with the vast amount of kids. It was more like a hobby for beatniks and misfits. Beyond that, the activity was quite scarce in Seattle otherwise, compared to southern California. Just a few of us punks, skating against the suburban machine in the Pacific Northwest.

Mom continued to have me drive the yellow van underage and without a license — I had to do all of the grocery shopping and drive my sister to dance class. Mom was near permanent bedrest; she couldn't do much to help me, nor *stop* me from doing most of the things I wanted to do, either.

I took the skateboard on my errands, and I usually found an embankment to check out or a good place for some street skating. I took my board everywhere, even to school. Not much bullying anymore, just spinning 360's in the parking lot.

One of my stupid high school mates took a piece of paper and drew a straight line on it in class. He claimed that it described one of our classmates who was a "goody-goody"—he was "straight." Then he drew a curvy line next to it and said, "This is how *you* and I draw a line… crooked." What a dunce, but I welcomed it, as the skateboard seemed to increase my perceived outflow of boorishness. At least I wasn't getting hassled for being a goody-goody fiddle-faddle boy anymore.

The "Aurora Bowl" was an ideally shaped drainage reservoir formed from blacktop. It was located behind the Aurora Village Shopping Center on the north end of Seattle, just about a 10-minute van ride from the house. We climbed the chain link fence to skate it. The large basin was controlled by the public works wastewater management, but the days that it held any backup water were long gone. Thank goodness for that "bowl," as it got me through being 15.

Electric jazz violinist Jean-Luc Ponty was my soundtrack at the Aurora Bowl, too, blasting the music out the Ford Econoline speakers with the van door pulled wide open—especially his albums: *Imaginary Voyage, Enigmatic Ocean, Upon the Wings of Music,* and of course *Aurora.* Hardly anyone knew about the Aurora Bowl—just me and my friends skated there. It was the best kept secret, before there were any skateboard parks in the Northwest.

Even though I was uninterested in playing much music myself, the skating which was taking place in my life that year meant everything to me.

"Rounder called again and said that if you are not interested in recording a fiddle album, would you be interested in a guitar album, since you won the national guitar contest at Winfield for a second time?" My mother goaded me.

I thought of the perfect dare for Rounder Records, too—so they wouldn't keep hounding me to make an album. Earlier that fall, on October 16th, 1977, the David Grisman Quintet with Tony Rice performed at

the University of Washington. We attended the concert and went backstage to say hello to David and Tony, as I knew them both a little, and I
was a huge fan of their new band album. David Grisman asked me to sit
in with them to play a fiddle tune, and so I did. We played "Sally Goodin',"
and it went very well, a big hit with their audience. As we were playing on
stage, Tony Rice was staring a hole right through me, too. I was positioned
stage right, so as I played I could see him easily out of the corner of my
eye. Grisman was standing next to me, in between Tony and I. Looking
over a few times at him, seeing if Tony wanted a solo on the tune, he held
off. What he did do was to give me some of the most driving bluegrass
guitar rhythm I could ever experience. Both he and David did. Afterwards,
Tony wanted me to try out his old Martin backstage, the D-28 that once
belonged to Clarence White.

"If Rounder wants me to make a guitar album, tell them I'll do it if they
can get David Grisman and Tony Rice to play on it with me," I told
Mom. *That should shut 'em up.*

She relayed the message back to Rounder, but of course, it was the ultimate dare, *wasn't it?* I didn't expect to hear back from them. In the meantime I had big plans.

THE "AURORA BOWL" inspired me and my skateboard friends to
find some genuine vertical terrain. Unlike the photos in *Skateboard
Magazine* profiling all the action happening in southern California's
abandoned backyard swimming pools, there were no drained pools for us
to skate, because there were hardly any backyard pools in Seattle. It was
not the swimming climate. We did find some rather large cement pipes
on an industrial parts and manufacturing lot just north of town. The place
had concertina wire fencing and security decals everywhere, but we figured out a way onto the premises. After a few escapades, it was all a bit
unnerving to make this a regular diet. But was it ever a rush while it lasted.
We got a taste of vertical.

My mother refused to let me spend my music money on building a big
skateboard ramp, the project scope for which I had my designs on. She
said that if I can get the lumber out of my father, then I could proceed to
build it in the back yard. Some crafty negations with my Dad ensued in
the mornings before school got underway—when he was good and sober.

It required a careful presentation and many deliberations over weeks. We had *his* "business" at night, and then we had *my* business in the mornings—after he woke me up. Dealing with Dad's multi-personality existence only fed my own. I *compartmentalized*, yet again.

I never wondered much why my mother allowed me to contemplate building an apparatus in the backyard that would risk life and limb. I only had to think back a few years before. My 10-year-old friends and I used to dig up the entire back yard, forming a labyrinth of underground tunnels. The moist and deeply layered Tokul soil created by the volcanic ash and glacier tills found in King County, made it possible to keep on digging using only a common shovel. Today, I occasionally think about those exceedingly narrow tunnels crisscrossing the yard just a few feet down—any of them could have caved in on us with no way out. I remembered how my friend would jump up and down on the lawn so we could check the amount of dirt filtering down on top of me while still inside the tunnel. We wanted to see how they were holding up.

When we tired of being underground, there was always the fir tree in the corner of the yard which seemed so tall that it touched the sky. We were bound and determined to reach the top of that tree. Cutting up 2 x 4s in two-foot lengths, my friend and I took turns pounding the next board into the tree. At about 30 feet up, one hand holding on to a short 2 x 4 and hammer, I grabbed the nailed-in board with my free hand, highest on the rung, only to have it come right out of the tree. After nearly losing my balance and tumbling to the ground, my friend confessed that he didn't hammer enough nails in that one because he "chickened out" over the height we had achieved. I reminded him that it would have been good to let me know that. I could've finished nailing in his board before tacking up the next one.

Years later, I developed pretty good cases of claustrophobia, and acrophobia.

Of course, skateboarding wasn't without its risks, and Mom was plenty aware of it. That year, Robert, a friend from school, lived a couple of blocks over from us. He took his skateboard straight down our neighborhood's steepest hill, dubbed "Zoom Hill." Going fast, he met up with a car coming across at the bottom, and broke his neck against it. Weeks later he came to school with a large metal contraption around his head so his neck could not move at all, the bolts screwed right into his forehead. For months he was like that.

The pledge to Dad was the following: supply me $1,000 of lumber so I could build a 25-foot halfpipe in our backyard, and then I would never ask him for anything of monetary value again. For $1,000 of wood, it could keep me out of his hair, and by definition, *buy* the better part of my happiness. I think he got a kick out of how relentless my accommodations were each morning when it was just the two of us at breakfast.

"Dad, I am telling you right now, between you and I: $1,000 of 2 x 6s and plywood for the skateboard ramp will satisfy me through high school—I will not ask you for a car, or anything."

I already knew I had the Ford Econoline to drive, and, it was quickly turning into the *boyz* van—the ultimate skateboarder *hang* for trips to the bowl.

Dad swung for it.

The towering wooden half-pipe ramp was magnificent to construct. As a junior, I signed up to build a house with the carpentry class, getting a bit more familiar with the trappings of a construction site. Sporting a leather tool belt, this work came a little more honestly than I wanted to admit. It reminded me of how close I was to swinging a hammer with some permanency. Indulging in a bit of a holdover from fiddle contests, I dipped snuff at our job site.

I designed my skateboard half-pipe monstrosity from scratch, operating from a set of blueprints I drew up—because Dad thought it should be down on paper before I started to hand-saw my way into this project. "Hand saw" as opposed to power saw. A few months were spent constructing it using no power tools. Part of the deal was to "protect those fingers." In wood shop that year, I was cutting into some wood at the band saw, when a couple of kids pushing and shoving each other came dangerously close to my zone. Something clicked in that moment. I laid the piece of wood down on the bench, grabbed my coat and never stepped foot into a woodshop again.

It impressed Dad with the degree of seriousness I brought to this, and he took note of my handiwork each week. Before I went to bed each night,

I stared out my bedroom window, admiring the ramp bathed in the moon-light, dreaming about what it would be like to skate it. It's all I could think about.

"Mark—fantastic news! Both David Grisman and Tony Rice said they'll record with you! They suggested to record in Berkeley, Califor-nia, at the same studio where the Quintet album was made last year. David Grisman suggested their group's bassist, Bill Amatneek, for the recording. The finances have been worked out by Rounder Records. Everything's ready to go!" Mom impatiently relayed the news to me.

The ramp was 25 feet from side to side, 12 feet wide, 12 feet high on one side, 13 feet on the other—with three feet of vertical at the top. I had an on ramp/off ramp with a sitting bench at the end of it. On one side of the vertical, I inlaid some pool tile at the top—the small little squares of tile with mesh mounting finished with grout. Atop the tile, I used real ce-ment pool coping for skaters to grind axles, and for tail taps. On the other side of the vertical, I installed plexiglass with patches of grip tape for trac-tion. A sitting bench was placed behind the glass and positioned about ten feet high, so onlookers can see people skate right across their faces, just a quarter-inch away.

My half pipe ramp took up half the backyard. Our Shetland Sheepdog, Frisky, loved it too, chasing the skaters back and forth on a path he wore in the yard around the ramp. It was a hoot—tireless as he chased us. This half pipe wasn't just the envy of the neighborhood, but of the skateboard-ing Pacific Northwest. Skaters came from all over to visit several times. I called it "Mark's Ark" and placed a sign at the top of the ramp with the lettering made from silver reflective tape we stuck on our boards: *Mark's Ark.*

"Well?" Mom demanded.

I was not that into my own playing anymore, actually—I was really down on it. I was burned out of anything that remotely whiffed of blue-grass. I just wanted to escape and skateboard my troubles away. When those wheels hit the pavement, or the wood of the ramp, it was the freedom I was looking for. Out there skating the streets on my own, I didn't have to care what people thought of me anymore.

My skateboard consumption was not without a great deal of discipline, either. I worked on my skating constantly, and considered it an athletic pursuit as pretext. I strived to get good at it, and committed myself to additional exercises and stretching regimens to improve mobility and strength. I practiced relentlessly on tricks and *moves* at the bowl and on the ramp.

"Tell them that I don't have any ideas for an album right now, but please tell them thank you for me!" I responded.

Mom was *not* about to tell them that. Not in the least. She sternly expressed to me how great an opportunity this was, and that she's going to insist I begin to think about an album for Rounder.

"All I'm asking you is to give me 30 minutes a day, that's all. Sit down with your cherished Herringbone guitar for 30 minutes a day and think about what you would want to record with David Grisman and Tony Rice. Just 30 minutes." Mom appealed.

There *was* actually something I could do—it more or less distinguished me from most others, I must admit. A kind of adroitness and finesse that came naturally I guess you could say, and I had known it for some time. My flexibility and dexterity were always hallmarks, and folks made comments to me about it; *"how about those long appendages!"* I could always make the big leaps. Unquestionably, I had some spring in the extremities. It kind of reminded me of how I ran to the point of takeoff, gliding through the air, and flying over all those Seattle mud puddles. It really felt like I could almost float through the air at times.

The current world record for the skateboard high jump was 4' 2". I figured out a cross-bar set with a fiberglass dowel strewn across it. I put together a longer skateboard out of a plank of wood, nice and thick, and slapped some used trucks and wheels on it. I practiced every day on the high jump.

The high jump trick is to approach the bar on the skateboard, leap up from the skateboard in a forward motion, all the while maintaining the board's same rate of speed. If you can clear the bar, which is the first step, you have to time your descent and land back on the same skateboard you took off from, meeting up with it on the other side of the cross-bar set. To complete the trick, keep skating without falling off for a number of feet. I worked up to clearing the jump at 4-feet. Then I finally beat the record by jumping at 4' 3". By the time I completed that height, though, the new record was announced in *Skateboard Magazine* at 4' 6". So, I worked on it some more. Ultimately, I was able to jump and make the landing, by clearing at 4' 6". The local newspaper came out and photographed me clearing the jump on the skateboard and tying the world record. No one coached me on it, I had my own training regimen. The high jump photo from the newspaper was always one of my favorites in the music scrapbook.

I had never been happier with my childhood life than when I was skateboarding. It felt like I could be the bad boy rebel all I wanted when I was skating the streets. It was an athletic pursuit. It was good for me and it took a lot of discipline to get better. I became very health conscious, really got into health food: brown rice, legumes, dried fruit, macrobiotic cooking... and all those other things I learned about from Eddie in Wisconsin. Mom wasn't a huge fan of me "stinking up her kitchen" when I cooked up my health food concoctions.

But I did give Mom 30 minutes on the *Martin* each day.

As she suspected would happen, within a short period of time I had the beginning to a couple of different tunes. I played her some of what I was coming up with and she thought it was beautiful, and just the right musical direction for the album. Some of it was rather *jazzy*. Soon, I had the intros to what were to be called "Fluid Drive" and "Markology."

Mom was right. All I needed to do was give it a few minutes a day and the ideas would start to come—and they sure did. I started to really get excited about the album, based on my own new musical compositions and creativity, instead of relying so much on my technical abilities which weren't going to be enough to inspire me anymore. I already had my latest versions of "Dixie Breakdown" and "Blackberry Blossom" from the second Winfield championship ready to record.

To celebrate my progress, I grabbed my skateboard and did a handstand on it for the entire length of a city block. Even the ladies who were sunning themselves across the street at the "call house" gave me a hand for that one.

BECOMING MUCH MORE impressionable than ever before, surprisingly, this year turned out to offer a new kind of restitution—a realignment of my own confusing identity. Who I was as a person was always shoved aside for the child musician I was on stage. But now, I attempted to leave that prodigy part of me behind, and put much more faith into the musical characters I revered. Even with the ample Joe Venuti himself, I was a devotee for the way he played swing violin. There was Stuff Smith's hard swing-style. Of course, the estimable Stephane Grappelli was at the top of my list. Then there was my desire to play electric violin in the manner of Jean-Luc Ponty, and especially sit in with him. I saw Ponty each time he played at the Paramount in Seattle. I even fantasized about playing second violin in his electric band with bass and drums. It seemed pretty far-fetched, but I put far more credence in all of these men now—their constitutions, their amplitudes—their vastness.

Many years later, I played "second violin" with Ponty and his band for my album, Heroes, *a tribute to my favorite fiddle players. "New Country" was always the best tune to skate to.*

Trusting in the extraneous adjuncts of my new favorite characters, those patron saints, and then *dreaming – imagining – transporting* myself next to them, became a lifeline and a way out of my own treachery at school and an increasingly toxic home life. Because of this manner of reformation, I could learn and excel in a good amount of musical genres, even without having hardly touched an instrument for a better part of a year.

It seemed like I could pull myself apart at the seams over something I was working on, and completely set aside the other thing I was doing earlier that day. Imperviously, I was accomplishing all the musical things I set my mind to. I was wanting to discover something far more grand in music—to be just about anything I wanted to be now.

I began to symbolize through appearances of my favorite characters. My proclivity to a "split personality" way of life was manifested in musical indulgence. Without the pervasive stresses I experienced, I wouldn't have to use so many master strokes to find a way forward. When I changed my appearance, I attained things more easily—to get where I wanted to go. I had dressed the part: from Texas bull rider hat for fiddle contests, to more recently, the Dogtown skateboard iconoclast Tony Alva, with kinked-out hair—I tried to become all of these artful personalities.

I became much more physically animated when I played fiddle especially. I might bend way over at the hip, appearing to look like a cow grazing in a field (as one reviewer put it). Then I'd snap my torso backwards and whip it to the other side, as I yelled out "ooh" a time or two. Occasionally I'd even stick out my butt some, and wiggle it a few times. Then I geared up for the same sequence all over again and didn't miss a lick. Playing this way reminded me of Terry Morris. The new sparkle and vivacity I was tapping into made my playing red-hot and charged.

Lately I had been submerging myself into the world of jazz violin, mainly because of its spontaneous creativity. I became even more of a devoted servant to the recordings of jazz violin legends, such as Grappelli, South, Ponty, Venuti. Stuff Smith and Ray Nance, too—improvising in their musical style and language on stage. For this music, I came off as more aloof and stoic. I tried to look more cool, and less kinetic than I had with the fiddle music. Jazz guitarist and professor of music, Al Galante, joined me for duo gigs around the area, while other performances with Seattle's Great Excelsior Jazz Band were scheduled. Jazz was my much more serious face—more studious. Compartmentalizing my artistic imaginations would help me accomplish vastly different musical settings, simultaneously. "Methodizing" was a trait I could rely on for any golden arrival in music.

It was going to be much less about me for a while and more about the people I preferred and wished to emulate externally—whether it was the musicians Clarence White and Tony Rice, or Stephane Grappelli and Jean-Luc Ponty, or the skateboarders like Alva and the other Z-Boyz Jay Adams, Shogo Kubo, and Stacy Peralta. Because, as a personality, I was too complicated to have just *one*.

With all of its curious undertakings and gross contradictions, my life as a kid was undeniably playing out like a symphony full of asymmetrical counterpoint.

When Weiser rolled around, I won the Juniors for the 4th year in a row, and did so without any preparation or practice. I was interested in other music, and they were still not going to let me enter the Open. People were getting a bit knackered over the Juniors. I was trying to tune it out. My mother came up to me in the cafeteria warm-up room:

"What's wrong with your back?" She pressed me.

"Nothing. What are you talking about?" I peered back at her.

"Well, you are holding your back like there's something wrong with you," she insisted.

"No, that's silly," I replied. "I'm not holding my back."

Then I got up from where I was seated to walk away. As I rose, I sure enough had my left hand holding my lower back. I was also hunching over a little (like I was an *old* man).

"There, you're doing it again!" Mom said, as I turned around to face her.

I began to laugh and shake my head. Benny held his back just the same way when he rose from a seated position. He actually did have a bad back. His was from all those years as an auto body repairman. Me, I had no excuse. I guess I wanted to be like Benny to such an extent that his externalization was imprinted onto me, at least for that week at Weiser it was. Then I moved my impressions to someone else. I was selecting and then *trusting* important artists. I needed to.

Tony Rice became that idol for me regarding the Martin steel-string guitar. When he played the guitar, Tony didn't *move* at all, not even his head. Totally rigid. Forbearance was not really my thing, as I was into flowing, bending, carving across the Aurora Bowl, and carving and flexing into my fiddle. But it didn't matter; I was getting into jazz and he was too. I wished to not move around when I played my guitar, just like Tony Rice.

All of this *portraying* was confined to a physical manifestation, but had little to do with my playing style, which fiercely remained its own expression.

The emulation was about personalities, not about their licks. For me, it didn't matter if that personality was a redeeming one, as long as I loved the man's musicianship. It was the work-around I used—how I coped with lots of new musical information I wanted to assimilate. I could project myself to those musical places I wished to go much more easily if I just *dressed* the part. The question was: *to hat or not to hat?* I wore hats either to emulate or to distinguish myself. Or to confuse people by throwing them off and keep them guessing.

I COULDN'T WAIT TO GET out of the house and record a guitar album—and without a hat on this one. I had three new original tunes, and the rest of the selections were mostly familiar, but with new arrangements. I wasn't sure if I had a whole album ready by May 1978, but I hadn't a moment to waste as long as both Grisman and Rice, and their bassist were ready to go—the majority of the David Grisman Quintet.

I had a tactical tune-up gig before the guitar album recording. On April 23rd, I played an opening set for Doc and Merle Watson at the Hub Ballroom at the University of Washington, the same venue where I sat in with Rice and Grisman. I got to try some of my new licks in front of a primed acoustic-guitar crowd.

Any diary entries contemporaneous to my experiences as a child musician are non-existent, except for one. When I discovered this personal accounting at age 16, synchronous to the making of my guitar album Markology, *I had to include it here, unexpurgated and unaltered, as I wrote it in 1978:*

"ALBUM NUMBER 5: After all the arrangements had been preplanned by the business boys at the exec. offices and the various musicians that were picked for the album by yours truly, the rest was more or [less] up to me. Behind locked bedroom doors is where the ideas pour out through the fingertips [and] where they rest anxiously atop the fretboard.

Months go by after cancellation and re-cancellation of the session dates, and finally my family and I board the Econoline and start for San Francisco. We take 2 days for travel and arrive at the Berkley Motel Plaza Friday night. The college town more appropriately titled Bezerkley is still full of the radical-ists strongly bred from the beatni[k] movement of the 60's. The Plaza gave us a place in an apartment-like complex complete with a kitchenet and the front room with the bedroom in the back. We would be staying there about a week so we proceeded to load the refrigerator with the nutrient oriented products I so commonly ingested.

We hit the blankets somewhat early to be ready the next day for some dubbing of intro's and outro's in the studio at 1:00pm. The next day after shower and breakfast was taken care of, we left for the [Arch Street] studio which was about 2 miles down University AVE. It was a big, old castle-like house made of adobe and tiles. The front room would be the room to play in since the dimensions of the room were made for acoustical instruments by a genius violinist that lived there many years ago. It seemed that he was losing his hearing in his later years so he had a room specially built so to be able to play and hear every note, so the story is told.

Upon meeting Bob Shumaker, our engineer, he took us to the control room where the taping would take place. In most studios the control room is directly adjacent to the playing room with a window in between so to communicate by gestures more freely, but this place had the control room down a flight of stairs, through a couple hallways, rooms, and doors so the communication is done by an audio system and also a one-way Video T.V. Monitor.

We all were quite impressed in that it was quite different than any other I've been to because it wasn't built purposefully for recording, but that the studio was built right into this mansion, complete with the gardener's quarters and everything. After explaining to Bob what I was about to do in the next couple of hours, we got organized and underway.

I completed 2 long introductions, one using multiple overdubs to sound like 4 guitars. We would complete the structures of the pieces within the next couple of days. For now this would be all I could do by myself and it came off smoothly. We got back to the motel around 5:00pm and within an hour or so, Dan Crary arrived from Los Angeles. He made the drive up and got a motel room next to ours. Dan is going to guest on the album for 3 tunes tomorrow night. He is considered one of the best flat top guitar players in bluegrass. I had called Tony Rice earlier that day and he showed up at our room about the same time. Tony is one of the hottest guitar players, currently playing with the David Grisman Quintet and he will be playing all through the album doing rhythm and some lead.

After a few hours of conversing, Tony took me to his apartment near Mill Valley across the San Rafael bridge. We spent the night listening to music and his new records that haven't been released yet. We played some while I played his old Herringbone Martin guitar that belonged to the late virtuoso Clarence White. Tony's wife fixed dinner and Tony took me back to our place.

The next morning Dan and I went over some songs we were to record and Tony got here about 1:00pm. David Grisman, an excellent mandolin player, who just [got] through with doing a movie score in New York, came about 4:00. And Bill Amatneek the bassist with his band came about the same time. We spent the afternoon making chord charts and rehearsing tunes, and we ate some dinner that my mom fixed for us. We all left to record about 7:00pm.

David, Bill and I started recording the rhythm track for a tune I wrote called Fluid Drive for 3 guitars. Tony, Dan and I will dub in our lead breaks later. One of the introductions I did yesterday, went to this tune. It took us an unusual amount of time to get this down because of the 8-beat stops where the rhythm quits playing. The idea was to have someone try tapping a secluded mic on a separate track [during] the 8 beats so the lead player will stay on the right beat through the stops. Well we got through it and got a good take [but] when I listened back to try to play lead over the top of the taps that Tony put on, it slowed down a hair right at the end. So we done it over again with Tony playing another guitar in another separate room through the stops. We can listen to him through head phones so the rhythm could come back at the right time. This worked real well and after the leads were in, we would just rub out Tony's track for the final production.

Dan, after waiting for 3 hours, finally got to do his break in the song while the rest of us rested down in the control room and listened. Tony and I would do our breaks some other night because we had to get Dan through because he had to drive back to L.A. that night... We said our goodbyes to Dan and thanked him for coming up. We told Bob that we'd see him the next day about 6:00 to start another night.

You might think that we had the whole day to blow in Sisco, well not really. After getting up at 1:00 and taking a shower, then you have to eat dinner about 4:30, that's enough time to play some guitar awhile. All the guys showed up around 6:00 or 7:00 at the studio. David, Bill and I recorded the rhythm track to a tune I wrote entitled Markology. The other intro I recorded Sat. goes to this tune. I played rhythm on Tony's guitar because there was a little buzz on my 6th string when I fretted chords up the neck. David and my chops were mixing pretty well on this jazzy piece.

After that, I dubbed in my breaks while I brushed over the structure to lay his down after I was done with mine. We recorded 3 more tunes that night which were Dixie Breakdown, Blackberry Blossom and one I wrote and recorded when I was 13, Picking in the Wind. We went through these pretty fast. By this time, quite a few people had gathered down in the control room. David had invited friends including a writer-photog for Guitar Player Mag. We got done recording the tunes pretty early around 12:00 midnight. I was going to finish some overdubs that needed to be done but I decided to finish that tomorrow. We just talked and listened to the tunes downstairs again.

Tuesday night it was planned for me to do some fiddling things, but that day we decided not to because we would have to cut down on guitar tunes we already had on tape. So what we did was we recorded Dixie Breakdown again leaving no holes for Mandolin and fiddle breaks since I won't do any fiddling on the album. We got that one in about 2 takes. After that, David and me did a duet on a Carpenter's song called I'm On Top Of The World. It started not so good and in an hour, we got a beautiful take. After taking care of my dubs on Blackberry Blossom and Fluid Drive, the recording was done. David said that he wished he could make an album in 3 nights." MOC – May, 12-14, 1978.

Guitar Player Magazine, May 1980, Vol. 14, No. 5.

"He plays something like Doc Watson, he plays something like Django Reinhardt... Mark O'Connor flatpicks bluegrass music in a clear, rippling style punctuated with unexpected chromatic flurries, effective syncopations, and blues bends: and that's just the first cut, 'Dixie Breakdown.' The rest of the LP is similarly impressive, and by no means confined to bluegrass... The title cut (with David Grisman on mandolin) is a virtually flawless, minor-key toe-tapper reminiscent of the David Grisman Quintet's first album. The up-tempo, eight-minute "Fluid Drive" opens and closes with an orchestral arrangement of layered steel-string guitars: with solos by O'Connor, Tony Rice and Dan Crary, it's every bit the flatpicker's paradise you'd expect.

Mark's maturity and his musical intuition are even more remarkable than his dazzling technique. Somehow in his relatively few years he has garnered the experience to allow him to, say, rip through a passage on his way to a chord change, appearing for a moment to accelerate too fast but then arriving just on time. He can continuously and effortlessly change his metric anchor, slipping from straight sixteenths into triplets, then into bluesy syncopations, and back to sixteenths for the last fragment of a breakneck run. He has a similar facility with melody: for example, he'll sometimes alter a bluegrass turn-around with jazzy, modal excursions. This eclecticism and the daring quality of his phrasing should interest even hard-core electric guitar buffs.

There's a Martin D-28 herringbone picture on the cover, and assuming that it's the guitar used on the LP, it sounds terrific."

Bluegrass Unlimited Vol. 14, NO. 11 May 1980
"The title tune 'Markology' sets the tone for the album; it's a 6 minute 27 seconds acoustic jazz number similar to what we've been hearing from David Grisman in past years. While a few of the titles have been common with the traditional scene, don't be fooled; some uptown arrangements along with O'Connor's uncanny sense for phrasing and putting together extended runs turn tunes like 'Dixie Breakdown' into modern showcase pieces."

"What is this?" My mother held up a hotel receipt.

"I don't know, what is it?" I replied.

"Why don't *you* tell me, it was laying on the floor of the van."

"I don't know, Mom."

"It's a hotel receipt," her anger growing. "You got a room with her, didn't you?"

I was in hot water, but I didn't know just how *hot* this was going to get. By the time I was 16, I finally recovered from my previous traumas over anything to do with girls—enough to actually find a girlfriend, and a great girlfriend at that. I had fallen for Jeanette Beyer, who was at the Omaha fiddle contest. We saw each other here and there at music events, and she had just visited our home for a few days as a "fiddling friend," so my mother had thought. But while she visited, we were sneaking around and holding hands, trying to hide our affection from Mom and my younger sister. I figured the romance thing would not fly with Mom, so we kept our new relationship a secret. Our fondness for each other was building to the point, however, where we thought the best idea was renting a hotel room for a couple of hours one afternoon—just a few miles from our house. We wanted to see what it felt like to be naked with each other. Maybe it was what they call *puppy love,* but I had never felt like that before—I was swept away by these new heartstrings that we both were experiencing. Jeanette had kept the hotel receipt and put it in her purse. It unfortunately fell out onto the van floor, where it remained for several days. The worst of luck.

At the very same time, my acne was getting worse and I was becoming severely self-conscious about how bad I looked again. As long as I skateboarded my blues away, maybe no one would notice what I looked like—many didn't. Jeanette was so pretty, a very sweet personality as well as a really good fiddler for her age. For whatever the reason, she was not bothered by my horrible complexion. I viewed her as a true blessing in my life to come along when she did. It took me awhile to even attempt a relationship after all the exposure to bluegrass musicians on the road. I was so very happy about Jeanette, my first love. We were planning to see each other again at other fiddle contests soon. She lived in Redding, California.

"You are to never see her again, you got that?" Mom scolded.

"Mom, it wasn't anything, you are over-reacting. She is a great girl—it's Jeanette, our fiddling friend," I emphasized.

"You will NOT see her again, not until you are 18. It's either her or *me.*"

My mother laid it down in no uncertain terms. If I "walked out that front door" to be with Jeanette, I wouldn't be invited back into our home again. My mother would *write me off.* On the contrary, if I decided to stay with my family, then I couldn't speak to Jeanette again.

A phone call to Jeanette was arranged with both sets of parents involved in the matter, as Mom demanded. She wanted to nip *this* in the bud for good. I hoped she was going to cool off a little by the time of the phone call, see the lighter side of it... but agonizingly, she did not. I thought I knew my mother better—I thought we were better *friends,* and working partners. She helped me so much putting *Markology* together. It wouldn't have been made without her—but all of this now staggered me. I had no idea what Jeanette's parents were going to say, especially if Mom was this upset about it. The phone call was contrived to be nothing short of humiliating anguish.

On the call, both of Jeanette's parents, surprisingly, were more or less fine with what had transpired. After confirming with their daughter that there was no chance of a pregnancy, their feeling on it was that if we continued dating, we should have access to some "protection," to be safe. They were supportive of our relationship continuing, as my Dad was. Listening in, he agreed with the Beyers. He wasn't that bothered by the hotel room rendezvous. But despite what three parents had to say, it was Mom who could not let it stand without severe reprisals. She considered what I did unforgiveable—not to Jeanette or her parents, but to my mother. As if she was a woman done wrong by a man.

Had I really become her surrogate spouse?

After all the psychology used to disentangle the kid living in a grown-up world, now there was a new impediment unfurling through our family home, and, it was as much about my relationship with my mother as it was about a new girlfriend. I was not to speak to Jeanette again as long as I was in my mother's house. Sweet "Jeanettey," the young, beautiful girl who had not only become my fiddling pal, but likely the biggest fan of my fiddling I could imagine—she was my love. She loved me. But, it's all done. This was over.

I thought about running away from home—and for many reasons. I could well survive out there with musician families willing to take me in, I dared say. I would have plenty of places to stay at least temporarily. Heck, even Norman and Nancy Blake wanted to adopt me. They approached me about it at Winfield the last time I was there—when they saw me by myself at a festival yet again. Norman took me aside to have a personal talk with me. "Mark, I see you all the time out at these festivals," he said, "with no parent around." Norman offered to adopt me, to live in north Georgia with him and Nancy. They would make sure I got to school, and there would be plenty of opportunities to play music with them and their friends. I assured him that Mom would be very sad if I left her, but I thanked Norman for his concern. That was back when I was 14.

But for all of that, I made the decision that I was not ready to lose a relationship with my mother over Jeanette, even though I believed that I loved her, and I thought Mom was so very wrong about it. Leaving home before high school was finished didn't seem good to me, after all Mom and I had been through together. I wanted no regrets the day I moved on. As soon as I graduated, one way or the other, I planned to be out of the house.

How I felt about my appearance, my recuring acne—I didn't see how I was going to find a girl to love me like Jeanette did, and that really broke my heart. Even if I could get a girlfriend, my mother would obviously be in the middle of that, too. I could not bear to go through all of this another time, so I had to forget about girls again. The new arrangement over Jeanette put in jeopardy my attending fiddle contests—one of the few musical activities I could get away from home to anymore. Jeanette seemed to be going to all those same contests I did.

My reliable escape routes went up in smoke. Things were going to pot.

MY BEST FRIEND AT SCHOOL had been trying to get me to smoke weed with him for a couple of years. I just sat there and let him toke without me. We tried our first cigarettes together back in 7th grade, in the woods behind the ravine. I stupidly—but fortuitously, as it turned out—took the biggest drag on a cigarette I could gather—then my lungs stopped working for a minute. It scared the pants off me, so my smoking cigarettes lasted all of a couple weeks.

But now it was time to get into some real *grass*. Most all the skateboarders, especially the good ones who came over to ride my ramp, like Rob, Eric, Peter, and Tom, had been smoking a lot of weed when we went on skating excursions in the Ford Econoline. If I was aiming to project a similar lifestyle to Tony Alva and the "Dogtown" Z-Boyz, I already had the crazy hair, and I suppose pot was the finishing touch. We ended up rolling our own, did the hash pipes, and got into some pretty elaborate water bongs. I only got high when I was away from the house, storing the hash pipes and bongs under the seat of our now ancient black Chevy station wagon—the car I usually drove to school. Living a little dangerously with the not-well-hidden paraphernalia, my loyalty and subservience along with my bong exhales, went out the *car* window.

How much more trouble could I possibly get myself in with Mom? Maybe one more of these showdowns would push me over the edge to just leave home, find Jeanette, and start my music career on my own at 16. *Mom can disown me if she finds out.*

She never discovered that I smoked pot during my junior year in high school. That she didn't smell weed all over my clothes every day is hard to deduce. Maybe she ignored it. My mother tearing me apart from my first girlfriend; my parents' unwillingness to be civil to each other in our home; and then there was my mother slowly dying of cancer. It was bad at the house and getting worse. I'd rather get high.

THIS WAS GOING TO BE an entirely different Weiser than ever before. By 1978, the contest officials were finally going to allow a 16-year-old to enter the "Open division" at the National Oldtime Fiddlers' Contest. I hadn't been practicing many fiddle tunes, but I was doing about everything else, including writing new music for the violin—music I was calling *On The Rampage*. I was inspired by what I could do with my new guitar tunes such as "Beserkely" and, "Markology." I wanted to follow a similar direction for the fiddle: a follow-up album of all originals.

Preparing for Weiser hadn't been high on my list. It wasn't even *on* my list. The very thing that both myself and many of our Weiser friends had been hoping for—that being a rule change so I could enter the Open division—now seemed utterly dreadful. I saw nothing but around-the-clock stress in Weiser in 1978. Jeanette would be there the entire week.

I was hoping I could just go to Weiser by myself that year, but Mom insisted on attending, and here she could barely walk from her cancer. She wanted the Ford Econoline parked out back of the Weiser High School gym—the back doors of the van opened so she could catch some of the jamming and socializing just outside. I felt horrible for her, but since I spent about every day with her that year, I was really looking forward to just being a teenager and hanging out with fiddling friends I didn't get to see often anymore, like Loretta and the new teenaged Grand Master Fiddle Champion J'Anna Jacoby—and yes, maybe even Jeanette. She was entering the Juniors along with Loretta and J'Anna. My Mom warned me to not speak so much as a single word to Jeanette; "or there will be a scene in front of all your Weiser friends like you wouldn't believe!"

It was extremely difficult for me to avoid Jeanette. In addition to her being nearly everywhere I went that week, she looked even more beautiful than when I last saw her. Jeanette had matured in just the few months since our forced breakup. She was now 15. Jeanette was very much in our friends circle, too, but very few people, if any, knew how serious Jeanette and I had gotten. But we were keeping the imposed breakup yet another secret. As soon as the teenage group of friends would gather anywhere around the contest grounds, Jeanette would walk up and I'd have to make a hasty exit. Weiser was six-days long, and it went on like this every single day. My kid sister was nosey that week. My socializing habits were going to get back to Mom, one way or the other.

For someone who didn't hang out with girls at school, this all was such a disappointment. I'd been going to Weiser for years now, and I was popular there. Jeanette very much wanted to talk to me, to discuss what happened to us, and what we might plan for the future. She wanted to know if she should wait for me... but I could not break away for even a minute without being discovered. All eyes were upon my every move. I couldn't speak to her because of my mother's orders and threats, with a potential scene in front of all these nice people at Weiser. It would just be soul crushing if Mom lost her mind there over this, someone who was bedridden and dying of cancer. I was not allowed to be any kind of friend to Jeanette, or to show any concern for her, or for us. It hurt me all over again. In time, I became even more mentally hardened by this experience.

In the meantime, here was the biggest fiddle contest opportunity unfolding right before my eyes. Finally, I was being allowed to enter the Open after winning the Juniors four years in a row. At 16, I was to be the youngest to ever compete against the big guns and old-timers at Weiser. Due to a rule change, they were going to allow contestants under 18 to compete in the Open, but only if they win the Junior division three years in a row. They didn't *name* the rule after me, but I was the only one affected by it, and the only one who benefitted from it by 1978.

Not to dismiss the good fans of the other competitors, most people at Weiser were pulling for the youngest person to ever compete in the Open division. The pressure I felt to come through on this three or four-year-long wager was intense; *could this boy win the Open?* Both Dick Barrett and Herman Johnson were entered, and as always, they were playing to win. As I got going in my rounds, I was pulling out the stops, too. But as the week wore on, the accountability from all sides was utterly squeezing me. Avoiding Jeanette at all costs day after day was very difficult to do. Appeasing my sick mother laying in the van outside the back door of the cafeteria, along with her getting so much sympathy from folks, and rightly so... was overwhelming as well. Then there was the competition itself. To think that a 16-year-old could beat both Barrett and Johnson at Weiser, a contest each of them had dominated since the 1960s, was quite a seditious idea for the status quo. The old way had been installed for generations. Now, a kid could take it over…

By Saturday, the night when both the semi-finals and final rounds were to take place, I was internally drained and emotionally broken. My two accompanists, Joe Sites and Rick Youngblood, tried to keep me in the frame of mind that I could win this thing.

There was another new rule instated that year: a time-limit of four total minutes for the round of three tunes. This was for the purposes of saving time throughout the week: there were 300 entrants that year. The audience was told to withhold their applause until the entire round of three tunes had concluded. For many, it was a straightforward adjustment. For me, a child performer for already several years, it felt awkward not to hear any audience feedback, especially after the energetic breakdown tune. It was yet one more issue I was having trouble adapting to that week.

The second to last round was set to be a fiddle contest thriller (the top eight). You could almost hear the packed-in crowd of 1,900 collectively hanging onto their hats as I played. I finished my breakdown, and it went smoothly. Again, recognizing there was no applause allowed, I immediately jumped into the waltz, saving any valuable time I could on the clock. Given the new rules, going overtime meant they would deduct points right off my total score. But when I launched into my waltz so quickly as I did, rushing right into the start of it, one of the worst feelings took over that I had ever experienced on any stage — I plum forgot what waltz I was going to play.

The waltz I kicked off was not the one that I warmed-up on, nor the one I had sent to the officiators desk… and to boot, it was in another key altogether from the one I had planned. The guitar chords Rick and Joe played were immediately discordant. Incompatible with me and with each other. I panicked. I was struggling to remember what waltz I intended to play, and at the same time, trying to chase the guitar chords down they could only guess at. The three of us played in three different keys for what seemed an eternity. My own instinct suggested that I couldn't just jump right back into the desired waltz, if I ever found it, because it would be a complete give-away — an admission that I spent the first 30 seconds of the tune trying to remember it. Instead, I began to improvise a new waltz entirely. I came up with one on the spot. It may have passed for at least something halfway decent, but of course my accompanists had no idea what tune I was inventing on stage—they just kept hunting around for more chords. Together, we sounded plain awful—a crash-and-burn right in front of 1,900 enthusiastic spectators who were pulling for me. I blew it. I was devastated. I lost Weiser right then and there.

The waltz I should have played, the one that was announced to the audience before my round began, implausibly was none other than Howdy Forrester's "Memory Waltz."

Of course, any of them who supported me, all of the friends, the teenaged fiddlers, my family… everyone realized that I had made my first major mistake in fiddling competition, and it was a grave one. Most didn't think I could stay alive and make the final round of five. I didn't surmise I would either.

In spite of my scatterbrained debacle in that round, I had played four very good rounds before it, and evidently I'd been edging ahead in points. The preliminary good showing gave me enough accumulated scoring through the rounds, and therefore some cushion to get into the finals. Part of me didn't even feel like playing anymore and just withdrawing. I felt like disappearing someplace to hide. I used to not cry about anything as a younger kid, but I had been doing a lot of crying that last few months over Jeanette. Tonight, I let the entire Weiser community down—the narrative of the kid going up against the biggies was toast.

After the top five was announced, in a right-about turn, many were heartened and frankly impressed that I made it through to the final round. Some reminded me what I was undertaking that evening *was* making fiddling history—just to make the top five of the Open as a kid. Some appealed for me to get back up there and redeem myself. Jeanette came up to me—her sweet smile and empathetic, beautiful presence… and told me: *"Mark, just play as wild as you want to now. Let it all hang out!"* Another added: *"Show this audience how good you can play that fiddle."* Someone else said, *"Give 'em a thrill up there, get the audience on your side!"* All of it brought about the seasoned child performer, the youngster who gets up on stage and gives the audience that thrill. I guess I did owe the audience a good show after what I'd just put everyone through, including my accompanists.

I shook things off, and, chose my final three tunes.

We were back at it again for the start of the final round. I was letting it fly… I put some tempo on, and stuck in lots more attitude. I was bending my body backwards and sideways as I played, reveling in every moment while I was up on stage. I had nothing to lose. It *was* wild and electrifying to the crowd—they went berserk. I emphatically redeemed myself and put in one of the bravest performances I had accomplished as a young musician. Everything important seemed to be on the line: my tenacity, dependability… my self-worth …I felt the weight of the world on my shoulders in those moments. This was about a great rally from even a greater setback. The goal was to play—not to *place*.

The top contestants took the stage for the awards ceremony. After they announced the 5th and then 4th place finishers, Dick Barrett was called for 3rd place. The sold-out auditorium went bonkers, screaming like no one has ever heard at Weiser before. You could tell Dick was pretty bound up, extremely uncomfortable. He knew I had messed up my round, too. He couldn't believe that he didn't overcome it with his own performances. So I put my arm around Dick's shoulder to comfort him on stage. My role as the kid consoler who must mind over his parent's care and every disposition they wandered into, catalyzed in those moments with the older champions. There I was, taking care of the adult competitors and their prospective hurt feelings—their moral harm.

They couldn't even beat me when I scratched an entire tune.

Then I looked over at Herman. He was standing there like he was seeing a ghost. I had never seen the man so nervous in all the years I was around him. Herman was all but spooked at what he saw was inevitable. I walked over to put my arm around him. To Herman, it was really all over but the shouting.

Unlike Dick, Herman didn't fully know just how bad I screwed up. Dick was one for the rumor mill and put his trust in it. Herman was typically above that kind of stuff, and remained composed. Herman grabbed my arm with both of his hands. You could tell that he wanted to win this thing, but at the same time he was proud of me for accomplishing this unimaginable feat with the fiddle at age 16. He never thought he would see this day come, for a kid fiddler at this level. As they called 2nd place, the silence in the room anticipating the momentousness was at once… deafening.

Herman Johnson remained undefeated going for his fifth national title: *"2nd place goes to Mark O'Connor."*

Idaho Statesman, Boise
"O'Connor has a world of talent that could win the championship." – Herman Johnson

FOURTEEN MONTHS LATER I called Jeanette to try to reconcile. I honored my mother's wishes in that regard, at least, and I waited. I asked her if I could see her again. She told me that she had a steady boyfriend now. She wanted to see me in person at least once, though, to see if I was truly there for her, before she split up with him. After our visit, she decided to come back to me. We dated for a few months, and she was the same loving, talented, caring, and beautiful girl as before. But by then I was emotionally rocked and unstable. I couldn't be a good boyfriend to her and told her, sadly, that I had to break it off nearly as soon as we got back together. It was all my fault—again. Both of us with terribly broken hearts.

Jeanette grew to become the Ladies National Fiddle Champion at Weiser. She went on to get married and to have a little boy. Soon after, her husband was killed in an avalanche in Avon, Colorado, where they made their new home. I consoled her often during that time; it made her feel good to talk to me like old friends with special feelings for each other. She eventually began dating a guy who showed signs of jealousy. She wanted my advice about it. I always told her to get away—don't need a jealous man around. Jeanette told this new boyfriend of hers that she kept in touch with me, that we would talk on the phone now and then. She had so much to be proud of; she had her son she loved dearly, ran her own boutique, and was well-situated in her own home.

One day, I received a call from her parents. It was the most dreadful of all calls: our beautiful "Jeanettey" was found dead in her home. Killed by gunshot. Her boyfriend shot her dead then turned the gun on himself and fell next to her. Her little boy came home from school to discover the gruesome scene.

VIEW of Puget Sound – On Entertainment, September, 1978

"Today at 16, Mark is six feet four inches tall; the skyscraper is still under construction. It's though his body is in a mad dash to keep pace with his burgeoning talent. It is a losing battle. I walked inside the O'Connors' barn-red white-trimmed home in Mountlake Terrace and nearly stepped on one of Mark's three guitars he had left neatly strewn about the floor (not an acquired trait, according to his mother). A strange light bathes the O'Connor living room, producing a shimmering silver pallor. The artificial light source comes from a three-tiered row of book shelves, elevated to eye level, and running wall to wall, containing more trophies in all shapes and sizes than the International Olympic Committee has medals.

Well, what have you been up to? 'Nothin' much,' Mark starts... 'Gotta new album coming out in the fall. Jazz guitar, Original compositions. It's my best so far, should appeal to the progressive bluegrass people.' Then without drawing a breath, 'Did a "To Tell The Truth" spot – both Kitty Carlyle and that other lady guessed me. Looks like I'll be touring Japan next summer...'

Don't you ever grow weary of winning fiddle and guitar championships? 'Nah, I like the competition of contests. When you're playing concerts, traveling a circuit, all you do is rehearse a little before each show. At a contest you've got to really concentrate, drive yourself to practice hard if you want to come out on top." At 16, he talks like a veteran, and he is.

Today his leanings are towards jazz fiddle of the Grappelli-Venuti vintage, and if Venuti is the Father of the Jazz Fiddle, Mark surely is its rising son... A master of disguise and courage. In recounting his sweating bullets in the finals at the National Fiddle Championships this summer: 'Someone came up to me afterwards, and told me they thought my waltz was beautiful, wondered where I found it. I told them I wrote it on stage, called 'Amnesia Waltz!' Funny, never has happened before,' Mark says shaking his head in disbelief, 'hope it never happens again,' he adds.

'I truly believe there's nothing that boy can't do if he sets his mind to it,' Marty O'Connor says of her son. 'But you know, he's always done things the hard way. He never knew how to do a handstand, and when he finally learned how, he learned by doing them on a skateboard – moving...'

Yeah, but can he fiddle and skateboard at the same time? I queried. 'Sure!' Mark piped. 'Ah, you cannot!' sister Michelle scoffed. 'You've never even tried it.'

I saw a twinkle form in the boy-genius' eye."

People Magazine – LOOKOUT A GUIDE TO THE UP AND COMING, 1978

"The versatile Mark O'Connor also took the National Guitar Flat-Picking Championship two years in a row against adults. A high school junior, he teaches the fiddle when not competing. With his career already launched, Mark is busy planning a 'heavy jazz album with drums and good sidemen' for next summer. 'I just ease with the breeze and go with the flow,' he says. 'That's my style.'

Guitar contests took a turn for the worse. Winfield 1977 was the last time I ever entered a guitar contest. After I won there for the second time, they implemented a rule that blocked me from participating for the next five years. In effect, it retired me at age 16. I lost the desire to worry about entering guitar contests anymore.

Music was still taking me everywhere around the country and in every setting one could think of. I was a special guest on the national television show *To Tell The Truth.* They had to guess who was the young champion fiddler. It was my first time in New York City and I loved it. I wondered if I could live in Manhattan one day. Local innovative bluegrass musicians Russ Barenberg and Tony Trishka watched me while I was there and showed me around. They accompanied me on the show playing "Sweet Georgia Brown."

MERLE HAGGARD PLAYED a special week-long engagement of Western Swing music in September 1977 at Harrah's Lake Tahoe. The country music superstar invited me to play 4th fiddle in the lineup sitting next to his main fiddler, Gordon Terry, and the two Western Swing pioneers Johnny Gimble and Tiny Moore, both had recommended me to Haggard for the shows. We were seated on stage, but rose to our feet when featured. On the tunes that Merle himself played fiddle on, I suppose you could say that I was "5th fiddle."

To apprentice in Haggard's band, though, with the heroes of Western Swing music, and backed by a Vegas-styled orchestra, was another good mentoring opportunity. I was getting well-schooled in this style of music which could serve me in all kinds of ways—maybe even in Nashville one day down the road—*if I could ever become a session player.* Playing with Merle Haggard singing his original songs up close and personal was another great experience, and constructing quadruple fiddle parts for those songs was certainly a novel idea. Both Johnny and Tiny were giving me some good harmony lines to play—each of them having played with Haggard over the years. The main reason for all the fiddles this week: lots of Bob Wills and the Texas Playboys on the set list. Haggard's recent number one hit, "Cherokee Maiden," was a Bob Wills cover. For this line of work, the "working man's poet" drafted in players who were the actual former Playboys from the 1940s.

I noticed that Merle Haggard transformed into a whole other character when he picked up the fiddle. He was able to evoke even the appearance of Bob Wills, along with Wills' well-known mannerisms. It was interesting to me that this kind of mimicking wasn't just limited to an impressionable teenager. I believe it helped him leave his own *Hag* orbit and step smack into the fiddling world—into the world of Western Swing—simply by acting it out through his series of physical responses. It was uncanny to see it. Merle's transformation into his favorite musical artist gave validity to what I found myself doing a lot of that year. Both Merle Haggard and I admired Wills, but coming from wildly differing perspectives, notably him being at the top of the music industry. Still, it demonstrated that we were students of the music and of its best musicians. Merle revered Johnny Gimble and Tiny Moore, just like I did. Wills had long since sanctified both of them as the leading instrumental proponents of his own musical genre.

Johnny Gimble, born in 1926, had been swingin' on a fiddle in Texas since he was ten years old. Starting out playing tunes like "Darlin' Nelly Gray," "Ragtime Annie," and "Ida Red," he soon became a big fan of Milton Brown's band that featured his fiddle heroes, Cliff Bruener and Cecil Brower. At about the same time, Bob Wills' new band was popularizing a sound later known as western swing. Johnny joined the Bob Wills band in 1949. Johnny brought his Texas swing sound to Nashville in 1968, and quickly was included in the "A Team" of Nashville's session players.

It is fascinating how Johnny Gimble's fiddling joins country and jazz right square in the middle.

After serving in the military during WWII, Tiny Moore became a regular in Bob Wills' Texas Playboys in 1946. A Texan, born in 1920, Tiny went on to become one of the only "electric" mandolinists in the world. By the early 1950s he married one of Wills' singers and headed to Sacramento to run Bob Wills' Point Ballroom. Tiny played with Merle Haggard's The Strangers for more than a dozen years. In 1970, he and Gimble joined Haggard to record an album of Bob Wills music, *Tribute to the Best Damn Fiddle Player in the World.* Tiny frequented many fiddle contests around the West and tried his hand at them into his later years.

Rounding out the fabulous assemblage of fiddlers was Alabama's Gordon Terry, born in 1931. At age 19 he joined the Grand Ole Opry and went on to record albums with artists such as Bill Monroe, Elvis Presley, and Faron Young. After serving in the U.S. Army during the Korean War, Gordon developed quite a surprising career as a professional fiddler. It included moving to Los Angeles in 1956, resulting in acting parts in films such as the western, *Hidden Guns,* starring John Carradin; releasing rockabilly singles like "Wild Honey"; recording a square dance album with Flatt and Scruggs in 1961; and opening a Tennessee theme park, Terrytown. The same year I played with Gordon in Tahoe, he released ultra-commercially-produced recordings *Disco Country* and *Rockin' Fiddle.*

The way Haggard worked his shows in Tahoe, like Wills would often do, was to point to you when it was your turn to take a solo. Gordon, Johnny, and Tiny were called on quite a bit, as one could assume, being his reliable standbys. Tiny doubled on his 5-string electric mandolin, and Johnny played swing on his electric mandolin as well, so they were working double-time. In other words, Merle called on me a great once-in-a-while. So, I had to be ready when he did. Sometimes a half-hour might go by before Merle was pointing at me: "Take a solo young man!" You just never know when it's your turn—when someone will finally point you out.

Merle Haggard was one of the most influential country music singers and songwriters in the history of the musical genre. With countless number one songs he penned and recorded, it was the fiddle that he first learned as a young boy and that remained his passion throughout his life.

Born in California in 1937, his early years were fraught by run-ins with the law. As a line from one of his famous tunes, "Mama Tried"—"*And I turned twenty-one in prison*"—had an autobiographical basis. When doing time in San Quentin for a burglary charge, he saw Johnny Cash perform his first-ever prison show. Haggard learned to surmount his own demons in prison and put his life into the lyrics of songs with his one-of-a-kind rich singing voice. When Wynn Stewart's "Bakersfield Sound" put both Buck Owens and Merle Haggard on the map with a new style of music that thumbed its nose at Nashville's crossover "countrypolitan," Haggard found a musical genre to believe in. Forty number one songs later, originals like "Okie From Muskogee," "Mama's Hungry Eyes," "The Fightin' Side Of Me," "Today I Started Loving You Again," he was only about halfway through with his chart topping by 1977, the year that found us all in Lake Tahoe together. His latest number one, "Cherokee Maiden," led us to that week along with a lot more music by Bob Wills.

The Bakersfield sound of country music was a part of *our* West Coast identity. Buck Owens became a fixture at the National Oldtime Fiddlers' Contest at Weiser for a few years, too. He missed my rounds along with the entire Open division—he was really there for the *Ladies division.* Front-row seat. He asked winner Jana Jae Greif to be the new fiddler in his band that night—and then his wife. She was on *Hee Haw* all the time after that. When it all came around to a divorce in a couple of years, ol' Buck was back. Front-row seat again at Weiser for his favorite: the Ladies division, and it led to another one. Winner Connie Bonar was asked to join his band next. We all were wondering if this would lead to the inevitable affair. The little town of Weiser was rocked by good old-fashioned country music stardom.

The 1970s on the West Coast were big years for country music. Los Angeles country-rock was at its heights with groups like The Eagles. Their song, "Hotel California," was released this same year, in 1977. But California country music had much earlier roots than the new country-rock sounds out of L.A. and even the Bakersfield Sound of the 1950s. I played some shows with Rose Maddox, the lead singer from the once popular 1930s hillbilly group out of Modesto: Maddox Brothers and Rose. They sang songs like their bawdy hit: "Sally Let Your Bangs Hang Down." It was the *Western* song that I swear Buck Owens was mouthing as he watched the Ladies division. The year that Jeanette won it, Buck wasn't there, but I am quite sure he would have been knocked out.

The Ladies division at Weiser was created to elevate the very few women who played fiddle music. But in time, there was no need for it anymore. The Ladies division hereinafter was viewed as antiquated in a generation that was ushering in many more female fiddlers. It was ultimately dropped for good.

Back at Harrah's, Hag had to be reminded to toss in a few more of his own hit songs during the sets, he got completely carried away with all the fiddlin'. Buck got carried away with it, too. *Those Bakersfield boys.*

The Seattle Times – Wednesday, December 6, 1978
"Does he practice a lot?

No, he spends his time writing his own music and perhaps working over a difficult musical passage, but he doesn't spend long hours playing through songs.

'My only real practice is on stage,' he said. 'I'm surprised I can get up and play without making a fool of myself sometimes.'

His hobby is skateboarding, and the backyard of this family's modest home has a huge plywood skateboard course in it that O'Connor built. Shaped like a U, it's taller than the house.

'In country music only a handful of [instrumentalists] have made it,' O'Connor said. 'I'm trying to broaden into different kinds of music. I have another album coming out next April with progressive fiddle music.'

'When I get out of school I want to do some traveling, to see what's out there in the world.'

There's an extensive collection of fiddle music [recordings], but, O'Connor says, 'If I want to listen to music, [Country] Western is about the last thing I pick. I usually listen to rock 'n' roll or jazz.'

O'Connor says he had an offer to play in a back-up orchestra in Nevada after he was heard in [Merle] Haggard's backup group, but he declined because the orchestra plays back out of sight, whereas the Haggard gig gave him a good taste of being up front where the crowd could see him."

L IKE A FAST-MOVING SCREENPLAY of circumstances and surroundings, from California-styled Western Swing with Merle Haggard, to the West Coast period of Tony Rice's guitar splendor, I was also enamored with another Pacific shore guy named Tony—a skateboarding star who gave me the idea for my first all-original music concept album. This project no longer relied on any traditional materials: *On The Rampage* was inspired by my years on a skateboard.

Away from the music scene, Tony Alva held my complete fascination. The bad boy boarder from Dogtown USA in Venice, California. Like him, thankfully, I had the kinky, frizzy hair mop with a similar puberty mustache. In prepubescence, I grew perfectly straight hair. But I had one very unique wish and I prayed for it often. I just wanted wavy-curly hair like some of the cool kids in school and the long-haired progressive hippie musicians in Muleskinner. And especially like Alva. Noticeably, I was granted this wish. *If I had just the one wish, I wasted it on kinky hair.*

Not all of my musical influences were rough and tumble figures. Occasionally there was a more sensitive and softer enchantment. I was revamping and liberalizing my violin vibrato for *On The Rampage*. I wanted to move away from a traditional fiddle sound to a "contemporary violin sound," but sounding it out on the old white fiddle—still, the only good fiddle I owned. I truly believed it to be a magical instrument that helped me win all those fiddle contests. In order to accomplish an appreciable difference, I rejected the use of a more "classical violin vibrato," turning back any vestige of a Dragoo influence.

I had altered my fiddle vibrato into more of a slower rate mellow pulsation. There was another Pacific coaster, Olivia Newton-John, a singer from the other side of the ocean and down under. She had just won the Country Music Association "Female Vocalist of the Year" over Loretta Lynn, Dolly Parton, Anne Murray, and Tanya Tucker, when I first heard her. Newton-John had a slower "Have You Never Been Mellow" vibrato to her voice. Her velocity seemed to match my approach on the slow tunes.

More meaningful than that, the relationship to skateboarding gave me the idea to compose an entire album, giving rise to a new style of fiddle playing in the process.

It always felt good to glide around on the streets, free and smooth—a skateboarding *state of mind.* It was also the new power source for the music I was composing. I was making a departure from the brown dirt southern cultural music influence, and exchanging it for a boatload of Pacific roots. My increasingly free-flowing fiddle style was inspired by the fluid skate moves I performed at the Aurora Bowl, embellished by a Newton-John violin-vibrato.

MY FIRST GOOD BOARD was a Gordon & Smith fiberglass chassis for freestyle skating. When I got more into slalom, and my mother didn't mind me skateboarding beyond the reach of our block, I got a new board by Alva's Zephyr teammate Jay Adams called Z-Flex. With that awesome blue-colored board, things got more intense with my desire to skate vertical. Getting into rigorous ramp skating, I moved to the first line of the new 1977 Alva boards. Finally, I followed that great board with a Kryptonics. It was during my era of the '70s that the new polyurethane wheels were developed—they made all the difference. Before that, the wheels were made of steel, and made for one very rough ride.

When I started skating embankments, any beautiful, peaceful afternoon found us at the Aurora Bowl doing tricks like frontside carves and "Bertleman" slides, especially the one-footed "bertslides" were cool to pull off. Gyrating up onto the high side of these slopes for kickturns, alternating backside and frontside, making cool cutbacks and 540s, altogether, was the combination of freedom and discipline I had always desired. It was there at the bowl when I found it. I owned all of these moments for myself. There wasn't another care in the world as I let it all go by the wayside — just practicing power slides.

When I wasn't at the bowl, I skated the streets and practiced freestyle moves. I got to the point where I could do a "hang-ten" nose wheelie the length of a city block. I liked to do one-footed nose, two-footed back and one-footed back wheelies—all of them. They were a little more academic, where the two-foot nose wheelie was *classic.* I believed it felt like surfing— hang-ten and *shootin' the tube,* even though I only *projected* surfing— never having the opportunity for trying it out. I had pretty good balance for a 6' 4" guy, no doubt. A lower center of gravity was preferable for board- ing. I *imagined* a lot.

My high center of gravity did not help me for many tricks—such as multiple revolutions of 360s. I could get up to about four or five backside and frontside, but no more—no matter how hard I worked on them. But when I carved the smooth lines out in the street with some speed, making slalom turns and generating pace even uphill without taking my feet off the board, that's when I felt like the suburban pavement was *my* domain.

I flowed with it, and people who saw me liked my smooth style. Always staying loose-limbed and light on my feet, I got really low to the ground, tucking my long legs so far in on radical crouch positions that the sides of my bare knees nearly scraped the asphalt when I turned. I did the surf-style boarding on the blacktop, just imagining myself on the actual waves of the ocean. But there was something about all the concrete and tar that made it feel so *real*—and really in your face—a kid's rebellion against the system, against the *machine.* My friends and I took the streets for ourselves. We skated them, daring all those vehicles of convention, no matter what hap- pened.

This was my world away from the pressures of being a child musician.

I loved all the great skateboarders pictured in the Skateboard Magazine (had the very first issue), the Zephyr Team, the "Z-Boys" especially: Alva, Adams, Peralta, and Kubo. But then I started to get the electric guitar mag- azines, too—Di Meola, Carlton, Benson, Beck, Ritenour, and Feiten on the pages, and it all came full circle again. Listening to my jazz-rock fusion tapes as much as I did, I thought I might get into electric guitar for the first time myself. Surely it was sacrilegious for bluegrass players... right? But that also was the reason why I was heading there soon.

McCABES GUITAR SHOP in Santa Monica booked me for a solo gig. Vince Gill agreed to play it with me, turning it into a duo. I was eying all the electrics hanging on the shop walls. Vince recently moved to L.A. and lived with his girlfriend Janice Oliver of the Sweethearts of the Rodeo. I stayed with them for a few days. Vince had already gotten into electric guitars.

But most of all, I begged for Vince to take me to a place where I could see the pro skateboarders in action. We lucked out and saw the great Dogtown skater Shogo Kubo do his thing in the big pool. I was just feet away from him, catching backside air right in my face. Vince was impressed by him, and also impressed at how this captured my complete and full attention. He had to chuckle, but it didn't prevent him from trying out my board when we got back to his pad. Vince ended up on the pavement a couple of times.

Later that night, Allen Wald, the jazz guitarist who played with Byron Berline and Dan Crary's Sundance, invited Vince and I to come down to his club gig at the pier. He was playing with the highly respected jazz-rock electric guitar player, Buzzy Feiten. I had listened to him on recordings and seen him in the mags. Allen got me to sit in. For someone who hadn't tried to play jazz-rock fusion yet, Allen's advice: "just play as fast as you can—this is the time and the place." Sounded good to *me*. All the while, I was making connections between West Coast contemporary jazz fusion music and skateboarding, and coming into my own. There was no better example than the Los Angeles based Jean-Luc Ponty. Whether he did or not, I connected his music right to his own neighborhood—the southern California skateboard culture I lionized.

As luck would have it, a kid from high school just happened to be a very good boarder—kind of a natural with it. Vince, a sophomore, was one grade below me, and we became inseparable after school, riding our boards most every day. If it wasn't raining, we were skating. But even if it was, we were prepared. We built a portable ramp that could fit in the back of the new red pickup truck my Dad had bought as his eventual work truck. Dad was slow to replace the old truck with the new, fearing it would get dinged up all too soon. It was the first new pickup he ever purchased. So the job of giving the red pickup's first scratches went to me. It took two to lift the portable ramp in and out of the bed of the truck. If the ground was wet, we headed for partially empty parking garages to set up the portable ramp. The thing stood about five feet high and had a metal pipe across the top for coping. We did our axle grinds on that. We didn't have to miss many days of skating during the school year in the never-ending rainy climate of Seattle.

Skateboarding was *our* high. We craved it. I needed it every day, even if I wiped out repeatedly and fell on my wrists—sometimes on every other ramp trick I attempted. Acquiring wrist braces was an investment that Mom was pretty high on, there wasn't any doubt about that.

ON THE RAMPAGE was recorded in Berkley during a week of sessions, all financed by Rounder Records. The studio musicians included Sam Bush, John Cowan, Bill Amatneek, David Grisman, Tony Rice, Glen Kronkite, Robert Claire, and Bill Lewis. I was so thankful, especially to Sam Bush and John Cowan of the Newgrass Revival. They took the time to learn all of my new tunes and study my fairly complex chord charts for the album in advance, and then they made their way out from Kentucky to California for the recording. It made all the difference.

For the album cover, I wanted to feature the splendid City by the Bay. The city was opening up a whole new world of recording for me, on my way to becoming a full-fledged young recording artist. I had an award-winning Bay Area photographer, John Pearson, conduct a sunrise photo shoot of San Francisco's most iconic image, the Golden Gate Bridge. I searched out a place above the bridge to pose for the album cover: Battery Spencer in Marin Headlands—a military bunker, tunnels and batteries protecting the harbor during WWI up until 1942 before it was decommissioned. As the sun came up, we photographed the cover shot. With the Golden Gate in the background, I skateboarded atop the cement bunkers while playing the fiddle. (Yes, I *could* skateboard and fiddle at the same time).

In the same way that the label didn't release *Markology* to the public for well over a year, Rounder held onto *On The Rampage* for another two years beyond that, but for a different reason altogether. They weren't too keen on how radical of a musical departure I was taking, and wondered who the audience would be. They were slow to figure out that tunes from my new guitar album such as "Beserkely," "Fluid Drive," and "Markology," would win just as much favor from music fans as the traditional tunes—the ones the label favored.

The new jazzy fiddle album identified me as a kid from the West Coast, and that is what I wanted. This was important for my new musical persona, but fans who followed me couldn't know my highly personal transformation in music for a couple of years. I had no ensemble to perform any of the music live. If that were to ever happen, it would require highly specialized players, and as far as I could see, only Sam Bush, David Grisman and Tony Rice were the musicians qualified to perform this kind of acoustic music on string instruments. It didn't leave many choices for putting a band together, even if I could afford to.

At heart, I was experiencing a lot of personal musical growth through my new passion for composing music, and at the same time, I was introducing a new brand of violin improvisational playing, something that would define my approach and style of playing—long into the future.

Side One: Come Ride With Me, Mark's Ark, Midnight Interlude, On The Rampage, Ease With The Breeze
Side Two: Rampology, The Dark Rain, Soft Gyrations, Tubular Explosions, Disco Fiddle Rampsody

"Thanks to the obsession I had with skateboarding during my 17th year, this music was able to flow out from me. As you listen, picture me catching air off a vertical wall. I'm still going for it."
-Mark O'Connor (1979)

WITH ONE YEAR LEFT of high school, I was looking for a good memory to take with me from my school years. In 1978, both the Mountlake Terrace High School's music program along with its music teacher, were not just of the mediocre variety—they were an utter disaster. Wayne Christofferson, the school's music instructor, had to be one of the shoddiest.

So I couldn't bring myself to be involved with any school music program, but there was a good shot at a work-around. I had been hiring Al Galante to accompany me on Seattle area shows, a sagacious guitarist in the style of a Kenny Burrell or Barney Kessel—but his main gig was teaching at nearby Edmonds Community College, where they ran a decent local jazz program. Meanwhile, the professor of voice at Edmonds, Frank DeMiero, headed up their jazz and chorus ensemble. He was taking his college group to the country of Panama for performances that year, and wanted me to enroll in the college program so he could take me along. It sure sounded good to me.

I had known Frank DeMiero for a few years. One of my Dad's bosses, Don, a construction contractor, paid DeMiero to teach me private voice lessons—two years of private lessons as a gift. An incredibly gracious man, Don was concerned about my musical future as an instrumentalist. He believed that it was going to be difficult for me to succeed in the music industry unless I could sing well. In all of my experiences as a child in old-time, bluegrass, and country music, his benevolence was the only financial scholarship I ever received. Don's message was loud and clear: *"learn how to sing if you want to make it."* Alas, I was to be an average singer at best and always kept my eye on the instruments.

DeMiero wanted to draft me into his college music program and offered me high school credit for enrolling as a full-time college student. "Right at the front of the stage and playing solos" is where he wanted me, as he described it. Yeah, he was *singing* my tune. If there was any way to get out of Mountlake Terrace High School and go to the community college instead, I was jumping for joy. My high school principal, however, said *not so fast.* He had a conversation with my mother about it:

"I'm glad that you have a talented son," the principal said, speaking to her privately in his office, "but we don't cater to talented kids in this school. We consider our primary job is to keep kids off the streets."

Mom was greatly disappointed by the message of his statement more than anything. *Primary job is to keep kids off the streets?* We could not accept Frank DeMiero's gracious offer to go to college for high school credit.

I had one more year of high school—the barren wasteland I had always disregarded. Going on six years without a single musical note played at

257

school, I continued to mull over what I might undertake—something I could be proud of for my final year. I didn't want to have such a downcast and hopeless school life be my final decree.

What if I taught a music class at Mountlake Terrace High for my senior year?

I talked to my mother about my cockamamie brainstorm. She actually liked the idea. I had credentials to push around to get someone's attention about it: five albums released (*On The Rampage* still to come), national championship wins, all of the professional band experiences I had. In an exercise of self-abasement and further shame, I met with the same school principal again. After giving the man the best pitch I had for teaching a music class in my senior year, this time he laughed me right out of his office.

I was about to make a speedy exit off this lame brain avenue, but I did have a good relationship with my school counselor. He never failed to encourage me to bring my music to the school. I thought, if anything, I could report back to him that I tried—doing it on my own terms—yes, but I did try. After hearing my same pitch, the counselor told me that I just might be on to something, and to not to give up on the idea so quickly. Taken aback, I asked what other recourse could there possibly be if the principal gave me the bum's rush? A slight smile came across my counselor's face as he told me I may be on firmer ground than I realize: "Go around him. Go to the school board, they just may listen to you there."

Some paperwork was drawn up and set into motion. It would require a design of what the music class would look like, who would participate, and what were the objectives for the class—*the program.* My mother helped me with the outline as well. My presentation in front of the Edmonds School Board was well-received, but they wanted me to probe into the class objectives more. They were mostly concerned with the lack of a performance or "assembly," so the student body could "audit" the work in my proposed class. I didn't anticipate that, but I probably should have. It did seem like they were interested, though. I started re-drafting the proposal.

Because of their requests for performances, I upped the ante. I changed the length from one period to two periods per day—thereby earning two school credits for myself and for the participating students. I committed to performing two school assemblies. I was trembling a little when I actually wrote that part down on paper: performing at my own school that I had long sworn off. Plenty of grievances… but not allowing me to enroll at Edmonds Community College for high school credit being the latest if not the most distasteful. They wouldn't even let me transfer to another school in the district. There was no way out. Imprisoned. Every day I had to attend a place that obliged me to despise it. The sentiment hadn't changed, even as I offered this program to the school board. My addendum:

Additional Course Objectives – 1978

a. Overall practice and refinement of songs which will increase music ability
b. Rehearsal of composed tunes from previous quarter
c. Some rehearsal of compositions of various artists
d. [Standard] Performance will be on a professional musician's level and ability
e. [Standard] This performance will show a refined result of 90 hours of rehearsal and preparation time. (i.e. this last objective will be left to Wayne Christofferson's judgement)
f. [Standard] Most of the pieces will be of a complex progressive jazz-rock nature
g. [Standard] Some of these pieces will be included among our repertoire at a 4th quarter performance

Astonishingly, the school board accepted my course—two periods for full credit. Through the grapevine, they also understood that there was some resistance at my particular school for this initiative, but they were not interested in "petty school politics" getting in the way of talented students thriving within their school system. What they were interested in, though, was "developing opportunities for students in their district."

Man oh man, I couldn't believe it. I finally found a way to bring my music to the school and just under the wire.

When I held auditions in the music room, the look on the principal's face was absolutely priceless. The look on the music teacher's face, Christofferson, even more so. As a new music instructor, I was able to give students two credits for taking my music class for *our* senior year of high school.

AFTER AUDITIONING several students in the music room, and because of the supplication for public performances, there were just two qualified to perform the music I wanted to compose for the class—Scott Bringedahl on electric bass, and Sean Swift on drums. Both of them were currently in a Jimi Hendrix-styled tribute band with another electric guitarist who'd already graduated. The schoolboard stated that it was up to me, the program's instructor, as to what students would participate, and how many. I changed the name of our new group from "ensemble" to "trio."

By then, I was acquiring some electronic music gear. Yes, I was *going electric.* I acquired a black 1969 Les Paul Custom guitar, MXR Digital Delay (the one that Jean-Luc Ponty was using in his shows), a Morley Volume Pedal, phase shifter and wah-wah. I already had the Polytone Amplifier from the Merle Haggard run at Harrah's. That would have to do.

For many musicians in Seattle, we were a Jimi Hendrix town. The African American rock music legend had a profound influence and superhuman hold on all rock musicians here in the 1970s—Scott and Sean being no exception. The three of us were excited about our jazz-rock trio format placing me on the electric guitar—the precise instrumentation of the Jimi Hendrix Experience: guitar, bass, and drums. My schoolmates couldn't wait to do some Hendrix with me, but I was fully committed to coming up with original material at this point. Hendrix, who was laid to rest across town in Renton, died from barbiturate intoxication a few years earlier. He left behind plenty of imitators. There was at least one local professional impersonator.

Randy Hansen held a concert in our high school gym that year in 1978. He was noted as an excellent rock guitar player. At the show, dimly lit by a couple of blue gels on one small light stand, Hansen and his rock trio took the stage for some blazing guitar and vocal renditions of Hendrix. He had an Afro and looked African American to us, so I had assumed he was a black musician. Years later, I met a him in person. He had become a fan of my own guitar playing and attended one of my Seattle concerts—but when I saw him backstage, he was white with straight hair. He must have worn some dark makeup that night I saw him at the school gym. The practice of white musicians in "black face" could still be seen in the late '70s. Curiously believing it to be a good idea, he still seemed to be devoted to

Jimi Hendrix as a musician. But like the old "black face" minstrels, this way of portraying another person to channel their music was a step over the line. For many white musicians in Seattle, the culture was rather to *sound* like a black musician when playing African American music styles such as blues, jazz, R&B, funk, soul... Hansen did that as well.

The idea of adopting physical attributes of another musician seemed absurd on one hand, but on another, I learned how to play so many styles of music by acting things out as a kid—personifying the music of established icons. Learning the various musical styles made me feel differently about myself—and some of the playacting caused my own persona to alter as I would shift to the next genre. By fully immersing myself into a genre of music, I could get *out* of my own way. I still lived this same musical schizophrenia, but it started to be less about an escape from reality and more of a career direction pursuit—an embracing of my multi-layered musical persona. This notion became such a natural high on its own for me that I even quit smoking marijuana in my senior year. The endless changing of musical channels seemed even intoxicating.

To their disappointment, I told Scott and Sean that we weren't doing any Hendrix for the class. *Too many people already knew it.* Our "Trio" was going to be much closer to a "jazz-rock trio"—like Al Di Meola, Stanley Clarke, and Lenny White, current jazz players plugging in with Chick Corea's Return To Forever. For me, the 1970s were also about jazz-rock fusion, and I was pumped to be on the first wave of it. All the same, we were gearing up for our own appearance in the school gymnasium—the same gym that Hansen played his "black face" Hendrix tribute that blew all the white school kids' minds.

Leading up to it, our first trio performances took place across the mountains in eastern Washington. We were featured alongside the "jazz band" on a school field trip. A split bill. As I listened to our school's milquetoast renditions of the "Rocky" theme song, and another one by Chuck Mangione, it preyed on the mind. Christofferson treated me like some rebel kid that whole weekend. Feeling restless, I couldn't wait to plug my Les Paul into my fiddle amplifier and drown out all the noise. Except for the noise out of several schoolmates claiming I was "the best guitar player since Jimi."

CROSSING BRIDGES

E ACH DAY AT SCHOOL, Christofferson checked us in to report our attendance, then he left. We were left to *rock out* in the music room, playing at the loudest volumes we could obtain through our amplifiers. Most of the teachers in the surrounding buildings were not very happy about it—you could hear us throughout the school grounds.

We played so blaringly loud in the music room that clouds of fine soot drifted down from the drop ceiling tiles. We breathed in these particles as we jammed and thought it fairly amusing. We blasted so hard it caused the ceiling to ooze all over us. Sometimes, we had to go outside just to brush our clothes off and shake out our head mops.

Later, we learned how dangerous those *asbestos* ceilings tiles were in our school.

It reminded me of those same square titles in the false ceiling at elementary school. When the teacher wasn't looking, us boys flipped our pencils up there and tried to get the extra-sharpened points to stick into those ceiling panels. Had to get the pencils nice and pointy to do it. Of course there was plenty of asbestos and silica filtering right down on us from our attempts. If I was caught doing this, or even worse than that, tipping my chair on its hind legs, I was sent to the principal's office to receive my corporal punishment—usually two paddlings. I was there in his office often: both hands on the chair with my legs extending—the butt sticking out to receive those "swans." That's what we called them, *swans.* When I came back from "the man's" office, friends would want to know how many "swans" I got. Just holding up the two or three fingers made you feel cool. But as long as those ceiling tiles were not "disturbed," and you never breathed in, the experts said us grade-schoolers should be just fine. It all made about as much sense as the many drills that had us ducking under our desks—to shield us from a massive Soviet nuclear attack.

In time, some of the kids started to pay attention to the music we were making, even though our style and the music's complexities were likely far over their heads. We were still electric, and loud. It counted for something. While we seemed to be alienating teachers, we were drawing a fan base of kids at the high school.

In the process, I became a *student* of the electric guitar, even though I was the one teaching the class. I was learning to bend and vibrate the lighter-gauge strings, exploring scales and modes for extended improvised soloing especially, and getting comfortable with the idea of *playing the amp* as opposed to an acoustic wooden instrument. But as instructor, I took Scott under my wing the most. I wrote the bass lines for the music and showed them to him in class. Since he didn't own a bass for himself, always borrowing one, I bought a blonde 1960s Fender Precision bass for him to play. It only set me back $250 and we got some great bass out of Scott for the class. Sean was a pistol on those drums, too. Smokin'.

There were some high school kids who snuck into the music room to listen to our rehearsals, some of them recent dropouts still hanging around the schoolyard. They seemed to love what we were doing and I didn't mind sharing the music with them. One particular day, I recognized additional high school dropouts sitting along the back wall—some of them were the very 9th grade gang who beat me up in Junior High—almost took my leg out. Having them in the same room with me again was the very moment that my school life came full circle. They weren't supposed to be in there in the first place, none of them were, but I didn't want to readdress the malfeasance and abuse of the past, nor ask them to leave the class room. In those moments, I learned even more so that music could bring healing to just normal, everyday people. If they were willing to reach out and meet me halfway, my music could reach back to them, whether I personally wanted to make this investment or not. Their regenerated appreciation for me now meant I didn't have to say a single word to build their trust.

After we built our set list to nine of my original electric rock-jazz compositions, we were ready for our first high school assembly performance.

Introduction by Wayne Christofferson, music teacher for band and choir; *Mountlake Terrace High School Assembly:*

"I guess we could have sold ear plugs and probably made a mint out there after we get done. You people up here will want 'em. Anyway, this is a good group. I can't even remember names... *what's your name?* This is Mark O'Connor, the guitar player. He was also senior celebrity for the most musically inclined. We have Scott Bringedahl on bass guitar, and Sean Swift on set. I'll let them take over."

Electric Metamorphosis (Composed by Mark O'Connor - 1979 High School class for credit)

"Bermuda Square," "Hectic Dance," "Invasion," "Lee's Tune," "Afternoon Eclipse," "The Devil's Spleen," "Lunar Shadows," "Blue Food," "Ballad."

The students loved our performance and we got a standing ovation from them. I would count my high school music class as one of the most extraordinary accomplishments I experienced as a kid musician given my history in the school district. Given *everything* in Mountlake Terrace.

But there was pushback and some sincere fallout. While I was the first student-teacher in our school district, no mention was made of my "Jazz Trio" class for school credit in the school yearbook. My name was omitted entirely from our senior yearbook.

ATTENDING A WORKING-CLASS neighborhood high school in the 1970s meant that the vast majority of the students at Terrace were not preparing to go to college. Nine out of ten students at my school did not attend college. Therefore, my school counselor who supported me teaching the music class, never even brought up the idea.

My mother, whose wish that my music income could take care of her and my sister, never brought up the idea of me attending college either. In the 1940s, Mom earned a two-year degree from the University of Washington, and still, she didn't have any of these aspirations for me as a parent. While I could have easily enrolled at Edmonds Community College after the fact, I wanted to at least take the summer and go to Nashville—stay at Bill and Bonnie's again and find out if I was old enough to make it as a recording session player. Under the threat of flunking out and being held back a grade, I was unable to tour much during my junior and senior years. I wanted to get out there and away from Seattle for a few months, to see what might pan out.

To attend my high school graduation ceremony, it was going to cost me a roundtrip plane flight doubling back across the country from the Grand Masters in Nashville. And yet, Mom insisted that I do so. I was making a strong case to just go ahead and skip it, but she wanted to *see* the cap and gown on.

At the ceremony, the students were not seated alphabetically, so of all things I found myself next to one of my classmates, Renee—the beautiful Polynesian girl I had a crush on in 3rd grade. Frankly, I had a crush on her for a few years after that too, through 7th grade at least, but she completely ignored me. I figured she was just one of the many girls who thought I was too ugly and pimple-faced to be seen with. As far as Renee's appearance, she grew to be one of the most beautiful girls in high school—popular, and a member of the cheerleading squad. While we sat together during graduation rehearsal, Renee told me that she kept the notes I passed to her in 3rd grade. (Out of frustration and disappointment, I had long since thrown mine away.) Then, unexpectedly, she kissed me on the cheek and said she was "proud" of me." We began holding hands during the ceremony. On the very last day of my senior year, one of the hottest girls in school is now going to *like* me? And right when I was leaving town and heading to Nashville for the summer. *That school assembly performance was a really good idea.*

Renee was deeply emotional about graduating and sad she wouldn't see *me* at school anymore. My reaction was like... *what?* I quit trying to say hello to her years ago, because she wouldn't really respond that much. But, here we are. We went on a few dates before I took off for Nashville. She was actually falling for me, and I was blown away by all this. I could see myself wanting to be her boyfriend very much so. She was frightened over my wanting to leave Seattle. I reminded her, "You could always move away and join me." She saw it differently. Since we both were from our shared corner of the world—the same schools, the same small Seattle suburb... why would I ever consider leaving, especially if a serious romance between us was in the picture. I definitely could see her point, I sure did. I could enroll at the local community college—she lived right there in Edmonds herself, just a couple miles from Terrace. Her world was right here, while everything I wanted, except for her, was as far away from this place as I could get.

Renee and I remained in touch, but I would have needed to glue myself to Seattle for there to be any chance of having a serious relationship. It was frustrating to have all of those years go by—and maybe we could have been together during my school years? I just had to shake my head— the incredulity over my unluckiness in my love life. How attending school would've been so much better, easier... safer. But I was predestined to bear loneliness and hurt in my personal life. As a young man, my fiddle and guitar themselves became my "serious relationships"—my solace and escape from the treacheries I confronted.

In my final days of being a Seattle resident, I spared myself of a beautiful and loving relationship with the prettiest girl in school to try my hand at musical *chance.*

In a few years, Renee was soon married and she started her family.

A FEW YEARS AFTER I graduated, Wayne Christofferson belittled my sister in choir—just because she was related to me. She felt so uncomfortable by his mental games that she had to transfer out of music during high school entirely.

Soon after, Christofferson was found guilty and sentenced to prison for child pornography.

A couple of my former classmates returned to Mountlake Terrace High School after that, this time as arsonists. They torched our school and burned it to the ground. Investigators determined that the "fire started in the student hub where musical theater programs took place."

What happened next was an entirely new structure for the Mountlake Terrace High School built on that same piece of ground, and with it, an unlikely rebirth. Like a phoenix rising from the ashes, the school transformed into something much better than its former self: new teachers and a great music curriculum fielding as many as two symphony orchestras replaced all of that despicable rubble. Their award-winning music program's "jazz band" went all the way to the national competitions at the *Essentially Ellington* finals at Jazz at Lincoln Center with Wynton Marsalis, a jazz trumpet master who would later become my close musical colleague.

More recently, I received a call from a Mountlake Terrace High School student who wrote for the school newspaper. This student was working on an in-depth article about the school's history of their now-successful music program, one that boasted an illustrious track record dating as far back as the late 1980s. In his digging around, he heard a rumor that I may have attended his own high school a number of years before that, in the 1970s.

"Are the rumors true? *Were you ever enrolled at Terrace?"*

After confirming that I was a student there, he responded by saying, "I couldn't find any records of that." (Perhaps they were burned in the fire?) After informing the student that I was a 1979 graduate, he reminded me that I didn't have an entry in the 1979 senior yearbook either. My history was essentially *erased* at the school.

I proceeded to tell the student journalist the whole story. All of these years later, it was rather cathartic detailing what had happened to me there.

Around this very same time, I had a performance during the Washington Music Educators Conference in Yakima, Washington where an orchestra director from the Mountlake Terrace High School approached me. She also asked if I had ever attended Terrace High—she heard something about it recently. I told her that I did. She said, "I don't think anyone in our music department knows this." When returning home, she jumped through some hoops to arrange for an official school visit, for me to speak to their students, and have me inducted into my old high school's Hall Of Fame. They had never inducted someone into the school's Hall of Fame who wasn't an athlete. The physical education teachers would oversee the proceedings.

During my induction ceremony I teared up when accepting the honor. The memories and the hardships of those years on that very ground all came flooding back. The school now was so much better than what I had experienced. I repeated the sentiment to the students and teachers there several times during my visit. What a difference. I was proud of all that they had accomplished since my time. As I observed the kids in the various music classes, I felt so much joy for them—getting to attend a successful and thriving public school with access to the arts. Most all of their programs were getting national recognition. It was hard to fathom this kind of success. I hoped that I had even a little something to do with ushering in this change for the better—a complete transformation.

I met a lot of the high school's faculty that day, all of them congratulatory. But no one said they remembered me from my time there as a student. I supposed those teachers would be in their 60s or even 70s by now— likely retired, I assumed. When a group of us were lingering afterwards, I asked the school principal about it. He told me, "There are actually two teachers here at the school who date back to your time here." Excited to hear this news, I asked if he could point them out to me. I wanted to greet them, shake their hand. Conspicuously, the principal looked down at the floor, and then said, "Unfortunately, they both called in sick today."

THE VERY WEEK AFTER high school graduation in 1979, I won the Open division at Weiser for the first time. I became the National Old-time Fiddle Champion at age 17, the youngest champion in the history of the contest. What a way to begin post-Terrace life. It already seemed like ancient history when Wayne Christofferson couldn't remember my name at the school assembly.

The Salt Lake Tribune, Monday June 25, 1979 (Associated Press)

"WEISER, Idaho — (AP) — Mark O'Connor, 17, of Mountlake Terrace, Wash., became the youngest fiddler ever to win the National Grand Championship at the National Oldtime Fiddlers' festival Saturday.

O'Connor who previously had won four national junior titles edged out veteran Dick Barrett, 60, of Pottsboro, Texas, for the top crown.

'I just wanted to play my best for this contest. I'll keep coming back as long as I can,' Mark O'Connor said after winning the top title of the week-long national fiddling event.

During the performance, he was accompanied by Men's Division winner Rick Youngblood of Pocatello and Bill Lyell of Gatesville, Texas.

The top crown brought O'Connor $1,000, a certificate and a trophy. His selections for the finals were 'Sally Goodwin,' 'Zenda Waltz,' and 'Black and White Rag.'"

Weiser American "Published in the Fiddlin' Capital of the World" June, 1979

"Asked where he was going musically he replied, 'They said I was at the top when I was winning the Junior championship...so who knows.'

As one woman quipped, 'If Mark hadn't won, there would have been a riot.'"

Golden West Bluegrass, Pat Powers of San Diego, 1979

"Every once in a while a phenomenon occurs in the arts and sciences, a talent with the body of a child and the ability of immeasurable educated and seasoned professionals. Such a prodigy was introduced to the subculture of fiddle music at Weiser, Idaho, in 1973, and the world of horse hair and cat guts has not been the same since.

...Each year Mark seemed to grow taller as if to accommodate his growing imagination and marvelous execution of fiddle tunes. Everybody knew him, listened with awe, and wondered what he could possibly come up with next...

Previously, the fiddling world had been astounded if a little unnerved at the vitality and creativity of the Texas style, championed by Benny Thomasson, Major Franklin, Herman Johnson, and Dick Barrett. This particular style took fiddling out of the category of accompanying hoedowns, its danceable tradition, and into a listener's music, an artist's arena of intricate improvisation where so much happened to a *Durang's Hornpipe* or a *Leather Britches* you'd find yourself losing the original melody in flights of fantasy. Then along came young Mark and took those tunes along with the venerable old *Sally Goodin* and the archetypal Texas showpiece, *Tom and Jerry*, and charted absolutely unknown territory with his incredible command of the instrument, his precision timing, his ability to take your breath away and then return you to the old familiar melody which would never be quite the same again."

Terry Morris' older brother Dale made the finals at Weiser that year. He informed me that he was going to take his newly purchased motor home all the way up to Calgary, Alberta, for what they advertised as the Canadian National Fiddling Championships. For the first time, U.S. players were allowed to enter in a Canadian national fiddle competition. I was welcome to ride up with him. I took Dale up on it.

On the drive up, we discussed our individual strategies in how to win the Canadian nationals. Dale's plan was unique. He wanted to play obscure Texas tunes so the judges might be deceived into thinking that these were obscure Canadian gems — *playing* the slight-of-hand card? My strategy was a little different. I planned on playing well-known Texas fiddle breakdowns — my normal course of action. But I was going to at least speed up my waltzes, speed up the rate of my slow vibrato, and play with less double-stops. All of it being my own observations of what was germane to the distinctness between these two styles: *Texas* and *Canadian*. For my tunes of choice, I assumed that ragtime was out. Maybe I could pick up a tune or two from the Canadian fiddlers when we arrived at the contest. I did have a few Joe Pancerzewski jigs in my back pocket, if I needed them.

Both Dale and I made it into the finals. Earlier that day, I heard a nice Canadian polka performed by one of the Canadian contestants. I taped it on my portable deck and learned the three-part tune from the cassette backstage. I went over the chords with an accompanist and was ready for the final round.

A bit of an unusual practice saw the competitors announce their own tunes over the PA. I had just one problem with it — I didn't catch the name of the Canadian polka I had learned from the tape. Fearing that other fiddlers, or even the contest officiators, would catch on to my hijinks, I didn't dare ask any of the locals about the tune's name. I was hoping that an idea of how to handle this would just come to me as I walked up on stage to play. I got up to the microphone, I hesitated for a second, and... made up a name: "My third tune will be—'Calgary Polka!'"

It worked. I became the first person ever to win both the U.S. and Canadian national fiddle contests. In time, even Canadian fiddlers began to know "Gaudette Polka" as "Calgary Polka."

MAKING MY WAY ACROSS the country to Nashville for a second time that June, I was hoping to make good in Music City with a much better advantage this time around—I was flying high as the fiddle champion for practically the entire continent.

I spent more time around session ace Buddy Spicher, hoping I could apprentice him and break into at least some studio work. The sidekick thing was not his idea, but mine. He remained fairly protective of his studio session contact list. I learned that even the top guys did lower-level session work, too, not always the hit records. They even played on song demo sessions (writers recording their new songs they wanted to pitch), but I wasn't scoring here either. Buddy's fiddle tune idea for the radio wasn't any farther along than the last time we worked on it.

The other session fiddle staple, Johnny Gimble, was currently on tour with Willie Nelson. I sensed an opening in Nashville for a new fiddler, at least while he was gone. But still, recording sessions looked like a narrowing prospect for me. At 18 they were.

My summer was filling up, though. I had some more appearances with Jim & Jesse booked, featuring me as the new national fiddle champion, and Dan Crary asked me to travel with him to Japan for a duo tour. It was to be my first trip out of the country, other than to Canada. Even by 1979, it was still infrequent for American musicians to perform in Japan. Regardless of Nashville's fair bets, I was excited about moving on from school and getting out of the house.

A RATHER IMPORTANT CALL is what it sounded like to Bill and Bonnie Smith. David Grisman wanted me to get back to him right away. He and Tony Rice had recently appeared on my new On The Rampage album, playing on a tune called "Ease With The Breeze,"—a simple three-chord folk-style tune I wrote. The rest of the album was much more progressive stylistically. For the bulk of the recording, though, I did not pilgrimage with the dynamic duo of Grisman and Rice together again. Things seemed to get a little strange on the last one. At one point during the *Markology* session, David said to me, "Hey man, if you keep playing guitar like that, I'm going to hire you for my band when you graduate from high school." Tony Rice was sitting right there pretending not to hear that—noodling on his Martin with a cigarette hanging from his lips. I did my own guitar rhythm on the new album for which I was relying on a good deal more.

"Mark, I have a proposal for you," David declared on the phone.

"Okay. I'm all ears?"

"So, remember when I said that I wanted to hire you after you graduated high school, man?"

"Ha-ha, yes, I remember that!"

"Well, here's the deal, Tony can't do our three week-long tour next month, so I need a guitarist to fill in."

"Great! I would love to do it!"

"I'll need you to come out to San Francisco to audition with my band before I make a final decision."

"Oh…wow. August turns out to be completely packed for me. I am doing a Texas-style fiddle album in Nashville for Rounder and I am doing this tour in Japan with Dan Crary as well. I am in Nashville right now, not in Seattle. Do I really have to come all the way to California for an audition? You already know how I play!"

David told me he was considering a few other guitar players for the spot, saying it was all a little complicated and that he could explain more later. He offered to pay my flight out for the audition and I could stay with him in Mill Valley for a few days. The tryout part of it seemed a bit of a drag—a few days? I never had to audition for anything before—well, except for Ted Dragoo—but of course, I had to make it out there for the audition. I would definitely want that tour in September—filling in for Tony Rice in the David Grisman Quintet. *Yeah.*

ONCE I ARRIVED IN TOKYO in early August of 1979, I couldn't help but be awed by how big our world truly is. My first trip abroad. Mom reminded me that my chosen profession of music may not earn me a fortune (she would know better than anyone), but it would allow me to see the world.

Dan Crary had been to Japan once before, so he was a good tour guide along with Robert Tanaka and his secretary Kay Kawaguchi, who presented the tour and acted as our hosts. We performed duo concerts in several cities including Hiroshima and the northern city of Sapporo. Getting acquainted with the local culture and customs was such a new experience. I learned to eat with chopsticks there, no other choice. I had never tried to eat sushi before either, so it took me a couple of days to get the courage up.

On that big day, the four of us walked into a restaurant in Tokyo, and I readied myself for eating raw fish. I grew up eating raw oysters from Seattle's Puget Sound, but somehow this seemed so different. It's all about what you're used to. I loved those raw oysters, too—Dad would shuck the oysters on the rocky coastline of the Sound. Our waiter had me choose among the fish swimming around in the restaurant's fish tank, located right at the front entrance. Each of those fish were between eight and ten-inches long. They grabbed my chosen fish, slapped it down on a wooden plate and drove a steak knife like a dagger right through the middle of it. With the tip of the knife lodged securely into my plate, the spearing caused its head and tail to natural curl up into the shape of a "U," (or a *half pipe*). Each end of the fish quivered uninterrupted throughout the meal—maybe an hour before the fish finally quit trembling. Sashimi cuts of its "cousins" were piled up all around it. I ate the pre-cut pieces, but couldn't dive into the traumatized daggered fish like they intended for me to do. My Dad would've been unhappy for not licking my plate clean. But my first sushi meal was accomplished—the occasion never to be far from my mind ever again.

Keeping with the ocean life theme, my secret mission was really about tortoises—as in guitar flat-picks made from a tortoise's shell. I only had a couple of real tortoise shell picks that I used on *Markology* and *On The Rampage*, but otherwise they were hard to find in the States. Being illegal and all—smuggling them in was not going to be a good look for Dan, so he wasn't interested in them. However, I was willing to take my chances. The tone that they could give a flat-pick guitar was much better than the imitation plastic that was common to most players. I convinced Kay to help me find some of these guitar picks in Japan—especially the thick triangle ones. Willing to please, Kay came up huge, the big payload. Out of a single music store I must've gotten a hundred strong. To evade tortoise-shell detection at customs, I put four or five picks in every pocket of clothing I had in my suitcase. Amusingly, some of them were stamped with an image of a green marijuana plant. If any of these were discovered at the border, emblems of funny weed stamped on them were not going to help matters.

Spending all the money made on the tour now, I bought my first suitcase with wheels on it. I had never seen a rolling suitcase before.

It was a great trip all around and so cool to be playing music with Dan for the Japanese audiences. He had a little bluegrass version of Mozart's, "Rhondo Alla Turca," that we charmed the audiences with. Dan was especially known for transposing fiddle tunes to the flat-pick. We were kindred spirits in this way. Dan willingly accompanied me on at least a couple of Texas-style fiddle tunes. In time, I spread this music out there around the world, like Benny would have hoped for. I was a musical ambassador for him, already.

Kay was wonderful throughout the trip. She hosted J.D. Crowe and the New South with Tony Rice there a few years earlier. I told her all about playing and recording with all of those guys back home. Kay really loved American music. I heard her sing some of it at one of Tanaka's steakhouses, her Japanese accent curiously reshaping the English lyrics. It was enchanting to hear something like that for the first time. Kay asked me what it was like living in the U.S. so I encouraged her to try it out for a while since she was so interested in all things American. I told her, *"You could always return home if you didn't like it."* It was a similar crusade I had been attempting out of Seattle, so I could identify with the dream to journey far away from where you were born.

Before long in 1983, Kay did journey to the U.S.—initially to Arkansas. At a bluegrass festival, she met Art Stamper of Kentucky, a first-generation bluegrass fiddle pioneer. Stamper played in the first Stanley Brothers band as well as working with Bill Monroe and Jim & Jesse. They were soon married. Kay Kawaguchi got to realize her dream of living the life of an authentic country musician in the rural South after all. For the rest of her years, she became Kay Stamper and remained in Kentucky on their family farm just outside of Shepherdsville.

Dan didn't buy tortoise shell picks, Japanese suitcases with wheels, nor did he eat sushi for the very first time. His perspective on our travels in Japan was on a much deeper level. Dan's capacity for comprehending the world helped me to learn just where we were not very long ago. Especially so when we visited the Hiroshima Peace Memorial Park. Helping me to contextualize the powerful emotional response I was having, Dan was not your typical bluegrass picker.

Dan Crary, one of the first lead guitar flat-pickers in bluegrass music, was a professor at California State University at Fullerton in "speech communications." Earlier in his life, he studied theology at a few prominent institutes. When he moved to Louisville to earn a doctorate in philosophy at the Southern Seminary, he also became a co-founder of the Bluegrass Alliance that saw Sam Bush, Tony Rice, and Vince Gill follow in his footsteps. Back in southern California, he became a long-time musical partner to Byron Berline. They teamed up for a few professional bluegrass bands including one called Sundance.

The grievous undertaking of the trip, and something that Dan very much wished to do, was to visit the museum in Hiroshima. Neither Robert nor Kay advised us doing so, considering we were their American guests and all. Robert even tried to talk Dan out of it, but Dan felt strongly that Americans needed to fully understand this history so it will never happen again.

The center of Hiroshima bore a single original structure, the only physical remnant after the U.S. atomic bombing during WWII. The justification for using such a horrific measure was to stop the world takeover of a once-militant Japanese nation led by their emperor and "god," Hirohito. The way things were going 34 years ago nearly to the day, on August 6th, 1945, was that America would prevail, or our democracy and the United States Constitution would be torn to shreds by the Japanese dictator. The photographs hanging in the museum of Japanese citizens running for their lives while their bodies were burning and skin melting, was a horror that penetrated the soul. I didn't remember seeing anything like those photos in our history books at school. To have Dan there, putting this contemporary hideousness into his own stoical perspective and historical framework, helped blunt my own purely emotional reaction to this. I was going to have nightmares, regardless.

In the seven years after the War, beginning in 1945, 350,000 U.S. troops occupied Japan in order to westernize it, but not at gunpoint. That was probably the difference in why it worked at all. The cultural seeds were planted in the late 1940s bringing western music to the ears of the Japanese. Just 27 years after the occupation was complete, that effort resulted in people like Robert and Kay answering to English names and all of those beautiful Japanese music fans there at our shows making two guys from America feel so welcome. We were standing on a street corner one time when two older Japanese ladies standing beside us started to giggle. As they kept looking at us, I wasn't sure what to think, but Dan had the biggest smile on his face. "Two tall white guys must look so strange to them," he said. Given the recent history, I was surprised by the heartwarming love we experienced in Japan, even at our show in Hiroshima. After all, Japan was a place that only recently was the home of a merciless enemy who wished our all-out destruction. I couldn't help but remember the Japanese war cry evoking Roy Acuff's name. I didn't mention it to anybody.

After my tour in Japan, I developed a keener interest of our elliptical world, one that I wished to experience through performing my music in the future. I hoped I could continue to reach out to more people in these ways—on all six inhabited continents. In time I would, but I was anxious to begin. It seemed to me that American music was quite a healer the world over. American music was introduced to the Japanese and it made all the difference. The universal attractiveness of music from my own country brought people and cultures closer together. That it did.

AS I PREPARED FOR A full-time career in music right out of high school in 1979, I couldn't help but be thankful for the creative musical experiences that set me on my way. I found my own Western Coastline musical persona with a new kind of musical expression realized on my two recent albums. Most importantly, the creativeness of writing music devoted to the unusual theme of West Coast skateboarding, but rooted by acoustic improvised violin-playing, was going to put my music on a unique course.

My ever-developing musical agility by age 17 became so interlaced as to carry on musical dialogues in any number of genres and styles simultaneously: the jazz-rock trio at school; dropping into Country music and Western Swing for a week with Haggard and his top men; trading bluegrass licks with Crary in Japan, and winning old-time fiddle contests in Canada. Any of it could happen within days or weeks, and without warning, or even a dry run. The power of *dreaming* and *imagining* so as to *transport* myself to the other musical place I needed to go, advanced as a way to learn new music as a kid. But more than that, it was becoming a musical *way of life*—a blueprint for a distinguished career in music.

Buoyed by the epoch of rebellious musical freedom, it seemed to both convey and heighten the multiplicity I was holding on to from the beginning. I simply could *turn around on a dime.*

The Texas-style fiddling learned from Benny Thomasson—I wasn't done with that either. It remained a mental sector of my mind I could just conjure up in a heartbeat—with almost no warning, or practice. With the finishing touches put to the contemporary jazz violin album, Rounder suggested I should get back into the studio for an all-fiddle-tune album and take advantage of my success in the old-time music genre—the stuff that Rounder Records liked a lot more. And since I was the brand new national fiddle champion, why not...

Late in August 1979, we scheduled a recording session with engineer Fred Cameron at Oak Valley Studio in Nashville. I wanted to record a collection of fiddle tunes that I'd been playing in contests the last few years. We also recorded a waltz I had written the year before, "Misty Moonlight Waltz." I debuted it at Weiser for my championship run, so the tune didn't hold me back any.

At a future date I recorded "Misty Moonlight Waltz" for the Grammy-winning album Appalachian Journey *with cellist Yo-Yo Ma. Together, we played it over the phone to violinist Isaac Stern in celebration of his 80th birthday.*

For accompanists, I drafted in some of my favorites: Jerry Thomasson on the tenor guitar and Buck White on mandolin. I overdubbed my own six-string guitar backup.

I had the distinct impression this recording may very well be my final traditional fiddle album. The newfound propensity to create new instrumental material meant that it was going to be hard for me to get off that train, now that I jumped on. If this was to be my last old-time fiddle album, I was glad to record this specific set of old tunes and contemporary themes within the traditional music setting—some of the more obscure contest repertoire I played. The album documented my unique renditions and the "controlled improvisation" I had been practicing for several years. The album cover was an old-time sepia toned photograph of me with a Derby hat on and holding the old white fiddle low on my chest. Soon, John Hartford adopted the Derby for his own stage appearances.

Side A: Soppin' The Gravy, Misty Moonlight Waltz, College Hornpipe, Calgary Polka (Gaudette Polka), Morning Star Waltz, Peaches 'n Cream, Skater's Waltz
Side B: Tennessee Wagoner, Yellow Rose Waltz, Medley: Speed The Plow / The Maid Behind The Barn / Teatottler's Reel, Jesse Polka, The Dawn Waltz, Wild Fiddler's Rag, Over The Rainbow

Byron Berline – Soppin' The Gravy album notes, 1979
"For anyone who likes fiddle music, and for those of you who don't know, just try this album on for size. You won't want to put it down... Mark includes an original waltz that is simply beautiful. Still playing his white-painted fiddle, at the ripe old age of 18 and a few inches over six feet tall, my ears are still disbelieving. I am sure yours will be too."

Benny Thomasson – Soppin' The Gravy album notes, 1979
"There is not room on this album for me to explain the extent of Mark's musical talents. I've met the greatest fiddlers in this nation, but to me Mark is the greatest one of all. I know you'll agree when you hear this album."

CHAPTER NINE

ME and STEPH

"…and Mark, you're probably going to like this part. We'll have a special guest fiddle player on the tour," David Grisman said to me on the phone call. "You don't mind playing with Stephane Grappelli, do you?"

The hand that was holding the phone to my ear, went numb. Then the handset dropped to the floor.

DAVID GRISMAN MET me at the San Francisco airport in late August 1979. That was a good sign, getting the personal touch from the "god of the mandolin." David told me that his violinist, Darol Anger, had taken a fellowship grant with his wife, Barbara Higbie, to study traditional music for six months in West Africa. His temporary absence from the DGQ (David Grisman Quintet) led to a tour collaboration with jazz violin legend, Stephane Grappelli.

David's relationship with Grappelli came by way of his film score for *King of the Gypsies* at Paramount Pictures. David arranged for Grappelli to play on the soundtrack, and it led to cameo appearances in the film for both of them. While in the studio recording the film music, astute thinking led to Grisman cutting a couple of tunes with Grappelli for a follow-up to the original *David Grisman Quintet* album, *Hot Dawg*. The album was billed under David Grisman (not the "Quintet"). Tony Rice and the rest of the band were still playing on it, though. *Hot Dawg* was released on a major label, A&M Records, just months before I arrived for my audition in San Francisco. The "Dawg music" that Grisman self-named was becoming a lot more famous.

I was still trying to wrap my head around the idea that Tony Rice couldn't play the three-week tour with Stephane Grappelli. As far as I could tell, he was going to be sitting around his Marin County apartment for the month. As to why, there were a few competing stories floating around. When we exited off of 101 into Mill Valley, David asked me if I was hungry. He took me out for the most delectable crab meat omelet I could've ever believed possible. I didn't think that fresh crab and eggs were even a thing, but in San Francisco… yes it was. He asked me if I wanted a *cappuccino* to top things off. I'd never heard of one of those before. I told him that I didn't drink coffee. "That will probably change," he said. Mill Valley was surely one heck of a hip place.

David's home was nestled in one of the hamlet's hilly and narrow, winding roads. It was pretty nice digs alright — on a street called Morning Sun. You could almost feel David's beautiful compositions coming right out of his home on the hill. It was interesting being back in Marin County again. My sister was born there and my Mom and Dad taught at Arthur Murray's Dance Studio a couple of miles away, just up in San Rafael.

I remember some of my early childhood living in Fairfax, set back just to the west of San Rafael. There were six or seven very specific reflections I carried with me from those preschooler days, and about all of them took place right there in that apartment. I could recall our black and white television and the images on it of JFK's assassination. I remembered my mother crying for days over it. I saw the Beatles debut on *Ed Sullivan* and Mom got me a Beatles haircut the following week. I had long hair as a toddler, anyway. Mom wanted a girl instead, so I had all pink baby clothes that she knitted. We lived on the second story, and I took a hellacious tumble on my tricycle down our flight of cement stairs. I knocked out my front teeth. Another odd thing — I didn't see the sun for days at a time because of overcast weather, all the Bay Area fog — so when the sun did come out I took shots at it with my toy pistol. Mom reminded me of that one.

I can think back to those lawn chairs we had for furniture, and Mom and Dad sleeping on cardboard boxes so they could be elevated off the floor. Not being able to afford a bed, Mom said that it made them feel a little higher. Higher class. At my first day at kindergarten in Fairfax, I must've carried some level of discomfort with me, and got in my first fist-fight — I was on top of the kid when they pried me off and was sent home. It was my first day of school.

A prevailing memory, though, had to do with floating cardboard boxes. Me and my little friend from the apartment building thought floating down the drainage ditch out by the busy road was good city-kid entertainment. Attempting to enjoy the more than usual rainfall one day, a gush of water swept us down the drainage canal more swiftly than before. It pushed my friend right into the corrugated pipe of the storm drain that went under the road, the spot where we always stopped ourselves before going in. This time the flood water came rushing up high into the storm ditch. He took the lead on that run. I was just behind him. But I caught the edge of the culvert with my little hands just like we did the other times. He did not. Once he was inside that pipe, his cardboard box got hung up. As I heard his yells and cries for help reverberate through that pipe, he drowned in there. My life was spared that day.

I was jolted back to the present when David offered me a toke from his joint. Maybe I looked like I needed one. But I had already quit smoking marijuana. Sean, from my jazz-rock trio, wanted to really *focus* on the music, and he helped inspire me to not smoke anymore. He didn't talk Scott out of it, just me. In terms of timing, though, it was a shame. David smoked the really good stuff—the Jerry Garcia-level dope. The kids back home would've given an eyetooth for this quality of grass. But for now, I'd have to settle for the contact high. If David smoked as much as he did on the day of my audition on a regular basis—that *contact* was going to be substantial.

The Grisman mission statement for his tour could be summed up as follows: the opening set was to be *David Grisman Quintet* material. For this part of the show, I had to become something on the order of Tony Rice. For the main portion of the concert: Stephane Grappelli material. For this part, I had to become something of a Django Reinhardt stylist. I had to wonder what kinds of guitarists David was auditioning for this gig. I wasn't aware of that manner of guitarist. It was a role where nearly no one on earth was really qualified. So on that account, I was big on my chances of getting hired for the tour.

THE FIRST DAY was just David and me. I began to learn the tunes for both sets from him. The new bassist was to arrive the following day. I had never auditioned for anything before. But learning all the tunes for a concert, while wondering if I was even getting the job, was quite a new consideration. Regarding the guitar position on this tour, I soon discovered what David was most interested in: my rhythmic proficiency and *dependability*. That is to say, knowing inside and out, the finer points of David's mandolin groove. It was paramount to getting this gig. Luckily for me, David doesn't have much of a poker face. His facial expressions let me know as soon as I was doing something rhythmically he didn't like. The reactions he expressed on his face were open and big-hearted, his curly black hair flopping about was akin to his exuberant smile. As he played his mandolin, he made a unique habit of fixating his engrossing eyes right on yours. What this meant to me in practical terms, was that he was *digging* it. If he began to scrunch up his face, steeled his eyes off to one side while overworking his furrowing brow, well, that meant he was "not digging it."

David's California style of speaking reminded me of my own skate-boarding lingo. He was both hippie and yuppie at the same time. There was nobody I had ever run into quite like the god of the mandolin.

Born in New Jersey just months before the end of WWII, David grew up in a conservative Jewish household. His father was a professional trombonist and imparted the love of music to David. He first learned piano and saxophone before turning to the mandolin at age 16. In the early 1960s he attended New York University and joined up with Maria Muldaur and John Sebastian to form the Even Dozen Jug Band. After a year with blue-grass singing traditionalist Red Allen and the Kentuckians in 1966, he went from folk to folk-psychedelic with Peter Rowan and Earth Opera. Two albums later, David found himself keeping company with the all-time psychedelic rock guru Jerry Garcia. Leaving Boston for the Bay Area, he guested on the Grateful Dead's *'American Beauty'* and assembled Old & In the Way with Garcia, Rowan, and Vassar Clements.

Next in line of the many bands David participated in was Muleskinner with Rowan, Clarence White, Richard Greene, and Bill Keith. This was the lineup when I first saw David play on TV. The short-lived group with Greene called Great American String Band acted as a precursor for his new expanded compositions in his own Quintet with Tony Rice. That was 1975—the very year I first played with Grisman in L.A.

I expected to see the Quintet's original bassist at the audition, Bill Amatneek, who played on my last two solo albums. Bill played some good jazz grooves on the first DGQ album, but David was looking for even more jazz chops on the tour, as he described it. Amatneek was replaced with a pulsing powerhouse bass player who came out of the folk/swing/pop Mill Valley-based Dan Hicks and the Hot Licks. This was Rob Wasserman.

After playing through some rhythmic grooves as a trio, it was clear that Rob was quite a force on backup jazz bass. Fearsome, along with a big, punchy sound, and pushing out some relentless momentum, the three of us still needed to find each other's groove to make it all click. At least that's what David was submitting. It likely meant that Rob and I needed to find David's strum and stick to it no matter what—even if we were playing in the "swing groove," which David didn't seem to be most of the time.

David liked talking about "band seniority." Occasionally, David enticed Rob to offer his thoughts about my playing as a part of my audition, because his month-long status of being a band member proved his "seniority." *So how am I doing, Rob?* I found it to be fairly awkward—his responses filled with shoulder shrugs. In the beginning, at least. This was a tall order, and I was very young for a role like this evidently. I was getting some jitters about the tour. Putting together a backing band for the violin legend, Stephane Grappelli, when none of us had any professional band experience with each other, was indeed some real high-flying. It was just weeks away.

It's so important to have the rhythm guitar and the bass in sync in every way. I found myself straddling David's groove and Rob's groove on occasion. As soon as Rob started to go into double time on the swing tunes (*walking* the bass), the feel shifted dramatically. I adjusted to playing more of a swing feel at those times, as opposed to David's bluegrass-style strumming. But I wasn't sure if that was what we were going for. I couldn't imagine Tony playing that kind of swing rhythm—closed chord, "gypsy jazz" *sock* rhythm for an entire tune, let alone the whole set. David did his own "Dawg"-bluegrass mandolin whether Rob was pulling me into more of a jazz feel or not. Of course, Rob was just getting used to playing with David, too. Like I was. Neither of us had this down yet.

We were putting together jazz standards—"Pent-up House," "Misty," and a Reinhardt tune, "Swing 42," for Grappelli. It started to feel more comfortable as we fell into roles that were more defined. David wasn't really focused on what kind of guitar solos I could take. That seemed to be his last concern, surprisingly. Nevertheless, it is what I was most worried about going into this audition, and what I was most excited about at the same time. Am I going to have to try to sound more like Tony Rice on the DGQ solos and then Django Reinhardt on the Grappelli solos? Some tall order, especially if all this was taking place inside a single set in major concert halls. The *split music personality...*, I mean, they got the right guy in that department. I was pegged. Grisman didn't want me to take any solos in the rehearsals, though.

On the third day of the audition, David added his second mandolinist, 20-year-old Mike Marshall. With Mike joining in on the rhythm, it seemed to get a little better, and the rhythmic sum of its parts now became the greater whole. I could relate to Mike a lot—musically and personally. He had great timing and groove, and some good solo chops, too, although he wasn't playing solos in the rehearsal either. I had met him a few months earlier when I sat in with the DGQ at San Francisco's Great American Music Hall during my *On The Rampage* sessions. Playing guitar and fiddle in addition to his fine mandolin, Mike had been in the band for a year.

Mike Marshall grew up in Lakeland Florida, where he won statewide mandolin and fiddle contests and played in local bluegrass bands. When David was suffering from painful tendonitis in his strumming arm, he remembered meeting a teenaged Mike Marshall and brought him in to cover most of the rhythm mandolin for the *King of The Gypsies* soundtrack recording. Doing the job at "rhythm mandolin," at 19 years old, Mike was invited to be a member of the DGQ.

At some point during that third day, David finally announced; "Mark's got the gig!" Mike and Rob congratulated me and welcomed me to the tour. When I asked David if the other guitar auditions had taken place yet, he said he didn't have to schedule them after all: "You saved me a lot of extra hassle!" David had an additional announcement for us, too. We were booked with Grappelli to do the *Tonight Show with Johnny Carson*. We had some serious work to become a real band in the next couple of weeks. The tour would get underway at the beginning of September, with three nights at the Great American Music Hall—David's hometown venue filled with his thoroughly discerning audience. The first rehearsal with Grappelli was scheduled in the green room at the Music Hall the day before the tour kicked off.

I called Mom to tell her that I got the job. I told her that I was going to do the national tour with Stephane Grappelli and David Grisman and that we were coming through Seattle to play at the big Paramount Theater, where I went to all of those Jean-Luc Ponty concerts. "You can see the show, Mom!" It was hard to believe that I was actually going to perform on tour with my violin hero Stephane Grappelli.

Stephane Grappelli & David Grisman Tour, 1979
9/5–9/7: San Francisco, CA (Great American Music Hall)
9/8: Seattle, WA (Paramount Theater)
9/9: Beaverton, OR (High School Auditorium)
9/11: Denver, CO (Rainbow Music Hall)
9/13: Los Angeles, CA (Johnny Carson Show)
9/15: Los Angeles, CA (Royce Hall)
9/16: Salt Lake City, UT (Symphony Hall)
9/18: Kansas City, KS (Uptown Theater)
9/19: Chapel Hill, NC (Univ of NC, Memorial Hall)
9/20: Boston, MA (Berkley Performance Center)
9/21–9/22: Long Island, NY (My Father's Place)

The tour pay for Mike, Rob, and myself (inclusive of all rehearsals) was $1,350 each. Perhaps this pittance is why Tony Rice refused to play the Stephane Grappelli tour? There were other reasons, as I came to discover. The Chapel Hill, North Carolina stop may have been a deal breaker for Tony, for an entirely different reason than I could've ever predicted.

THE TOUR BEGAN September 5th in San Francisco, but it was the rehearsal with Stephane Grappelli on September 4th that I was most anxious about.

David Grisman booked a benefit concert at the Great American Music Hall on August 29th, just a few days before. It was also a chance to test drive the new lineup for the DGQ tour. David Balakrishnan, a jazz violin colleague of Darol Anger, sat in with us on a few tunes. Being a friend of the band, he had hoped to meet Stephane Grappelli for the first time himself the following week. A Bay Area-based jazz string player and composer, Balakrishnan went on to become the founding member of the Turtle Island String Quartet. Grisman invited him to stop by the rehearsal in the green room.

For the DGQ material, Grisman's hometown audience was going to be a pretty tough nut for me to crack. They had grown fond of the original lineup with the inclusion of Rice, and the Music Hall was their stomping grounds. In the same way that Old & In the Way was brought around,

Grisman debuted his namesake act in the hall, the Great American String Band, back in March of 1974, and Jerry Garcia was along to play it. What a cool venue for some good string music.

The Great American Music Hall was constructed in 1907 on O'Farrell Street in downtown San Francisco—one year after the big earthquake. A French architect designed the Music Hall's interior to be a rather elegant theater. The décor featured ornate balconies, marble columns, and ceiling frescoes. The hall was originally a Victorian burlesque and minstrel show theater called Blanco's, named after a Barbary Coast house of prostitution. In 1936, Sally Rand took the theater over to feature erotic fan dance and bubble dance shows. It all closed down during the War, only to re-open in 1948 as a jazz music club. When jazz began fading in popularity, the oldest music hall in San Francisco almost saw demolition. But in 1972, Tom and Jeanie Bradshaw purchased the 470-seat theater and turned it into a national touring venue for all styles of music—from Stan Kenton to the Grateful Dead. Tom Bradshaw renamed it the Great American Music Hall.

The jury was out if David's audience liked me playing guitar with his Quintet. At least that's what it felt like. It was quite an interesting experience as a newly-turned 18-year-old, feeling real angst from the suspense of performing in order to meet perhaps unreal expectations. But maybe they were just wondering where Tony was? Like I was, too, frankly. Tony Rice's reputation (and shoes to fill) there in San Francisco, was more considerable than I ever thought much about before. I was taken aback by it. Replacing an original member in such a young and iconic band was already humbling and disquieting, even if it was for a single tour—but this was *their* biggest tour, by far.

I got to know Grisman's manager, Craig Miller, a little that week. He was fairly optimistic about the "new sound." It "wasn't what he was used to," he contended, but he expected it would develop and get rhythmically tighter as we went. Craig was a drummer. Without being able to understand all of these growing dynamics, I started to sweat over things a bit.

We were to meet with Stephane Grappelli for our first and only rehearsal. The band arrived plenty early to get warmed up on some rhythmic grooves in the green room located downstairs from the performance space. David divulged that band members were not to take solos at the rehearsal with Grappelli, so we could really lock down the rhythmic feels and the arrangements with him. Time was precious. It sounded reasonable. Maybe it would waste Grappelli's time to have him sit through guys' solos in the band, even though it can be how musicians get to know one another.

With that being said, David was going to play solos in the rehearsals so he could test what happens to the groove when he went in and out of the rhythm section. This was the principal reason why he had Mike on second mandolin. When David dropped out, another mandolin was right there to take it up with the same rhythmic intensity and character. It was reminiscent of '30s-era Grappelli/Reinhardt and the Hot Club of France. While Grappelli played violin solos, it could be just Reinhardt accompanying him. But when Reinhardt played his own guitar solos, he had his two guitar-playing cousins come roaring in behind him for rhythmic support. It took two of them to equal the majesty of their famous gypsy cousin.

We waited nervously for the French jazz violin legend to arrive, the man who charted the course of this music long before any of us were alive.

STEPHANE GRAPPELLI WAS BORN in Paris, France in 1908. His mother, who was French, died when he was three. His Italian father, a Latin scholar who taught philosophy, had no choice but to put him in a very poor Catholic orphanage. When his father returned from the War, Grappelli moved back in with him. Soon he bought his son a ¾-size violin. Having no money for lessons, Stephane was self-taught on both the violin and the piano. By the age of 14, he was earning a living playing piano and violin to accompany silent films in a Paris movie theatre. He was introduced to jazz at a music emporium next to the cinema—where, for a few centimes, one could put on headphones and hear the newest tunes to hit Paris. "Lady Be Good," "Tea For Two," and "Stumbling" excited and amazed him. He played in back-alley cabarets, street-side cafes and hotel lobbies until age 17, when he began playing in dance bands. Jazz artists like Bix Beiderbecke, Art Tatum, and Louis Armstrong, along with jazz violinists Eddie South and Joe Venuti, were all major influences on his style.

At 20, he was playing with Gregor and His Gregorians, a 17-piece band. Shortly after, he was hired by a montparnasse club as alto saxophonist for the big band, and violinist for the tangos. In 1931 at age 23, he encountered the Belgian gypsy guitarist, Django Reinhardt. They didn't actually play in a band together until 1934 at the Hotel Claridge in Paris. One day between sets, they suddenly started playing "Dinah," pretending to be Joe Venuti and Eddie Lang—great jazz violin and guitar duets from America. At about this time, French jazz critic, Hughes Pannasié, organized the Quintette du Hot Club de France and employed Stephane and Django. Their new quintet became the premier European jazz band, thrilling audiences that flocked to hear them. They performed extensively and recorded hundreds of 78s from 1934 to 1939.

Grappelli and Reinhardt had several reunions after World War II, but the partnership ended with Django's death in 1953. Earlier, Reinhardt had tried to make a career in the U.S. and Duke Ellington featured him on shows, but nothing took hold. Stephane continued to work in Paris and London, teaming up periodically with other fine jazz musicians. But by the 1960s, his career had faltered as well. The art of Stephane Grappelli was nearly forgotten.

Times were hard again. As in his youth, he had to take gigs playing solo piano in restaurants and hotels. For a few years he didn't play violin at all. He rarely performed with guitarists after Django, until English guitarist, Diz Disley, persuaded him to return to that sound. In 1973, Grappelli debuted at the Cambridge Festival in England, reviving his string band jazz with two guitars and a bass.

This is the group I saw two years later.

At age 65, Stephane Grappelli had a brand new music career.

WHEN STEPHANE GRAPPELLI bound into the green room, you could just feel the mythical presence of him. He was now 72, and I might add a *young* 72 at that. He looked like he was plenty full of salt and pep. David was 34, Rob 27, Mike 20 and me, I had just turned 18 a month before—but I had a feeling that all of us were going to struggle to keep up with Mr. Grappelli.

Grappelli exchanged hugs with Grisman. He was reacquainted with Mike, having already played with him a few times as part of the DGQ. Then Rob and I were introduced to the great violinist. Grappelli was ostentatious, he was colorful, and very French. Whatever it was, he seemed to be an opposing character to Joe Venuti. I wondered if they liked each other at all. At 18-years-old, I will have played with the two living giants of jazz violin.

Taking our seats in a loosely assembled circle of chairs, most of us did the best we could not to just stare at the man as he gathered his violin from his case and prepared to play. After diving in on the materials—tunes like, "Shine" and Grisman's own *King of The Gypsies* medley of "Tzigani / Fisztorza / Fulginiti," and with David himself handling the task of showing Grappelli his arrangements, the band was sounding and feeling pretty good. Of course Grappelli was magic—there was nothing like the man himself, sitting right there to inspire us. He was truly leading the charge.

When we got to the 3rd and 4th tunes for the show, "Satin Doll" and "Sweet Georgia Brown," Grappelli looked over at me to take a guitar solo. But Grisman waived me off and just came right in with *his* mandolin solo instead. When we finished the tune, Grappelli suggested there should be some solos from the musicians in the band. But unreasonably, David shut the request down. Having to explain himself in the open, David succinctly described his concept for the tour, the violin and the mandolin were the two featured instruments.

Grisman had it plotted from the outset. I was not to play a solo on the Grappelli sets. This is why he didn't care about hearing my solos during the rehearsals on the swing material. He made me all about the rhythm guitar. Would Grisman have let Tony Rice take guitar solos if he had taken the tour? I wished there was more honesty about it up front, and not all the gameplaying. After hearing Grisman's justification for the violin/mandolin-only shows, Grappelli simply shrugged his shoulders, and fell quiet. He didn't disagree with David—but he didn't say it was a good idea either. I wondered what Grappelli was really thinking. But I was ready to jump in if anything changed—I was soloing very well on the guitar at that point in my young life.

In Grappelli's own concerts, he was exceptionally generous in featuring his guitar players as soloists, both of them. I would even argue that at his 1975 concert I attended in Victoria, Canada, the solos by his two guitar players, Diz Dizley and John Ethridge, as well as the bassist Jon Burr, combined for more stage time than Grappelli's violin solos. He enjoyed seeing the younger bandmates take off on musical tangents, too. Grappelli was proud of them, from what I saw, and it was sweet to see the vim and vigor created by his playing off each of the band members. It was enjoyable watching Grappelli while he watched his guitarists go for it on stage attempting to one-up him if they could. There were a lot of external reactions between the four of them—winks, nods and smiles. The back and forth was a charming aspect to the Grappelli concert. I came to know this manner of band member dynamic as integral to all jazz performances. Here, Grisman was cutting off that potential for our shows.

At that point, David Balakrishnan poked his head in the door of the green room. He immediately made eye contact with Grappelli, who was sitting directly across from the doorway. Balakrishnan made an odd face as he went all bug-eyed on Grappelli. Startled by his own entrance, he head faked, and then awkwardly backed out the door, closing it behind him. In his French accent, Grappelli remarked, *"What is theees?"* Balakrishnan slowly opened the door again, peaked around the edge of it while doing another couple of head fakes… It was one quirky way to introduce yourself to the jazz violin legend. Regardless of how and why, Grappelli didn't like it. Not at all. He turned towards Grisman and asked him to *"make sure this man at theee door goes away!"*

Grisman tried to reassure him that Balakrishnan was a friend of ours, a local jazz violinist. But that didn't impress Grappelli. It took about five minutes to convince him that this guy was all right to let in the room. I made a mental note not to bulge my eyes out at Stephane Grappelli, or for that matter anyone I wanted to have like me.

Whatever I was to do, I didn't want to lose this job. I was pretty much staying quiet and unassuming. After working up a couple more swing tunes, the grand old man played like silk with endless improvisational perfection rolling off him like it was nothing. We took a 20-minute break.

As Grisman and Grappelli were having some conversation, I took Mike aside and asked him about the non-solo situation for band members.

"What do you think about not getting to play any solos on the tour?" I was looking for a sympathetic response.

"I'm the wrong guy to ask about it," Mike said. "I haven't been asked to take very many solos in this band for the last year!"

On practical grounds, Mike was hired only as a rhythm mandolin player, even for the DGQ material. I clearly had no one to commiserate with over the issue.

Stephane Grappelli had asked for me to take some guitar solos, but I was not allowed to. Grisman thought it that important to overrule the top dog of the tour. I was only left to believe that this collaboration was not so much about the "Quintet," but a way to improve Grisman's solo career status by drawing the most amount of attention to himself as he could. Being a young impressionable musician, I found it really disappointing, and I had not seen that approach before in all the years I had been playing with groups. What was the lesson here? I always hoped that the music came first, but now that I was entering bigger leagues, maybe career considerations do get in the way. David might be concerned that Mike and I would grab some of the spotlight and take attention away from his soloing before a largely jazz-oriented audience coming to see Grappelli.

Perhaps Grappelli's audience wouldn't know who Grisman even was?

I never saw that kind of insecurity in the fiddle and bluegrass scene like that. I noticed that David learned the heads to the jazz tunes, and played the jazz-like harmonies of the melodies, but largely his own solos were left to his standardized approach for a bluegrass tune. He wasn't really trying to incorporate "swing" or jazz playing, and phrases like I was wanting to do on the Martin guitar. But maybe that wasn't the point of this collaboration. Maybe it was supposed to be *jazz-meets-bluegrass,* and I was just not seeing it yet... But the more I tried to see—the more it looked like violin-meets-mandolin—and the rest of us were simply "the backup."

I was still learning the ropes, trying to understand what it meant to be a high-level artist in the music scene. Perhaps this exalted station of musicianship and artistry that I found myself in, capitulated to a synthesis of supreme confidence that Grisman seemed to possess, and a good amount of self-doubt and insecurity that he was revealing as well. I certainly understood both—I had much more confidence in a fiddle or guitar contest, but much less in social interactions as of late. I was petrified to even utter a word to Mr. Grappelli, yet... Maybe that would change in a few days. Nevertheless, Grisman was co-billing himself with the legendary violinist playing jazz music; Grisman needed to make sure he came off well on this tour.

Whatever was developing, I was going to continue to make my presence known on the tour and chip away at any looks I could get, seeing if I might add even a small guitar ride somewhere. Merle Haggard would just point at you when he wanted you to take a solo on stage. Maybe Stephane Grappelli might do the same thing? There wouldn't be much that Grisman could do about that on stage—if it happened. I had to be ready for anything to come.

I WAS OUTMANEUVERED on the pay scale as well—$1,350 pay for the month of non-stop rehearsals and concert hall performances in 1,500 to 2,000-seat halls. That low wage got Mom's attention. I received $1,000 for winning Weiser just two months before. Thank goodness for fiddle contest prize money—it was going to keep me afloat financially during the tour. My mother framed it for me succinctly:

"I'm glad you're getting to tour with your musical heroes, but you are getting taken advantage of financially. I can get you solo performances for $500!"

She wasn't happy about it, and kept reminding me of it on the phone. Easier said than done, of course. My income was still her business, so it seemed. She handled my bank account, payments from Rounder, tax filings, and my sister was helping her on all of it, too. My music was still a family affair. Mom now had a permanent hospital bed in our living room back home. She couldn't climb the stairs to Michelle's bedroom any longer.

I tried to lighten the mood: *"I'm getting paid by the solo,"* I said. It didn't go over well—"you're underutilized, Mark." So, toss that grievance in, too. Mom made me call her every few days. She needed to hear my voice and wanted to keep her hooks in me too. Mom knew I was itching to escape the household—and there I was in the City by the Bay and on my own—occupationally (so-called), for the first time. Her negativity took some of the sheen off my newfound position. It was difficult to balance all of the messaging coming back and forth—in all the many ways it was landing. I wasn't but a few weeks into this new and idiosyncratic environment when I started to become fatigued and emotionally sapped by a lot of it. Before long, I was getting more nervous each time I turned around. Is it good, is it bad—right or wrong? Can I please everyone at the same time, and still do what I thought was best?

There were many head trips, mind games, and agendas all mixed up with the fine artistry I found in San Francisco.

With about ten minutes left of the break, the band members were milling about in the green room waiting to get back to rehearsing, and Mr. Grappelli finally had a quiet moment seated in his chair. David had already moved over to one side of the room. In an understated tone, and quite unexpectedly, Mike directed a comment towards Grappelli:

"Stephane, you know that Mark plays violin, too?"

"Who plays violin?" Grappelli asks.

"He does. Mark," Mike points towards me.

I began to turn about every shade of red that I used to when I was 11.

"Well, I must hear you play the violin at once!" Grappelli said to me.

Gathering my wits about me, I responded: "Mr. Grappelli, I was hoping I could maybe play for you in a week or so, once the tour was underway. I want to make sure I had all your tunes down on guitar first."

"No, I must hear you at once! Where is your violin?" Grappelli implored.

"It's out in the car," I sheepishly answer.

"Please, go get it now!"

My mind was reeling and I was overwhelmed by this sudden undesired attention. I was cornered.

"Mr. Grappelli, could I please have five minutes to warm up before I play for you? I haven't played it in a week," I beg.

"Take five minutes then," as he motioned with his right hand for me to get going.

I was absolutely freaked out. I saw how Grappelli dismissed the young jazz violin player just moments before. I remembered my "run-in" with Joe Venuti, too. Grappelli is still cut from that same old legendary jazz violin cloth as Venuti is. If this goes wrong, Grappelli could ask me to be replaced on the tour if he didn't feel comfortable around another *jazz fiddler* who might me looking for lessons or to steal his licks. He might suspect I'd be "bug-eyeing" every fingering, every bow stroke… and I suppose that I would. I just didn't know how he would take to having an additional violin player in the group before getting to know and trust me as his guitarist. It might just wig him out and become a nuisance for him while touring. This is exactly why I didn't want Mr. Grappelli to know I played violin until we were already past the first rehearsal, after we were already on tour, when there was little way I could lose this job.

Despite those concerns, I was outed as the other fiddler. Outed by Mike. Not to blame him, really—he had no idea I was intending on hiding the fact I played the fiddle from Stephane Grappelli, for at least that first day, maybe longer. Grappelli would've found out at some point soon, I was quite sure of that. But things were just strange enough already, and I feared they could get worse. At this juncture I had quite everything to lose.

I grabbed the keys and walked out the theater's front doors to find David's car. I had left my white fiddle in the back seat, hidden down in the legroom. I carried it in a small profile case. I definitely didn't want to take that violin case into the rehearsal and have Grappelli spot it. So uncharacteristically, I left it in the car. As I made my way back to the Music Hall, I decided not to play anything jazzy for him, as it might throw him off. It was too much of a gamble, so I planned to play one of my Texas fiddle breakdowns, "Grey Eagle." I thought it could show off my ability to play well, but in a style that Mr. Grappelli wouldn't have any knowledge of, and therefore be the least threatening—if there was any issue of being a bit tender over all this.

This time, I'm the one who took the quick peek around the door of the green room—I asked if Mike could grab my guitar and visit me in the bathroom down the hallway. I wanted to go over the tune with him. We had already messed around a little on some fiddle breakdowns at that benefit concert the week before—I discovered that he could play this kind of Texas-style rhythmic accompaniment just fine. After playing through the tune just a single time, we were ready. The two of us headed back and were prepared to play. Mr. Grappelli, however, had something else in mind. Promptly, he produced a page of sheet music.

"Play this instead," Grappelli asked.

"Mr. Grappelli, we just went through our tune. Can we play it for you first?" I pleaded. *I thought I had this all figured out...*

"No, I want to hear you on this instead," as he points to the page.

We didn't have any music stands in the green room because the band had memorized everything for the tour. So, I put the page of untitled sheet music on a chair just a few feet away from him, and God only knew what he thought of my white-painted fiddle. *Was he staring at it?* I didn't even want to know. I kept my head down.

Hunched over the page of sheet music, I eyed the first bit of it. The key was A major and the phrase started with the C# in third position on the E-string. I played the first couple of lines half-speed with a softer dynamic. Grappelli could probably see that my bowing was smooth and rhythmic and that I played with good intonation, even when I was noodling around with it the first time through—all bent over like I was. Largely out of shape with the reading, I still could eke it out okay. I began with the top line again from the first measure, but this time with some tempo and more volume. I recognized it as the harmony line to his intro of the old swing standard, "Tiger Rag," that he recorded with Django Reinhardt. That second time through, I was able to put it into the fast rhythmic tempo and swing that I suspected Grappelli would have desired.

There was a bit more music to read, yet halfway through, Stephane Grappelli halted me from where he sat by grabbing my left forearm.

During the entire episode, Grisman was standing about ten feet back, just outside of the rehearsal area. As I negotiated Grappelli's hand-written sheet music, I gently raised my head to glance up at the greatest jazz violin player ever to walk the earth—and he was smiling at me.

"Young Mark, you and I will perform this together on the tour— *two violin!"* Grappelli made it known to the entire room.

I about fainted. I felt the same rush, the similar jelly legs I had when I first won the Grand Masters. Right there in the green room below the Music Hall, I won the biggest prize of them all. In the space of something like a minute or two, and just a few strokes of the bow, I was invited to trade violin licks on stage with my biggest jazz violin hero—the best there ever was.

Again, I peered over at David. He was not smiling that much, not nearly as much as I was smiling. After all, he was the bandleader for the Grappelli shows and what just happened here was clearly not his vision for our tour, by any stretch of the imagination. The 34-year-old veteran, David Grisman, outmaneuvered me on my guitar role as well as the low pay—arguably easy pickings given that I was the teenager. Stephane Grappelli, on the other hand, saw that I might be talented on the guitar, and questionably, was not allowed to take a guitar solo on his portion of the show. So, the 72-year-old veteran then outmaneuvered the 34-year-old to get me featured. Grappelli brought it into plain view that Grisman was simply not utilizing his players well enough. After all, Stephane Grappelli was the top draw of this tour and these were big concerts coming up, even for him—some of the largest in Grappelli's career. He wanted to go over well with *his* new touring band. Grisman was not the only person to decide who was going to share the spotlight on a Grappelli concert—and what a spotlight this was going to be for the kid with the old white-painted fiddle.

Stephane embraced me as a young violinist in those few minutes. The trajectory of my fiddling career took a major turn that day in the green room, just below the Great American Music Hall.

STEPHANE GRAPPELLI insisted we try the duo-violin tune with the full ensemble *tout de suite.* He wanted this to be *his* arrangement, so Grappelli was doling out the directions now. Mike was still holding my Martin, so he was asked to continue on guitar, with Grisman on "backup" mandolin. The intro section was just two violins alone. The blowing sections modulated to the key of G and I had the first solo out of the chute. On the run-through, I went for it—to prove that Stephane made the good call. Grappelli's facial expressions seemed to indicate that he liked what I was going for. He looked over to Grisman a couple of times, his visage signaling approval, his deportment signaling, *"I told you so,"* or *"what were you thinking?"* Then he motioned for me to take a repeat chorus, and then a third. Ah! It was a fast tempo too, and I was digging in… and the grand old gentleman was "digging it."

Grappelli played once through his improvised solo and then we did some trading four's—ultimately whittling the four bars down to two's. It all felt so thrilling, and pretty darned terrifying as well. Listening to Stephane Grappelli for years didn't mean that I had figured out how to match my fiddle with his. He played deceptively on the front of the beat, (and here I thought I could do that already). But I didn't play on the front edge nearly enough for this assignment. I had to go for more, and more.

While we played together, it felt like I was taking off from the crown of a San Francisco high rise and flying unbridled through the air. I could already tell that this violin duo was going to be one of my enduring highlights in music.

David could easily sense what was being accomplished now—a new musical relationship born in those moments. A new mentorship that was uncommonly significant. A violin mentor and a protégé took flight right before everyone's eyes in that green room. Ultimately, and without much delay, David Grisman loved it and embraced it too. In a lot of ways, he had his hand in it. He was astute enough to recognize that the ship had already sailed, so he might as well take as much credit he could for the lorryload. Despite the messy process, this was where all the unique characters in our ensemble ended up that day.

After "Tiger Rag" was rehearsed, it was like a pressure valve getting released for all of us—everyone was free to be themselves. There was a musical purpose for the tour now, beyond career considerations and monetary demarcations—it was about music again, about mentoring, and long-term musical relationships. It was the handing down of the music itself, just as I experienced with the older fiddlers when I was 12 and 13. I had a new violin teacher now, as Grappelli took me under his wing. I didn't mind who took credit for the pairing, I just loved that it happened to us.

When I joined him on violin for each night of the tour, Stephane made sure that he introduced me himself, even though I was emerging right out of the band lineup, and was already introduced during the opening DGQ set. Stephane wanted to distinguish me as *his* guest.

Stephane Grappelli at the Boston performance - September 20, 1979
"I thank you very much indeed, thank you so much. Now we are going to play the first composition I play in 1934 with Django Reinhardt. That's a few months ago. (cough) Excuse me. When I remember 1934, it make me cough. ...on that occasion because it was the first time we were playing for the Hot Club de France. So now we are going to play with my young friend Mark, a transcription for two violin, of 'Tiger Rag.'"

GRAPPELLI BECAME MY FINAL violin teacher, and he liked spending his available time on the tour to mentor me in jazz violin. He also mentored me in being a worldly person and artist. Stephane always insisted that I walk with him everywhere in each new city we arrived, to go out to eat with him, getting up early to meet him for breakfast, and going to the art galleries and museums of most any kind. We even swam in Salt Lake together on a day off. The two of us swam out about a mile on the lake. No way to sink either, there was so much salt in the water. It was remarkable. I was floating around on the salt water next to Stephane Grappelli. There were enjoyable moments, profound moments... but funny ones too. That night at a Salt Lake City eatery, with the whole band together, Stephane ordered wine with the meal, but Utah didn't quite work that way. It being a control state for alcoholic beverages, the waiter informed him that the restaurant wasn't allowed to serve wine. Stephane uttered; "What is this Utah? I never want to come here again!"

The following day I bought a couple of T-shirts for us that read; "Eat, drink and be merry, for tomorrow you may be in Utah." The only time I ever saw Stephane wear a T-shirt, he wore that one.

Irrespective of the Utah brasserie, Stephane showed me how to be the world traveler, through and through (as long as he got his wine, that is). Having whetted my appetite for world travel in Japan just a month before, I began to calculate the ground that Stephane walked — the well-traveled universal artist. In those weeks on tour, I had made a profound association with the most well-known jazz violinist. He blessed me from the start — the audiences were blown away by the spectacle of the legend and his protégé jazz violinist going at it on those blistering tempos, with him motioning me to go again and again, and again. The crowds loved it every time. Even the discerning SF crowd — he helped me win them over — together. After we finished our violin dialogue on stage, he sometimes put his hand on my face like a grandfather might do. He favored this opportunity so much, just as I did. He was the mentor I needed to put me over the top in a giant-sized world. I was cherishing our performances together that changed my life.

David was getting the billing, marketing, and some good money from the tour. His career was on the uptick. Stephane's attentiveness, however, was mostly directed towards me for the rest of the way. So both David and I were getting something significant in the end. Mine was supremely intangible, a mentor-student relationship that Stephane afforded nearly no violinist in his entire lifetime. I became one of only a couple of violinists he cared to share his time with to teach. Those players included Jean-Luc

Ponty, and another French jazz violinist my age, Didier Lockwood. But the list ends quickly after that. My jazz violin friend from Boston, Matt Glaser, got a few lessons in, and classical violinist Nigel Kennedy, boasts a few as well.

For all intents and purposes, I pushed aside the insult of David paying me miserably for a month-long successful concert hall tour. Heck, I would have paid *him*, just to get some lessons from Stephane Grappelli and play those couple of violin duos with him each night. Sometimes he would want me on violin with him for "Sweet Georgia Brown," as an encore.

Even in my mother's condition, she insisted that Dad drive her and Michelle down to San Francisco for the premiere. It took everything she had to do so. Mom took photos of us on stage from her seat, and got to meet Stephane as well. It was such a beautiful moment to share. Mom drove me up to Victoria to see him when I was 13, and now look at us.

I invited Benny Thomasson down to the Portland show. He had just moved back up to Washington the year before. Benny started to make plans to come back to the Pacific Northwest after we bailed on moving to Nashville in the winter of '77. After the concert I got to introduce Stephane to Benny backstage.

When they met to shake hands, I swear I felt the earth *shake.*

After speaking for a few minutes, I could tell that Benny needed to sit down because of his bad back. He motioned for Stephane to have a seat, too. Stephane insisted, "After you." Then Stephane asked Benny, "What is your age, may I ask?" Benny responded, "71 years." Stephane said, "I am 72, so I will sit first!"

Those were dreamlike moments for me. I never thought I could ever have a mentor and teacher after Benny. We spoke by ourselves for a moment in the hallway. It was just a few months back when we stopped by Benny's new trailer home in Washington, on the way home from my recording sessions in Berkeley. He was living on a small section of a farm owned by the Wallace's, a fiddling family who were good friends of ours. I wanted to play him the new mixes from *On The Rampage.* Benny just loved them. He was beaming ear to ear as he listened to what I was doing on the recording. He was always proud of me, even though my compositions were very far removed from the Texas fiddle breakdowns that we both shared and loved.

"Mark, you sounded incredible up there with Stephane, all of you sounded incredible. It was all just great. Are you going to be all right now?" Benny asked me.

"Thank you so much Benny. Yes, I am going to be all right."

"I want to make sure that you are taken care of and that Stephane will take over with you." Benny made sure.

I eased his worries because he knew that I had struggled over the last year or two with him away in Texas. He had come all the way back to live in the state of Washington again. His son Dale, however, had moved back east years before. It was not fully understood by anyone why Benny returned to the Northwest other than he wanted to make sure he was still my teacher and mentor. The conversation we had in Portland after the concert, bore this out.

"I believe you are in good hands, Mark."

"Thank you so much, Benny, thank you for everything. You will always be my teacher," I answered as I said goodbye to Benny for now.

Soon after the Grappelli/Grisman concert in Portland, Benny and Bea said their own goodbyes to the Wallace family, packed up and moved back to Texas for good.

IT STILL SMARTED A BIT that I couldn't take a single lead on the guitar until a small ride for our encore tune of "Sweet Georgia Brown" (the nights I wasn't playing fiddle on it). At the conclusion of the Grappelli set, the audience was like, you mean this guy can also play jazz guitar solos, too? Our electric mandolin-playing friend, Tiny Moore, sat in one night in San Francisco on "Satin Doll." I was hoping David could give that Tiny Moore spot to someone in the band for the rest of the tour, but he did not. The leads went right back to his violin/mandolin combo.

Our *Tonight Show* appearance acted as a summation of how Grisman conceived the music. Because Carson admired Stephane Grappelli, he gave us two tunes back to back—announcing us as "Stephane Grappelli and the David Grisman Quintet." When it came time for David's first mandolin solo, the camera zoomed in on me for the longest time, assuming that the guitar solo was coming. But it never did. The director finally found Grisman through the camera lens, but this was *the program* we followed for the entire tour. During the bows on the *Tonight Show,* Carson wound up the segment by prophetically thanking "Stephane Grappelli and David Grisman," and dropping the "Quintet." It was unfortunately typical. We weren't featured on either tune, therefore Mike, Rob and I didn't deserve much of any status.

With some outside pressure, Grisman deduced that the concerts were going to need some additional dynamics from the band in short order—more staging and more variability. Additional musical attributes were critical for the shows to come off as well as he wanted. Those concert hall audiences were as big as any that Grappelli or Grisman had ever drawn. Rather than have more band soloing, David continued the *fiddle theme* that had already begun, by having me play one of my Texas fiddle breakdowns to open the concerts. With Mike on guitar and Rob playing bass, we whipped out a little "Grey Eagle," the tune I was going to play for Stephane in the green room but never got the chance to. In response to this auxiliary element of the show, we shortened the DGQ portion to just a few tunes, bringing out Stephane to start *swinging* as soon as possible. The audience demanded it.

Stephane had to play a lot on these shows, working hard without any other solos from band members to relieve him. In addition, David asked Stephane to play a solo piano encore, for even more variety, and demanding even more endurance from the 72-year-old. He *was* a consummate jazz pianist indeed, playing in the style of his favorite 1930s and '40s jazz piano great, Art Tatum. (Stephane pronounced it: *Tai-toom*).

Another noteworthy artisan for the tour was our sound engineer, David's long-time friend, Billy Wolf. He was an accomplished sound man. Notwithstanding his long-time work with progressive rock bands *Grateful Dead* and the *Mothers of Invention,* he's got some ears for acoustic music. The soundchecks were so very long, he wanted to be thorough—30 to 45 minutes dedicated to each instrument. Not quite as much for the piano, but someone else had to play it—Stephane was not going to soundcheck the piano every time. There was another objective with such detailed soundchecks—David was having Billy tape the concerts for a potential live album. Billy carted a Nagra reel to reel tape recorder aboard all the flights for the tour. But Stephane didn't take it quite as seriously. Soon, Stephane didn't even bother to soundcheck his violin either. He was already playing so much on the tour—carrying more than half of the solo load each night, both the heads of tunes and the extended improvisations. I soundchecked the violin through his microphone each time, increasing my own onstage prep duties. It was the least I could do.

On the road I befriended Billy Wolf and asked him if he could mix my two new albums, *On The Rampage* and *Soppin' The Gravy*. He was going to give me some top shelf mixes for my teenage releases.

D AVID DROPPED THE "Quintet" part of the billing for the live album; "Stephane Grappelli/David Grisman Live." Yes, it was a systematic demotion of the band. I couldn't help but think this must've been part of the dynamic with Tony Rice. The question still remained over why Rice refused to do this month-long tour, when he was just sitting at home. But I was sure glad that I got to play the tour in his place.

At each venue, Stephane requested Scotch whisky on the rider. He was accustomed to taking only a sip or two right before he went out on stage. During the tour, David kept nudging Stephane to take a hit from his hand-rolled joints, until finally, Stephane rolled over, "Yes, why not!" From that point, Stephane made sure he took a few puffs of Grisman's weed right before each concert began. It was rather amusing that Stephane at 72 was smoking pot, and his 18-year-old protégé was not partaking. But that's how it went.

Along the way, a few journalists asked whether Stephane had ever played bluegrass music before. Sometimes he related their questions to the act of smoking *grass.* Another time he answered: *"I don't play this grass music. I do not ride theee horse."*

The music I was experiencing, though, was a whirlwind of great consequence and an avalanche of so many emotions. Also, these weeks on tour were without much sleep. Stephane wanted me to get up early to meet him for breakfast, before taking off on our walks. He insisted on this congeniality from me, while the others got more sleep, at least. Squeezing in jazz violin lessons with Stephane along the way, the long soundchecks I did, answering the extra band calls for rehearsals with David... I was taking it all in, and not wanting to miss a second of the action. The call and response sessions between us were worth all of it and more.

Each morning, I woke up with my left hand in the shape of a claw. It was well molded. Appearing rather ghastly, it took my youthful hands only a few minutes to recover each morning. The bulkier jazz chords I was playing on the Martin D-28 all night, and trying not to buzz out a single one of them, was really pushing me. The strength necessary for both the musical and physical stamina of the tour, flying most every day, as well as the emotional investment made, was considerable. It was intensive in a way I hadn't been accustomed to, evidently. The workload and stress got me run down physically and I caught a nasty cold that challenged me even more so.

I had updated my apparel for this tour, trading in my bull rider for a new and much smaller jazzy fedora. I outfitted with a vest, cream colored shirt, some dress shoes. It was the first button-down shirt I felt chippy enough to wear consistently—and only for the stage. As I was playing guitar on the opening DGQ set in Chapel Hill, a town solidly in the middle of North Carolina bluegrass country (and a place that would've certainly appreciated Tony Rice more than me), I roused up a horrendous nosebleed from the head cold I was carrying around. It was horribly unattractive—blood getting all over my old Martin and my stage uniform. It began to really gush. Shaken up by my torrential outpour in the middle of a band tune, I hurried off the stage for the restroom. A few minutes later, I returned to center stage to find David not happy with my fleet-footed exit. In that instance, I didn't know what else to do. It was the first time that David showed some anger and frustration towards me openly—he let me have it after the set. The *ghost* of Tony Rice was calling.

It was not the first stage *faux pas* from me on this tour. The nosebleed came on the heels of even a better lapse of judgement—this one, self-inflicted. A week earlier, back at the Music Hall in SF, we learned that the great classical violinist Yehudi Menuhin was in the audience to see Stephane perform. I grew up listening to Menuhin on the family turntable, as he was my mother's favorite violinist. Grappelli and Menuhin had dinner together just before the show while we were handling the soundcheck. They had done the duo projects together—classical violin meets jazz violin. I wasn't a big fan of those recordings that so many others liked and appreciated. That jazzy *Bach's Double*—I don't know... not as good as just "improvising on the repeats." However, it sure did introduce Stephane's playing to a huge audience. If I ever had the chance to do an album with a major classical string-player I concluded, (someone like a

Yo-Yo Ma), I would want to use my own compositions to find that uncommon musical place to meet.

During the opening DGQ set, I spotted Menuhin at his table down near the front of the stage. In between tunes I grabbed my white fiddle and scurried down the steps off to the side of the stage and into the audience. I definitely wanted to get Yehudi Menuhin's signature on it. I was well armed with the Sharpie just in case I would run into him that night. In the hurried environment, he scribbled his name right over the top of Mack Magaha's signature, the fiddler from Porter's Wagonmasters. You could make out the *Yehudi* part of the signature, superimposed over Mack's, "Yehudi Magaha!"

David gave me a bit of a talking to after that little deal as well. Definitely the actions of a young guy who didn't know how to be just a band musician yet.

During the tour, some in the audience would toss bouquets of flowers up on stage during our encore. I had never witnessed this before at bluegrass festivals, or wherever I'd been. I got all caught up in it—kind of *lost* my marbles over it I guess. For my follow-up *faux pas* I grabbed one of the bouquets off the floor during the curtain call and ardently thrusted those flowers right into David's face—just so he could take a good whiff of them. After he turned his head away, I tried Stephane next. I bustled those flowers sloppily into his face so he could smell them, too. Stephane turned away to cough. For some absentminded reason, I didn't think I was trying hard enough and thought the violin legend may have missed the opportunity to enjoy the fragrance. So, as Stephane brought his face back around, I lobbed them up Stephane's nose one more time. He took his free hand, and swatted those flowers away in short order, then he took his same hand and shooed me away, right in front of the cheering crowd. After this was all over, was I ever going to feel like an idiot. But as the crowd continued to cheer, I didn't see the end of this yet. I went over to David with that same bouquet, and thoughtfully upheaved it into his kisser all over again. My "good gestures" were met with similar bad reactions. I was just a little too excited.

Because of the big commotion I stirred up back at the first concert, Yehudi Menuhin was compelled to find me in the green room after the show. He was clearly intrigued by my enthusiastic gesture towards him.

Most of all, Menuhin complimented me on my fiddle playing. As he smiled at me, he did a little air bowing, then pointed towards my hands: "Great job," he said, as he gave me his good slack-jawed facial expression. He didn't care to meet David or the other band members. I asked him if he wanted to. He said to tell Stephane, "I found the concert lovely." He detailed that they had dinner together, and that he was well apprised on everything going on with Stephane: "Not to bother him further and to let him rest." And with that, Menuhin left the Music Hall. I got to play fiddle for Yehudi Menuhin. A sweet bit of testimony from the iconic classical violinist, it was the first and only time I would ever see him.

There were a lot of fast moving parts on this tour all right. Every time I found myself in another corner, seemingly all hung up, I figured a way out that was better for the music in the long run. The great adventure I found myself in during the fall of '79 ranged from utter incoherence to utopian bliss, sometimes all within a solitary day. At times, the journey resulted in blasted outright genius. When the collective "we" finally arrived at the brilliance of it all, we learned to find our way, together. Stephane sure forgot about that bouquet of flowers incident—like it never happened. I could do no wrong in Stephane Grappelli's eyes from here on out.

San Francisco Examiner – Thurs., Sept. 6, 1979

"O'Connor, especially had his work cut out for him last night. Not only did he have to fill the mighty shoes of Grisman's otherwise far-famed regular guitarist Tony Rice, he also had to confront a series of fiddle duets with Grappelli.

And, undoubtedly, the evening's high point came when Grappelli and O'Connor (separated by [over] 50 years in age) shared the lead and solo work on two old warhorses – 'Tiger Rag' and 'Sweet Georgia Brown.'

Pushed into a competitive role, Grappelli responded with astonishing finesse and originality. After each taking extended choruses of solos (on "Tiger" especially), the pair of violinists came to grips with each other. First they split four-bar solo breaks, then took it down to splitting two's. Grisman's mandolin led the supporting mini-ensemble in rhythmic backup and goose pimples crept up my neck as Grappelli and O'Connor had it out.

Neither won, nor lost; the audience of course gained the most and the two musicians embraced at the end of the pair of duet-tunes."

Stereo Review – September 1981

"The high point of many David Grisman Quintet concerts these days is the segment in which the group plays together with jazz violinist Stephane Grappelli, and a new live recording from Warner Bros. captures some of that magic...Grappelli introduces 'Tiger Rag' here as the first composition he played with Reinhardt, back in 1934, then lapses into a mild coughing fit; recovering, he says, 'When I remember how tough 1934 was, eet make me cough.' The tune has been rearranged for a second violin, played by the quintet's Mark O'Connor... O'Connor is an excellent violinist and an incredible guitar player, and at an age so young it's obscene."

Album Notes For On The Rampage by Stephane Grappelli - 1979

"Sometimes there are in life good surprises. On the occasion of my last meeting with David Grisman (with whom I've had the joy of discovering another aspect of music for David is a living god of the mandolin), there was, in his ensemble, a young musician who absolutely astonished me. Among other things, he plays the mandolin, and also he accompanies the group on the guitar. But it is when he plays the violin that I feel the great musician that he is, despite his young age. I predict for him a great future and I hope to live long enough to see the fruition of his great talent. He is 17 years old and his name is Mark O'Connor."

CHAPTER TEN

DAWG GONE IT

THE GRAPPELLI/GRISMAN TOUR itself turned out to be another audition, it would seem—for the permanent replacement of Tony Rice in the David Grisman Quintet. I didn't really know it at the time, because I was just hired for the one tour, the one Tony refused to do. Still, there were casual references from Grisman along the way: "Hey man, I might just hire your ass if you don't scare the shit out of me like that!" This repartee came after my nosebleed incident on stage in Chapel Hill, North Carolina. I figured it was just his way of eliciting my best behavior. After all, I had just turned 18, and over-the-top *antsy* to be that indisputable musical soloist on stage. And maybe Grisman was just brooding over DGQ dates in the South, as I came to find out.

After the final Long Island, New York concert of the Stephane Grappelli tour, I caught a flight home to Seattle while the others went back to San Francisco. Stephane flew home to Paris.

Within a couple of days, David got back in touch with me by phone. He and Tony Rice hadn't resolved their differences, so he wanted me to come down for a pair of California dates: October 5th, 1979 in Palo Alto at the Keystone and on the 6th in Sacramento at UC Davis. David offered to fly me down and pay me $200 per show. I needed to arrive a few days early to rehearse quite a bit more DGQ repertoire. He had me stay at his house again because I had a whole show to learn.

My mother insisted that Grisman's offer was plainly not as much as I was worth. The low pay was glaring to her—I guess it was to me as well. For the intricate and highly-specialized nature of this music and musical presentation, and especially, the effort it took to prepare—I mean, was Grisman making five times more on these? More than that? But despite it, I reminded her I didn't have much else going on that week, anyway. Mom promised she could get on the phone and line up some solo gigs for me in the next few months. But in the meantime, back down into the thorny matrix of the David and Tony show in Marin County.

When Tony Rice first heard about the tour with Stephane Grappelli, he was supportive of the idea at first. He was up for the tour, reportedly.

That was up until the day David called me to replace him, just a month before the tour got started. According to bandmates, Tony's feelings hardened as he arrived at Grisman's house for a band meeting. He threw a fit. Slamming his hand down on the table, Tony exclaimed that he had "moved out to San Francisco to play 'Dawg' music, not to play that old shit." Meaning that he wasn't into playing older tunes, or swing tunes? Up to that point, Rice had remained grateful to Grisman for the invitation to join up a few years before, to play "Dawg" music. Rice even suggested their new band should be named after David himself: the *David Grisman Quintet.*

It was peculiar, because I was learning some of the DGQ material from their first album for those two California shows, and there was plenty of jazz and swing grooves there, complete with walking bass lines. David's tunes such as "Blue Midnight," "Fish Scale," and even Tony's tune that he contributed to the album, were *swing.* In fact, Tony called it "Swing 51." At least the title of it was influenced by Django Reinhardt: *("Swing 42").*

None of it made much sense.

Now that the Grappelli tour had concluded, Tony was ready to resume his old guitar role with the DGQ. However, David was having second thoughts about Tony, given their exchanges over the past few months. David used *my* arrival into the arena, dangling me as Tony's replacement in the balance—a bartering chip. As they haggled over reuniting, David threatened he just might not need his band's founding guitarist anymore. Tony was my musical hero, too—I trusted I would only play the DGQ dates that Tony didn't want to play.

With Darol Anger still in Africa, the Quintet was temporarily a quartet for the California shows. David changed his attitude about my guitar role dramatically—looking for my personal investment into his band. Not only was he going to feature my guitar solos on most every tune now, but he asked me if I could bring some of my originals to the shows—including two selections from my new guitar album that he played on, "Pickin' In The Wind" and "Markology." He told me he was also writing a tune for me to play on fiddle: "Bow Wow."

I was learning to feel more comfortable with David's tireless canine-friendly tune names. As soon as he *picked up the scent* for my guitar solos, though, it got me about as excited as treeing a squirrel. Without Grappelli or Rice on the stage with him, he needed more activity from the band members. The *lead Dawg,* wanted me to be a "swing dawg" now.

It was just the two gigs—really fun stuff to solo on. Got a good guitar workout, too. Likely, this was the last time I would replace Tony Rice. He definitely wasn't giving up the DGQ spot. As for me, it was back home to figure out what was next.

AFTER RETURNING HOME to Seattle, I got yet another call from David. He briefed me again about Darol Anger returning from Africa soon, and that meant he was lining up a "Quintet" run of dates, starting the 1st of December. On the subject of Tony… they couldn't work it out. It was over. Right there on the phone, Dawg offered me my first full-time band job.

I didn't exactly jump for joy, really. David detected some hesitation in my voice. My mother was laying right there in the living room, nodding *no* to me. Mom did not want me to join the David Grisman Quintet.

Clueless to my mother's recalcitrance to his band, David instead understood that I was most concerned about *replacing* Tony, my guitar mentor. David attempted to ease my apprehensiveness. He divulged some of the interesting paradoxes confronting the band. My taking over the guitar spot, as David explained, meant it was going to be much, much better for the Quintet. David went into some details he hadn't shared with people even inside the band. Tony had refused to ever perform in the Southeast again. Perplexed by that, I'd always wondered why the Quintet had largely played up and down the West Coast since its inception. It was all a bit preposterous. Of course, we had just played a southern date in North Carolina, at Chapel Hill. I remembered the nosebleed very well. I'm sure David did, too.

David decided to let me in on the little dark secret that had plagued their band from the outset. Tony left J.D. Crowe and the New South quite suddenly in 1975. That group had just recorded the seminal bluegrass album of the generation with Ricky Skaggs and Jerry Douglas in the lineup. It took Tony four years of performing and recording with J.D. before they finally assembled that combination of great bluegrass musicians. Previously, the New South had some clunky Nashville-based recordings with

Tony singing bluegrass songs over drums, steel guitar, and electric bass. There weren't many guitar solos on that stuff either. Back then, J.D. told David, *"Plug in and join me on the charts!"* Ever since, David's catchline became his own never-ending, *"Unplug and join me on the charts."* David used the line when he wished to boast about his recent and quite unprecedented chart success as a string band.

The improved and "unplugged" New South finally had put all the pieces together, and played just a couple of months of bluegrass festivals with the lineup. I saw them at the Pickin' Parlor during that run, and hung out with them for a day at the Whites'. Immediately following it, they played a short sold-out tour in Japan in August, the one that Kay worked on for them. Right in the middle of their Japan tour, Tony announced he was leaving the New South and going straight to California to start a new group with Grisman. He decided he wanted to play string jazz—more or less, out of nowhere. The only problem: Tony didn't know how to play jazz music yet—he would have to learn some jazz chords, at least.

I always thought the Tony Rice timeline seemed so sudden and more than a little suspicious. David had few, if any, shows booked for the entire year back in 1975/76. Tony's sudden departure from the New South prompted the immediate exodus of both Skaggs and Douglas, to form the ephemeral bluegrass band Boone Creek. In other words, the best bluegrass band of a generation, presumptively, held together not even a year. It dissolved because of Tony's swift exit.

Grisman continued with the saga on the phone. Mom was laying there wondering why I was so silent and captivated: Tony reportedly had an affair with a woman in the Southeast that *may* have produced a child, David said to me. The woman's brother lost his marbles over the affair when Tony didn't hang around to own up to it. At a southern bluegrass festival during the summer of 1975, the brother showed up at the New South's dressing room trailer with a baby in his arms. After getting the attention of J.D. and a couple of band members, he had a message for Tony: he came to end Tony's life. The brother even threatened to shoot Tony while on stage, if he had to. Rather than cancel the set over the violent threat, Crowe soberly instructed his band thusly: *For this set, we'll spread out on stage a little, and use separate mics for the trio singing.*

Tony believed these threats from the woman's brother were to persist. Rice fled across the country trusting the man wouldn't follow him all the way to California and carry out his promise.

I was curious if Tony had hooked up with this woman after one of those bluegrass festival gospel sets?

The pact Rice made with Grisman was that the DGQ would rarely appear in the East, and especially not in the South where Tony had this ongoing threat. Four years after their pact was made, David finally booked the band for a few dates back East, its first time on that side of the country. But Tony swore up and down that he saw that very man at their one show scheduled in the Southeast: *The North Carolina show.* It led to such an elaborate undertaking to protect Tony—even the clandestine getaway car was summoned. There were band members sitting on either side to shield him from view. Tony refused to attempt another DGQ performance in the South after that.

It was not just about "playing that old shit," as it was more widely understood—it was about playing any "old shit" east of the Mississippi River.

David believed that with four years gone by, Tony's paranoia about the contract on his life had run its course—at least from Grisman's perspective. Cutting off performing in literally half the country was now too much to ask of the Quintet. They did what they could to protect Tony, as he demanded, but with an 18-year-old who could play the music at the same level stepping in, it was time to move on.

It all made sense now. Tony went incognito. Moved to Marin and grew his hair long, no longer played bluegrass and he quit singing in public. Tony learned to play jazz guitar instead, and denied any bookings in the South. He disavowed bluegrass festivals for his new band they were launching and maybe he didn't even want his name billed. Why, he even named his band after the other guy. *I think we should call us the David Grisman Quintet.*

THE DAVID AND TONY SHOW sounded like a can of worms, but for artistic reasons, I was still interested in taking the position—of course I was. But at the same time, I still held out the idea, even if it had somewhat dimmed over time, to establish myself on the fiddle in Nashville, too. As I justified everything, playing with Grisman was one thing, but being a member of this elite Quintet which had earned a well-deserved reputation, took it to another level. David made his pronouncements to me that it was going to be *all* about the Quintet going forward. This move back to being more about the band, rather than about David as a solo artist, was worth the financial sacrifice, as I saw it.

I tried to convince my mother.

It was arduous to defy Mom, and she put up quite the fight, crying for hours at a time and exhausting all the justifications and elbowroom she could muster, just to soften me on the idea. The guilt she poured on me, the recrimination over leaving home for this job with David Grisman, given her ailing health and accelerating cancer, was enormously disheartening for me to withstand. Michelle was 14, and required more breathing room, too. The intensity of our home life made it unreasonable for the four of us to live together any longer, especially when I had a good opening now to just go on and move out.

It was agonizing to see Mom roundly scorn my first full-time job as a musician to such a magnitude. She cast Grisman and his manager, Craig Miller, the bad guys—the enemy. That's exactly what she did. She rebuked them for luring me away from her, while at the same time, compensating me so miserably that, in no way could I help our family's ongoing financial crisis with her healthcare. Nor could it even keep me afloat, unless something dramatically turned for the better.

Craig offered to help me on a couple of budgetary issues with Rounder, and to obtain Billy Wolf to mix my two recent albums for a reduced rate. Mom resented Craig moving in on *her* territory. She had always been the person to deal with Rounder. It was so awful to see her take it this far. She did this kind of stuff with my former girlfriend, but to see her do this with musicians and my music career—it was so senseless. Together, Mom and I had put in so much good work on my musical trajectory, ever since I was a little kid. She was a warrior. Half of her body may have been consumed by cancer, but her other half stood in opposition with unremorseful blows to my own common sense. If she could have stood erect, I don't know if she would've physically allowed me out of her grasp. At least she wouldn't have for the David Grisman Quintet.

My mother always held out for me to hit it *big,* with herself as my manager. This hope was never dashed, even though she was bedridden by then — my poor Mom. By her terms, if I could assume that family *provider* role, it was when I could truly assert that I had "made it" as a professional musician. She reminded me how she sacrificed her own life for my music. She drove all those summers across the country for me, with my kid sister in tow.

After years of working as a child musician for the very cause she repeatedly stated, it led me to a different conclusion than hers. She was trying to tie me down, to stay with my family, and I was resisting her.

I just wanted to run away from home and join a band.

If I didn't go and join up, I felt like I'd lose my sanity in our Mountlake Terrace household. There was too much friction, anger, resentment, guilt, and abuse there. I knew if I stayed, something awful could happen if one of the four of us just *lost* it. I didn't trust anyone, including myself, to keep it all in check. I told each of my family members there was simply one too many people in our home now. One of us had to go, and that person was going to be me. I was the first child to reach 18, and I was to be the first one to leave home.

However distressing Tony's personal and musical issues were, I was facing similar stresses. The Bay Area would have to make room for both Tony and me — two Herringbone Martin guitar players living in Marin County. Let it begin now.

As long as I was featured in the band as a soloist, and *not* just a rhythm player, it would be a fair restart. David was looking to give me plenty of room, and a lot more solos on the guitar, to change the nature of my role.

It was fine with Dad for me to drive his red pickup truck down to SF. I wanted to take all my instruments with me. "Why do you need all of those? You're coming back in just a couple of weeks," Mom was forecasting where and when from her hospital bed. Dad never saw that red truck in Seattle again. Taking it and parking it in my new home of San Francisco, helped me to go ahead and make a break for it. After spending Thanksgiving of 1979 at home… I ran away.

IT WAS COOL TO MEET UP with Darol again and start Quintet rehearsals without any equivocation. I listened to Darol and Barbara's engrossing tales of their travels to West Africa.

It turned out that both Darol Anger and I lived in San Rafael in the 1960s during the very same years, but, of course, neither of us had any clue of that before.

Eight years older than me (he was born in 1953) Darol graduated from San Rafael High School, where he played violin in the school orchestra. A Youngbloods rock concert in San Rafael's Bermuda Palms Hotel is where he saw a local progressive group as the opener—Seatrain. It featured both Peter Rowan and fusion violinist Richard Greene. The performance represented an introduction to a new kind of fiddle playing Darol had never experienced before. After attending the University of California in Santa Cruz and taking a class in country music roots, he dropped out of college to play bluegrass in pizza parlors for a few years. In 1975 at age 21, Darol was at the right place at the right time. David Grisman was just forming a new group with Tony Rice, and reaching out to the local fiddle talent to fill the new violin position. As they say, the rest is history.

As we rehearsed with the Darol back in the DGQ, of all things to happen, Tony Rice began to call me and Mike Marshall incessantly. Tony was assembling *his* band now. He already had a name for it—Tony Rice Unit. Leaving one hornet's nest in Seattle for another, I was stumbling into a whopper of one in Marin County. Tony was doing a nice job of roping Mike in for the proposed traveling ensemble. It meant Mike would finally get to play solos. Mike was palpably excited about joining up with Tony and supported me enlisting, too. The attractiveness for me, according to Tony, is that I wouldn't have to play 2nd fiddle to Darol Anger with "the Dawg." I would also get to take as long of a fiddle solo as I pleased, playing it suspended on top of a great acoustic music rhythm section—Mike, Todd Phillips on upright bass (yet another former DGQ member), and the dreadnought drive from Tony Rice himself. I certainly couldn't argue with how great that rhythm section would be to improvise violin solos over. Tony *was* the best player in the David Grisman Quintet.

TONY RICE WAS BORN IN Danville, VA, but his family moved to Los Angeles when he was still an infant. His father, Herbert Rice, played mandolin and guitar and had a family band with Tony's uncles, the Poindexters. The were called the Golden State Boys. It was Tony and his siblings Larry and Ronnie's introduction to bluegrass and country music.

The three Rice children eventually formed a band and played at L.A. haunts such as the Ash Grove, Troubadour, and at Disneyland. Another Los Angeles-based guitarist, Clarence White, had a profound impact on Tony during those formative years. Tony eventually purchased Clarence's old Martin Herringbone after Clarence was killed.

Moving around the country during his late teens, Tony found himself in Kentucky replacing Dan Crary in the Bluegrass Alliance, a band that at the time, featured a teenaged Sam Bush. Soon after, Tony landed the lead singer role for J.D. Crowe and the New South. By late 1975, though, Tony was in California learning to play jazz, and eliciting the help of jazz guitarist and instructor John Carlini, a music friend of David Grisman: Music theory, diminished and augmented chords... all the jazz harmony you would never find in "My Old Home Place."

I learned from Tony that Carlini was on the audition shortlist for the Stephane Grappelli tour. Tony would've preferred that it had gone to him. If Grisman would've simply gone with John Carlini for the tour, there wouldn't have been such a mutiny amongst the pirates in the San Francisco harbor. The "taking a backseat on fiddle to Darol" that Tony was clinkering to me about was just noise. I didn't feel that way at all. I was the guitar player in the band, and that was fine by me.

I was a little surprised that Mike was considering leaving the DGQ so readily, given that the Grappelli tour was in our rearview mirror by only a few months. The state of play for me was more blurred. I was getting to be featured on guitar in one great acoustic band, and I could be featured on violin in another great acoustic band. Different sides of the same coin, but could the two sides coexist? Mike and I cobbled together a plan. If we stayed well-organized as a tag-team, we just might have the upper hand. United, we seemed to be quite in demand. Our justification was on a practical level. Both Mike and I needed *far* more income to survive the season in San Francisco.

While David did have at least some shows on the books, they simply didn't add up to enough to keep us afloat. Tony was willing to split the show fees with us, divided up evenly—that is, when there were bookings to be had. Tony had no concerts scheduled, nor very many leads—and no agency. This was all new to him, too. Mike and I thought we could buy some time at least. We let Tony know that we planned to keep playing all the dates on the books with David.

Under the cover of night, Mike and I joined Tony and Todd for rehearsals at his apartment in Corte Madera, Marin County—just a couple exits north of Mill Valley off the 101. We rehearsed regularly for nearly a month. Tony Rice taught me most every tune he'd written—"Devlin," "Is That So," "Mar West," "Mar East." Ultimately, we had an entire concert's worth of material rehearsed and ready to go. Meanwhile, we kept our activities and whereabouts secret from David. Why make waves when we didn't know if the "Unit" would amount to anything more than a fragment? Musically though, it amounted to something beautiful.

Tony and his amazing guitar work, along with Todd and his upright bass following every one of Tony's nuances, was very special. I hadn't witnessed that kind of high-level synergism from the combination of those two instruments. They had played together for years and it showed. The acoustic groove between Tony, Todd, and Mike was thoroughly enticing to play violin solos with. As well, Tony was playing some of the finest guitar solos I'd ever heard him play in those rehearsals at his apartment. It was awe-inspiring to hear Tony play like he did. That unique and unmistakable sound he had, with so much *dreadnought* tone and projection… and his impeccable sense of time on top of it. Cool tunes too, they were great to jam on.

Tony wanted Mike and I to take as long of a solo as we wished, and on each and every tune at that. Whatever it was we were *saying* in our solos, as he described it, we were encouraged to keep it going and wrap it up when we had said enough. I wondered if Tony had heard about our dottily short, choreographed solos during the Grappelli tour.

Tony was motivated. He had something to prove going up against Grisman as a new hometown rival. Rice had managed to put together an instrumental string band that *could* rival the Quintet, absolutely. To be precise, it was the only other group like the DGQ in the world. It was rather helter-skelter bouncing back and forth between the rehearsals with both bands, just four miles apart—between these two acoustic music leaders who were determinedly at odds with one another. For me as a multi-instrumentalist, I could truly benefit from the ideal components of each undertaking. I had to pinch myself, having all this going on immediately after moving to San Francisco. It sure got my mind off how I had to leave home.

Tony was still a very young guy himself at 28. He seemed a lot older to me, though, but that's how it is when you're still a teen. Everyone who's a little older than you seems so much older. For the last two years, I had really looked up to Tony as a kind of big-brother guitarist. Beyond my personal stake in his band, or in the Quintet, I remained interested in what Tony was thinking, and what he was going to do next as a musician. Rice had his mind set on playing only new acoustic jazz-styled music. No singing, no bluegrass—he was done with that stuff. No desire to sing any song. As I knew then, there were probably circumstantial rationales for it—involving bluegrass music in the southern states, at least. Tony sort of mirrored my own *snappish* musical personalities. He definitely looked the part to play West Coast hippie Dawg music—now *Tony Rice Unit* music.

The makeover worked out for Tony. For all practical purposes, I too was done with bluegrass bands, and so was Mike. Bluegrass was all in the past for the three of us, and now it was time to become the Parker, Miles, and Coltrane of string instruments—so we *dreamed*. Similar to Tony's trajectory, bluegrass was Mike's training ground. Mine was a lot of things, with bluegrass being a big one. We were all moving forward, and it was time to really stretch out—play on the other side of the beat or whatever we could experiment with. The better we got on the instruments along the way, the more into jazz we found ourselves heading.

Tony wanted to book our first gig at the Great American Music Hall and make a sizable statement in town. Yet another string band debut at the hall. Start big, he thought. Tony figured he had the best string band he could've envisioned. I could tell he was fervid, eager—Mike was, and so was I. But an unfortunate development took place which was going to end it all before we even played our first show.

Rather than play at the Music Hall and test the waters, publicly and otherwise, especially after we did all the artistic work to launch this group of musicians, Tony felt comfortable in asking Mike and me to make the big decision. He wanted us to flee the "Dawg," and, *bay* his "Unit" for good.

Tony was absolutely dogging us about it, too. Seriously, he was stone cold grim-faced. He wanted us to choose. He put his foot down. He was threatening us that we were out of his group if we didn't "leave Dawgy" — immediately. Or, we could "remain in David's dawg house." He was leaving us no other option. No other way out.

We tried to lighten the mood with him. But Tony insisted it was time for us to pick up the strong scent of his "Unit" or get the hell out of the woods. Mike and I, however, informed Tony that we were hoping to hunt in both expeditions, that there were still plenty of racoons to tree whether we remained just a couple of Dawg dawdles or Unit strays. After all, we still needed to afford food in the Bay Area, unless we resorted to procuring our own coonhounds to *tree* our meals. To say that Tony took the news well about us not wanting to switch out our lead dog, would be like saying that Grisman doesn't use enough dog slogans.

Tony started directing some of his ire my way:

"OMAC, you should be playing just one instrument if you're going to be respected. You have to stand for something."

Tony liked nicknaming players close to him. He called Mike "Gator" because he was from Florida, and he called me "OMAC" after my own indie record label. Yeah, no *gay dog* here. I am no *rounder.*

Hoping things would simmer down after that, they didn't.

Rice went into a cussing tirade that even surprised Mike I think, someone who had lived with him for a good while the previous year. Rice went on to call Grisman all kinds of expletives. Our professed barks back to him were put down as mere dawg whimpers and whines. With the same precision care he showed the Bulova Accutron 214 Spaceview Swiss watch he wore on his left wrist, Rice delivered one of the best recruitment lines I've ever come across:

"You can either be grown-up musicians with me, or you can be Grisman's fucking pups!"

After a month of rehearsing undercover, and not for a single dime in pay, Mike and I realized our master plan was never going to work with those two. Tony called Craig the next day to vent about the shared-musician status we proposed. Then David jumped into the pack with his own four-letter words for Tony — trying to snare and run off with Quintet band members? "Let him get his own fucking band," David added.

In the end, David didn't cast too much blame on us for rehearsing with Tony. Maybe he thought it was a close call, and that we nearly grabbed hold of Tony's Unit and didn't let go. But just to make sure we stayed around, David gave us a few items to grip our attention.

1. There was another tour being proposed with Stephane Grappelli. 2. Warner Bros. Records was going to release the live album from the Grappelli tour as David hoped. 3. In a few months, we were to begin work on a brand new studio album of "Dawg" music for Warner Bros. Records— featuring the new Quintet lineup.

Without a promise of good-paying gigs, and with no major record contract or management/agency on tap, Tony wasn't in a great position to convince us to leave Grisman. But it revealed how serious he was to get out there under his own name and move out from Dawg's shadow. After naming his former group after the other guy, he wasn't going to take the chance of burying his own again. The Tony Rice Unit was destined to go on without us. One of my fiddle contest friends, Fred Carpenter, came right in and landed the job. I figured staying with Grisman meant a high-profile, national career in an established band, one that I could be proud of my membership in—the *Quintet*.

L IVING IN THE BAY AREA was expensive, no question. I lucked out on my first apartment in Sausalito, just a couple exits south of Grisman and Rice off 101. A couple of bar-singer buddies of Mike's from Tampa moved to the Bay Area soon after Mike joined the DGQ. Jeff Pinkham and Steve Mastro were playing duo gigs in local bistros, and renting a nice bayfront apartment together in upscale Tiburon. They had it for rock bottom rent, too. After Craig approached them about the new DGQ guitarist needing to share a pad, they said, "Sure, c'mon." It was great timing. A cot in the living room for another month, then I could take Pinkham's bedroom when he headed back to Tampa. I guess he was giving up on SF for making a living in music. I could already relate.

Our fabulous new digs didn't last long, though. I got us all kicked out by playing mandocello on our deck in the middle of the night, under the light of the moon. I liked playing for the seals out there a-barkin' away. Likely moonlighting with the wrong barking mammal.

It was so beautiful there—the few months it lasted.

With no place to go, I slept in Darol's living room in Oakland for a couple of months. Craig was looking around for another place. He finally came up with an available bedroom from a rock-band friend of his in Terra Linda, just an exit north of San Rafael—a quiet suburban neighborhood on Monticello Road. The rent was $100 a month. The man—John Harrison a.k.a. Johnny Lankford, a.k.a "Crazy Johnny."

Standing just about 5' 6", Johnny's head of hair looked like it had just sprung out of Queen's "Bohemian Rhapsody" video. His live-in girlfriend, Bobette, wore her most hermetic of spandex each day, and she played the part of the sexy chick rock groupie in most every respect. They both seemed pleased to have me as their new roommate. Johnny, a pianist and synthesizer player, led an amateur rock band that sounded a little like the English progressive rock group Yes. Their band, named Timmy, had a daily routine: rehearsing every evening in a local sound studio, and, never playing any gigs at all. They just rehearsed their original material. Timmy was funded by a well-off hippie dubbed Sponk, who owned A Brown Sound, a place where you could get your speakers re-coned. He also leased out rehearsal studios for local bands.

Many professional rock musicians came over to the house to smoke pot with Johnny and Bobette, some of them from nationally known bands. I still didn't partake in any of it, but, similar to Grisman, Johnny had the killer weed. Van Morrison's guys hung out at our house, Morrison himself lived over in Fairfax. Members of the Grateful Dead swung by periodically. From Novato just up the road, Mike Varney, the guitar shredder with The Nuns came by a lot. He talked about his *Rock Justice* opera he was working on with Marty Balin from Jefferson Airplane—it was playing down at the Old Waldorf for a few nights that first month I arrived. A local band that had just gotten signed, Huey Lewis and the News, were over at our place constantly, it seemed. They had one of those rehearsal studios right next to Johnny's.

Our low-profile neighborhood abode on a quiet, ordinary suburban street was *grand central.* At the time, I didn't really understand what was the big attraction. Was it just good grass, friendships, a great musician connection? Turns out, Johnny was a big drug dealer, and I had never connected those dots. Hard drugs, too. Johnny's dealing was all done discreetly—all of it taking place while I lived there, right under my nose. I never knew the extent of it until years later when he got busted by the *fuzz*. A sting operation at the old homeplace. Johnny was thrown in jail for many years—everyone in the house was rounded up until it could all be sorted out. Craig bought weed from Johnny, that much I knew, and that was how Craig knew about the spare bedroom.

If I had known that Johnny was a hard drug dealer for the area, using the very place where I slept and kept my instruments—as the "trap house," I don't believe I could've ever moved in. All I ever witnessed was Johnny selling some weed to friends on occasion. Johnny must've sorted all the hard drugs for his customers in his bedroom. I'd never gone in there, and he always kept his door locked up.

The reality for me as an 18-year-old: this place was the new crib. Johnny's trap house was my first home away from Mom and Dad. I should've never played my mandocello in the middle of the night out on that deck overlooking Richardson Bay.

Because Grisman didn't have many concerts booked, there was plenty of downtime at Johnny's and Bobette's. I began to compose music in my bedroom. I started making 4-track demo tapes and it resulted in a kind of grudging antithesis to David's guitar approach for me on that first tour. My new tunes did not contain *any* rhythm guitar whatsoever—the acoustic was utilized for cross-picking parts with my flat-pick. Johnny took a lot of pleasure in the new music I was coming up with. I could overhear him bragging to his friends (customers), about what I was up to in the back bedroom.

Unlike Mastro and Pinkham, my new roomie was not a big David Grisman fan. He liked Craig, the manager, but not David, the artist. Sometimes Johnny made fun of Grisman's music, calling it "old people's music." He parroted David's new tune, "Dawgma," by scatting the melody in a *"scooby-dooby-dooby-doo."* It didn't assuage him any when Grisman insisted on playing an additional slow-downer version of the same tune, calling it "Dawgmatism."

Oh well, Johnny was a rocker. Nevertheless, he became a strong cheerleader for my own musical creations—the project I was to name *False Dawn*.

One of the perks of being in the DGQ and having the Great American Music Hall as our house gig, was that I got to see any concert I wanted.

Tom Bradshaw let me in for free. I sure did take advantage of that. Over a period of a year and half, I saw almost every touring jazz musician perform, from Ella Fitzgerald to Joe Pass, from Dizzy Gillespie to Ornette Coleman and a young Pat Metheny. One night I saw a jazz piano-trio double-bill of McCoy Tyner and Bill Evans. I studied jazz up and down during my time in the City by the Bay.

I invited Johnny to go with me on occasion, to check out some jazz, but he wasn't big on seeing much live music, and especially not jazz. But there was one jazz-rock band he was plain nutty over, and would see any-time they were in town—the Dixie Dregs. I shared his enthusiasm, as I was into electric fusion myself. They were coming to town soon, to play at the Keystone Korner. It was all Johnny could talk about for weeks. He gath-ered a group of his musician friends to see the Dixie Dregs at the club. He claimed he knew them, too—Johnny having grown up in Georgia. The Dixie Dregs were based in Atlanta. I tagged along. I guess he *sort of* knew them after all—they gave him the nickname: "Crazy Johnny."

The band was good. I loved Steve Morse's music, his guitar playing, and they still had the violinist from their records, too, Allen Sloan. The whole band was tight. Johnny carried on and on about how they were the tightest band ever, and Steve was the best rock-fusion composer in the world. He was right. Morse was a genius musician, similar to Grisman and Rice, but with electric music. Morse was even younger than Rice, age 25. I was casually introduced to all of them after the show.

The following year in 1980, the DGQ played two co-billed shows with the Dixie Dregs. They took place at the Neighbors of Woodcraft Hall in Portland on May 13th and the Masonic Theater in Seattle on the 15th. Steve Morse watched our opening set in Portland and liked my guitar and fiddle playing, he told me. Backstage, he placed his noted customized Fender Telecaster around my neck after the show, and I messed around on it some. We ended up hanging out at the hotel all night talking about guitar and violin music as I continued to pick on his Tele—acoustically with no amp. Later, I found out that Steve almost never lets anybody touch his guitar. But if he did, they would have to wash their hands good and clean before that were to happen. But instead, that night he just gave it to me to dink around on.

For the Seattle show, everything was unchanged from Portland. Morse watched our set, and then went over-the-top complimentary about my playing. That night, he told me that I was the best musician in the Quintet, and that I should play far more violin than they're letting me play. Ah, the story of my life, never getting to play enough. Grisman was finally in the same room as Morse so they could meet and have some kind of exchange. While members of both groups were gathered together, huddled in the back hallway, to my dismay, Grisman flogged Morse's music in front of everybody there.

"I like your group, but it sounds like you could use some new material. I've got plenty of tunes, just let me know if you want to check some out."

Steve laughed nervously and quickly bid everyone goodnight. It was an unexpected, one-sided deliberation. But at least I had Morse's phone number in Atlanta before his speedy escape.

Everett Herald - Saturday, May 17, 1980

"Virtuosity, poise and power — The Dixie Dregs/David Grisman Quintet concert at the Masonic Temple Thursday was an amazing display of those three qualities and more.

Virtuosity was obvious in the set by Grisman's acoustic ensemble of bass, violin, two mandolins and guitar. The Dregs had the corner on power with their amplified fusion of jazz, country-rock and classical forms. Both acts have incredible musicians.

Following the set by Grisman's group, one of The Dregs remarked, 'It's great to be playing with real musicians,' and laughed, 'I guess you can tell who we've been playing with.' He probably meant that The Dregs' Southern rock and boogie roots were showing. How many groups can share a bill with a heavy-metal band as well as with a string quintet?

Musicianship of the quality heard at the Grisman/Dregs concert is a rare thing. Maybe it's just as well. The concert business would [go] to pieces if more audiences could compare the shallow posers with players like Grisman, Morse, O'Connor and the rest."

S PEAKING OF THOSE NEW TUNES, David was coming up with some tantalizing material for *our* new album. In addition to "Bow Wow," on which I would be playing the fiddle, two of the eight tunes for the record in particular were very big guitar features for me, with solos that stretched to several minutes long. "Barkley's Bug," finally broke the dog theme—going feline. (Barkley being David's cat). Secondly, and substantially, there was his long-form composition titled "Thailand."

In all of my interactions with Tony Rice that year, I didn't want to continue feeling bad about taking his coveted guitar spot. What's more, it was my time to see if I could not only match Tony's eminence on a DGQ recording, but maybe add something new. I admired him as my mentor, but I wanted to put my stamp on the Quintet as the new guitarist—I had a real opportunity to put something significant down on tape. His "you have to stand for something," regarding my trying to excel on more than one instrument...I wanted to prove Tony *wrong* on that. I thought that was pure folly. I not only wanted to affirm that I was one of the best young fiddlers, but that I was up there with him on the guitar as well.

For "Barkley's Bug," David had me arrange a lengthy double-acoustic guitar solo on my Herringbone Martin. And for "Thailand," David let me take a several-minutes-long improvised guitar solo. Together, my playing on those two tracks represented some of my best guitar playing on record. In that year, 1980, I took advantage of the opportunity given to me, and I exceeded most every expectation put on me in those circles. I was happy with the artistic result. Grisman, to his credit, let me do *my* thing. At least for now.

S O HOW DOES ONE MAKE A LIVING as a member of the David Grisman Quintet? I figured out that you pretty much didn't—other than the endorsement deal for free D'Addario strings. Not this year. Darol, Mike, and I created a trio and booked some gigs on the side. We even went out of state for some, but it still wasn't enough. When June rolled around, I let David know that I was taking off for the big fiddle contests and I'd be gone a few weeks. There was nothing on the DGQ schedule anyway.

In June 1980, Buddy Spicher organized his fiddle contest again at his Franklin, Tennessee ranch, the weekend before the Grand Masters. With the close proximity to the big one, he hoped to draw an even bigger field to vie for his $800 first prize. Thankfully, I won it this time. I entered the Grand Masters Fiddle Championship again—Porter Wagoner and Roy Acuff were running the show as emcees. I made sure to play some fiddle for Roy in his dressing room, as always. After coming in 2nd place for a couple of years, and playing way too jazzy, I compartmentalized "old-time" fiddling instead. Financially I had to. Spurred on by great Texas-style backup guitar work from Texans Bobby Christman and Rex Gillentine, I won this championship for the second time. It earned me another $1,000. Next up was Weiser, Idaho the following week.

Darol and Mike were curious about my fiddle contest prowess and they wanted to try to play *their* hands at some of it. Earlier in the season, the three of us entered the California State Fiddle Contest together. As serendipity came our way, the DGQ boys came out one-two-three. Darol was 2nd and Mike, 3rd. Would our luck carry over to Weiser? Mike and Darol were aiming to bust in and see what they could drum up in the little dusty Idaho town. They drove up from SF to the storied fiddlers' championship while I flew in directly from Nashville. I met up with them when the week got under way.

I didn't expect that Weiser would deal me and the "East Bay contingent," as David referred to Darol and Mike living in Oakland, a winning straight. Much stiffer competition here than in California. For myself, I expected to win it. As defending champion I went about my work, carving into the breakdowns round after round. Six rounds total. By then, I knew the American fiddling repertoire backwards and forwards even though I hadn't looked at hardly a fiddle tune the entire year. But it didn't matter when it came to the contests. I showed up in June like someone whose mind wasn't occupied by a single other thing. Somehow, I found myself even better at Texas breakdown fiddling than I was the previous year. The more time I spent on other styles, or even other instruments, the better my fiddling seemed to get.

For the second year in a row, I won the national title, and another $1,200 went into my wallet (the prize money increased this year). The Weiser fiddling judges were much tougher on Darol and Mike than I would've liked. Mike edged out Darol this time, but they both came out somewhere near 20th place. This stuff was not their forte.

Jam Interview: Mark O'Connor by Bob Burtman, Winter 1980

"Listening to Mark O'Connor play guitar last October 13th with the Dave Grisman Quintet, I was struck by the incredible ease with which he manipulated the strings, the fluidity with which he laid down the rhythms and leads. And though he must be sick of people dredging out the world "prodigy," one can't help but be amazed at Mark's lengthy list of accomplishments at age eighteen...

I spoke briefly with Mark after the Quintet's set. As he shrugged off one achievement after another, 'Well, I just sorta started playing, and then sorta started winning festivals,' etc, I was thinking to myself, holy !*&#+, what is this guy gonna come up with in the next ten years? Whatever it may be, you can bet it will maintain the incredibly high standards of creativity Mark has already established.

Q: Do you play as much fiddle as guitar these days?

A: 'No, that's one sad thing for me. I haven't practiced fiddle in a year. I played in a [couple of contests] this summer. Lucky thing for me—I don't know what it is—I think fiddle is my natural instrument because I'll get up there and only warm up a little bit, and just play. It takes me about a week to practice up and enter contests. I don't get to play the fiddle like I used to, for sure, but then I play more guitar.'"

The $3,000 I picked up in prize money within a couple of weeks' time, along with on-location record sales at Weiser, easily bought me another three or four months of survivability in the DGQ. Financially speaking, Grisman should've been thankful for my ability to play fiddle breakdowns because winning fiddle contests was clearly keeping me in his band. Otherwise, I would've had to convince him to give me a bedroom at his cool Mill Valley pad, and while he was at it, buy me those crab omelets and cappuccinos every morning at his neighborhood cafe. Yes, I was starting to drink coffee, as he expected.

While I couldn't cover living expenses by playing in Grisman's band, he did own a bevy of incredible mandolins that I took advantage of. In our concerts, we performed a three-mandolin tune on stage from his first Quintet album, "Ricochet." I had to borrow one of David's good mandolins on a permanent basis for that—in order to remain practiced. As a result of having a great mandolin around, I got very good at playing it that year. *Apologies to Tony about the multi-instrumentalist idea.* In September, there was a big deal going down in Kerrville, Texas regarding all things mandolin: the World Mandolin Championships was to take place. I played more mandolin around David and Mike during that time period. It was kind of funny that my progress kept them on edge just a little. David said to me, "Hey man, cut that out! No mandolin for you!" I was working up tunes for the championships. Hopefully the de facto Texas contest boycott would not extend to another instrument?

Mike was a little quieter—he didn't say much to me about my increased mandolin skills. One time I just went up to Mike wanting to play him something I was preparing for the world championships. He said, "Yes, let's hear it." After I played him "Russian Rag" composed by the classical mandolin virtuoso Dave Apollon, I asked him if there was anything I could improve? He had learned "Russian Rag," too (Grisman hadn't worked it up completely). We were all devotees of this early 20th century classical mandolinist. Mike advised that I could get a bit more bark out of my full chords. He demonstrated. Mike had certainly exercised that muscle for the last two years. Taking note of the tip, I worked on it more, and I felt ready. The winner in Kerrville would get some cash and take home a handmade Luke Thompson "Buck White" model mandolin worth several thousand dollars. I wouldn't have to keep borrowing Grisman's.

The whole idea became a little more provocative when David let me know his plans for being a judge at the mandolin championship in Kerrville. He hoped there wouldn't be an issue—my entering with my boss judging? It is not like we were kin or anything. After all, I'd played in fiddle contests with Benny judging a few times, he being my long-time teacher. Fiddle contest propriety was far more established than any mandolin contest, certainly.

When I arrived in Kerrville in September 1980, the fiddle contest money from June had nearly run its course. By now, Grisman had reduced our pay to $100 per show. We played just ten shows all summer as a band, including our first appearance at a new hippie fest in Colorado called the Telluride Bluegrass Festival. Grisman was finally able to book the Quintet at bluegrass festivals. Because of those Tony Rice *conditions?* Anyway, ten shows added up to no more than a $1,000. I desperately wanted this win in Kerrville. And frankly, I had a great shot at it.

Waiting in line to register at the check-in table, I was well motivated. Playing in a band with two of the best mandolin players in the world, I was ready to prove my worth as a mando player. But zippy as greased lightning, the officials who avowedly promote the playing of the mandolin, weren't going to give me an opportunity to play one after all. They heard I'd recently slipped into the Tony Rice position of the David Grisman Quintet and that was unfortunate. Some of them believed it was my automatic disqualification from the championship—if my employer was my adjudicator. A non-starter? Some thought differently, though. I thought differently, too. My main employer that summer was not Grisman at all. ...by three-fold, I was paying federal income tax on prize money from fiddle contests.

Over the dustup chafing in south Texas, I sought more back-up help from Buck White himself, but he ultimately wanted to stay out of this. The coordinators of the contest were the folks to drop the hammer. Grisman pledged to them he would judge it fairly. Still, *no* was their answer. David graciously added that he'd even remove himself as judge altogether so I could enter the competition. He'd seen how many months I prepared for it, but they didn't want that either. His name was advertised as being a judge. They were not going to lose David Grisman just so I could enter their mandolin contest. Frankly, Grisman would've judged me tough. No rubber stamping me to the title of World Mandolin Champion. Being in his band as guitarist and fiddler, the redress would have been relentless.

There I stood, the first person in history to win national titles on both the fiddle and the guitar. Adding the mandolin title would make it a record seemingly out of reach, maybe for all time. Perhaps I could've accomplished it all as a teenager on top of it. Whatever my cost, I was removed from the competition. The ongoing interdiction in Texas contests leached over to include the mandolin. They invited me to stay for the festival and "sit in" with folks. For free. That was the last thing I was going to be doing, given what they just did.

I got on the next flight home. David could have his fun adjudicating mandolin players without me around. I don't know what hurt more—not being allowed to enter the mandolin contest after practicing so much for it, or that I just spent $300 on a plane flight.

The financial pressure of just staying afloat in the Bay Area and trying to prove to my mother that I had everything under control as a young adult, was increasing my stress load day and night. I tried to keep thinking positively about my place in the band and any benefits I was receiving from band membership, mindful that I was in the "prestigious" Quintet, and it could pay off. At least it seemed impressive to people there in Kerrville—being a member of the Quintet meant something to some of them. I hoped I could see that worth soon. In addition to the financial concerns, I alienated my guitar hero, Tony Rice, in taking over his position in the band which he founded. I didn't know what I was going to tell Mom about being turned away from Kerrville. Tell her that David was the spoiler?

There's always next year, they said.

It took another two years for me to return to Kerrville and complete the trifecta by winning the World Mandolin Championship in 1982.

THERE WERE MORE NOTEWORTHY times with the DGQ. The Quintet created an all-mandolin ensemble to play at film director Francis Ford Coppola's birthday party at his home in SF. We read old mandolin sheet music scores for it, and played an all-mandolin rendition of Nino Rota's "Speak Softly, Love," the theme song from Coppola's first *Godfather* film.

The *Tonight Show with Johnny Carson* had us back —just the Quintet this time. David had me play "Bow Wow" on fiddle as one of our two selections. Johnny remembered us from Grappelli and tossed the bone.

There was the time when we played on the PBS television show, *Austin City Limits*. Jethro Burns, Johnny Gimble and Tiny Moore played their own set, too. It was a nice opportunity for us since the previous lineup never did much, if any, TV. Maybe the familiar Tony Rice blow-by-blow? With the cameras rolling, one of my strings slipped all the way out from beneath the bridge pin to where it was flopping around. It happened near the beginning of my guitar solo in "Dawg's Rag," playing on a new hand-made Somogyi guitar. I motioned to David for help—for somebody to take my solo over from me—but no one was reading my stress signals. Therefore, I swung around with my back to the audience. I took several hand twists of the tuning peg and tuned up the guitar string to the exact pitch I needed in about three seconds flat, and smack in the middle of my guitar solo. I did it without even hearing the pitch of the string as I was off mic and the band kept playing full speed ahead. I dipped back into my solo, hardly a couple of measures missed—guitar perfectly in tune. The escapade reflected how much I understood the physicality of the guitar during my time with the DGQ. Like people said about my fiddle, the guitar became something of an anatomical appendage.

Members of the Quintet were asked to record with young Bela Fleck for his second album, *Natural Bridge*. The sessions in January 1981 were at our favorite recording facility, *Arch Street Studio*. Bela scheduled Tony Rice to play guitar on the recording while I was to play the fiddle. However, Tony backed out the day before the session. Bela told us that the issue was over the DGQ. More than a year had gone by since he was out of the group, and Tony was still overwrought about the whole thing. Bela asked me to play guitar and drafted Darol for the fiddle spot. Bela credited me with saving his project at the 11th hour. He couldn't have done it without a progressive bluegrass guitarist. Developing my own brand of rhythmic accompaniment, and recording guitar solos on Bela's tunes such as "Apple Butter," "Crossfire," and the title track, the album demonstrated how I was earning my stripes on contemporary bluegrass guitar.

We got to tour with Stephane Grappelli again. It was the big payoff for all of my dedication to the DGQ. This time, however, we weren't Grappelli's band, but an opener. He had his own group along—guitar players Martin Taylor, John Ethridge, and bassist Jon Burr. It was a bit of a demotion for us. I wondered if Stephane had gotten to know us all as jazz and swing soloists, perhaps it would have made a difference in choosing his ensemble for his closing set. David went from bandleader and trading each solo with Grappelli throughout the show, to… playing "Sweet Georgia Brown" for the finale along with the rest of us. Either way, it was great for me as far as the fiddle went. There I was trading licks with Stephane on stage for a couple of tunes each night and grabbing some more lessons on diminished and augmented scale work with my great jazz violin mentor.

My crowning achievement during the DGQ years was making my Carnegie Hall debut playing with Stephane Grappelli on October 11th, 1980. Adding to the prestige of the evening, none other than classical violin-great Isaac Stern was in the audience watching us. He served as president of Carnegie Hall and was its chief protagonist. Exactly 20 years before, Stern led the effort to save Carnegie Hall from the wrecking ball. The newly built Lincoln Center was surely going to make the old hall obsolete, so many said. I became close to Isaac Stern, he being yet another mentor in the coming years.

On occasion, the Quintet opened for some other musical titans, including my violin hero, Jean-Luc Ponty. There were also the opening slots for Chick Corea, Gary Burton, Bonnie Raitt and David Crosby. On our way through Canadian customs for a Corea and Burton concert, Grisman remembered he had quite a bit of pot in his mandolin case. David and Craig suggested that the band members ingest the stuff, rather than flush it down the toilet and have it all go to waste. Not sure what I was thinking, but I figured it sounded like a reasonable idea since it came from management. I was going to try to help out. After digesting that ball of hash—the potency of it…well, I didn't know where I was by the time we arrived in Canada. It was one mighty hallucinogen. I couldn't walk off the plane without somebody holding me upright.

Anyway, there was something about my existence in the Bay Area as it wore on. I felt much more eclectic—more incompatible than I'd been before, and it wasn't because I was swallowing balls of hash. That was just the one time. But my normal every day mental make-up was feeling like I was stoned out of my gourd. A bit of a *space cadet.* I tried to refer to it as a natural high. On the way up to Grisman's house for a rehearsal on Morning Sun Road, I was pulled over for coming across the center line on one of those little roads too many times. Made to get out of the red pickup, I failed to walk the line. Flashlight in my eyes, I was told not to drive anymore taking whatever I was *on.*

"But I'm not on anything."

The officer had a look again at my pupils with his flashlight.

"I don't believe you."

I was finding myself more detached from people than I had been—even within our music circles. After a year in SF, I didn't really have many friends. Just Johnny, and maybe Bobette, I wasn't sure. Even with Mike and Darol, I didn't relate to their social hang as much as I wanted to, or should have. Before that year, I always had a good time in the social music scene, but I was becoming increasingly unhappy and depressed.

I liked hanging around with the hippies in Berkeley, I thought. I'd drive over there for some cheap Turkish or Indian food. One time while I was in an Indian restaurant, a woman came up to my red truck parked out on the street and started yelling at it. The pickup was parked just outside the front window. Before I knew it, she was hitting it with her purse. I thought she was going to scratch my Dad's new truck all up so I asked the waiter if we should call the police. The nasty stares in that restaurant were directed my way like I was some kind of miscreant. A guy walked past my table and said, "And the circle connects." I didn't have much of a clue to what it meant, but the clear message was I should just let the crazy lady hit my truck with her purse. Sorry, Dad. I felt like she was slapping me in the face with her purse instead.

330

When the DGQ was over in the East Bay, playing for some small event, David wanted the band to have dinner at an Indian restaurant. Not having a place in mind, he went with my recommendation—the place with the crazy lady and my red truck. I thought the food was pretty good. But David didn't care for it, and he sure let me know. He moaned and groaned about it the entire dinner, saying he would never take a restaurant recommendation from me again. He made sure we all knew it.

Not being able to get ahead with the Quintet was really getting to me. Musically, I had the intuitive gift of being magnanimous; however, as a young person, I wasn't sure if I was becoming absolutely jaded—even disillusioned now—by this environment. It was hard to imagine staying on without become marked and scarred.

I JUST DIDN'T KNOW HOW FAR my career could ever go under the tutelage of David Grisman. Mom's health was getting worse—I needed to call her often, as she insisted I do. The phone charges on Johnny's utility bill were eating me alive, actually, they dwarfed my rent payments considerably. The opening slot the DGQ played on that second Grappelli tour—a big tour, too—only paid me $1,200. It was even less pay than the first one. Grisman started me out with $200 dates, which my mother rejected out of hand. Now it was down to $100 across the board. I didn't tell her about the pay cut and just kept my money down in SF for food. Where was all of this heading?

Sometimes I drove up to an overlook across the bay as it joined the great Pacific. It was the place where I took the cover shot for *On The Rampage*. The record was still being held up by Rounder. They didn't know what to do with it so I kept reminding them that it was "sort of like the music I play in the DGQ." They didn't think it was a selling point. I would drive my red pickup there in the middle of the night and just sit for hours—thinking about everything. Eventually, I'd fall asleep in the cab of the truck only to wake up in the early morning hours and not have any recollection of driving up there in the first place.

Other times, usually in the middle of the night, I drove the red truck around the Bay Area, never being fully aware of where I was heading. I was just zoning out and surprising myself where I ended up. I spent most of my nights now just getting lost in the red truck. I imagined performing my own music one day and having an audience that cared about it, like they did for David's music. I liked driving across those bay bridges in the middle of the night, too—the San Rafael bridge especially—the windows in the pickup down and wind swirling my hair about. No traffic, no tolls— the time I felt most free in SF was right there, *crossing bridges.* Crossing all of those bridges. The symphonies in my head during those midnight excursions were glorious. My musical dreams were pure reverie, some kind of genuine golden dream for me had to be out there in the distance. In the meantime, I had put all my faith into the Quintet. And not without a sincere personal price to pay. I tried to be there for the David Grisman Quintet, but I wasn't sure if it was ever there for me.

I was petrified of dating girls again. Becoming more socially isolated, I couldn't even bear to ask a young lady out on a date for fear of rejection. The experiences of my childhood with girls had unwelcome repercussions—the imprints bored right into my conscience. I was becoming more difficult to deal with, or to even relate to. All of the guys in the band were either married or had live-in girlfriends. I thought about calling up Jeanette in Redding, but frankly I didn't know who I was as a person anymore. I identified myself as a musician only. If I was looking for something in a woman, it would be far more transient, I assumed. I still had some loose-screwed set of morals, wanting to be honest with Jeanette, but I wasn't sure what my life was all about.

Darol's wife, Barbara Higbie, was taking fiddle lessons from me on a weekly basis. She was a good musician, her main instrument being piano. The wife of a fiddler wanted me to teach her fiddle, and I was flattered that she wanted to. Barbara was 21, she was pretty and fun to be around. As the lessons continued over that winter, it seemed like Barbara was beginning to flirt with me. Of course I had to reject it all out of hand. She was married to the fiddler in our band. I confided in Mike about the situation with Barbara, and he seemed to be all ears. Then Mike and Barbara started to have an affair. Darol found out about it and filed for divorce. I feared that the affair could break up the band, the Quintet that I invested so much of myself into, a group with hard-to-replace personnel. But Darol wasn't that ruffled at Mike over it and it didn't cause any issues in the band, thank goodness, although it was hard for me to understand. Instead of Darol being upset, I was upset about it. I ended the fiddle lessons with Barbara in short order. She wanted to talk to me about everything, to explain what had happened, but I didn't want to hear it. She really wanted our lessons to continue but I told her that I didn't want to see her, I didn't feel good about it. The whole thing made me queasy. It could've been me, and where would the Quintet be if that were to have happened? Something told me that while Mike got a free pass with Darol, I may not have. I could see double standards everywhere.

More than anything, I was apprehensive about women because of my own appearance. One of the main issues was that my acne was worse than it had been, even back in school. I had pock marks and scarring taking its toll right on my face. I had no health insurance, couldn't afford a doctor. I hoped and prayed that it would all just go away. In one particular incident David tormented me about my skin condition while on a plane traveling back from a show. He was wondering if my mother had an accident while she was "carrying me." He was reading a book about the Elephant Man, and pointed to a photo. I wanted to vomit. My only solace in that moment was that Rob had nearly as bad a skin complexion as mine. I wanted to tell David, why don't you pick on him? I didn't. David had a perfectly smooth complexion himself; he looked like he probably never had a zit in his life. I thought about my poor mother in so much pain; she was so fearful of everything. Instead of throwing up, I just wanted to cry. So many times, I prepared myself to believe that I was only as good of a person as my music would allow me to be. I had little else to offer anyone, especially so in David's group.

One day, I was tooling around on my skateboard on the street in front of "Crazy Johnny's." My board was still an escape. This particular afternoon, an older man walking along waved me over to the sidewalk to have some conversation. After a nice comment on my boarding skills, and about what a nice young man I seemed to be, he asked me to stop what I was doing to speak with him. He had something to tell me: "I have a rinse solution that can get rid of that acne on your face." I was startled, because it wasn't a topic of conversation usually. I mean it was probably the elephant in the room, but went unsaid—unless it was from David. The man continued: "It will work like a charm. Where do you live? Right there?" as he pointed to Johnny's house. "I'll drop off a case of it for you."

I let Johnny know about the container being dropped off at our front gate. I described what had just happened out on the street. Animatedly he said; "Oh Mark, this is magical! It's magic! It's going to work, you better believe it's going to work!" Within weeks, by golly, my face started to clear up. It was some kind of home brew that he must have been peddling to potential customers. He claimed that he created the solution himself. I had no clue what was in it and, I still don't to this day. Within a few months, I was feeling much better about myself. Girls, for the first time that I could remember anyways, started noticing me. I couldn't quite believe it. Like Johnny said, it was "magic." Maybe my social life could turn the corner, at least in this department. I'd been truly lonely for some time.

There was a bluegrass group in Sacramento, South Loomis Quickstep. They had me play some fiddle on their album, all of them really fun guys—Ted Smith, Rob Bonner, Brian Cutler, and Allen Hendricks. They were friends, so perhaps I did have more friends in the area than it felt like sometimes, but they weren't just down the street or anything—a good 100 miles away. That fall, South Loomis booked several arts and crafts shows named the Harvest Festivals. They asked me to join them for a few. The shows took place in convention centers up and down the West Coast, leading right up to Christmas. Grisman's schedule indicated that we only had seven concerts booked for November and December combined—three of them were local gigs. So I had plenty of weekends off for the Harvest Festivals. South Loomis actually paid me more money to *sit in* with their band than I was getting for concerts with the DGQ. On top of it, I had some decent luck bartering my albums at the crafts booths. I was trading for things like coral mushroom lamps, and sea urchin lamps, and a bunch of hand-carved items. I got a lamp for my bedroom made out of a twisted tree stump. A jewelry box, made from another tree stump, was perfect to hold my tortoise shell picks. I loved things like that. I was able to get some Christmas presents there for the family.

With my skin clearing up, too, I noticed that some of the girls at these Harvest Festivals wanted to talk to me more, especially after seeing me play on stage. I felt less like the freak kid musician who people gawked at, and more like a young dude just hanging out. It felt really good for a change. One of the Loomis band members had a girlfriend who was strikingly beautiful. They lived together in Sacramento. She was paying a lot

334

of attention to me during the San Francisco Harvest Festival. We went strolling together, window shopping at the arts and crafts exhibits—sometimes we would stop to talk for quite a bit, just the two of us. She seemed really interested in me, like I had seldom experienced from an adult woman before, let alone a woman who was so beautiful. She was probably about five or six years older than me. She wanted my phone number and asked if she could attend an upcoming *Quintet* concert of mine. I said; "Sure, we're opening for Jean-Luc Ponty at the Berkeley Community Theater on Nov 14th." The perks for being in a well-known band?

She came to our concert in Berkeley by herself. Here I was getting to play on the same bill as my *other* jazz violin hero, the one that I skateboarded to during my days back at the Aurora Bowl, but all of that seemed to take a very distant back seat that night. She told me that she was attracted to me. I couldn't believe it—she was putting some moves on me. She wanted to stay overnight, wanting to work a little bit more on me—making me feel more at ease about what was developing between us. I was really on edge, she could tell. I had to let her know that I really didn't have much privacy at Johnny's house.

I agonized… *isn't she Brian's girlfriend?* I mean the last thing I needed was to end up like Tony in that department, too. First Barbara and now this. All of the interest in me came from bandmates' girlfriends? Craig's wife came out on the road one time. I called over to his room to pick something up. His wife said to come on over, and she met me at the door with no clothes on. Before I knew it she was hugging me in the hallway. I had to back out of that one goggle-eyed. She must've been on something.

Nothing came of it regarding the girl from Sacramento, but without much else to go on, I was building at least some self confidence in social circles again. The old man's " face rinse" from down the street, and a little *filling out* from all the working out on the ten-speed bicycle began to make a big difference in how I was projecting myself.

This didn't mean that my new self-assurance was going to impress Grisman much, though. On the contrary.

WHEN WE SET OUT TO record the new Quintet album at our trusted Arch Street Studio, undeterred, both David and Craig suitably confirmed that the band members' fierce advocation for a "Quintet" album was indeed heard and addressed. It was to be called *David Grisman Quintet '80*. Of course, Darol, Mike, Rob, and I were thrilled about that. High fives to each other, we were proud of our band and *our* album. We had steered David back to the Quintet mentality with a strong and committed band membership role along with performances around the entire country. It was something the DGQ couldn't do before. We even played gigs in the South those days.

The photo shoot for our album took place on the roof of a downtown San Francisco skyscraper. Not one with a crown, like I imagined flying off from during that first rehearsal day with Stephane, but just your flat-on-the-face, variety skyrise rooftop. We started with shots that had us all bunched together—kind of like any normal band promo pic. Craig and the photographer had David move to our right by about five feet. We shot some there in that position. Then they had David move ten feet over. *What's up with all this?* I wondered. Ultimately, they had Grisman positioned 20 feet over to our right while the four of us remained clumped together in our places—*our stations.* "That's a wrap," they called.

When the LP was released on Warner Bros. Records, the cover of the album had David pictured by himself. The panoramic photo stretched all the way around to the back cover of the LP, and that was where you'd find the rest of us. Not much bigger than a couple of specks. Now we understood why Grisman was 20 feet away from the band. I didn't get to be featured on a front cover of a Warner Bros. album like I was led to believe. In one way or another, it did not turn out to be a "Quintet" album after all—as they expressly promised it was. "Our album" was a "David Grisman" solo album. *"Quintet '80"* was just the *name* of the record.

(Years later I signed a long-term deal with Warner Bros. Records as artist/producer, and I appeared on the front of many album covers).

The gamesmanship was unreal. Why couldn't David and Craig be more big-hearted when it came to this stuff, I worried. Just as I was feeling better about becoming more social, more supportive of our band's efforts, I retreated again—further isolated to becoming more defiant, and even reckless. There was a part of me that just started not to care as much—about a lot of things. One night after a band rehearsal at David's, as I was loading up the red pickup, Darol and Mike were getting into the car they drove in together from the East Bay. After acting weird and dismissive at rehearsal, I stood at the door of my truck and began to cry. I got their attention to tell Darol and Mike I loved them, and I was really feeling down. I didn't follow the successes of our album, or *his* album as was the case. I just couldn't bring myself to have much concern about it anymore. I wasn't even sure how high the album charted.

(Unplug and join me on the charts).

S KIING BECAME A NEW ESCAPE from my Bay Area reality, as we got fully into the winter months. Yes, it was a little expensive, but it was just a day trip from our house up to Lake Tahoe. I needed better outlets for my increasingly confined fighting spirit. I was going bonkers without a better platform for my pent-up energy.

Grisman got together with bluegrass singer Herb Pederson and booked a run of small club dates in January 1981. They wanted to perform ultra-traditional bluegrass music with me on fiddle. While I was definitely not into playing straight ahead grass anymore, I desperately needed the $100 a night it was paying for the week-long run. Against my best instincts, regarding my sanity, I said yes. While it might have had the appearance of a welcome change of pace, Herb, Sandy Rothman the banjo player, and even David, henpecked me into fiddling more authentic bluegrass than I ever cared to play. It was so odd that Jim & Jesse loved my fiddle explorations, and so did J.D. Crowe; but when it came to the West Coast bunch, you had to get it just like the records from the 1950s, or it wasn't good enough for this outfit. A "memorial band," or something? David and Herb named us the "Bluegrass All-Stars," quite the egotistical designation.

Morning, noon and night, the three of them argued about details of the original recordings—and nothing about self-expression. It was like bluegrass boot camp that I had no interest in. Where was Old & In the Way anymore? I had no idea Grisman was *that* into traditional bluegrass, or traditional anything. I didn't know what was going on, I felt like I was sliding backwards; I had already been in top bluegrass bands, and this wasn't a top bluegrass band by any stretch of the imagination—evidenced by their trio singing. It only got worse for me when I had to sing bass on the Flatt and Scruggs song *"Hot corn, cold corn, bring along the demijohn.""*Gotta get it just like the record, Mark." But I was done with parodying. Maybe I was ready for drinking somethin' out of that demijohn jug?

Billy Wolf had just finished mixing my *Soppin' The Gravy* album, so I had the chance to give it a spin for David at his house. I was well satisfied with how it came out, and since it was "traditional music," I thought David would be into it. Digging it. When the LP had played, David surprisingly didn't have much to say about it other than commenting on the style: "Sure is its own thing." He added: "It's quite parochial." *Really?* Well, I didn't see it like that. There's a myriad of musical influences for Texas fiddle tunes: Western Swing, Mariachi and Ranchero, Venuti-styled jazz violin, Appalachian fiddling, and Celtic fiddle tunes, Ragtime... blues... show tunes. Every bit as diverse as the underlying instrumental nature of bluegrass—even more so. I even had a Canadian *polka* in the sequence of tunes ("Calgary Polka,") "Skaters' Waltz," "Over The Rainbow." *Parochial?*

At the time, I thought it was a gross misunderstanding of the musical factuality, the certitude—the heart and marrow. But it was also clear I was becoming depressed, and perhaps overly sensitive to a lot of things. I was making a distinction between the band experience and the rough and tumble competitions where I didn't care as much what other fiddlers thought of me. Everything here was far more personal and even intimate. Maybe David felt it was right to keep me in my place? But I hoped he would remember that a Texas style fiddle tune was good enough to kick off the first Stephane Grappelli tour—once upon a time.

Grisman really liked me polishing his picks. It sounded like a good *rookie* job. I had all of those tortoise shell picks I brought back from Japan. My criticism of tortoise, though, was that they routinely got scuffed up from the act of picking on the strings. This produced tiny notches and gashes on the pick's edge. It would scrape against the strings—you could both feel it and hear it. When the edge was new or nicely polished, it made a world of difference to me. In that smooth state, I could pick as free as the wind blew—a shimmering tone when buffed out and glistening. A triangle pick with all three edges wouldn't last me more than a couple of tunes on stage before it felt like I was playing with a wood rasp.

I had picked up a tube of metal polishing compound at the hardware store and kept it in my Mark Leaf guitar case at all times. Taking the inside of my wide, leather guitar strap, I squeezed out a dab, and then in a back and forward motion I polished the three sides of the tortoise shell pick, front and back. I made sure that I stroked it against the leather at the angle where the pick usually *met* the string. There were six playing edges to each pick. I had it down to where I required six picks to get through a show — one pick for every three tunes. It was a hassle, but it really worked.

Showing off my stash of picks as well as my polishing regimen, was definitely my mistake. Observing what I was doing before each show, David asked me to prepare his tortoise shell picks the same way. The ones I had given him. Therefore, I had an additional couple of picks to polish. Wherever I was, he'd find me and lay down his picks for me to shellac. Part of me wanted to insist that he take my strap and compound, and do it himself. But I couldn't bring myself there. I had plenty to ruminate on as I polished picks for upwards of 30 minutes before each concert. On top of everything, I was Grisman's *pick-shine* boy.

We were back up in Montana for a show, and David had his picks all buffed to order. Whenever the DGQ performed, at a minimum there would be a few people in the audience to invariably yell out Jerry Garcia's name: *"Jerry Garcia!"* It seemed customary for any Grisman show by 1980 — his connection to Jerry and Old & In the Way was indelible. By now, the one-time fruitful partnership resulted into an ongoing feud over the rights to the recordings they made together. The audience wouldn't know about all of the sausage-making, of course. In response to one of the "Jerry Garcia catcalls," David goes up to his microphone and I thought he said to the auditorium full of fans, "Fuck Jerry Garcia!" Then he stared me down immediately after it. It's his usual habit. Grisman will say something to somebody else, but stare at me like he wants me to react to it — or learn who's the boss and who's the shithead. I'm going, hey don't look at me. *I didn't tell him to say that...* But I never could bring myself to speak out much at age 18. David must have been highly stressed out to take stuff to such an extreme. If I were him, I'd be forever grateful to have assembled a band to play his music as we did, and to have paid them next to nothing to do it. *"Don't look at me, David — I'm just your pick-shine boy."*

One of the rules my mother enforced growing up was not allowing me to ski in Seattle, speaking on the topic of *unreason.* The mountains were just an hour away from home. She was worried sick about me breaking something, and jeopardizing my music career. It was so thickheaded. I mean, at the very same time, I was skateboarding vertical on the ramp out back. Well, that changed quickly once I moved out. Skiing was a hobby I took up as soon as I got out of the house.

"Crazy Johnny," Bobette and I got in the car and headed up to Tahoe for a day of skiing. It was my first time to ski at Heavenly Valley. Johnny and Bobette were well suited for the bunny hills, so after an hour at that tempo, I told them I was heading farther up the mountain to find something faster. I went looking for the "black diamond" runs. I wasn't a good skier, was still very inexperienced really, but I thought of myself as a bit of a *hot dawg* at the same time. I liked going fast down mogul fields and *shellacking* over the tops of them. I wasn't even sure it was really "a thing," but for some reason I could pull it off. I buffed the tops of those moguls down a black diamond run… just like a good *pick-shine boy*.

I thought about how cool it was that Johnny and Bobette looked after me like they did, as "crazy"—and *illegal*—as they were. They treated me like a good friend, and in some ways like a member of the family. Dysfunctional family number two. They were proud of me and that meant so much. This was a critical period. I was looking for support for what I wanted to do in music, not just what everyone else wanted me to do.

David always referred to himself as "your ol' Dad," nodding his head back and forth as he placed his first finger across his mustache to make his own appear to be crooked. (He mimicked a fan and the way he appeared and behaved at a past gig with Tony Rice). God, I got tired of that mocking joke. He constantly joshed me, "This is your ol' Dad." But it reminded me that I was still looking for that "ol' Dad" figure in *my* life. I had those wonderful grandfather figures that mentored me—the fiddlers whom I saw every so often anymore. But there were no middle aged men in my life who were there for me on a personal level, and altruistic for what my own artistic aspirations might be. I was still a teen, alone for the first time with my real family hurting in another household a thousand miles away.

Johnny believed that my musical compositions and creativity were superior to Grisman's, and deserved to be recorded and performed; that Grisman had the career, and mine would come one day. All this was hardly a resounding endorsement, considering the source, but at times it felt to me like it was all I had. It was obvious that the very good audience feedback I received in the band, as well as the favorable critical reviews, didn't make me happy about my participation. But in so many other ways, this band meant everything to me. I was really struggling.

On that same run in Montana, one of the concerts was close by to a ski resort, so I made sure to pack my ski pants. I got to the slopes the day of our show, but ran out of time to go to the hotel and change into my show clothes before soundcheck. As usual, soundcheck went long and I didn't really want to forfeit dinnertime either. I was pretty hungry. Had to shine those picks, too. It looked like I was going to play this gig while still wearing ski pants. As we were about to go on stage, David looked me up and down and said, "You're not wearing that are you?" I told him that these were my stage threads for the evening. Then David lost it, I mean he really did. He lost his shit on me: "Listen man, I am so tired of you fucking with me, I'm just about ready to fire your ass right now and just get it over with!" Darol, Mike, and Rob ambled off and pretended to be busy. What got to me the most was the anger he drew on. It's like he's on the verge of a boiling point, and maybe my mere presence increasingly brought him close to that boiling point. Did he detect in me some lack of commitment to his band? When I dropped everything else to be there. I wanted us to work more, not less.

Sometimes I had a novel approach to someone's fury. I had a lot of training on the social anthropology with my father:

"Since we're playing a concert in *real* ski country up here, I thought I would pay tribute to our fans by wearing my ski pants for them."

David paused for a second, like he knew I was giving him a total line of B.S., then a smile came across his face. "Hey man, I'm sorry." He patted me on the shoulder. "You're not fired."

And fat chance he could find someone to replace me on the guitar spot anyway.

Most everyone around me assumed that I should be an adult by now, but I was still the kid who couldn't save himself from what lay right in front of him. I had a lot of growing to do in order to cope. I was perplexed why the music business seemed so difficult to me now. Sad and lonely, I felt stuck. Musically speaking, I wanted to feel more free with my music. Instead of playing for free. Practically.

I took off skiing down the black diamond run.

The rush of skiing so incredibly fast over the moguls was a stupid, awesome thrill. I guess I was still looking for speed in my life. Yeah, I was looking for it. That was the freedom I knew. I wanted to run as fast as I could to find it, the freedom I could smell and even touch once in a while. I always had to go really fast—whether it was running home from school, driving on the SF bridges in the middle of the night, or on those paved streets riding my board, and yes, playing my instruments with a good amount of momentum. Speed was always the best. In recent months, it was my ten-speed bike making it over the steep hills to San Rafael, or taking it out on the open highway to the coastline, past George Lucas' Skywalker Ranch.

That one time was hilarious when I was over there. A bunch of leftover *Star Wars* characters hanging around the place. C-3PO in the corner. They wanted Johnny to bring by some dope, and I went along. Everybody was looking for some freedom.

I made it down the hill. Good. However, I was going about as fast as I had ever been on skis—even at the bottom of the run I was going that fast. Most of the skiers were moving a lot slower down that mogul field, because they actually had skied the moguls. It looked like the trail was flattening out, so I planned to just ride it out, even though the trail was narrowing all of a sudden. I didn't have the room to put on the brakes. Why would the trail narrow like that? WHY? I was going too fast to be on that narrow of a path now, just about 15 feet wide. The way out of this was being choked off. I was going too fast to figure out how to turn out of it. If I started skidding, I could crash into the rock on either side. I told myself to just ride it out. That's what I had been telling myself for a few years now. *Ride it out.* Suddenly, the trail veered to the left. It was SHARP TO THE LEFT. I couldn't make this turn: I CAN'T MAKE THIS TURN. I was boxed in yet again...

This time, I finally went off a cliff.

Salt Lake Tribune, Sunday, September 2, 1979
"The newest addition to the David Grisman Quintet is 18-year-old Mark O'Connor. Playing both guitar and fiddle, Grisman refers to him as the 'Mozart of bluegrass.' For the past two summers, O'Connor has won the national

fiddle championship in Weiser, Idaho. He cut his first album when he was 12-years-old.

'He's a child prodigy, he plays everything. I met him when he was 13 at a bluegrass fiddle show. He was playing his Texas-style fiddle,' says Grisman. 'Mark fits into the band very well, he's one of those guys who knows a lot of music. The guy is from planet music? He's too exciting for me to talk about. I start sounding like an advertisement.'

O'Connor replaces Tony Rice, Grisman's longtime guitarist.

'Tony quit the band because he didn't want to do this tour,' says Grisman. 'He felt stylistically incompatible with Stephane. He's going off in his own direction, doing some things he's wanted to do, which I think is good and fine.'

Grisman describes his own role in the band as that of a 'benevolent dictator.'

'I tell them what I want. I had a sound in my head and that's what I want to achieve. I was in a lot of groups that were so-called democracies. It just doesn't work.'

'I find the better the musician, the more he wants to be told what to play. The guys right now are eager to do that. I regard my music as classical music.'

'True professionals learn to work with direction. However, I don't like to nail down every note.'

'[Dawg] was a nickname I acquired. People just started calling me that. I always had trouble titling songs, so I thought, 'why not attach a meaningless word to the songs and let the music define the word.''"

Edmonton Journal, Saturday, July 26, 1980

"His boss says he comes from planet music. It's his music and abilities as an acoustic musician that set him above the average bluegrass picker. O'Connor is to acoustic music what Bjorn Borg is to tennis or Michaelangelo is to chapel ceilings. 'This guy's an absolute natural,' says band leader David Grisman. 'He does things it takes people years to learn. He's got it.'

Grisman, one of the world's premier mandolinists, says he's afraid to let O'Connor get close to a mandolin, and he's only half joking. 'Mark is so good it's scary.'"

Guitar Player Magazine / April 1981 By Jon Sievert

"Today, at an age when most musicians are in the infancy of their careers, Mark O'Connor, now 19, has already built a reputation among his peers that few will match in a lifetime...he became the guitarist for the David Grisman Quintet in the fall of 1979.

Mandolinist Grisman, who for 20 years has had the opportunity to observe at close hand virtually every prominent flatpicking acoustic guitarist, calls O'Connor 'the most imaginative, versatile, and adventurous guitar player I've ever worked with. Mark speaks in many musical languages. He has a way of mixing elements of bluegrass, rock, and jazz that I've never heard before. He doesn't have any stylistic boundaries, and you can't really say he's a direct descendant of anybody. He's got his own thing, and that's the most you can say about any musician. Mark is a state-of-the-art guitarist on acoustic, and probably electric, too – and anything else he touches. Buddy Spicher, a prominent Nashville fiddler, told me he thought Mark was the greatest fiddle player in the world.'

Part of Mark's prodigious talent comes from the coordination in his hands, which he believes have been physically altered from playing for so long. He has extremely long thin left-hand fingers that actually stretch between 1/4" and 3/8" out of their sockets. (His joints even allow him to bend his fingers to touch the back of his hand.) His left-hand fingers are longer than those of is right, and he has a reach of seven frets. Both thumbs are very wide and flat, which Mark believes is the result of pressing the neck with his left thumb and gripping the pick with his right one hard enough to pound out the volume.

'I like the strongest, most powerful rhythm imaginable, and that's what I think is the downfall of most acoustic players' he explains. 'There are very few who can really punch it out. I punch the guitar like people punch snares on a drum set, and when I take a solo, I play so loud I distort the sound on the monitors down on the low notes....I love loud music, and that's why I listen to rock. Steve Morse of the Dixie Dregs is fantastic, and I think Steve and I are actually going to do a duet album in the reasonably near future.'"

CHAPTER ELEVEN

IN FOR A CHANGE

FLAT ON MY BACK, I regained consciousness. The first thing I recognized was the clear blue sky above me. It looked so beautiful. I stared straight upwards for a few minutes, recognizing that the wind had been knocked out of me. As my eyes continued to focus straight up towards the sky, I gathered my outstretched arms off the slab of rock and brought them up to rest on my chest. They remained there for a few more minutes as I was trying to fully come to. I must have hit the rock slab very hard.

I didn't remember flying through the air at all. I drew a complete blank on it. The terror must have shut me down entirely. Later, my skis were recovered in the snow drift at the edge of that narrowed trail. I was 25 or 30 feet over the side of the cliff and I had no idea how long I'd been there. Regrettably, no one else knew I was there either. Nobody saw me go over the edge. No one had come to help.

Lying flat, staring skywards—with my two hands resting on my chest, I started to regain some of my breath. I took deeper breaths, trying to come through the shock. I tilted my head to the left ever so slightly—I saw my left arm. At first, it was reassuring to see the arm of my ski jacket extended out from my body—just lying there unfolded on the gray rock. I saw my black ski glove placed on my left hand, planted there. I turned my head back to look straight up at the sky again, and concentrated on my breathing. This was when I realized something was dreadfully wrong. How could I possibly be seeing the left arm of my jacket, outstretched like that on the rock slab with my gloved hand over there—when my left hand was actually on my chest?

I fought off being panic-stricken—but I was for a moment. I maintained that I must to try and keep it together and not let my mind race. I had to try, at least, and investigate my condition, but I was horror-struck as to what I might find. Methodically, I looked straight up towards the blue sky again. I moved both of my arms slowly down and out to my sides, to where they should be resting outstretched on the rock slab again. The immediate thought: either my mind was tricking my body into something that was not real — or my left arm was detached from my body.

I looked tentatively over to my right and wiggled my fingers inside my glove. They moved. Slowly, I took that right arm, little by little, and brought it up to my chest. I looked over to my left again, and wiggled the fingers of my left hand. Nothing. I took the right arm and reached all the way over to nudge my left hand's glove. There was no feeling in that hand. I was touching something utterly lifeless. The best word I could use to describe what went through my mind in those moments — *heartbroken.* Absolutely heartbroken. I knew I had really messed up this time, and I just may have snuffed out my future as a musician. The forfeiture of any promise, the sense of devastating loss I was experiencing, was terrifying as I laid there alone. Alone on the side of the mountain. I had done a horrible thing to myself, and with only myself to blame.

I started to scream for help, but I couldn't yell loud enough. I had no idea how long it would be before someone discovered me. Johnny and Bobette could presume I'd be skiing the remainder of the day until the last lift down. There would be no way for them to know I went missing until this place closed down for the night.

Thankfully, after about an hour, paramedics found me at the top of the mountain. It took about another hour to get me down to the bottom in a rescue toboggan. They told me to hang onto my arm and hold it into my body. There were still ligaments attached, but it appeared that the arm was horrifyingly snapped off.

My body was still in shock. I couldn't feel the sum total of the pain until I got in the ambulance at the bottom, when the shock began to wear off. As the medic truck took the corners at a good clip, that whole area of the arm started to really throb because it was separated. Pulled apart. I still had my thick black ski jacket on, and my cream-colored sweater beneath it so I couldn't see anything. Once inside the emergency room, a male nurse had me try to hold up my arm for X-rays — in a couple of different positions. I was begging, *"Is this absolutely necessary?"* Thankfully, and not a moment too soon, the official doctor for the Olympic ski team burst into the room. He chastened the nurse for having me lunge my severed arm all over the place — he only needed one X-ray. Straight on with the arm against my body, as I held it together with my free hand.

The doctor explained that my upper left arm was completely broken apart (the humerus), that the two ends had been previously separated by a good amount of space. But miraculously, the ligaments were holding on. The technical name for the break was a *Diaphyseal Fracture.* Through all of the trauma up on the mountain, with the various locations of the limb, the main tendon and nerves were stretched but still intact, and that was very good news. If the trauma had snapped the arm from a different angle, the tendon and nerves could've been damaged and that would make it a 50/50 proposition for full recovery from surgery, the doctor said.

I informed the doctor right away that I was a professional musician—I had concerts that I absolutely had to perform. They were coming right up. He listened to me for the moment I spoke about pending shows, and then told me what was going to happen instead:

"This will take a while, three or four months to heal. It's a painful area to have this fracture. How they found you on that cliff—consider yourself lucky to still be with us."

The doctor for Team USA continued with his prognosis. The weight of a cast would just pull on the arm and keep the bones apart. The best route to go is to tape up my arm with a strong medical tape, from the shoulder down past the elbow for the purposes of holding the arm together, somewhat. That alone wasn't going to be enough, though. A lightweight splint was applied for some protection from a direct impact, but I was going to have to use my right hand to hold my left arm in place for the duration. The ends of the fractured arm were going to have to find each other and begin knitting themselves back together over time. I was going to have to keep that arm as still as possible.

Recovery would involve being seated upright—inactivity was essential. I was going to have to sleep upright, too, propping up my left forearm with a hard cushion so the arm was stable once I nodded off. No baths or showers—just wash cloths. When I walked to the bathroom, I'd have to do so carefully, hunched over and not allowing the arm to bounce off my stomach. I'll have to keep holding the arm together with my free hand, otherwise the weight of the forearm would just pull the bones apart.

There will be intense pain once the shock wears off completely. I'll be on an opioid pain medication, Demerol. It's addictive, the Doc reminded me, so I should bear that in mind.

NOT QUITE SURE HOW I made it back to Seattle, but I got there. I'd be sitting in Dad's black leather chair for the next three months, alongside my mother's hospital bed to my right. I wore a poncho—the loose fit made sense. I didn't have to stare at my bandaged arm. I remained on daily doses of Demerol.

After several weeks of not being able to play music, my high school friend, Scott, brought our old electric bass over so I could practice right hand technique and thumb slapping. I had given it to him during our school project. At least it could occupy a few minutes of my time, otherwise I was pretty much out of it. I couldn't concentrate on much else, being heavily drugged up.

I watched a lot of tennis on the black and white TV that my mother still preferred over the newer color sets. ESPN was recently launched and there I followed the teenaged John McEnroe, and Jimmy Connors, Bjorn Borg, Guillermo Villas, and Ivan Lendl, on the tennis circuit. Tennis was a game that I had never tried before, but it looked a lot safer than what I'd been into lately.

"Mom, look at us, aren't we a sight to behold?" She reminded me that I will recover, she will not. "Oh Mom," I told her. "You'll be fine."

David Grisman was waiting for me to heal up and make it back to the Quintet. In the meantime, they formed as a quartet, moving Mike over to guitar to play the gigs on the books. About six weeks into my recovery, David called to see how I was healing up. When would I be ready to return? I repeated to him the same thing I said before, that the doctor said three to four months. Without being assured that I'd be rehabilitated to the degree required for playing musical instruments, David was worried about the DGQ's first European tour slated for July. "I'll be ready," I promised him on the phone. "The doctor said I'll be healed up by June."

With my continuing commitment to all things "health food," I figured out a daily cocktail of bone meal as a source of calcium, and dry *horsetail root extract.* The herb was expected to increase bone density. I needed to get some bone mass growing back around that break and cement those two ends together—as fast as possible. I had the six-week check-up X-ray and it revealed a bulb of bone mass growing around the break, nearly twice in size as the humerus bone itself, although you could see right through the new formation like a mist. My Seattle orthopedist muttered under his breath that he had never seen anything like it—and certainly in this kind of recovery time. I told the doctor about the daily bone meal and horsetail root supplements, and he simply shrugged his shoulders in response. Implausibly so, I was thrilled that it might work.

David phoned our house in Terrace the following week during my seventh week of convalescence. He asked me how I was doing at this point. I told him it was going very well and I had just got back from the checkup—the doctor was blown away at my progress;

"They're going to take this tape and splint off a month earlier than expected," I told David.

"Can you play, though?" he asked.

"We'll, not right now, but I can move my fingers fine, I will be able to play."

"Well, that's great, Mark. But I'm thinking about the European tour and the quartet is actually sounding pretty good."

"I'll definitely be ready way before the European tour—two months before at this point. It'll be my first trip to Europe, too, and I'm so ready to get out of this splint and play!"

"I hear what you're saying, but it's not a guarantee that you'll be ready, right? I mean, you're not down here rehearsing with us. We have a gig tomorrow night at the Music Hall. We need you but you are not here."

My heart started pounding—*is he preparing to drop me from the Quintet?* I was sitting there still broken apart, and my mind was really not in a good place.

I wanted to prove to him that my hands still worked and that I'd recover soon. I told David I was flying down to San Francisco to prove it to him and everyone there, that I still could move my fingers and play. Mom overheard the conversation as she was laying right there in the living room. She didn't think I was serious, though, about flying in my condition. But she wasn't in a position to stop me from going, either. I had decreased my Demerol intake by then, but I still had to hold my arm together when I walked. I religiously held that arm together as if it was the last thing I was ever going to do. I couldn't take the chance with the weight of the arm pulling at that newly forming commissure. Having no free hands meant I couldn't take an instrument with me, or even a bag. I planned to fly down and back the same day—that day being tomorrow.

After diligently walking through the airports, the airline ticket remaining in the pocket of my poncho the whole way, I grabbed a cab and got over to the Great American Music Hall. The quartet was on stage, so I went straight down to the familiar green room where my luck had dramatically changed for the good not so long before. I waited on the sofa for the band to finish their first set. Soon, the guys came down, along with other friends. Jon Sievert from *Guitar Player* magazine, who had just done an in-depth article on me for the publication, was there. Everybody was glad to see me, even if they were a little taken back at my appearance *and* my condition.

Cutting to the chase, I asked David, "Could I see a guitar?" Mike gave me his. Remaining on the couch, I carefully positioned my splinted arm outwards while resting my left forearm along my thigh. I tucked the guitar neck in around my left hand which was resting there. In this position, I could place my fingering hand around the fifth fret fairly well, and still flat-pick with my right hand around the sound hole area. I was able to play in that very position across all six strings, and I dare say, probably as good as any acoustic flat-picker in the country—at least on the fifth fret. Jon and the others stood gawking.

Next, I asked to borrow Darol's violin. I positioned the fiddle neck to where my resting forearm on top of my left leg could grasp the fingerboard. I bowed a bit of a tune. My fingers could move to all the pitches, even with some dexterity and accuracy. The nervous system was A-OK, and I proved it in the green room that night. If this display of gallantry couldn't save my job with the DGQ, then nothing would. Each of my efforts earned a round of applause from the gathering there, and I was so very glad I was able to do it. After the room began to thin out, and the quartet was getting ready for their second set, David and Craig said they'd be in touch. I didn't stay to see them play, I had to leave to catch my late evening flight back to Seattle.

Once I was back home, the hours ticked by the following day anticipating their phone call. I had knots in my stomach—waiting with bated breath. Finally, they made the call.

While they were impressed with what I had accomplished during my rehabilitation, and thanked me for coming all that way to San Francisco in the condition I was in, their feelings about the matter remained unchanged. I was neither rehearsing with the band nor making a contribution to the music; therefore, it was "unfair to the *other* bandmembers to wait on me any further." In addition, they liked the *sound* of the quartet, and wanted to go ahead with the foursome in Europe.

As to what happens after Europe regarding reassembling the Quintet again, they were unsure. They didn't want to ask me to wait around another five or six months to see what the future looked like regarding my involvement with the group. They felt it was inconsiderate to ask that of me, so they offered me severance pay of $1,000.

HEARTBROKEN ALL OVER AGAIN by the effort it took to get down there to SF, and the plane fare, unmasking my injury for everyone to see—I put my condition on display like some carnival spectacle. It hurt my psyche and threatened to set me back even more. Certainly, the lack of loyalty shown, nor any affirmation of what I sacrificed to be in the DGQ in the first place—financially and otherwise—alienating friends and mentors like Tony Rice, harming my mother appreciably by leaving home and joining up, and then sitting there with a broken arm, it all was taken for granted and without much empathy raised. So it felt. I was getting to know, rather intimately, the matter-of-fact ways of the music profession. *We need you when we need you—or we don't.*

This would've been my first time to go to Europe. I wanted to play there so badly. Perhaps it would've made waiting around for DGQ gigs to come in over the last year-and-a-half all worthwhile. I was using the European trip as a motivation to get healed up, too, to get back to playing. I had put in an incredible recovery time after the doctor's prognosis, but it only seemed to matter to *me*.

I called Steve Morse to commiserate.

Steve and I already talked that first week after the accident once I was back home in Mountlake Terrace. I wanted to let him know what had happened and that I couldn't record a duo project with him any time soon. It was good to talk to him and he encouraged me to hang in there. He gave me a few updates on his side of things. They had recently dropped "Dixie" from their band name because their new record company, Arista, insisted on it. That was cool, I thought. It lifted my spirits to talk to him, one of the very best guitarists in the world. To have Steve like me as much as he did felt really good. He was pulling for me to fully recover, and in record time.

"Steve, I am out of the Quintet. They won't have me back, I'm so unbelievably distraught. I just wanted to let you know."

I began to whimper a bit on the phone.

"Man, that's really a bad deal, a real bummer," Steve sympathized. "There has to be a way to get that gig back. Who could ever replace you?"

"Well, they became a quartet and moved Mike over to guitar."

"It's not as good of a band without you in it." Then Steve paused. "Let me think for a minute...

"Would you be interested in coming to play with us? Would you want to be a Dreg?"

As I was fighting off my tears, I was now feeling a bit of a jolt. I told him, "of course I would!" He then said:

"I don't know how I would do it, whether you could just be added, or maybe replace one of us. I'm going to have to figure this out. If I can get this to happen, which I'm not sure I can... when would be the earliest you could get down to Atlanta?"

Once I hung up the phone, I sat there for several minutes, stunned. *What just happened there in the space of a minute or two?* Mom was wondering the same thing. "How can you be ready to play in a month?" she asked me. "You told him a month." I didn't know for sure, of course. But the orthopedist was very happy with my progress, and said that this tape could come off my arm maybe in another few weeks or so. "One more X-ray and maybe this all comes off," I assured Mom.

Steve called back in a couple of days.

"Well Mark, if you're serious about joining up, you are officially now a Dreg!"

"Oh my God, Steve, that is incredible! I can't believe it. What instrument do you want me to play?"

"Both violin and guitar. I want to take full advantage of your assets," Steve declared.

Allen Sloan was leaving the band, and I wasn't sure if it was a mutual decision or not. They had a band meeting and discussed the change. The Dregs had an extremely busy schedule of shows coming up, so they needed me to start right away. Allen wasn't going to want to stay around to play many more of them. I might even have to learn Dregs repertoire while on the road.

"Steve, I really want to. I'm getting out of this splint, maybe in about a week," I reminded him.

"How soon can you make it down after you get the splint off? We can add you into the lineup on the run starting April 18th at the University of South Carolina," Steve pushed.

"That's just under two weeks from now, though. I will try, I'll do everything I can to get down there by April 18th. Thank you so much, Steve! I'm so excited for this—I'm so grateful."

LOOKS LIKE I HAD JUST TWO more weeks to recover from that broken arm and get out of the splint. Steve and the others let Allen go—they did that to get me in the band. I had to do everything within reach to get there, to play in the Dregs as soon as humanly possible. The following week, my orthopedist said the X-ray looked great. He showed me how the bulb of new bone growth had built up around the break, but now it was a mass of solid white bone. It appeared to be filled in with nearly the same density. "That is one fast recovery," the doc told me. I reminded him of the horsetail root.

"Now, getting the medical tape off is going to be uncomfortable, and you may want to look away until we get you all cleaned up."

Not only half the skin came off my arm along with the medical tape, but my arm had atrophied in that three months' time, down to the bone. I couldn't believe that it was *my* arm—it looked like a diseased, emaciated piece of tissue just dangling from my shoulder. I still had so far to go in recovering from this. Having the arm taped for three months had caused a real mess. How in the world was I going to travel to Atlanta and play shows with the Dregs in under a week? To play with one of the best bands in the world?

Immediately, I began to do arm exercises. I couldn't bend my left arm from the right angle it had been stuck in this whole time. I just had to keep trying to bend it, the doc said, and eventually the elbow will start to give. I progressed rapidly, though. I really couldn't wait to take a bath, it had been so long. I slowly paddled with my arm in the bath water for hours.

I had one appearance coming right up that week, judging the Northwest Regional Fiddle Contest. Flying over to Spokane for the contest, it was great to see so many fiddling friends urging me back to health. After many requests to play something, I sat down on stage, rested my forearm on my left leg, and fiddled a tune for the audience in first position. It didn't go badly, and it sure felt nice to perform again. They paid me $250 for adjudicating that weekend. I just kept exercising that arm, all day long.

Within the week, I could bend my arm farther but only by just an inch or two. It was still noticeably bent. Luckily, playing the fiddle and the guitar requires the arm to be bent to some degree. I wore long-sleeve T-shirts so I didn't have to look at the arm, nor have anyone else see it either.

My older half-brother Larry's wife, Francy, had a decent violin which belonged to her father. She brought it over for me to check out. He was willing to sell it because he didn't play anymore. I thought a violin like this would be much more suitable to play in the Dregs than the old white fiddle. I would need a bridge pick-up on it to keep up with a loud rock-fusion band. "My father says it's worth $3,000," Francy said, "but he would give it to you for $500 on the condition that you pay him the rest whenever you get famous!" I took that deal. It was a German copy of a Maggini violin, made in the late 1800s. My cousin, Mike Mills, owned a local music shop in the Seattle area. I had gotten my Polytone amp and MXR digital delay through him for the high school trio. They outfitted the new violin with a Barcus-Berry bridge pickup. I was going full-scale electric on the fiddle for the first time.

I was spinning my Dregs LPs nonstop that week. Fantastic music. I was so happy to sign up to be in this band — *Free Fall, What If, Night of the Living Dregs, Dregs of the Earth* and *Unsung Heroes.* They were all excellent. I had most of these in my record collection before I'd even met them. Steve was quite an impressive jazz-rock-fusion composer—his guitar playing was simply out of this world.

I had kept "Crazy Johnny" abreast of the progress with the broken arm. When I informed him that I was becoming a Dreg, he pretty much flipped his gourd, as expected. In nothing flat, Johnny had an apartment for me to rent in Atlanta. His older brother, Tom Harrison, lived in their mother's old house in a high-end neighborhood called Buckhead. The basement apartment was available to me for $250 a month. Tom lived alone. He would have the place ready for me when I arrived. What a find. I guess it was all meant to be.

My mother was happy for me to get back to my music, but she couldn't say she was a big fan of this "electric stuff."

"But Mom, you liked my electric rock trio in high school?"

"Yes, but that was your music. I know you're excited about this, so, I will try to like their music more, if you are playing it."

There was such a sense of elation, combined with some loss and resignation. I was so excited about a fresh start with a new group that really wanted me. But I was saying farewell to the beautiful acoustic music I got to play on my Herringbone Martin and my old white fiddle. Perhaps one day again soon, I could create music for my acoustic instruments. It helped me a great deal that I could *imagine* and *dream* about that. I could see the course that my life was taking in the meantime. It was to work with composer-band-leader bosses who put their persuasive and unflagging instrumental compositions front and center with no apologies. People who demanded that their music be performed and recorded, at almost any cost. The power of my own ideas helped me stay connected to the things I'd loved for a long time, even though I wouldn't have much time to participate in them.

MOM WAS PRETTY HAPPY that I was healing up, too. I just about drove her crazy, sitting next to her in the living room day and night and moaning for three months straight through my pain and misery—not being able to play my instruments. During this time, though, we got to know each other a little more—as two adults. We were finally on equal footing, so to speak—and both of us physically in bad shape. Michelle was at school all day, driving herself to dance class and hanging out with her friends most every afternoon. Dad was working until late hours, but would continue to act up against my poor Mom at night. As I sat in his black leather chair crippled up with a broken arm, I decided there was no way this pattern was going to continue. I told him, "Dad, we can't do this." He tested me a couple more times, taunting my mother;

"I need to recover in peace and quiet! Mom needs to recover, too. You will have to live somewhere else for a while."

Mom wasn't so sure if my panacea was too harsh.

"Tough, I'm doing this for my own sanity, then."

Dad moved out to stay with his sister, Birdie, in West Seattle. It gave Mom and I some mental quietude. We got a chance to talk some about her personal life, things I never knew much of before. Because she was *Mom,* I never had a chance to learn about her own history, which she mostly kept to herself.

I knew so much more about my Dad's family because we took all those summer trips back to eastern Montana when I was a little kid—visiting my three uncles on the ranches where Dad grew up: Uncles Dan, Jim, and Richard. They all talked about the old days on the ranch in Poplar, Montana, like it was a rite of passage. Dad's American story begins a couple generations before—my great-grandfather Dan O'Connor and his brothers coming over from Ireland during the Great Famine. They homesteaded initially in St. Paul by the 1840s, and then to eastern Montana for sprawling ranchlands. Bordering Fort Peck, initially a trading post in the early 1800s, the O'Connor neighbors were the Sioux and the Assiniboine peoples. The Blackfeet and Crow areas were just beyond them—all about the time of statehood. Dad was the 2nd youngest of 14—several of the siblings were now living in Seattle, like Birdie. I was proud to learn that Uncle Richard became a decorated hero in action during WWII. He was our favorite uncle back on the Montana ranches—he chose the horses for us city kids to ride on the range, nice and easy. He broke and trained all of them himself. Richard even had a herd of wild Mustangs on his land. Mom admired their ranch culture a lot. This life seemed beautiful to her, like some place she wished she could've escaped to.

When he was 16 and *his* father died, Dad was too young to inherit the family ranch, which went to his three elder brothers. He didn't want to work for them either, so he headed to the big city. Those family vacations at the ranches were before our summers turned into music summers.

But Mom was far more secretive about her and Granny's recent past, and for good reason. Granny, having the sensational name of *Helen Adriance Storm,* grew up on her family's Memphis plantation in the 1890s, raised by her parents' former slave nanny. Her father, my great-grandfather, was a Memphis probate judge and a member of the Tennessee legislature in the 1880s. At the outset of the Civil War in 1861, as I learned to my disappointment, he and other relatives living in the upper southern state of Tennessee joined the Deep South and took up arms as Confederates. My great-grandfather owned a plantation, and reprehensibly, he owned slaves. On December 6th, 1865, when the 13th Amendment to abolish slavery was ratified, some of their former slaves stayed on with the family for employment because they were "treated well as slaves," Granny conveyed to us, "unlike some of what happened with the other slave masters they knew." Her "nigra nanny," as Granny fondly recalled her, was someone she loved very much.

By 1917, WWI saw Granny and her older sister, Mary, move out West. Granny and her new husband homesteaded where the city of Lynnwood is today, just north of Seattle. As the years went by, they gave parcels of their land away to welcome neighbors settling in the area. Otherwise, if the family could've held on to their initial acreage... well, who knows. Mom had done her own extensive family tree research, mostly at the Seattle Public Library, where she found it all on microfilm. You could describe our family heritage as both sanctioned and successful—aspects of it full of glory from blood-and-guts hardships; other parts, well... seditionist, degenerate. ...outlandish. But all of it was central to the history and the founding of our country, The United States of America.

My 13th great-grandmother, Sarah Rapelje, whose parents came over from the Netherlands on a wooden-hulled ship, was the first white child, and Christian, born in the state of New York. Her parents established the first Dutch colony in the Hudson Valley, called Fort Orange. This is where Sarah was born in 1624. Two years later, her family and other Dutch settlers purchased Manhattan Island from the Canarsee Indians of the Manhottoe for a reported 60 guilders (or $24 worth of merchandise). Soon this island became New Amsterdam, and the Rapelje family helped settle the southern tip. Sarah was granted a large tract of land by Dutch authorities at Wallabout Bay in Brooklyn. Even though Manhattan island was ceded to the English by 1664, and became the Province of New York, my 13th great-grandmother's final home was the village of Boswijck which eventually became the modern Bushwick in Brooklyn. A personal chair of hers is in the permanent collection at the Museum of the City of New York, and a medallion given Sarah upon her marriage to Hans Hansen Bergen, was donated by family descendants in 1926 to the Brooklyn Museum of Art.

Sarah gave birth to 15 children by two husbands. It was reported at the time that one of her female children was kidnapped by Native Americans in the Hudson Valley. This was during the years when the Dutch first created an alliance with the Mohawk Nation owing to fur trading. As allies, they ran out other tribes from the area such as the Mohicans. The younger Rapelje eventually married one of the chiefs of the Mohawks, and their offspring were educated in Dutch settlement schools. Many Mohawks were converted to Christianity by early missionaries and priests. These people—the Mohawk chief and his family—are my direct ancestors.

The Mohawks as members of the Iroquois Confederacy, largely took the side of the British during the American Revolution. After the British ceded to the colonists, the Mohawks were driven north into Canada, but my family headed south.

As Mom researched the family tree, the documentation on microfilm was both comprehensive and accessible, as most all of our relatives were public figures, and were written up in newspapers for one thing or another. One of our ancestors was a surveyor responsible for drawing the Delaware state line that is observed to this day. As the family migrated south, eventually Granny was born in Memphis in 1891, my mother was born in Seattle in 1930, leading to my birth here in 1961.

"Why didn't you talk more about your childhood to us, Mom," I prodded her.

Mom finally opened up to me about some of it.

First there was my grandfather, the father-figure who Mom loved. Henry Stanley MacDonald saw me for the final time when he was 85. I was just one-year-old. He told his daughter that I was a "very special boy," according to Mom. She said this wasn't just typical grandparental doting— she believed him to be both smart and somewhat extrasensory. His premonition helped to explain part of why Mom dropped everything else in her life to promote me as a child musician. Grandfather was eccentric and an academic. He was interested in mysticism, and spent time writing articles on a variety of topics from space exploration and extraterrestrial intelligent life to futuristic robots and science fiction. The central issue in his family life was that he refused to hold down a job that paid a wage; therefore, he wouldn't take care of Granny and their three children: John, Betty, and my mother Martha (Mom being the youngest by ten years). Mom's two older siblings quickly diminished their own father to nothing more than a quack, and extricated him from their lives. But not so for my mother. He was her favorite.

After John and Betty left home as young adults, Mom was the only remaining child at the house by age 8. Granny divorced my mother's father to marry a man who "at least kept a regular job and put food on the table," as was described reputably by John and Betty. Mom was scared to death of that man, however—her new stepfather. Tragically, he began to molest my mother, with Granny's shrouded consent. The child sexual abuse lasted for more than a year. Horrified over her own childhood conditions, I asked Mom, "At what age did all this begin?" She whispered, "age 10," as her voice broke. A tear came down her precious cheek as she laid there on her living room hospital bed. She told me about Granny walking into the room once while Mom was being raped by her new husband. All she would do was say, *"excuse me,"* and back out of the room, politely closing the door behind her. I asked Mom how she could even stand her own mother to this day, given this horror she is describing? Mom said she had long since forgiven Granny, and she never fully blamed her for what happened. Mom even defended her;

"It was her second husband. It was unheard of in the 1930s and 40s for a woman to have two divorces," Mom said. "Granny had no skills to make a living and take care of me. Your grandma believed it was the best she could do for me."

The molestation ceased before Mom was able to get pregnant. She tried to escape the hideousness of her family life by way of school work. She studied very hard—her desire was to be an academic just like her real father, who she greatly missed. Granny forbade Mom to ever see her biological father all of those years; however, Mom found ways to visit him in Seattle—even as a young girl. Along the way, she developed a love of classical music as a teenager, just like her Dad, and she sought out a couple years of piano lessons for herself. At a time when a very small percentage of women went to college, in the lower single digits, my mother did so in the late 1940s, earning a two-year bachelor of liberal arts degree at the University of Washington.

Discovering another artistic escape from her pained life, she developed a love for Hispanic and Latin American culture. During the 1950s, Mom got into Latin dancing such as the rumba, cha-cha-cha, samba, and the mambo. Her excellence as a student led her to teach dance at Arthur Murray's and that is how she met my Dad—on the studio dance floor. Lawrence O'Connor was not the Latin man she was hoping for, but they fell in love. She got pregnant with me in late 1960 prompting Dad to leave his wife and three teenaged kids (June, Tim, and Larry Jr.). He married my mother and started his second family.

It made more sense why Mom led me to study Flamenco guitar as well as classical guitar as a child. Mom always wanted to live her life vicariously through me. Her health was getting heartbreakingly worse, though, and I couldn't know how fast she was going to deteriorate.

As I headed out the door to the airport for Atlanta this time, she had her pyramid-shaped wooden box I had given her—resting there on her stomach. It was a Christmas present that I traded some albums for at the Harvest Festival. She prayed for her health using this pyramid box, with important items placed inside such as notes she wrote to herself. She kept long tabulations of how much my fiddle contest prize money would be worth one day if I kept winning. If I could keep the money, that is. She believed the impossible was possible... that even a knife could become more sharpened while inside her pyramid box. Once I noticed some scissors in there. She was always writing things and thinking of stuff like that. Like father, like daughter.

CHAPTER TWELVE

THE BASH

In The Groove by **Steve Washala, 1981**

"Mark O'Connor who has seven solo albums to his credit, O'Connor is the winner of virtually every fiddle contest you can think of. The world-wide champion played on the current David Grisman/Stephane Grappelli album on Warner Bros. Morse heard O'Connor play guitar before on a Dregs-Grisman bill but his fiddle playing on one tune totally blew him away. Morse then wondered if it was a fluke or not. After [a couple of] gigs, the two hung out backstage when Morse prodded him to keep playing. 'At first I thought he was lucky to do one tune real well but everything he played was perfect.' They talked of having Morse be a guest on his solo album, 'but before we got a chance to do that he was in the band.'"

ARRIVING IN ATLANTA, my new landlord and roommate, Tom Harrison, picked me up at the airport. The suburban house he acquired from his mother was located on Stella Drive in northwestern Atlanta, an upscale area called Buckhead. The home sat directly across the street from Chastain Park Amphitheater, an outdoor venue where music concerts took place each summer—the Atlanta Symphony's summer home. One day I'd perform my own "The Fiddle Concerto" with them at that place, but that's another story. Tom introduced me to my new basement apartment, complete with my own bathroom and small kitchen. Essentially, I was going to live alone—Tom spent all of his time upstairs. My new digs—cozy and quite comfortable—was a big step up from the small bedroom at Johnny's. I was plenty thankful to be there.

The following morning, Steve Morse drove his motorcycle over. With his Telecaster in a gig bag on his back, Steve rode down my driveway and parked it at the bottom. We hugged hello. It was amazing to see him after all I had been through. With my self-esteem laying at the bottom of the gutter for months, I couldn't help but believe he was rescuing me into this new fairy-tale and pristine world of music-making. Self-conscious over my diseased-looking twig of a left arm, I persisted with long-sleeve T-shirts. I wanted to hide it from him, and I still couldn't straighten the arm out—the sloppy clothing hiding the appearance. I kept both arms at soft right angles as I stood there speaking—so one arm didn't draw attention from the other. The issue actually never came up much that day. After taking a quick survey of the surroundings, Steve congratulated me on finding a nice place to live so quickly. He was impressed with my resourcefulness, a quality that he looks for in musicians, as I was soon to learn. Steve wore a black leather jacket and blue jeans, his straight blond hair pulled back into a ponytail like many of the hippies I knew on the West Coast. I reminded Steve that it was "Crazy Johnny's" brother's house—*the guy from San Francisco.* Eliciting his name brought a few chuckles. Hoping to give Johnny a bit more credibility than he enjoyed with the Dregs, currently:

"I didn't have any time to move my stuff from Johnny's house, so he offered to load it all up in my red pickup and drive it across the country to Atlanta," I elaborated. "He wanted to visit his mother and brother anyway."

The red truck had a flimsy canopy on it—not much protection to have instruments like my 1945 Herringbone Martin guitar, the 1924 Gibson K-4 mandocello, and my old white fiddle, in the back of it for several days. For the purposes of the *Dregs,* my black 1969 Les Paul Custom from high school was under that same canopy. I hoped that "Crazy Johnny" and the red truck would make it to Atlanta in a day or so—he was on the road and heading this way.

Since I had no furniture, we sat down on the reddish-brown shag carpeted floor while Steve began showing me Dregs tunes. I had my new violin ready to go. Steve played his converted solid-body Telecaster acoustically while he taught me the repertoire we were to perform. He didn't want to use an amp or anything, we just dove right in. There was just a couple of days before our first show together in Charleston. He probably knew we weren't going to get everything down to play a whole show in just a few days—but we were going to get as much as possible. I had tried to pick out some of the violin lines from my Dixie Dregs records before I left Seattle, but the violin was so tightly woven into the mix, it was difficult to distinguish which was the guitar, violin, or synth line a lot of the time. Steve was there to show me the music now.

The unison lines with the guitar and the violin were crucial, as Steve demonstrated to me that morning—it was the signature Dregs *"sound."* As a classical violinist by training, Allen Sloan, the guy I was replacing, spent an inordinate amount of time perfecting his violin parts to emulate each note of Steve's guitar interpretations, phrasing, rate of the vibrato, and even the exact timing of the note bends on the guitar. Admittedly at first, I was thinking that the goal of perfectly matching Steve's vibrato and bends on the violin was a bit frivolous to spend much time on. I was more worried about the kinds of solo spots I was going to play, the different chord changes I was to jam out on. I could emulate those lines, yes, but to do it to that fine of a degree that he was looking for… I wasn't so sure about.

Steve was absolutely sure. This was part of the gig. *Welcome to the band.*

Everything was taught to me by ear, and from Steve's memory. He didn't use any recordings, even as a guide to demonstrate something. There wasn't any notation to be shared, and Steve didn't want me to learn the music that way. To make the process *seem* a little less overwhelming, he declared that there were surprisingly few meter changes in his music— most everything was in 4/4. That didn't make the music any easier to attain though—it was a continuous flow of ferociously deceptive counting required for many of my lines, most of them played syncopated in all kinds of different ways against the fixed beat. Steve painstakingly went over them with me, pounding out the straight time with the side of his shoe on the carpet. There was nothing that was going to be nuanced or interpreted with him, it was to be perfected. Steve recalled it all from his own memory bank. He not only mastered *his* parts of the music, but also the counter lines on the violin he was showing me, the keyboard lines, and even the bass parts. It was a real mind blower as to how all this knitted together on his electric guitar. It was all there laid out on his fretboard and under his fingers. He could nearly play all four instrument parts just with his two guitar hands. I was not fully aware of this before, but he not only wrote all of the pieces for the band, he wrote each line for every instrument.

The music we launched into learning right away was from the new album, *Divided We Stand,* released on Arista Records. The record was out the very month I joined the band—my job was to promote the album that featured Allen. Steve wished I could've been on the new album, he told me, but it was already finished and that was that. Picking out those lines from Steve's floppy electric guitar strings, with the clacking of his pick being twice as loud as the pitch of the note itself, was excruciatingly difficult. I could barely hear what pitch he was bending to. After the first day of practice, Tom told me he had a guitar amp right up the stairs we could use, but Steve didn't want it. Luckily I had my large brass practice mute that I could put on top of my violin bridge to bring the volume of the violin way down to equal his Fender solid-body. What a crazy way to learn this music, I thought.

Steve wanted to open up the shows with the first track, "Divided We Stand." I learned a lot of the new album's material—much of it on that first day of practice: "Cruise Control," the country tune "I'll Just Pick," the funky "Kat Food," the heavenly "Day 444." For the shows, Steve wanted to play one of my fiddle tunes with him as a duet—it was to replace the more baroque-sounding duos he always recorded featuring Allen. I showed him "Limerock." He ended up playing the dickens out of it on the electric. I smiled. Benny would love this.

My instruments arrived from California in the red pickup, thankfully, and just in time before hitting the road. Johnny made it all that way. I was so happy to see all of my stuff in Atlanta, and in one piece. I had my black Les Paul now, ready to go. Steve wanted to turn one of the new tunes, "Rock & Roll Park," into a two-guitar special. On our floppy electric guitar strings with no amp sound, we started working on the duo guitar leads. Like the violin, Steve really wanted me to fully match his phrasing, bends, and guitar vibrato—precisely. I still could barely hear the pitches he was making on the unamplified Tele, nor the ones on my Les Paul, but it was obvious as well that I needed to develop the technique of bending the note and using arm vibrato at the top of the pitch like Steve was known for. The one year of playing electric guitar in my school jazz-rock band wasn't quite enough electric guitar technique to get me over the top on Dregs music. I could play an acoustic steel-string for sure, but I was in the land of Steve Morse now, another kind of guitar player who was just starting to dazzle the electric guitar world. Steve wasn't interested in playing on Martin guitars with me—instead we were going for Duane Allman meets Hendrix, with a little Mahavishnu Orchestra and McLaughlin laced throughout. My biggest problem: I didn't have a left-arm for the "arm vibrato" he used.

Not yet. I let him know that the vibrato was going to take a while. He let me get away with just matching the bends for now. On this day in Atlanta, Georgia, getting schooled on electric guitar technique by Morse began in earnest.

The musical talent of Steve Morse was astounding to see up close, as he tore apart his tunes to teach them to me. Being the Dregs new co-lead soloist on violin and guitar—standing beside the guitar god on stage and hitting the ground running the very next day, was more daunting than I ever thought possible at this juncture in my musical life. I had already worked closely with Grappelli, Grisman, Rice, Haggard, Gimble, Crowe, Jim & Jesse, Vassar Clements... some of the early bluegrass greats, and the best contest fiddlers in the country no less. I thought I had already seen most of the musical tests I could come across during my teen years, but I had one year left of them, and this was incomparable again. A new kind of musical training was in store; I had just signed up for actual music boot camp. Steve was 26 years old, a young musical genius who held a Fender Telecaster rather than a conductor's baton—the musical leader and creative mind behind The Dregs.

STEVE MORSE HAILS FROM MICHIGAN. He and his family moved to Augusta, Georgia when he was still very young. Steve's parents were both educational psychologists—his mother being musically talented while his father was a minister. They supported their two sons in music and encouraged them joining up with rock bands from the start. Steve's final high school band in Georgia included his older brother Dave on drums and Andy West on bass. They named themselves *Dixie Grit.* Steve and Andy spent plenty of time honing their instrumental chops after the band broke up, sometimes referring to themselves casually as the Dixie Dregs. Soon after, the two friends enrolled at the University of Miami.

Steve studied classical guitar at UM and had the opportunity to create a music lab which was a little different from the jazz music prevalent on campus as created by his fellow students Jaco Pastorius, Pat Metheny, and Bruce Hornsby. Steve's lab was called "Rock Ensemble II." He wrote and taught music to other students, including University of Miami violin student Allen Sloan. His independent class was nearly the mirror image of my own efforts in high school. After graduating, Andy, keyboardist Steve

Davidowski, and another UM alumni Rod Morgenstein, joined up to form a full-time band with Morse under the name Dixie Dregs. The new band played Steve's original music as well as rock covers by Cream, Zeppelin, Frank Zappa, and music from Georgia's legendary Allman Brothers Band.

One of the band's early shows took place at Nashville's Exit Inn club in 1976. An Allman Brothers Band show happened to be in town the same night. After their show, some of band and crew came to the club to check out the new instrumental band they had been hearing about. Twiggs Lyndon in particular, the Allmans' road manager, was rightfully impressed. He led them to a record deal with Capricorn Records close to home in Macon, Georgia. The label relationship saw the release of three influential Dixie Dregs albums before the company went belly up: *Free Fall, What If,* and *Night of the Living Dregs.* Next, the major label Arista Records signed the band and wanted them to drop the "Dixie" for broader appeal. They released *The Dregs of the Earth* and *Unsung Heroes* on Arista Records before I joined the group.

Most all their albums sold in the neighborhood of 100,000 copies, similar to Grisman. Customarily, they were on the jazz charts in *Billboard.* Critical acclaim had been building dramatically for the band, mostly from the rock music scene, and a nationwide cult-following was coalescing around the group, too. Terry "T" Lavitz, a jazz keyboardist and friend of Rod Morgenstein's, was invited to join the band just a couple of years before me. T was a recent graduate from the Berklee College of Music in Boston as he stepped into the shoes of earlier band keyboardists Davidowski and Mark Parrish. Par for the course, I was by far the youngest member at age 19. T was second youngest at 24, Steve was 26, while Andy and Rod were both 27. At my age, the other guys in the band seemed much older to me. They also wielded a lot of authority in the band regarding the finances, logistics, and most of the decision-making.

Being signed to Arista by the legendary label president and record mogul, Clive Davis, was leading to more commercial opportunities for the band at the time I joined. That meant we had opening act engagements that summer for southern rock bands: 38 Special, Molly Hatchet, and the Marshall Tucker Band. Surely we would have opened up for Lynyrd Skynyrd were it not for the fatal small plane crash that had recently killed several of its members.

The Dregs management team was an upscale Atlanta firm called Kat Family Management, led by powerful entertainment attorney Joel Katz. The band's principal manager, Joel Cherry was an entertainment lawyer who worked in the Katz firm. They were all about the business of moving the band ahead and building their profile on the national scene. The Dregs were positioned to break into the mainstream.

IF I TOLD YOU THAT I WAS READY for my first Dregs gig at the University of Charleston on April 18th, 1981, that would be some Georgia jabberwocky bluster. I shouldn't make a complete list of excuses, but one of them included trying to play with just half an arm. My mobility wouldn't allow me to lift anything above my head, yet—therefore, I couldn't put that hefty Les Paul around my neck without some help. On stage, "Microwave," one of the two band roadies, lifted it over my head for me.

The band's road crew consisted of Jeff Burkhart, who had recently replaced Twiggs Lyndon as road manager, and in that role collected the money at the end of the night. Multi-faceted Jeff also drove the equipment truck, set up the stage, and was a rather kinetic lighting director. I developed a new appreciation for that part of concert production. Jeff was a great guy who happily welcomed me into the group. The other roadie, Mark "Microwave" Mytrowitz, would do anything to try to make me feel comfortable at the shows. He remained on stage and took care of the band's gear and anything we needed during the sets. Our sound man, who traveled with the band in both private aircraft and vans, was David "Dopp" Colvin. Like me, he was a new addition to the band.

To fully comprehend the Dixie Dregs culture, it's important to know that it wasn't as much about music conservatories like UM and Berklee with their jazz or classical music programs, *this* band had much more to do with the lifestyle of southern rock bands. The Allman Brothers Band, along with the legacy of Duane Allman's rock guitar, had a bigger impact in the Georgia music scene than Jimi Hendrix did in my hometown of Seattle. Twiggs and the current road crew looked at Steve Morse as a kind of reincarnation of Duane Allman, who tragically died in a motorcycle accident in Macon at the age of 24. While the Dregs music was considerably more highbrow, interwoven with unremitting counterpoint and technical wizardry, there was enough southern rock & roll in the Dregs, and especially in Steve's electric guitar playing, that the band's heritage was most definitely rock, not jazz.

To understand the Dregs ethnology and what I was walking squarely into as principally an acoustic musician, it's to better understand Twiggs, as he singlehandedly shaped their way of life on the road. One of the tunes I learned that first week from Steve was named for him—"Twiggs Approved." Twiggs, an ex-military man, was a no-nonsense road manager who ruled the rock club concert circuit with an iron fist. For his bands, he could build and outfit most anything a southern rock show required on the road, from constructing Hammond B3 organ cabinets (that the Dregs used on stage), to configuring his band truck he named Black Hearted Woman—a roadster with a split rear axle, a lift gate, complete with seating benches that could transform into bunks sleeping seven. Throw in some PVC pipe that the bandmembers and road crew could "*piss* into," to prevent a stop every hour, the *Dixie Dregs* on the road traveled this way just before I arrived.

While still road managing the Allman Brothers, Twiggs established a big part of his reputation. One particular night, he was having trouble getting the gig pay from a promoter in Buffalo. After a physical scuffle culminating with Twiggs grabbing a butter knife off a nearby table and sticking the club promoter in the stomach with it, the internal bleeding of the man led to his death, and Twiggs was booked for murder. He got off partially with an insanity plea. After doing some time, he was released from the asylum and went straight to the Dixie Dregs as *their* road manager.

Twiggs, an avid skydiver, had a yellow jumpsuit with the Dixie Dregs logo stitched into it. Hours before a show in Albany, a year or so before I joined the band, Twiggs made an arrangement with a few other people for a jump. The band watched as Twiggs' parachute didn't come open that day. He fell to his death. Steve told me that he and Andy ran into the woods to find his body before the authorities could arrive. Twiggs wore a substantial diamond ring and Steve retrieved it from his hand before the police could take it for themselves—as he believed would've happened. The band went on to play their opener set that night, as they couldn't afford to cancel, but they have grieved over the loss of their close friend and supporter to the very day I joined up.

LEARNING THE DREGS MUSIC within just a few days, would be one of the more difficult things I had tried to accomplish as a teenager. I had to grab a lot of the parts back stage, and on stage during soundchecks. The altogether rushed soundcheck at Charleston, acted as my first full band rehearsal. This show was followed immediately by the University of Tennessee in Chattanooga, Ole Man Rivers in Avondale, Louisiana, then over to Birmingham at the Rams Head, all successive one-nighters.

Birmingham News, April 24 ,1981

"New Dreg fiddler Mark O'Connor, who in only his fourth gig with the band, completely upstaged his fellow music-mates.

He joined the troupe within the past week, replacing Allen Sloan, one of the original Dregs, who left just after production was completed on their latest album, Unsung Heroes.

O'Connor had one of his arms in a cast... after a skiing spill, and it didn't come out of its shell until Saturday. But he appeared well-healed as he led the Dregs with his blitzing riffs on the electric violin.

O'Connor, only 19 has already been twice proclaimed as a Grand National Fiddling Champ, and he showed off his skills superbly.

Many times during the night, Steve Morse, Dreg guitarist and producer, just stood back – with hands on hips and a dumbfounded grin on his face – and shook his head at O'Connor's feats."

The band owned a rehearsal house that had burned to the ground just before I arrived. A lot of the band's equipment was charred or in ashes. Some faulty wiring. They chose it as the site for our first promotion photo with me in the group. We stood next to Rod's scorched drum set, the band in paramilitary fatigues.

The onstage music gear for me was to be supplied by the band, but it was burned. Steve had an old Ampeg amp head at his house he wanted me to use—a high wattage tube amp for a clear violin sound, he explained. The band already had an endorsement with Fender, so they supplied me with two new speaker cabinets, with four 12" speakers in each. The cabinets were stacked right behind me on stage, with the amp head on top. Combined, the rig stood nearly as tall as I was. They gave me a sizeable Peterson Strobe Tuner in its own road case. Allen used this. Steve gave me one of his extra *Ernie Ball* volume pedals. I had brought my own Morley pedal that I used in high school, but he insisted that I use the Ernie Ball for its straightforward circuitry. "It didn't color the sound," he said. But with a Barcus-Berry violin pickup and its limited sound quality, I didn't know if it mattered much.

As harrowing of a start as it was for me, musically and logistically, it was ever more so doing it with the bad arm. There was the setback of not being able to play for three months, too. My fingers were just a few degrees slower than before, and getting it all back to 100% was still a process unfolding. The band's single engine Cessna plane was yet another stress point. All scrunched in that little plane, shoulder to shoulder—protecting my arm in there from bandmate's bodies—was a little nuts. There was no room to take my violin on board—I had to put it inside the wing of the plane. My new fiddle was going to get a little chilly out there on the wingtip at 10,000 feet. And it turned out that our guitarist, Steve, who wrote all of the songs, was also our co-pilot.

In the meantime, I kept learning tunes on the road from Steve every moment we could snag together. He spent every available minute teaching me his repertoire. Steve selected tunes from each of the previous albums for me to perform with the band. From *Dregs of the Earth,* I learned "Road Expense," "Pride O' the Farm," "Hereafter," "The Great Spectacular," and "I'm Freaking Out." I didn't know what was more difficult, remembering all the melodic lines, or trying to nail the unisons with Steve as perfectly as he wanted. I was learning all these tunes by way of an unamplified Fender solid body guitar and my violin with a brass mute on it. But within minutes, I was playing this stuff on stage with the loudest band I had ever imagined playing in. It was one crazy shock to the system. To my ears, it was so loud up on stage I couldn't really distinguish much of anything. I couldn't make out my intonation. If I was playing a harmony line, it might be as much as a half-step off. And I couldn't tell you if I was a half-step below the pitch or above it. This was how loud my new band played.

Steve was good with the volume on stage, plainly—and here I thought that Grisman's acoustic mandolin technique was fairly loud. Some of the bandmates wore ear plugs. I resorted to it after the first couple of gigs. In playing the violin, though, it made it even harder to hear pitch. The ear plugs removed the high-end, the very register I needed to hear in. I went back and pulled out the plugs.

I had another ploy to try and evade bad intonation, and I put it quickly into action. As technically accurate as I always tried to be, there was always the possibility of just *faking it.* I employed my strategy to get through the initial shows. If there was trouble hearing a pitch on a unison or harmony line, I backed off my volume, simply by the weight I applied to my bow. Why stink everything up with poor pitch? I'll just duck out. Steve caught onto it right away. That manner of dodging my lines was not going to fly with him. I had to keep hunting for it and deliver for the Dregs.

Steve traded players at the violin position on his team. He bargained and worked hard to trade for me, so that meant he wanted those lines tight. To him, achieving that level of perfection meant I was taking this job seriously and was not just along for the ride. He wanted this kind of discipline from his new player. Off stage, we worked on the unison lines between his guitar and my violin by far more than anything else we did, except maybe for the two-guitar unisons. We continued our backstage drills.

MY STAGE RIG WAS A MESS, despite the nice gear. It was just plagued with bad cables, bad patching... I had no idea how it was wired nor how to fix it. The 1/8-inch cable that came with the Barcus-Berry violin pickup was not cutting it either. Steve wanted me to move around on stage a lot, coming over to the center to join him there, jumping up on the drum riser at the end of the shows. This small cable came out of the plug and often broke. It was before the widespread use of wireless packs which aids the player with more freedom of movement. The choices that were available sounded awful, Steve said. He wanted us hard-wired in. I was one of a very few electric violinists on tour during those years—it was all new territory.

"Microwave" tried his best to fix the violin rig each time it crapped out. Unless I was turned on and ready to go, Steve wouldn't start the next tune without me—so he would stall and wait for my rig to work. The mishaps were happening every other show it seemed. Occasionally Steve would have to set his guitar down on the stage, laying it flat on its back. He didn't have a guitar stand, as he played just the one Franken-Tele with all of his customized pickups and switches. He would come over to re-patch every-thing in my rig while some in the crowd stood at the front yelling for us to play. My heart was racing in those moments—holding up the show and feeling helpless as I waited. I hadn't any idea why my rig was always on the fritz. But it was *his* amp head after all.

We were on a non-stop tour schedule. I learned more tunes in rock-club-bathrooms or the tiny crevices they called dressing rooms—always unplugged and straining to hear Steve's Tele acoustically in the quietest place we could find. Sometimes when Rod was sound-checking his drums, all the booming through the P.A. penetrated backstage to the point where I could barely hear what Steve was showing me. It was hectic, and nail biting—finding both Steve's guitar licks and my own sanity. The cocka-mamie process took an amount of musical patience I hadn't demonstrated before. It seemed so ridiculous to have to do it this way, but nevertheless, this is how it went. I learned tunes from the *Night of the Living Dregs* album from Steve on the road, including "Punk Sandwich," "Country House Shuffle," and "Leprechaun Promenade."

"Where's Allen?" was yelled from the crowd as we took the stage, oh…, just about every show. My time was consumed with the very difficult task of learning all the repertoire while on tour, and this was the greeting await-ing me each time we took the stage: "Where's Allen?" Just like "where's Tony," from the last band. Some fans made it tough on me replacing an original band member. I was the brand-new guy in every city we were go-ing to play for the better part of a year. Taking over from a founding mem-ber of a well-loved group with a cult following was more difficult than I'd ever imagined. It would also be a year before there was a Dregs album with me on it—so fans could even know there was a change in the lineup.

Instead of rooming together in hotels, as we did in the DGQ, the Dregs opted for low-end motels and individual rooms. I got into the habit of go-ing to sleep with the television on each night. My ears were ringing so badly after the shows, I awoke in the mornings with the TV set blaring at me. My youthful ears showed signs of recovering after a few hours, though.

Trying to help me understand why we had to play so loud on stage, Steve explained how the domino effect begins with the volume of the drums. My interpretation of it was as follows: The kick drum sets it all up, then the bass rig matches the kick. The guitar and keys follow by sounding the alarm, and then there was my little fiddle at the end of the switch.

For more than a few reasons, I couldn't play as well as I was capable of, still. Listening to a board tape from one of the shows, I was flat on about every line I had with Steve. I just didn't hear it that way on stage, with the audience screaming and everything—there was so much noise. I sounded bad; at least I thought so. My solos were a little better, maybe… but they were so short, I didn't have enough time on them to really *feel* it.

AS EVEN CHANCE WOULD HAVE IT, the Dregs' hometown gig in Atlanta was just my 5th show with the band, and it was a big one—The Fox Theater. The audience was chock-full of hometown Dregs diehards. In a gesture of accommodation, the guys had Allen Sloan play a few tunes with the band—so in a sense, he could say goodbye to his long-time local following. The awkwardness was a forgone conclusion. I may have felt better about it if I was happier about my playing. During our set, I dug in as hard as I could.

DownBeat Magazine – 1981

"This particular performance [at the Fox Theater] was especially noteworthy because of the presence of a new violinist, Mark O'Connor. Among the 19-year-old phenom's string of plaudits are accolades as two-time National Open Fiddle Champion at ages 17 and 18, and twice Grand Master Fiddler of the World at ages 13 and 18. One of his many solo albums features laudatory liner notes by Stephane Grappelli. He is extremely proficient on guitar as well, giving regular Dregs guitarist Steve Morse all he could handle during a jam on 'Rock & Roll Park.'"

My new roommate was in the audience and commented that I did really well on the violin, but Tom thought my electric guitar playing on "Rock & Roll Park," could use some work—the guitar tone especially. He said I played it like a bluegrass, or jazz player. Well, that critique could be taken either way, I suppose. I was still playing with very little guitar vibrato. I didn't have the left arm strength to accomplish the arm vibrato that Steve uses and wants. Painstakingly getting there, I just wasn't used to playing this kind of music professionally. A couple of years playing heavy gauge strings (.014 - .060) on a dreadnought, there just wasn't much of an opportunity for vibrating any of those strings on the Martin the same way. I plainly had more work to do. Playing guitar through my violin rig wasn't helping me much in the way of rock electric guitar tone. It was set for a clean sound, so I couldn't get any grit on the guitar—not compared to Steve's wall of crunch about 15 feet to my right. I was going from 0 to 60 in the oncoming fast lane of rock 'n' roll guitar.

The Atlanta Constitution, April 27, 1981

"If the music offered few surprises, the personnel did...the tall, gangly violinist was surely not diminutive Dregs veteran Allen Sloan.

Not long into the concert, the audience learned that Mark O'Connor, a 19-year-old former Californian, was Sloan's replacement. Recent indeed: This night wrapped up O'Connor's first week of shows.

O'Connor belied his rookie status with the band as he pretzelled himself around his fiddle and traded licks bow-for-pick with Morse. No wonder. The new kid's no newcomer to music: he has performed with violin great Stephane Grappelli and boasts six solo albums.

But the predecessor wasn't absent Saturday night. Sloan pinch-hit on three numbers...explaining his departure after seven years, Sloan said that 'things have a way of growing apart after a long while. I want to work on some things for myself. I want to clear my head.'"

The gigs kept coming. Athens was the following night, then to Buffalo and Albany. I heard all the stories about Twiggs again—being back in the place where he lost his life.

The biggest challenge for me in this band—I had to become an electric player for real. After all, this was "the greatest band in the world," according to about every Dregs fan I came into contact with. On the day of the show, some fans might discover that I was the "new guy." They would almost chide me rather than congratulate me. Dregs fans weren't going to allow me to wear my invitation to the lineup as a badge of honor. They often told me, "You *do* know that you get to play with the greatest band in the world?" As if I didn't know that, and as if I didn't deserve to be there. That is—until they heard me play in the band that night—at least by the end of the show.

The Red and Black, The University Of Georgia – April 29, 1981

"Morse is also thrilled with the addition of 19-year-old whiz kid Mark O'Connor to The Dregs, a national fiddle champion and guitarist of whom Morse has long been a fan. O'Connor is 'the most striking musician I've ever seen as far as being ahead of his time and being talented. We're still ecstatic about [him].'"

Steve's phrasing was polished. Given the frets, he had all his licks perfectly *in tune.* I was coming up short on violin in that department because of the amplified volume on stage. I still wasn't hearing pitch well. Actually, I didn't think I was earning my keep until the second to the last song of the set. The Dregs turned me loose on what Andy intro'd to the audience as a "drug-induced bluegrass tune, 'The Bash.'" On this tune, Steve let me solo each night until my atrophied arm nearly fell off. This was the two to three minutes I had to bring the crowd to me, and I brought them. It was the longest violin solo I got out of the entire show, by far—a country-blue-grass fiddle groove I burned down the barn with.

After coming up a little short for most of the show, I had to deliver on that one. My "Bash" solos always put a smile on Steve's face, and it kept me in good favor with him. The crowd went berserk for it, too—that didn't hurt. I ended the solo with all kinds of fiddle flurries and double shuffles. It was as if we wrote "wild applause and scream your blasted head off" on a cue card—it was an automatic audience-getter. I always had a hunch the audience was just waiting for me to cut loose on some improvisational soloing at any point. Backstage, though, I was still learning more lines from Steve—music from the *What If* album: "Take It Off the Top," "Odyssey," "Ice Cakes," "Night Meets Light," and "What If."

Birmingham News, May 7, 1981

"One who's won the Dregs over is 19-year-old electric violinist Mark O'Connor. '[He's] so good,' Rod Morgenstein bubbles, 'that they keep having to change the rules for him. As a gifted young teen, O'Connor dominated all junior fiddling contests he entered,' Morgenstein says. 'Then they made an exception for him and let him enter as an adult at 16.' Morgenstein carries on. 'He won the national title two times in a row and now they won't let him enter anymore. And listen to this. His arm was in a cast for months because of a skiing accident. He got his cast of on a Saturday, and the next day he flew to Atlanta for a rehearsal. And he was great. The guy's fantastic.'"

I really wanted to be more of a soloist in the Dregs, but Steve was not going to open up another tune for me in the show. I got the same length of those short solos as Allen played. I wondered if that was ever going to change for the better, but it didn't look like it. I was still perfecting more lines with Steve on the road from the *Free Fall* album, including the title track, "Holiday" and "Refried Funky Chicken."

Steve lined me up with his favorite local guitar repair shop, Bert's Guitar Shop, to get some custom work done on my Les Paul—an additional pick-up install to dial in a few more tonal options on stage. I needed to make improvements on my electric guitar tone. While we were at it with the guitar overhauling, my 1/8-inch cables for violin weren't going to survive my tripping over them as I moved about the stage back and forth. A couple of times I finished a whole section of a tune, unplugged—my 1/8-inch cable laying on the floor snapped off. Bert Foster helped me design a jack on the side of my violin using the clamp of a violin chin rest. The wooden housing allowed for a 1/4-inch guitar cable to be used instead. The pickup installment as well as the violin jack set me back $300. Unfortunately this was not considered a "road expense"—the name of another Dregs tune long since removed from the set list. The jack on my acoustic violin to accommodate a regular guitar cord was the first of its kind.

THE DREGS WERE A CORPORATION where each member drew a weekly salary no matter how many shows we played. My draw was $292 per week after taxes were taken out. At least it was steady income, but we were working hard for that money. I was playing shows with the Dregs for $50 each. If we played a club and turned the house doing two shows in a night, it would come out to $25.

My mother insisted I call her every other day now, as she was in a lot more pain than before—my phone bills were racking up. The band members acquired a newfangled device, a Porta Touch Tone Dialer, that you hold up to a rotary pay phone's mouthpiece. Curiously, you key in your account number to get on something called the Sprint network and altogether bypass any switchboard. The recent technology was mindboggling. It made long distance calls a little cheaper, and you could avoid the "collect call." But still, I could barely stay afloat financially.

After a bunch of non-stop shows (18 shows), learning more tunes every available minute, we finally had a day off in Philadelphia, the day prior to our show at the Walnut Theater. Steve moaned about our day-off on the road, which I on the other hand was kind of looking forward to. It was good to give my arm a day's rest. Steve wanted his free days at home. He asked me,

"Do you want to do some busking?"

"Come again?" I asked.

"Do you want to play on the street with me and make some extra money? If we're on the road, we should be working."

"Okay then," I replied.

As we were accessing what street corner to carry out our impromptu street-performer evening, we happened to notice that the David Grisman "Quartet" was playing in Philadelphia that very night—at South Street's Ripley Music Hall. What unbelievable irony. So I suggested that we busk Grisman's audience in front of that music hall—it would be a bit waggish of us alright. Steve thought it was a good idea, too, that is if Grisman's audience wasn't miserly. I assured him, definitely not so—he's got the yuppie Deadheads.

On yet another day off that Steve wasn't happy about, we were offered free tickets and backstage passes to see the Grateful Dead in Connecticut. None of the other Dregs wanted to go. I went with our two roadies, Jeff and Microwave, who were very thankful, because without me, they couldn't get backstage at a Dead concert. The entire arena was filled with people swaying back and forth to the music—it was one big hellacious acid trip. And talk about long solos—maybe Steve knew the solos were going to be sizeable and didn't want to bother? Jerry's Himalayan-sized guitar solos made the length of my "Bash" solo feel more like a speed bump. After we made our way backstage, we came face to face with the most incredible spread of raw oysters. I stood right there and ate many of them. Garcia was hanging out with us, and the Dead entourage invited us to drop some acid with them. However, I felt like it was time to head back to the hotel, I had a lot more music to input. Jeff always kidded me that my wanting to leave kept him from "partying with the Dead" as his job was to get me safely back to my motel room, and making sure that I was in shape to cover those lines.

Steve had a little Pignose amp with him, the one with a 6" speaker. We just needed to pick up some batteries for it. For some reason, he never used this amp for teaching me all of that repertoire. I never knew he even had it until that night, but it was in the road truck all along. We set up outside Grisman's gig. There was quite a line of folks to play for—many of them recognized us after a few doubletakes. Some didn't, though, and might have thought we were authentic street musicians.

Grisman's road manager finally came out to see what all the commotion was about. Word had drifted back to the DGQ dressing room that Steve and I were busking their crowd out front. Ultimately, we were invited inside and sat in on one of David's tunes "16/16." Steve took his solo through the Pignose on stage. The DGQ's reaction to seeing me was pretty interesting. It was a little like they saw a ghost again. Grisman told his band that my broken arm kept me from continuing with the group and going to Europe. I'd already played 20 shows with the Dregs before their European tour even got started.

In the meantime, Steve was counting up our earnings that night. We had to "take off the top" $4 for the batteries in the Pignose—our overhead. That left $50 to split two ways. I made as much on the street with Steve that night as I made with the Dregs the previous night at the Agora in Youngstown.

We had another two days off after our Philly gig. The band flew home to Atlanta while a new country singer-songwriter, Rodney Crowell, flew me all the way out to Los Angeles for a double-scale recording session. I made more in that three-hour session than I did for a week on the road with the Dregs. That got my attention.

A session player?

MEETING UP WITH THE GUYS back on the east coast in New York, the band was booked on the national television show, *Tomorrow with Tom Snyder*. We played "Cruise Control" and "Pride O' the Farm." By this point, I was starting to find my way into the rock scene a bit more. I uncharacteristically wore sunglasses on the TV show—maybe I wanted to look a little *cooler?* My hair was longer (and bigger) than it had ever been before, and I had adopted a new kind of hat wear, a suede leather hippie hat. While in NYC, the band met with Clive Davis at his Arista offices. Donning sunglasses at the record label office, too, I was introduced to Clive as the new member of the band. Andy told him that I was a "cool guy." My new "rocker" personality wasn't just about appearance, I was becoming a little more defiant and rebellious, and I demonstrated it more outwardly. I guess I left my shyness back in SF.

Perhaps my rebelliousness was similar to how the Dregs dealt with our record company and management. But some of my defiance turned towards the band itself, though, especially when they denied me the time off I asked for in June.

We had 15 more gigs in June, mostly in the Southwest: Cains Ballroom in Tulsa, the Paramount in Austin, Rainbow Theater in Denver, Uptown Theater in Kansas City, and we opened for the Jefferson Starship at Popular Creek in Hoffman Estate, Illinois, finishing off the run on June 20th. It was wild to be sharing the bill with all of those pop and rock bands I was listening to in high school. It was impressive how high Mickey Thomas sang, the same range as Grace Slick. I always liked the high tenor male voices in bluegrass, too. The violin, of course, is high-pitched.

By now, I was playing much better—getting used to the new material and our sound on stage. I had already asked both Steve and management for the third week off in June so I could enter Weiser and defend my national fiddling championship title for the third year in a row, something that no other fiddler had accomplished in the history of the contest. Not even Byron Berline and Herman Johnson had done that. While management accepted my request, and Steve did too, actually, it was the other Dregs who minded, a lot. It came to a confrontation with T, Rod, and Andy. When the band had a moment to ourselves backstage, T Lavitz blurted out,

"I'm glad you get to go to your fiddle contest, but what are the rest of us supposed to do that week?"

"Have the time off? We played 18 cities in May and 15 cities in June!" I reminded them.

Andy and Rod entered the fray. Collectively:

"Maybe you don't understand how the band works. We're getting paid a weekly salary to play all of the gigs that are booked for us."

"Look, all I am asking is for one week off for the entire year, that's it. I want to defend my national fiddle championship title for the third year in a row."

I suppose it was an understandable complaint in one sense—what if each of us wanted to take our own week off? But let's be real. How many of them had something that cool going on? They were looking for an *all-in* from me, and I understood that. After two months in the band, I was all-in, for sure, except for that one week. It was the first sign, though, that the rock instrumental band was getting a little nicked over how much attention their *fiddler* was getting, or demanding. That being said, I was not going to give in, not about attending the contest at Weiser. I felt it was that important. Steve came to my defense, to his credit. He knew how I joined the band far before it was medically possible for me to play. It showed him how much I wanted to be there. I'm not at all sure the others knew the real condition my arm was in when I showed up on that first gig two months back—hiding my emaciated appendage from them as much as I could. I wanted to instill some confidence, not sympathy.

Good Times – Dr. Pepper Music Festival – Jefferson Starship/The Dregs, June 27, 1981
    "New violinist Mark O'Connor was absent (something about a fiddling championship...), and former Dreg Allen Sloan filled in his old slot."

With all the fuss I made over getting that week off, I really needed to *win* Weiser—and I did. Long hair, sun glasses, hippie hat, arm on the mend and all. This time, I beat three Texans to do it: Dick Barrett, Dale Morris, and Ricky Boen, all of whom made it to the top five. No one had ever won it three years in a row; therefore, I was the first fiddler in Weiser history to be asked to sit out the Open division the following year. In my case, it wasn't all bad. This way I wouldn't have to beg my bandmates for another week off for a while. Hardly trivial, I also won $1,200. It was more than a month's salary working with the Dregs.

When I met up with the band for Summerfest in Madison, Wisconsin, I assumed the guys would be pleased to hear of my success. They were certainly playing up my fiddle championship status in the press releases, and on stage, milking it for all it was worth. For their benefit, too. Instead of twice-champion, the front office can "market" me as a three-timer. Andy's introduction of me on every show included the national fiddle champion reference. Their wholesaling of it could easily continue on track.

We were opening for the Marshall Tucker Band that night. I walked into our dressing room to greet the band, and Rod was going through his rudiments—paradiddles, flamadiddles, and various rolls on his practice pad like usual. I knew about some of those drum rolls as Sean taught them to me in high school. I practiced for months that year on a practice pad, too, while watching TV in the living room. It was the same kind of 8-inch practice pad that Rod carried around. I was becoming a bit of a closet drummer. Once in a while, Rod let me try out his lefty drum set at the end of soundcheck now. It felt good to be back with the band and to take the stage with everybody again. Joel from the office had already informed the guys about my win in Idaho.

Without interrupting his flams, Rod blurts out; "Mr. Champion, Sir," with a big smile across his face. Wow—the Dregs mockingly bestowed onto me a new nickname?

Nevertheless, the Dregs were headed to the Bay Area next. We were at the Old Waldorf on July 17th, but we had the week off before the show. That allowed me to go out to California a few days early and win the Western Regional Fiddle Contest in Salinas, picking up another $500.

That same week, David Grisman booked me for a recording session to play some violin on his next album. A quick recovery between the "Dawg" and I... And guess who was playing guitar on that session? None other than Tony Rice. No hard feelings all around—now that I had another full-time band to play with, and a great one at that. The three of us being unattached and liberated, now made things much easier. We were in a more comfortable position and not in each other's hair. David had written a tune for me to record on his new "solo" record with Tony driving the rhythm behind me.

As soon as I "went electric," the acoustic boyz made up.

"Crazy Johnny" was loving our SF area shows. We had about six of them around the Bay Area that week and he was at all of them, Bobette, too. Once we were past the "where's Allen," part in every new town we played, I was able to have an effect on the audience in a positive way. On one of those Bay Area shows, we got word that the Dregs' UM chum, the jazz guitarist, Pat Metheny, was in the audience to see us. I was a big Metheny fan, had already seen him play a few times in SF when I lived there. I was currently listening to his and Lyle Mays' album, *As Falls Wichita, So*

Falls Wichita Falls." I really liked that album, it was so dreamlike, ethereal. New Age music was coming on at that time and good musicians were getting involved in some of it. I remembered pianist, George Winston opening up a few shows for the DGQ, and guitarist, Alex de Grassi, too. Like Metheny, it was something I wanted to tap into more. But Steve and the Dregs were the polar opposite of it. That night at the club in downtown San Francisco where I first saw the band play, we walked onto the stage to hear "where's Allen?" cat-calls springing from the audience. A tag-team of three people screamed the phrase in unison for the entire room to hear. I was so embarrassed that Pat Metheny saw that. But I ended up winning over the crowd with "The Bash," and that may have impressed Pat all the more.

Washington Post, May 16, 1981
"The five band members are immensely talented, and guitarist Steve Morse and violinist Mark O'Connor are nothing short of phenomenal, particularly on a number of extended trade-offs."

At Davis Daily, California Aggie, University of CAL. July 29, 1981
"O'Connor fit right in, which wasn't too surprising, considering much of what the Grisman Quintet does acoustically, the Dregs do electrically. O'Connor's violin and fiddle sparked the band, and was, especially during solos, breathtaking."

Music Connection – Country Club – Richard S. Ginell
"Clearly O'Connor was the missing link, the catalyst that singlehandedly pushed this band over the hump from near greatness into something resembling the real thing. The next album ought to be a real killer."

BY AUGUST, THE BAND TOOK a week off the road back home in Georgia. I finally had a little time to settle in. Tom introduced me to the tennis pro across the street at Chastain Park. Folks called him "Buster." I began to pursue a safer athletic hobby—tennis. In this case, my broken arm wasn't the one holding the racket.

During my little kid days with the bluegrass bands, I had visited the Deep South plenty of times, but I'd never lived there before. I was able to get hold of a small TV of Tom's and turned on the local news to see what went on in Atlanta in 1981. The first local newscast I saw had a segment about rock record-burnings. I thought they were digging up old newsreels

382

from a decade or two earlier, until the segment showed a closeup of the recently-released *Foreigner 4* album melting away in a huge bonfire on a nearby city street. If it weren't for laying my eyes on that album cover, I swore it had to have been archival footage. "Rock music is the music of the Devil," they cried.

Yeah, the "Devil Went Down To Georgia" all right. Charlie Daniels had just come out with his country-rock classic featuring the fiddle.

One day soon I was going to create its sequel with Charlie Daniels, Johnny Cash, Marty Stuart, and Travis Tritt—"The Devil Comes Back To Georgia."

An older fiddler, Dallas Burrell, rang me up to give me a big Georgia welcome. He was a fan of my earlier fiddle albums. Now that I lived there, he informed me I was "Georgia's biggest fiddling star." I wasn't sure about that, but it did remind me to give Randy Howard a ring and let him know I had moved to his home state. I had just seen him at the Grand Masters. Dallas seemed like a sweet ol' guy. He wanted to invite me to an old-time fiddle jam session that friends of his held at their barn on a monthly basis. It was the biggest jam of its kind in the area—"a lot of folks attend," he said. "Sure," I told him—"if I was in town, I'd come on out." After checking in with his friends about me getting an invitation, he called me back to say it was going to be a no-go.

"Well, Mark… they asked me if you still wore your hair long, and I had to tell them that you did. They don't allow any man into the jam session with hair touching his *collar.*"

My hair kept getting longer and bigger, too—we were just getting started. I was in an 80s rock band, after all.

That same week, Steve invited me over to his farm in McDonough to spend the day. He was working on a new double-electric guitar tune for us to perform. I dropped by Burkhart's to grab the Les Paul out of the band truck, threw it in the red pickup and headed out to the Georgia country-side. Steve was schooling me on the electric guitar all over America, why not on his farm, too? It was about a 45-minute drive.

When I found his dirt-country-road driveway out in the middle of the sticks, I came up on Steve's mobile home situated on some 40 acres. The property had a runway for his own small plane, and his live-in girlfriend had a couple of horses in a small horse barn. I drove up to their house, took the guitar with me, and joined Steve inside. Once again, no amps at his place, either. We were playing acoustic on the solid bodies again. He had quite a new tune going—all kinds of cool guitar lines, with specifically-timed string bends and a lot more arm vibrato. The tune laid out like a practice etude for electric blues-rock guitar. I was going to get better just by playing it with him, "Blood Sucking Leaches." As I understood it, this was a tribute song to our management, agency and record company all combined. By this point, I was starting to get the arm vibrato down, and Steve was happy with my progress. The intense sound of this vibrato was really *in-your-face*. That was the goal, I think.

Here's how you do it: While you play a note on the guitar with your third finger, you bend that note up one whole step and shake your entire forearm while you're at the top of the pitch in a kind of *throbbing pulsation*. It's really like a thrusting gyration. I loved it. It sort of looks like you're flipping the finger, then pulsating your finger in the air for extra emphasis. Although we were using mostly the ring finger for this technique, the second finger wasn't out of the picture, by any means. Steve himself shook that second finger plenty, and it could be well-placed in a tune called "Blood Sucking Leeches." I told Steve that I really couldn't manage the pulsating second finger, though. Nothing against the way it looked. That part of it I respected well enough. But I had an accident with my second finger back when I was ten. I showed Steve the scars underneath the fingernail. You could still see the meatloaf through the nail.

I was in my friend's parents' car at the time, sitting in the back seat, on the right side. I had this habit of bringing my left hand over across my body and sticking my fingers into the gap between the window and the beltline strip—the "window fuzzies." His Mom slammed the right front car door shut. For whatever reason, it caused that backseat window gap to contract, and it pinched the second finger of my left hand in the door. It was really painful, and it was smashed all right. After my fingernail turned dark blue, with a considerable amount of swelling beneath the fingernail, the doctor at our town clinic said that we needed to drill a hole in it to relieve the pressure. My mother held me down on the doctor's table so I couldn't wiggle free. He took a drill outfitted with a small bit and drilled a hole right in the middle of the fingernail.

After a week or so, the hole didn't relieve the pressure like the neighborhood doctor had figured it would. The finger was blowing up like a balloon. Mom took me back into his clinic, where he announced that the nail had to come off. While he and my mother held me down with the weight of their bodies, and again without enough anesthetic (not a painkiller in sight), he took a pair of scissors and cut my fingernail off my finger. This took a little longer, all the while I was screaming bloody murder. He gave me a rag to bite on this time. It was categorical torture, medical treatment from the dark ages. With no health insurance, there was little money to spend on stuff like this.

He had a splint made from tin placed on my second finger, and wrapped it with white tape. It was there for a good long while. When I dropped my hand down, the blood rushing to that area made it hurt, so I kept it up with the middle finger pointed straight towards the sky. It looked as if I was flipping everyone off... and I was. Because of that small town doctor's office, the fingernail didn't grow back correctly from his scissor disfigurement. The flesh beneath never fully reattached to the fingernail again, even after years gone by. Bending the guitar string up with a lot of force behind it, while vibrating at the top of a whole step or minor 3rd interval and the forearm pulsating and gyrating, remained quite uncomfortable. The nail would surely separate from the finger if I pushed too hard. Steve advised me that it was just going to require *more practice.* Yeah, "just more practice." I ended up referring to it as the "F-you guitar vibrato." It sounded like it, too.

After a couple hours of learning "Leeches," Steve's ode to the music industry with plenty of F-you vibratos, was well in hand for now. Steve wanted to go outside in the hot Georgia sun to play some games. He was talking about sports games. Steve asked me if I was into guns. "Not really," I told him. "I've only shot a gun once in my life." That was at the old fiddler Garland Cunningham's farm in eastern Washington. Steve put his target up and went first. Not bad. But when I leveled his rifle, I got one of my bullets right inside the bullseye—beginner's luck. Steve walked over to the target himself to see exactly where my bullets had entered, as if he didn't believe his own eyesight. It was pretty obvious from where we stood, but once he was at the hay bale, he did confirm to me that it was a good shot by giving me a thumbs up. All right. Good. I was kind of impressed with what I was able to do, but honestly, I was hoping the gun shooting would be over soon.

I told Steve that I didn't want to keep shooting rifles. "Have you ever used a bow," he asked me. I looked at him, "Duh, you hired me right?" "No... archery..." A bow and arrow. Now, this was something I was into back when I was a younger kid. I didn't have one of those fancy bows that Steve had, but I did quite a bit of target practice in the back yard before I had the skateboard ramp. Steve fetched his bow. After we lined up the target, I was able to get more arrows in the bullseye than he did. Okay, so it was my lucky day. It was getting quite hot out here—I was thinking of calling it a day. Maybe heading home so I could look at "Leeches" some more. I didn't have it on tape or anything—all in the memory bank like Steve had it. But first, he wanted to know if I liked to wrestle.

Ahem... what?

I actually did wrestle some in junior high before I was removed from PE. I pointed to my recently-broken appendage. "Bum arm, remember?" Wrestling with Steve Morse? Two sweaty boors on a farm and getting it on... Steve looked a little disappointed. "Hey, cheer up, I got one good arm," I told him. "I could arm wrestle you." As he glanced at my lanky extremities, an exacting smile came across his face. Steve wore tank tops on stage to show off his rather developed arm muscles, so I didn't quite know what I was getting into. Whatever it was, maybe this whole experience at Steve's farm was just a one-off, all saved for the new guy in the band.

I could beat Steve in arm wrestling, too, as it turned out. My arms were a bit longer. He claimed I had an advantage with my "length." So we decided to *air* arm wrestle while standing up. I had that one, too. For months after, Steve challenged me to *air* arm wrestle him on the road, and I won each time. Believe me, I was not some big weight lifter. For a heat check, I tried arm wrestling my roommate—kind of feeling like I was invincible by now. Tom giggled at my spindly body the same way that Steve did, but took me down without trouble. So... about my visit to Steve's farm—*had it come to an end?*

Steve had a couple of bicycles. "How about taking them for a ride on that country road?" Now, I rode bikes constantly in Marin County for the last couple of years. I used to take the ferry across to Alcatraz Prison and ride around the island in the harbor. I hadn't ridden since the ski accident, though. We got the bikes all adjusted, my seat way up in the air for my height, and we took to the old highway. I didn't think we were going to race or anything, just ride for a while and maybe have some less-competitive *fun* together. I slowed up a bit to adjust something with my gears while Steve went on ahead. When I got it all straightened out, I began to catch up to him, and was just about to pull even. When I came up on Steve's right flank, he peered over, and then he opened it up. So, here we go—we are in a race. Steve flexed up, his arm muscles tightened like he was doing one of those F-you's on his guitar. He got that grimaced face going. It was sort of like being on stage next to him and playing off-key. We just flipping went for it. I passed him pretty handily—he could not catch me. I had more horsepower in the long legs, I guess. As I flew by him, he yelled out to me: "MR. CHAMPION, SIR!"

Upon returning to Steve's farm, we packed up the bikes. He wanted me to lower my seat, for storage, so he tossed me the wrench. I wasn't sure how the big day was going for me, with my new boss and all. But Steve wasn't ready to turn in just yet.

"You might have me on the bicycles, but how about some off-road dirt bikes?" Steve urged me with his big hardliner grin. "I've got a couple of bikes and an extra face mask for ya." I looked at Steve, in awe. "You win, Steve! The last time I was on a motorcycle I went over the handlebars and my head came within a foot of a car." I nearly lost it all on that day, on one of my visits to Spokane. I swore I'd never ride one again.

I came away from that day knowing a little more of what "Pride O' the Farm" was all about. Doubtlessly competitive—I suppose I was, too. I wondered if T Lavitz faced a similar band initiation in those Georgia backwoods? Or was I the lucky Dreg?

It turned out that both Steve and I had birthdays just a couple weeks before our notable blockhead sporting events day. Uh-oh, that meant we were both *Leos*. I had little knowledge of Zodiac signs at the time, but when Tom was told about the little sneak preview and the Leo birthdates, he prodded. "I really hope that works out for you two."

FINALLY, I WAS STARTING TO FEEL much better about a few things, at least. My arm was growing back, I could do ten pushups, and yes, easily handle my own guitar onstage now. My improving *rocker* appearance was starting to attract girls at the Dregs shows. I finally had time to notice, as I didn't have to be learning Dregs tunes in between sets like I did for the first few months. I started wearing short-sleeve tops because my arm had finally filled out. Steve always wore tight satin rock 'n' roll pants on the shows, so I matched him with my own tight satin pants, too — balancing the stage.

After our first set at The Bachanal in San Diego, Andy came up to me and asked, "Are you checking out that beautiful girl looking up at you? She's got it for you, man." I had no idea. The house changed over, so I figured she was long gone. Much of the time, though, probably half the audience paid to see our second shows at those clubs, real diehards for the band. After we took the stage for the second set, I looked down in front of me and there she was. She smiled up at me — beautiful, to be sure.

We spent some time getting to know each other after the show, stayed up all night outside on the motel veranda until we had to leave in the morning. We decided there was something good going on, so Shannon planned on visiting me in Atlanta in a few weeks.

The San Diego Union, San Diego, CA –August, 6, 1981

"A new fiddler, Mark O'Connor, who recently succeeded longtime member Allen Sloan, has emphasized the Dregs rural orientation. An accomplished and stage-wise musician, the rangy O'Connor easily matched Morse in solo savvy. But the show reached its peak when the two cooperated, first in a disarming and sweet duet rendition of a folk tune, then when they traded fiery, 'Orange Blossom Special'-inspired solos in 'The Bash.'"

She was a Southern California girl all right, and Georgia was quite a culture shock for her, too. We had three coliseum openers with ZZ Top in Jacksonville, Lakeland, and Miami, Florida that week. Shannon came along. While I loved ZZ Top's fierce bluesy rock 'n' roll, their crowd was plenty fierce in another way — hot-tempered. Fistfights were breaking out everywhere. The security personnel assigned to the front of the stage were punching guys in the face, just to push them back from the barricade. This was our show's crowd control. It was repulsive to be performing for a scene so barbarous. The backstage hang was bawdy too.

388

During ZZ Top's set, Shannon abruptly fell ill, doubling over in pain. It was serious, and she agreed that we needed to get to the nearest emergency room. It turned out to be a pancreatic attack. While I waited in the visitors area, the place was quite active. Many blood-soaked folks came in through the front doors, a lot of facial injuries, some knife wounds, and lots of overdoses. I hadn't spent too much time in an ER before, but I thought I would ask one of the receptionists if this was a usual evening there in Florida. She told me, "It's been busy like this all night. We must have admitted 40 people from the rock concert at the coliseum." I couldn't bring myself to tell her that I'd been on stage providing the entertainment for all the *fighting.* It was the first time I noted that the Dregs just might be barking up the wrong tree. *Why not a career like Weather Report and Return to Forever?* Shannon recovered, but our relationship didn't, and for many reasons. She and I weren't ready for anything serious. In spite of all of it, the Dregs rocker scene was still a good way to meet girls.

O N SEPTEMBER 14TH, I HAD AN entirely different kind of lady for my date—a lunch date at the White House with First Lady Nancy Reagan.

Merle Haggard was asked to choose a young artist to feature at a White House performance for President Reagan, and he chose me. Since that appearance with him at Harrah's, he obtained my *Soppin' The Gravy* album and was studying my fiddling up and down. He told me he was learning things off it, couldn't stop listening to it. After the illustrious invitation, I got a haircut and went to lunch with our country's First Lady. My performance was to take place the following March, but the lunch celebrated the kick-off to this series of four performances all filmed for *PBS: Young Artists at the White House.* If the Dregs were a bit unnerved by *"Mr. Champion, Sir,"* what could they be thinking about *this?* Merle Haggard was there and introduced me as a talented young musician who was deserving of a performance before the President of the United States. I was pinching myself the entire time. Was I really at the White House being distinguished like this? I thought back to the Tahoe run with Merle as a 16-year-old. About twice per show, he'd call on me for a solo, and I guess I *was* ready. One of the other young soloists for the series was nominated by the classical pianist Rudolf Serkin. He chose a 19-year-old violin prodigy Ida Levin. The same age as me. One day I was going to meet up with her again at chamber music festivals, the places where I would perform my own string quartet compositions. But not now.

Our band's manager was taking care of all the business regarding the White House functions. There was no money in it, but he thought it was rather extraordinary to be lining up those events for me. PBS wanted to film B-roll in some of my musical environs. They came to shoot a Dregs gig, of course. The PBS producer definitely wanted to shoot me in a fiddle contest. There weren't many big ones that time of year, but we did find one—the Sun Bowl Winter-National Fiddle Contest in November. It sounded ideal. Only one issue I could see—it took place in El Paso, Texas, the very state where I was never to win. The three judges were the top of the heap, though: Benny Thomasson, Herman Johnson, and Byron Berline. Maybe my luck would turn around with the quality of judging? It was a huge purse with $1,500 first place as well.

It ended up making great television... because I won it.

I finally won an Open division in Texas—the biggest prize money the state has ever offered in any fiddle contest.

MEANWHILE, BACK IN DREGS LAND, we had just played at the Agora Club in Atlanta for Halloween night. I had dressed up as a *joint*, and I wrote "I'm Smokin' Tonight" on the front of my costume. Steve dressed up as a psycho killer. I was thinking that I should have classed up my costume act a bit... you know, the President of the United States thing and all.

While on tour, occasionally we were in 15-passenger vans. During long drives, I tried to grab a seat up front to accommodate my long legs. On one particular trip, our driver was smoking cigarettes. The secondhand smoke started to really bother me. The smoke was stopping up my ears and my head. Sometimes when he lit up unexpectedly, I bolted for the back of the van, surfing over the back of the seats to get away. One of those day trips found me in the back row trying to evade the cigarette smoke, when Andy turned around towards me to declare that he wanted to discuss business.

Andy was the de facto businessman for the band. He had one of those Halliburton briefcases that he carried everywhere. When our road manager got paid in cash, which was typical for clubs, Andy had a pair of handcuffs to secure the briefcase to his wrist with the cash safely inside. Even when we were at the motel, the thing was cuffed to his bed. A few months earlier, back on one of those ZZ Top gigs, every one of our five motel rooms was burglarized while we were at soundcheck. All told, they got away with "$7,000 worth of items"—the amount our manager claimed in the insurance forms. For me, it was some cash that I had in my own hand bag. The other guys had some jewelry, watches, clothing, electronics, and a few family heirlooms stolen.

The rest of the band seemed rather attentive after Andy's announcement. "Business? Okay shoot," I replied. Andy reminded me that I was *netting* $300 a week with the band. I corrected him: "It's $292. Believe me, I count every dollar of that check—half of it goes to my phone bill for my mother." "Okay then, $292," Andy continued:

"How would you feel if you made $292 a week, while the rest of us were making $450?"

It took just two seconds to make sure how I was going to reply:

"Well, I think that sucks! I'm out here traveling to the gigs, playing the shows for the fans just like you all."

It was an awkward way of telling me I was about to become a full-fledged member of the band—a position that I already thought I had achieved. Evidently I hadn't earned it yet. They claimed that they weren't sure if I was committed to the band, so they hadn't been cutting me in as an equal on the show money. "Really guys? You're quibbling over a few hundred dollars that I need to pay my rent?"

The guys had a comparison for me to consider. Back when the five of us were invited to see the Rolling Stones at the Fox Theater (the best straight, no frills, rock 'n' roll show I'd ever seen) our friend Chuck Leavell from the Allman Brothers was playing keys with them. He was certainly not getting a cut of the band like the founding members of the *Rolling Stones.*

"You mean to tell me that you are comparing *this*...," as I pointed to a 15-passenger van on the way to play another two sets at a club for $25 a show "...you are comparing this to the *Rolling Stones?* They're multimillionaires! I can barely pay for my phone bills calling my sick mother!"

I took the opportunity to offer a comparison of my own. I reminded them we had just played a two-night gig where the club turned into a *trans stripper* joint by day. The club owner offered me a free lunch at the bar which I desperately needed to take him up on. I had to gulp down my soup while a partially naked man dressed up as a woman stood hovering over me doing a cakewalk striptease on the bar counter. He or she recognized me as a member of last night's band and crouched down to make sexual gestures towards me as a part of the performance. The club owner, who showed some salty fascination for what was taking place, walked over to me and said, "I think she likes you." He paused for a minute, admiring his daytime performer. "Look at the size of that *Adam's apple* on her," he declared as a smirk came over his face. I left my remaining peas and carrots in the bowl and ran out of there trying not to spit up more peas and carrots on the way. Scared out of my wits, I ran the four of five blocks back to my motel room every bit as fast as I had run the distance in 7th grade. I showed up to the gig that night literally one-minute before we had to go on stage — hoping that *she* wasn't waiting there to find me. *How about a little "Night Meets Light" in the set, boys?*

They left me alone to recover after detailing that little yarn — more than a little shaken up over getting stiffed for the past seven months. Only now, I was made a full member of the Dregs. Yes, my income was increasing, finally, but I was being completely misled at the same time. Never knew I was getting so much less pay than the others — a "trial period" for the entire time. Since they were prepared with ridiculous justifications for what they did, citing famous rock bands, they conveniently omitted the most obvious comparison — how long was T Lavitz's trial period? Was I still paying the price for being just a teenager?

On another day during that same run, our driver lit up another cigarette in the van, after he was told not to smoke inside the vehicle anymore. This time, I had a painful attack in my head from the smoke drift. It was a sensation I'd never felt before. The stabbing pain was over my left eye. Again, I dove back over the seats to the very back row. This time I was doubled over. I held my head while my body was throbbing, trying to manage the pain, the stabbing pain that lasted a couple of hours. Then it just disappeared on its own. My overall stress was increasing, my temper was at a boiling point, my patience was flagging, and now this unexplainable head pain from cigarette smoke. ...and we were a club band where people smoked from end to end.

STEVE HAD BEEN BUSY composing for the new record, to be titled *Industry Standard*. The recording schedule was to take place during seven weeks in December of '81 and January of '82. I'd been allowed to sell my new *On The Rampage* album at our merch tables because I was up there on stage, but wasn't featured on any Dregs albums for fans to listen to walking out the door. I only sold two or three per night, anyway. Andy, Rod, and T told me I wouldn't be composing any music for the new Dregs album. It was going to be all Steve. "That's the way this band works," they said. My viewpoint: I thought it was a missed opportunity for the band to not take advantage of another composer's voice, on at least something. Most democratic bands share the writing if people could make valuable contributions in that department. But it wasn't the case here. So... we had a lot of stuff to learn from Steve that fall.

They were also wanting to add a couple of vocal songs to the new album, which Steve would write, of course. They thought the band could get more radio airplay with some vocals—at least that's what radio disc jockeys kept telling us each time we were interviewed, "Give us a vocal and we can play your record more—we love you guys." The label was looking for more airplay for us, too. The topic of conversation turned to who might be the singer.

Of all the craziest things, Englishman Eddy Offord, engineer and producer of the British progressive rock group Yes, just moved to Atlanta. He purchased an abandoned movie theater on the south side of the city and turned it into his recording studio. We reached out to him to engineer and co-produce our album, and he signed on. Offord was the producer of such legendary Yes albums as *Fragile, Close To The Edge, Tales From Topographic Oceans* and *Relayer*. After hearing about our search for a guest rock singer, Eddy thought that Jon Anderson himself might do it, the lead singer on all of those Yes albums. He was interested, it seemed. He came to see us at a show and we talked a little with him afterwards, but the guest spot idea didn't pan out, for reasons unknown.

We reached out to rock music star Patrick Simmons of the Doobie Brothers however, and he was available to do it. It's remarkable how many fans in rock music circles the Dregs have—known as the "best band in the world"—it was not exactly hyperbole. Pat was up for it, if he could co-write the song. We had him write the lyrics while Steve added the music. Pat wrote about fast cars called "Ridin' High." He had just broken up the Doobie Brothers to begin his own solo career so that meant Pat was working on his first solo album, *Arcade*. I couldn't help but think about how many times I heard my pals Mastro and Pinkham sing Pat's #1 song, "Black Water"—Pinkham handling John McFee's fiddle lines that anchored the vibe. The fiddle had a hand in a few recent rock hits, this one being Simmons' iconic rock classic. We were finding a musical bridge to artists like Pat Simmons, already a big fan of the fiddle.

Along the lines of top rock classics with fiddle, all of us liked the progressive rock group Kansas and their lead singer Steve Walsh. They featured their own violin treatments with founding member Robbie Steinhardt—especially so on "Dust in the Wind," from four years earlier. I had really liked that one during high school as the violin played such a prominent role. Even some school chums had to admit they liked the fiddle a little bit more after that. We visited Robbie Steinhardt for an evening while on tour in Florida. A few of us took a dip in his partially indoor/outdoor swimming pool. You could swim all the way into the kitchen—going underwater to clear the house's exterior wall. Robbie was a fan of our band, and it was pretty cool to hang out with a big rock star who was a violinist. Steve Walsh was into singing a song on the album, so Morse wrote "Crank It Up," a song that Andy, T, and Rod contributed lyrics to—about being on the road and playing gigs.

The band asked me if I wanted to be included on the lyric writing for it, if I had anything to contribute. But I didn't think it was a good idea for any of us to be writing lyrics to a song we hoped would be a hit song. None of us had any experience writing hit songs. We were good instrumentalists, yes, but Merle Haggard, or that new writer I did a recording session for, Rodney Crowell, we were not. My suggestion was to have Walsh write the lyrics as well—and there would be more incentive for him to get behind the song, too. The fellows belittled the idea: *"How hard could it be to write lyrics to a rock song,"* they quipped. I had another idea then—to record a previously-released hit song or even a classic, but with our own musical treatment, *"There's nothing wrong with doing that,"* I proposed. But once again, I was outvoted four to one. An equal member of the band, now, but I just couldn't win any votes.

AFTER FULLY UNDERSTANDING the recording schedule for *Industry Standard,* I realized that band members were going to have several weeks off. Steve's timeline included a week to track all of the songs with the central purpose of getting Rod's drum tracks down on tape. Following the drums, there would be a week for Andy's bass overdubs, one week for T's keyboard work, and ten days for Steve to play walls of guitar parts and leads. Coming next was my week of overdubs on the violin and guitar. Add in a few days for vocal performances based on availability, and then Steve and Eddy planned to mix the album for another week-and-a-half. So… the "tightest band in the world" was going to record a completely overdubbed album. The guys said it was how they always did it.

More than a little ironic, I'd been wanting to do an all-overdubbed album of my own—a solo album with me playing all the instruments. I was looking at an entire month off during the band's seven-week recording period, but with nothing to do. Steve told band members that he didn't want us hanging around the studio when we weren't needed—didn't want all of the cooks in the kitchen. Fine. It was the perfect opportunity to record my next solo album, *False Dawn,* for Rounder Records. It would feature the music I had composed in the Bay Area during my time with the DGQ.

I asked Tom about both a recording engineer and a recording studio in Atlanta. A smile came to his face. "You have to get Sam Whiteside. He's recorded Allman Brothers albums—he's the best recording engineer in Atlanta." Whiteside was the house recording engineer for Capricorn Records: *Win, Lose or Draw* by The Allman Brothers Band, *Let It Flow* by Elvin Bishop, *Highway Call* by Dickey Betts that featured Vassar Clements, were all credits for Sam Whiteside. Given the mutual Capricorn history, the Dregs must've known Sam, but I didn't bring it up to the band. I was keeping my recording on the down low so as to not irritate any bandmates more than I already did.

Sam led me to Paul Davis' Monarch Recording Studio in Alpharetta, Georgia, and for a pretty decent friend's rate, too. The studio was just about a 30-minute drive from Buckhead to the north. Paul Davis himself was a laid-back southern hippie and a hitmaker. Songs he wrote, sang, and produced, like "I Go Crazy," were a part of the soundtrack to my high school years, just as the songs by Kansas and the Doobie Brothers were. Paul's current, "Cool Night," was atop the *Billboard* charts during the time period we took over his studio for three weeks. Like the Dregs' approach to recording, my album was going to be all overdubbed, with one very big distinction—I intended on playing all the instruments.

Rounder Records gave me a budget of $10,000 to make the recording, the same as my previous album budgets, and this recording was going to use every penny of it. My first winter in Atlanta was going to be a busy one—back and forth between two different recording studios.

B ECAUSE THE DREGS BEGAN to split the money evenly, except for Steve's writing royalties, I was getting an equal cut of the *Industry Standard* album advance. While Rounder's budgets were limited, the major labels like Arista, were supplying artists and bands between 60k and 80k for album budgets. The band was taking a significant amount of our album budget for ourselves—$6,000 each plus another $2,400 in session payments. The rest went to recording expenses and to Eddy Offord, and a percentage saved for the management cut. The $8,400 I was to receive, more than made up for the previous seven months of underpayments on the road—thank goodness. I could finally put something in the bank now.

By comparison, Grisman did not share the recording advance with the Quintet. It was all beginning to make much more sense now. If David signed the "Quintet" to Warner Bros., like the Dregs were signed to Arista, the band itself would be entitled to split the recording advance. However, David signed himself to the record label as a solo artist—so he kept the entire advance to *Quintet '80* for himself. Perhaps his take was the equivalent to what each Dreg got, times five? It could never be a "Quintet" album with him taking in all that bread, it had to be a David Grisman album. Grisman signed himself to WB as a solo artist, based off the success of the *Quintet* while Tony Rice was still in the band. I guess you'd have to interpret that level of hustle from of a mandolin player-composer, while at the very same time, his bandmembers could barely keep afloat in the Bay Area (without winning fiddle contests).

Steve demanded he write all the tunes for the Dregs album. So, he was getting all the songwriting royalties. For any recordings released before 1978, songwriting royalties paid 2.7¢ per song—but that was moving up dramatically. The very month *Industry Standard* was recorded in December 1981, songwriting royalties increased to 4¢ per song. With an average of 100,000 in record sales for a Dregs release—$40,000 goes to Steve just in mechanical royalties—let alone what BMI was going to pay him from radio play. No wonder he wanted to write every single tune. And that went for Grisman, too.

The large amount of individual earnings for Grisman and Morse had to be factors in how they dealt with their bands. Grisman wanted my tunes for the stage concerts, and that didn't pay anything extra. Steve wanted "Limerock" only for the stage, too, not for the album. If we recorded that traditional (public domain) tune, I could've shared in a song royalty for arranging it. These bands were *far* from a democratic process—regardless of what the band was called or what audiences perceived the group member's credentials to be. Learning about the music business while you're being squeezed out—can be a little gloomy.

I was getting an education up close from the *bosses* who ran their outfits with an iron fist. Morse and Grisman were savvy young business men who knew how to work all the angles, separating themselves from the pack (their bandmates), but using each one of us to increase their own salt.

It is why David owned a house in Mill Valley, CA while I had a $100 bedroom at "Crazy Johnny's" trap house. Similarly, it is why Steve had a 40-acre farm with horses, his own air plane and runway, while I had a $250 apartment in Tom's basement. We were playing the same music, the same gigs and, getting the same attention from the fans, and the press, but in the financial hierarchy, I was a hired hand playing for minimum wage.

To most people in the music industry, though, I came off as one of the two indispensable stars of the Dregs.

AT ISSUE NOW was getting to play much on *Industry Standard.* For my debut recording with the band, I was hoping to get featured a little, since I wasn't allowed to compose anything for it. When you compose, it can be a lot easier to write yourself a substantial part. To start with, there were just nine tunes for the recording from Steve, adding up to barely 35 minutes of music. The perennial acoustic guitar/violin duet that Steve always did with Allen, this time went to Steve Howe for a two-guitar duet called "Up In The Air." Eddy Offord delivered on this one. Howe was the legendary guitar player from the group Yes, but this was a duo slot that Sloan enjoyed on each record, and one that vanished for my Dregs album debut. I daresay it was a duo that many of our fans were anticipating for Steve and I to do together. Evidently, our duet busking didn't cement the idea in Steve's mind for more. The classical guitar piece from the two Steves turned out to be unusually short as well. Our Steve *removed* the other Steve's solo section, placing it coolly on the cutting room floor. The overdub from over in England was poorly executed, it was determined. Rather than heaving "Up In The Air," it was great politics to keep it on—an "industry standard" you could say. Stylistically, though, not in a million years. Or at least 250 years. The tune still sounded like the previous Morse/Sloan duos—two Steves packing their lutes and hopping into a time machine for the Baroque era.

Well-rehearsed, the band tracked at Eddy's theater studio to start everything off. Playing the only acoustic instrument (besides the drums), I was cordoned off in the tiny projector room atop the old movie theater. The drum set and the electric amplifiers of Steve and Andy could never find me way up there. The meager crevice—ugly and decaying, was, by early December, freezing. This week was all about the drums anyway. I sure did love Rod's drumming—he played 'em like they were his own percussion symphony. Looking across the theater studio from up in the projector room and seeing Rod get his drum tracks down for the record was pretty cool. I was becoming even more of a "closet drummer." We had done several double bills with the band Little Feat, and their drummer, Richie Hayward, became another favorite. I loved watching Rod's reactions to seeing Richie play. In some ways, Rod was becoming my favorite musician in the band.

DIGGING OUT MY 4-track tapes from Marin County, I got busy reviewing the instrumental parts I planned to record for *False Dawn*. I assembled an assortment of instruments I wanted to play: electric bass, some hand percussion, and a battalion of stringed instruments. I had picked up a black sunburst 1962 Fender Precision bass (an Impeach Nixon sticker on the face of it). I borrowed a fretless bass and a cello from Andy. He played cello in high school orchestra, but it was Andy's cool flat-picking on the electric bass that suggested I could do the same without having to work up the more typical finger technique yet. I also came across a rare 1932 Martin archtop 12-string, a refinished instrument I picked up for next to nothing. For the Mossman guitar I won in Winfield, I put super-thin gauge strings on it and tuned it up a fifth higher—a "high-strung" guitar. Back in San Francisco I found a very small, inexpensive 1923 Stew-art/Martin tiple—an odd, miniature guitar-shaped instrument more re-lated to the mandolin family than guitar, I thought. Joe Deetz, a guitar luthier at the Fifth String in Berkeley, converted the tiple into a tiny six-string guitar so I could practice in airports when traveling with my former group. I kept this "soprano" guitar tuned an octave higher from a standard guitar—the strings extremely taut. The high E-string was the thinnest you could find to tune it all the way up. I had two Martin tenor guitars in the mix (one from the 20s), my Somogyi custom-made guitar, and, of course, the 1945 Herringbone Martin with its original transition bracing. *False Dawn* was going to feature a wall of acoustic guitars.

The architecture of my rhythm section incorporated standard steel-string guitar on one side of the stereo, and the "soprano" guitar (tiple), on the other side. In doing so, it created an exact octave of all my guitar parts—mostly cross-picked. As I inventoried the instruments I wanted to choreograph into a "mountain string orchestra," I was still missing a cou-ple of key components: a good mandolin and mandola. Randy Howard from down in Milledgeville had a nice Moyer F-5 style mandolin he let me borrow. For a mandola, none other than David Grisman let me borrow his—an instrument built by John Monteleone, one of the top mandolin makers in the world. His Monteleone mandolin was photographed for the front cover of *Quintet '80.*

I was eager to highlight a lot of my DGQ-era mandolin and mandola skills, instruments I hadn't played much over the last year. I used to play mandola with Grisman on his tune "Opus 38." The two mando instru-ments joined my own Gibson K-4 mandocello and the Givens to create a fetching little mandolin section.

WHEN IT WAS TIME FOR my Dregs overdubs, Steve wanted me to stay in the projection booth so my sound could match the live tracking violin already on tape. The nagging part was that Steve was never going to keep a single thing I played from the live takes. We were going to redo it all. We had an entire empty theater for me to record in—a stage I could've played on—but I got the projection booth. They brought me a space heater, hoping to calm my nerves and warm my fingers. That said, I had to turn off the heater during takes because the thing made too much noise. I was about fit to be tied.

Steve let me in on his little "trade secret" for recording violin. Once I successfully recorded one violin part, perfected it, and got it down on tape the way he wanted it, whether it be a counter-melody to Morse's guitar, or matching his guitar lead line pitch for pitch, bend for bend and vibrato rate for vibrato rate, I was supposed to triple-track the violin parts recording all of them another two times. Steve wanted to triple-track every violin line on the album, performing it all in my claustrophobic dingy hole up in the rafters—truly an exercise in futility.

"Why, Steve!?" I exclaimed. "My violin is already a double of the electric guitar lines—no one will ever hear this triple violin tracking."

"It smooths out the tone to triple-track it," Steve emphasized.

"No, it does not! You not only have the acoustic phasing stuff from all the flutter echo and standing waves in this little projection room here, but you're using the same exact mic for each pass, using the same mic position, in the same location of the room—same instrument. Doing it this way takes the soul right out of the instrument, out of the player. The uniqueness of it is crushed."

Some of those things I had just learned at the recording engineering course in Seattle during my recuperation. Other points were thoughts of my own. But this is what was really going on—a recipe for having the violin's volume attenuated in the mix. It's why I couldn't pick out a single violin line from the records when I was trying to learn the tunes before I joined up. My additional effort in triple-tracking every violin line, only secured its burial in the mix. If we truly wanted a "smooth" violin sound, I needed to get out of that small projection booth and put the violin down there on that big open stage where Rod recorded his drums. *Let the instrument breathe some.*

Instead, Steve had me come down to the recording console area so he could show me how he was combining the three violin tracks where one of them would be featured more prominently—song by song, line by line.

"That seems just pointless compared to the effort it would take to execute this all week, Steve. The violin is going to be washed out completely with all of your guitars and T's synthesizers."

Steve heard me out, giving me his trademark grimace as I shared with him my approach to recording the fiddle.

"Wouldn't it be much better if the guitar melody was off to one side of the stereo, and my single violin track off to the other side. I mean like ten o'clock and two o'clock? You could actually tell that there were two musicians playing together, two personalities uniting and jamming— rather than just a wash of miscellaneous sounds where you can't distinguish the two musical identities."

Steve spoke next. He cautioned me that he was the album's producer, not me.

I was trying to save myself a lot of work and frustration over something that no one will ever hear, or discern. I needed to get through the week without any mounting state of mind. With the decaying hole of the projection room, and its temperature conditions, I was already halfway to making this a bit of a scene—if I wasn't careful. I still wanted to play my best for our record and for Steve.

NOT GONNA BE TRIPLE-TRACKING violin lines on *False Dawn*. Just no need to do that. You'd have to have an entire section of violins (as in an orchestra) for it to develop to another separate and substantial character all its own. My octave doubles of the standard guitar and the soprano on each side of the stereo mix was more interesting sonically, by comparison.

I loved the acoustic sound that we were getting at Monarch Studios with Whiteside at the controls. I positioned myself in the middle of our large main room to do my overdubs. I had various mic stations around the room, too, so there could be slight acoustical tempering and sound variation with each instrument I overdubbed. It was quite a comfortable studio to be in by comparison, and it was temperature-controlled; I didn't have to retune my instruments every five minutes.

I was every bit the perfectionist that Morse was—slaving over my re-cording in those ten-hour days, getting each part down so tight that it was the very best I could possibly do. Sam was a saint, and so easy to work with. There was never tension between us. He liked what was going to tape, and was particularly looking forward to seeing how it all came together once we got each instrument in the musical puzzle fully revealed. Since I wasn't getting to record the aforementioned obligatory duet with Steve on *Indus-try Standard,* I recorded my own guitar and violin duet for *False Dawn.* I played both the guitar and violin on "Rose Among Thorns," a piece I wrote on the night that John Lennon was assassinated.

TWO BULLS IN THE CHINA SHOP were the two vocal songs for *Industry Standard.* To put that kind of capital into vocal songs for an instrumental band, but not having any prior success writing pop songs, was, I figured, a real risk. We should've brought in an outside lyricist, at the very least. In any case, my violin was nearly non-existent on the songs Steve came up with. Even Morse's marvelous guitar leads couldn't save these two songs.

Steve Walsh sang "Crank It Up." It was rousing to see him do his thing in the studio. No tiny projection booth for him—he was properly right up on that theater stage. Morse was encouraging him to sing as high as he humanly could. Walsh was such a fan of our band, he was wanting to please. For a couple of high-pitched "Crank It Up" harmonies in full chest voice, he had to get down and do a few pushups right before we rolled tape. In spite of the extra effort, he received a phone call from his manage-ment while in the studio. It turned out that his record contract prohibited him from singing lead for any other record label. They were going to en-force it. Maybe they heard what the song sounded like by then? Walsh was very apologetic; he had come all the way to Atlanta for nothing. Of course, our hopes were dashed. The band schemed together—what if we kept Walsh's "Crank It Up" background vocals and credited some miscellane-ous female background singers? We did.

After a slapdash search for most any singer we could find, famous or not so famous, we had just a couple of weeks to get it all done before the album deadline and the start of our next tour. Alex Ligertwood, who sang with Carlos Santana, came in at the 11th hour to sing lead. Alex was excited to do it—he sounded great and was able to play some promotional dates with us after the fact. And about his boss, what a beautiful tone and vibrato Santana brought to the guitar. Later, I discovered that Carlos grew up playing with the Mariachi violinists in his family band. No wonder.

But the nagging feeling remained: was either song very good? Were the songs anywhere close to the level of our instrumental musicianship? The question loomed for me, even though the others refused to confront it. Instead, the band insisted on comparing our new vocal songs to the lowest common denominator out there: *"radio said they'd play us if we had a vocal."* Well, maybe they expected a really good song from a band like ours. The race to mainstream acceptance shouldn't have meant we had to sacrifice living up to our full potential—no matter the genre.

"Crank It Up," had the best chance of getting on commercial radio stations between the two—but neither of them met any "industry standard." But like a fully committed band member, I was along for all the *cranking it up,* and the *ridin' high.*

F ALSE DAWN WAS RIDING on my foundation of classical music as a child with my own new acoustic musical explorations. I put long recording days in, and Whiteside was right there with me every step of the way. The primary hardship was my own perfectionism—believing that I could get it better, tighter, and more inspired—and getting the most tone out of those great acoustic instruments I was playing.

Sam believed that Monarch was a great place to cut the album, but now he felt that *False Dawn* deserved to be mixed on the best studio console in Atlanta. For him, that meant Cheshire Sound. It also meant that I would have to go into pocket and spend most all of my Dregs recording advance to finish mine. Sam convinced me to spring for it, that the album we were making was worth it. So I didn't get to keep most of that newly-earned $8,400 in the bank after all, continuing with my established tradition, which is the clear intention to spend any money I could've saved and put it right back into the music. Cans of beans and peanut butter-cheese sandwiches were always an option in the kitchen cupboard at home.

W ITH MUCH FRUSTRATION OVER the *Industry Standard* recording thus far, I couldn't wait until my guitar overdubs on "Blood

Sucking Leeches." If the majority of my violin lines ended up being obscured, at least I can say that I recorded twin electric guitars with the guitar god himself. It was a lot to show for eight months of Steve and me woodshedding in every "dirty can" in every filthy club we played across America. I was anticipating the moment when Steve and Eddy would finally help me dial up some good guitar tone for the recording. Perhaps an opportunity to plug into any one of those great old amp heads lined up for Steve's guitar dubs. Between the two of them, they either owned or rented every guitar tube amp known to man—from Marshalls to Fenders and everything in between.

When we finally got done with the week of violin overdubs, analyzing every single Morse pitch, Morse phrase—tone, bend, and vibrato, and then tripling it all, I was more than ready to head down onto the theater floor and get ballsy with electric guitar. I had "Leeches" under my fingers now for a good three months; it was one of the first tunes Steve wrote for the project because he wanted to expand our double guitar repertoire. By now, I had the arm-shake vibrato well in hand: the F-you's with my meatloaf second finger were comin' right at you.

"Well, it looks like we are finished, Mark! Congratulations!" Steve told me.

"Thank you! But we still got the guitar stuff to do on 'Leeches,'" I reminded Steve.

"Oh, that's right," Steve paused for a second. "I'll call you."

Later that week at the *Half Moon Café* where I saw John Hartford play, I ran into Jeff Pinkham. He and Steve Mastro followed me to Atlanta—thought they might fish some new waters in the city's club scene. After the show, I told Hartford about our Dregs recording and that our engineer is none other than Eddy Offord, the producer of Yes. I described our studio being an old converted movie theater. John seemed really curious about it. "Do you guys want to drop by the studio tonight to check it out?" I asked. The three of us hopped in my red pickup and popped into Eddy's theater/studio. I still had my front door key on me, of course, and we snuck in quietly and took a seat in the back of the auditorium. Steve was doing some guitar work down near the stage where they had the control board set up—the studio monitors were turned up very loud—nothing surprising there. Of all things, "Blood Sucking Leeches" was up on the 24-track.

"This is so ironic," I whispered to Hartford and Pinkham—letting them know that this is the tune I'm going to play electric guitar on.

However, something was very wrong with what I was hearing. It appeared that Steve was recording *my* guitar part—himself. At first, I was assuming it might be a guide track. He and Offord had no idea we were in there. When enough time went by, and it was obvious that he was going for "keeper takes" on my guitar parts, I told Hartford and Pinkham that I needed to talk to Morse about something and if they would excuse me. I walked down to where Steve was recording. I surprised him.

"Hey Steve! What's up?"

"Oh, hello, what are you doing here?"

"Thought I would drop by and show my friends the studio," pointing to the back of the theater.

"That's not cool without checking with me, they shouldn't be in here."

"Oh, okay… So, what's going on with my guitar parts?"

"Yeah, we were running out of time and thought I'd just put on the parts myself," Steve said.

"Really?" Beginning to fume inside. I continued:

"I had prepared and worked on this for months! Me playing the other guitar will make it sound like there are two different guitar players, the whole point of you writing this tune for me to play with you, right? You know, the Tele and the Paul thing we always liked?" (He was recording my guitar part on his same "Franken-tele.")

Steve wasn't going to hear anything more on the subject. He asked me to leave and take my two friends with me—that I was bumming him out while he's trying to finish the record and with a looming deadline. I didn't even tell him that it was John Hartford looking in, I was too embarrassed over it all. Offord sat there trying to busy himself minding over a technical issue. Hartford turned to Pinkham and said, "It doesn't look like things are going too well down there." "Morse seems like a real dick," Pinkham added.

I'm tellin' you, I was hopping mad. I was blazing. The escapades at the studio were not good. As Steve turned away from me and walked towards the recording console, I walked back towards my friends. *"We need to leave, now."*

Similar to *Quintet '80,* I wasn't caring much about the future of *Industry Standard* all of the sudden.

My best violin solo on the album was likely on "Assembly Line," where Steve allowed me all of 12-seconds for it. On the rest of the tune, I couldn't distinguish if there was even a violin on the track, but it took a half-day to get all those parts down. He mushed out my sound with triple tracking and blended that behind the guitar and synth. All that extra time I spent could've gone to my guitar overdub, if the deadline was an issue. The album I was hoping would introduce me to Dregs fans as the new member of the band, featured mostly Steve's guitar and very little of anything that was my best. He was positioning himself to be the next big rock guitar guy and wanted all guitar-playing credits to be his, that was obvious. Pinkham echoed the sentiment. I knew my place now: Nothing more than his backup band.

Back on the other side of things, in due course, my *False Dawn* album was to be held up by Rounder. They were contemplating not even releasing it at all—dismissing it to my colleagues and even to music journalists as being "too far out."

After sitting on it for a year, Rounder sent the tracks to Norman Blake to get his opinion on the music, to see if it was worth releasing. Later, Norman told me what he said to the folks at Rounder about it: *"It is the work of a musical genius."* The album was released soon after.

False Dawn
Side one: Flight Home, False Dawn, Floating Bridge of Dreams, Rose Among Thorns
Side two: Point of Crossing, Conversation With A Friend, Thanks and Goodbyes, An Empty Hall/Into the Walls of Mandoness

Rod Morgenstein April 5, 1982
"There was a lot of soul-searching. One side of it was, naturally, the Dregs sell out. But the whole point of the band is to take on all kinds of music. We decided, why look on vocals as an evil, but instead as just an extension of what we do."

Billboard's Recommended LPs - Mark O'Connor False Dawn
"One-man string fantasias in which the fiddler, guitarist, mandolinist and percussionist weaves rich ensemble settings through overdubs."

406

The Atlanta Constitution – The Dregs, Industry Standard

"'We just wanted to do something different. No one in the group feels we've sold out,' Steve Morse said. 'Everyone kept challenging us. They said it was getting to be a predictable pattern. Clive Davis (Arista president) told us to avoid being too predictable. I couldn't understand the logic (because) we try to do a variety of music, but we all agreed if we could do something really different and yet still acceptable to our ears, we'd do it.

'In having a commercial type vocal (Alex Ligertwood of Santana sings 'Crank It Up' and Pat Simmons, formerly of The Dobbie Brothers, is heard on 'Ridin' High') we're trying to get played by stations that swore up and down they loved the band but said they could never play us unless we had some vocals. Everyone said you have to have vocals. We get that about once every 20 minutes.'

That brings up the subject of just how The Dregs are handling their new vocal numbers onstage. Morse laughed, 'We did 'Crank It Up' on this trip, sort of making light of it. We have a tape of the vocal only and we play along with it and set up a mannequin with a Dregs shirt on up at the microphone.'"

Backstage Magazine – Mark O'Connor, False Dawn

"Let's talk about False Dawn, I was told by the people at Rounder that it was pretty far out.

'Far-out? Is that like groovy?'

I think they meant 'far out there musically.' How would you describe it?

'It's a section of music in my life, and I probably will never do anything like it again. When I wrote it, I was 19, and it's a collection of my influences.'"

El Paso Herald-Post – The Dregs, Industry Standard

"Steve Morse's lead on FM hit Crank It Up is that song's only saving grace, since not even the humorous use of a mannequin as a stand in for the taped vocals of Alex Ligertwood could keep the song from exposing its obvious limitations on stage.

Newcomer Mark O'Connor was a delight on the violin and guitar. His forays into the diverse elements of the band's music – rock, jazz, classical, bluegrass, country – were exercises in how to master an instrument."

Independent Music Magazine – Mark O'Connor, False Dawn

"Although O'Connor's virtuosic mastery of numerous bowed and plucked instruments (augmented with sparse percussion) is truly awe-inspiring, this record is by no means just a flashy technical tour de force. It is his depth and maturity as a composer of extended, interwoven, labyrinthine melodies, not always hummable, yet consistently ear-catching, that sets this album at the fore of new acoustic music."

The Florida Times-Union, Jacksonville, FL – The Dregs, Industry Standard

"The problem with Industry Standard is a matter of restraint. The live Dregs are bristling with ideas and tricks and eclectic nuttiness from bluegrass to jazz. None of that wild sense of exploration is here, which is too bad. It could have made a more exciting record."

Jazziz Magazine – Mark O'Connor, False Dawn

"False Dawn, O'Connor's latest release, is by and far the best album to have come out of new acoustic music and will hopefully set a standard for this music...O'Connor intricately orchestrates all the instruments, utilizing unique time situations to attain a rich textural blend of high-pitched violins, mandolins and guitars, and deep bopping bass and mandocello lines. [David] Grisman says it's "like real modern classical music—a tapestry of orchestrated sound." O'Connor calls it his "acoustic rock" album, but to classify it as rock, jazz, or classical is an injustice to O'Connor's melding compositions. Let's just say this is great music, because he definitely forged a style all his own and has best captured the spirit of all that new acoustic music could ever hope to achieve."

Garden State Nite Life, NJ – The Dregs, Industry Standard

"For the first time ever, The Dregs have included two vocal tracks on record – 'Crank It Up' (sung by Santana vocalist Alex Ligertwood) and 'Ridin' High' (sung by The Doobie Brothers' Pat Simmons)—but in actuality, these were unnecessary tracks. With vocals covering up much of the instrumentation, the band's vast performing assets are diminished substantially when, in fact, their combined playing talents are what makes The Dregs stand out above their contemporaries."

The Arizona Daily Star – Tucson – Mark O'Connor, False Dawn

"It's a quantum leap for guitarist/fiddler Mark O'Connor. "New acoustic music" has hardly been named, and already he has provided it with an album against which all others must be measured. His own albums, however, tended to stick pretty close to a traditional acoustic sound—waltzes, polkas, folk songs, etc.—albeit done with style and grace.

But with this album, O'Connor has literally done it all: pulled together his many influences; written all the songs (perhaps the most graphic area of improvement); produced the album; played all the instruments; vaulted into the stratosphere on his own power.

Playing some 20 instruments from the violin, guitar and mandolin families, O'Connor has created layers of music with moods stately or sprightly, sometimes skittering along and sometimes soaring, always touchingly beautiful.

With 'False Dawn,' O'Connor has reminded us all that he's the one to watch. Not even the sky's the limit for him now."

408

THE BASH

"O'Connor, whose fiddling persistently soars over the whole hard-driving ensemble, is the country's champion fiddler. He's so accomplished, he seems to be able to play more than is required for some of these pieces."

THE DREGS WANTED TO BE taken seriously as a rock band; instead, we headed straight into the world of contradictions and absurdities. The band still insisted on using pyrotechnic flash pots on the small club stages—explosives that our roadies set off on the musical climax of "Cruise Control," our final tune of the night. Burkhart and "Microwave," ignited them every show we did, no matter how small of a space we were in. Flash and boom. I was reminded to stand as far back from them as I could on stage, because Sloan had his leg broken by the operation. As I became more assertive as an equal member, I asked for those flash pots to be discarded. They were positioned just a couple of feet from people's heads at the front of the stage. "Let the music be the show, we don't need it. Weather Report didn't have 'em." Once again—outvoted four to one.

Down the road, the hard rock band Great White played at a club in Rhode Island called the Station Concert Club—a place just like the Dregs would've played. Many of the established music clubs were not abiding by regulations and safety standards—certainly many bands themselves weren't. We had those same flash pots and ignition powder just feet from stage curtains, and no one around was specifically licensed for this work. The pyrotechnics of the Great White show turned the club into an inferno, causing the deaths of nearly 100 people. The roadie who set them off went to prison.

OUR PILOT DOUBLED as our merch guy. He flew the band in a two-engine plane to Plymouth, New Hampshire—a show at the State University. The band decided to skip the soundcheck at the Agora in New Haven the following night and stay for a full day of skiing. Burkhart and "Microwave" had already driven the band truck through the night and were setting up the equipment at the Agora. I was not itching to get back on the slopes, but I met a girl at the gig, and she encouraged me to go skiing with her. *Get back on that horse...* The whole band ended up hitting the slopes together. At day's end, we thanked my new friend for a nice day on the mountain, and headed to the Plymouth city airport to meet up with our twin engine. By the time we arrived at the hangar, it was not only sun-down on a Sunday, but the airport was shut down altogether.

After probing our pilot with the idea of taking off without any ground crew around, he informed us that we had to have the engines preheated because of the below-freezing temperatures. After looking around a bit, we couldn't find the engine warmers he needed. Jeff got in the cockpit to start up the plane, but the engines wouldn't turn over. One of us had a hair-brain idea—that our small hair dryers in the carry-on could possibly un-freeze the engines. If we got one of the engines unfrozen, Jeff confirmed, he would take the plane up to get the other engine started in mid-air—then land the plane to pick us up. Our immediate problem: we needed some AC to run the hair dryers. Nearly pitch dark outside, one of us found an outdoor AC receptacle located near the bottom of a small hangar's out-side wall. The band pushed the plane over to it, about 100 feet away. We got two hair dryers trained into the left engine. On that bitter cold night, it wasn't the warmest air coming out of those little dryers, but Jeff thought it could be just enough. We gave 'em about 15 minutes. Jeff got on board to crank it up, and bingo. That engine turned over.

Just when Jeff was going to take the plane up by himself, as planned, some band members insisted that we all should get in with him—not let him go up by himself and *"risk his life for us."* The "all for one, one for all" motto was dusted off for the occasion. I thought it was about the stu-pidest idea I'd ever seen come out of a group of grown men. I told them no way, but I was immediately outvoted again. Even T, who was frightened by those small planes to begin with, was saying to me, "We can't have Jeff risk his life for us, Mark!" Even though he was a pilot who could make those risk assessments by himself and determine what to do based on his training and experience.

I didn't want to go up in that airplane. I thought Jeff's suggestion sounded reasonable. As the others were boarding the plane, some looked at me like I was downright uncompassionate:

"What are you going to do out here, stand there and freeze to death?"

"Actually, I'd go over to that pay phone, call a taxi and head to a hotel for the night—postpone the Agora," I answered.

"C'mon Mark, let's go, we're already behind schedule—we need the bread," they said.

In the dark and the freezing cold, we all loaded into that little plane. The Dregs went up in the air on just one of two engines. Each of us prayed in the ways we knew how. Some actually believed, after the fact, that we might not make it this time. That's how idiotic it was. All for yet another club gig.

We were in the air for just about five minutes before Jeff got the second engine started. All of us screamed for joy. Our celebration was soon dampened, however, when the plane wouldn't heat. It was freezing inside the plane. Jeff yelled back to us that we lost the power distribution system which controlled the heating. We were without heat in the plane, and it was going to be an hour-long flight at 10,000 feet in the dead of a New Hampshire winter. Some of them told me not to fall asleep because I could pass out and maybe lose consciousness. If one of us looked like we were dosing off, another would poke and jab him to make sure he didn't.

After this harrowing experience, we were met with a van at a local New Haven airport and we got to the Agora just an hour behind schedule. We went onstage at 11 p.m., and I earned my fifty bucks.

New Hampshire was not the only place we risked our life in a small plane. On our way to a gig in New Orleans, we were attempting to fly through a thunderstorm. En route, we made a rough emergency landing at a small airport where we planned to wait out the storm. The thunder and lightning weren't retreating anytime soon, it appeared. After about an hour gone by, Steve announced that we were heading back up. This time, T and I looked at each other. *"We're renting a car,"* we told the others. They made it to New Orleans, thankfully, but we did as well, a couple of hours later than them but still on time. This gig was actually a good one *not* to miss—a double bill with the electric bass virtuoso, Jaco Pastorius, on his "Word Of Mouth" tour. Steve was all worried that Jaco's jazz audience wouldn't like us. I assumed it had something to do with Steve's history at the University of Miami where Jaco was in the jazz program along with Metheny and Hornsby. Steve didn't seem like he related to that scene much.

Later, back in Atlanta, Lavitz and I were carpooling to the airport together. On the way, we picked up Jaco Pastorius hitchhiking to the same airport. We asked him if he had another ride that fell through, or something. "No," he said. "I'm just catching my flight." All Jaco had with him was his bass in a gig bag placed over his shoulders, and an airplane ticket in his pocket. It would be one of his final tours. That year it was announced he was officially diagnosed with bipolar disorder. Beset by problems stemming from alcohol and drug abuse, Jaco Pastorius wound up penniless and homeless. He wouldn't last past his 35th birthday, dead from injuries in a physical altercation with a club owner.

WHILE I WAS GLUM about some of the things that were happening with band life, on the flip side, I had some very good things of my own developing. Speaking of jazz music, I was getting a cover story in the venerable *DownBeat Magazine* (June, 1982 issue). This was a pretty good thing, and completely unexpected—a fiddler getting the cover story in the largest jazz music magazine.

DownBeat Magazine – June 1982
"Mark O'Connor – Classical, Country, Fusion, Jazz-Rock Fiddler"

"Steve Morse said, 'and Mark and I would meet back at the hotel to jam. I realized he was the best violinist I'd ever heard—he played so in tune and so smooth—and that just stuck in my mind.'

He has, after all, already captured the hearts of the fiercely loyal followers of the Dregs, fans who are closer to fanatics...There's no denying the fact that Mark O'Connor has done more in 20 years than most people accomplish in a lifetime, and its remarkable how level-headed and adjusted he is. Trumpeter Wynton Marsalis and he could probably swap stories and feel as though they were talking to a twin."

Another weighty event on March 7th was my "command performance" before President Ronald Reagan – *Young Artists at the White House.* What must my bandmates be thinking? One of my feature tunes was some more of that jazz, "Sweet Georgia Brown." Along with Jerry Thomasson joining me on tenor guitar, I traded fours on that one with Tiny Moore, only after giving the presidential audience several courses of my improvised swing-fiddle solos. I couldn't get the Dregs to open up more than one tune for some of my extended improvisation, but I got to play several courses in front of the President of the United States. I even played a solo guitar tune on the Martin. The entire event, hosted by opera soprano Beverly Sills, would be edited for television the following month. Merle Haggard gave me this monumental opportunity. I couldn't help but think of my parents and what had to be running through their minds. Although my mother was too sick to attend the performance, still Mom knew that the President was watching me play the fiddle from just a few feet away.

New York Times, April 23, 1982

"Public television's 'In Performance at the White House' closes its current season Sunday at 10 P.M. with a performance that takes place not at the White House but at a ranch in California's Santa Ynez Valley. The occasion was taped early last month, and the list of 400 guests was headed by President and Mrs. Reagan, whose own ranch happens to be nearby. The young performer is Mark O'Connor, a 20-year-old fiddler, whose virtuosity is impressive. He plays, and the joint can't keep from jumping. President Reagan, wearing western garb, makes a brief speech to observe, among other things, 'I think the music we heard today reaches the heart of America.'"

The White House
Washington
April 21, 1982

"Dear Mark:
The President and Mrs. Reagan thought you would like the enclosed as a souvenir of the wonderful days they spent in Santa Ynez, California.

They so very much enjoyed hearing your wonderful performance and everybody here will be watching this Sunday night as the television show goes on the air nationwide.

From all of us, warmest congratulations.

Very sincerely yours,
Mabel H. Brandon
Social Secretary to the White House"

# # #

Steve drove his motorcycle over and parked it at the bottom of the driveway—the "Franken-tele" in a gig bag on his back. But this time, he sat on the floor of my small basement apartment, not to teach me more Dregs tunes, but to listen to my new solo album. I still didn't have any furniture. I did have a new stereo, though—the ultimate test drive was playing my new *False Dawn* album for the boss. Steve wanted to see what I was up to in my off time. He decided to practice his guitar while we listened. Anytime Steve was stationary, the man was inseparable from his guitar. But *really...?* I was glad I had the extra wattage in my brand new stereo so I could drown out the pick-clacking at least. I purchased the new stereo that very week, just so we could listen to *False Dawn*. He didn't know that. It was one expensive playback, but I wanted to prove something to him; that I could play guitar, that I could compose, and that I was a perfectionist in my recordings. As I cranked it up, he was intrigued by what he heard.

Steve elaborated. He made a reference to how resourceful I was to put it together, getting the budget from the record company, producing it, and finishing it. That was the main thing—finishing something. Goal oriented and getting the job done. He was impressed by people who had a big work ethic, were industrious, having the ability to see something through in a timely fashion to its completion. Steve was a can-do type guy. He also realized that his fellow centerstage "Leo" also had some drive to succeed artistically, at all costs—just like he did.

W E HAD SOME TV SHOWS to promote *Industry Standard* in Los Angeles: *History of Rock 'n' Roll* was taping our segment on March 22nd with Pat Simmons. We flew back out to L.A. a few weeks later on April 18th for Dick Clark's *American Bandstand.* Alex Ligertwood met up with us for an on-air appearance of "Crank It Up." Pat Simmons couldn't make that one, and it looked like "Ridin' High" wasn't going to get the nod for a single by Arista anyway. Not ridin' very high. It meant that "Blood Sucking Leeches" was our second tune on Dick Clark. Not even sure if the rest of the band fully understood I didn't play guitar on the album track. Never brought it up—too embarrassing. For the job of playing on *American Bandstand,* it was going to be "finger-synched" to the recording. I had wondered if I should ever play "Leeches" on stage. But it was a fool's notion if I was going to remain in the band. It was still a great rock guitar tune.

Before the taping, Dick Clark knocked on our dressing room door, walked in, and took a seat. We talked about releasing our new single and what it was like on the road, what attention we were getting. He asked about "the girls," and if they were "liking the band." If there was ever a

414

band that drew more musician dudes to their audience, I don't know who it would have been. I had him sign my suede hat right there in the dressing room, "America's oldest teenager." I used to watch his show on the black-and-white as a little kid, but I don't think there was much nostalgia from the Dregs for this venue — none of us felt like this was quite our bag. It really wasn't.

There was a never-ending stretch of club gigs for the band that Spring. I tried worrying about less those days. Wore my gym shorts on stage most of the time. Our own bottom of the barrel, though, was the stage manne-quin with a mic stand in front of it for "Crank It Up." *How could really good musicians stoop this low?* During our unison solo section, Steve and I approached the mannequin and played off it as if it was a real person. As Steve goes, we go.

On May 10th, we were out of our element once again on the national pop/disco TV show, *Solid Gold.* There was nothing about us that was disco, or solid gold. "Crank It Up" was solidly tanking at radio by now. Rock stations wouldn't play us like they had "promised" — not with that song at least.

As we made it down to the Golden Bear in Huntington Beach on May 11th, the entire band was beginning to chew over where our new rock band facade could really get us. In between the two sets, Andy and I met up with jazz-fusion bassist Jeff Berlin for Mexican food down the block. We were in the mood to let off some steam and maybe commiserate with a top mu-sician friend over our new self-imaging. Berlin was best known for playing with jazz-rock fusion drummer Bill Bruford. Berlin was a serious guy, and just the right one to air our grievances with.

After the first margarita, we began laughing more comfortably at our own expense — over mannequins and *Solid Gold* TV tapings. Surprisingly, Andy backed off unconditionally defending the decisions by the band at every turn. I was hitting more margaritas as Andy started to vent about re-cent turns the band had taken. By the time we were done, Andy was howl-ing about the mannequin segment, and, how drunk I was becoming. We still had a second show to do. Up until that night, the last time I had per-formed in an altered state was in fiddle contests against Texans.

Trailing behind West and Berlin, I shuffled my way back over to the Golden Bear. I was feeling a little like *anything goes* — with a strong dose of: *I don't care about all the shit anymore.* When it came time for the twin guitar tunes, I was less inhibited on my Les Paul than before, not nearly as jittery. Maybe all the *American Bandstand* guitar rollicking loosened me up. I'd always felt intimidated, and lately even a little frightened to be standing next to Steve on stage with an electric guitar around my neck. My guitar being omitted from the record unquestionably reinforced that. But I was feeling a little differently about things on this night. I had to.

I purchased an inexpensive Tom Scholz's Power Soak and was experimenting with it some on stage. Created by the guitarist of the rock group *Boston,* the creators of some very good rock songs by comparison, the gadget allows you to overdrive the amp while attenuating the volume to a "reasonable" stage level. The amp head *works* harder, driving the tubes to do more and to distort the sound naturally. I thought it was ingenious for what I needed on stage with that powerful Ampeg amp of Steve's that refused to distort. I loved this Power Soak, but Steve was dead set against it. He just didn't like any pedals and gadgets. Or so he always told me. *"It alters the natural sound of the instrument."* Steve's heavy hand on my stage rig was wearing thin anymore—very thin. His call for no pedals began to ring hollow. All I had to do was look over there at Steve's big-ass pedal board placed right in front of him on the stage floor. I had to start laughing about all of it that night. Like the joke was on me all along. Just one more *cut loose* at the pride o' the farm? If I was going to continue as a guitarist in this group, I needed to try to take some ownership of my own sound for once and for all. It was never more obvious to me than it was on the second show at the Bear. I was looking for a little more grit with my Les, following Steve's wall of crunch coming out of his Fender and huge speaker stack—twice the size of mine. For this set, my F-you arm vibrato was going to be ballsier, and nastier. The left arm was ready for the shaking—my forearm was set to stun mode.

I played my guitar solo section for the umpteenth time in "Rock 'n' Roll Park," but on this night, I got some nice fast runs in there, some good bends and a lot of pretty mean arm vibrato—all with a very cool tone coming out of my amp and out to the house. "Dopp" was lookin' for me back at the sound board, too, he was hoping that I would step on the gas a little more with the guitar. Impressed with my new sound, I played it more naturally—like I played the violin on stage. I hammered my guitar solo home and I got a big cheer from the crowd after it. I was thrilled by how it was feeling, even in my unclear state. As hazy as things were, I definitely could recognize people screaming and cheering. I wasn't too drunk to know what *that* was.

I finally broke through after a year of holding back. Getting a big hand for my electric guitar solo standing next to the maestro was something of a new experience. I looked over at Steve, my tutor, to see if he was enjoying the moment with me, but he was staring straight down at all his stupid pedals and gritting his teeth about something. Okay, I thought: after all this time with him schooling me, maybe Steve simply *missed* my first really good moment on the electric guitar. I moved on.

A few more tunes into the set, several people who were standing at the front of the stage pointed at my bow arm with looks of horror on their faces. I looked down to see that my right hand was bleeding all over the place. I was squeezing the frog of the bow so tight, it had crumbled in my hand from my grip—the jagged edges cutting into the palm of my hand as I played. In my altered state, I didn't even feel it. The fans close to the stage were grossed out over my blood flying everywhere as I bowed my fiddle. After they saw me scramble back to the stage wielding a second violin bow from my case, they gave me another hero's cheer. I just couldn't lose that night. I was in top *rocker* form on every level. As we got off the stage, there was another cute beach girl just hanging out near the backstage door. I had a date for the rest of the evening—everything was looking very good.

Getting out of our gig clothes backstage, the change room had a row of lockers with a gym-like bench running down the length of it. Separated by five to ten feet from each other, we entered our individual lockers we selected before the show. I yelled out to the band, "good one tonight!" Steve placed his guitar on the bench while he retrieved his hard shell case out from the locker. I noticed that he hadn't commented on my broken bow and bloody hand, like the others had. Then he slammed the locker door shut about as hard as he could. It made quite a clamor in there. Everyone looked over at him. Rod asked, in a serious tone: "Steve, everything all right?" Steve flipped his guitar case down onto the cement floor, bringing it flat onto the hard surface with his foot, producing another booming noise. Then he aggressively kicked his guitar case across the polished cement floor where I had to stop it at my ankles.

Steve could've shoved it even harder at me than he did—it was a *measured* hurl. He wasn't looking for a fight or anything, and yet, he looked at me and said, "So you're trying to play faster than me on guitar, now?" Without hesitation, I fired back; "I finally played a guitar solo that the crowd applauded for. Why did you spend all that time teaching me electric guitar if you didn't want me to improve?"

I found that cute girl and got the hell out of there. We had a motel right across from the beach. She and I hung out all night, going back and forth between the room and the beach. To top off my rebellious, drunken rocker altercations at the Golden Bear, she went and gave me some short-term VD to cap off the exciting evening—a full-scale rock and roll experience.

Guitar Player Magazine: Steve Morse, June and August, 1982
"How has Mark O'Connor influenced the band?
'First of all, we're very glad to have the best fiddle player in the world in our band, and we all enjoy doing the country tunes more than ever because he really burns them up. We love his solos. One effect he's had has been psychological: Everyone has become more self-conscious, possibly from his ultra-competitive upbringing. He's a champion at many things. But I think he's adapted to us and vice-versa very well, considering we've all been in bands and he's always been solo or a hired sideman.'"

A few days later we were back in the Bay Area again. I met another beautiful girl at the Santa Cruz Civic Auditorium. Patty and I became fast friends. We could talk for hours. That's what I wanted the most, a lady friend at this stage of my life. I think I could've fallen in love with her, too, but I was so messed up by then, I was no good for any girl past a one-night stand, and not even that. By early 1982, I was still under the drinking age. I couldn't wander back into the very clubs we were playing. Patty could, though, since she was a couple years older. I was always embarrassed that I couldn't get into clubs and bars on the road. Being 20 and a member of a club band was so very frustrating to me, especially when *girls* were hanging out. I was ready to be 21 so badly, but it was still a ways off.

Steve and Rod didn't drink alcohol or take any drugs. On the other hand, T and Andy wouldn't turn down many offers for hits of cocaine that I ever saw. As the band got a little more notorious, there seemed to be more people wanting to *turn the band on* backstage. I asked Andy and T what coke was like? They were into it. There were even concerts where

418

fans held out spoons of coke for the band as we walked up the flight of stairs to the stage. I remember one time, five coke spoons being thrust towards us from either side of the staircase. Looking for further escapes from the band reality, I began to do some blow along with them. It made me feel better about the current undertones. After doing a line, I felt like I could carry on a conversation with about anyone in those clubs—even with Morse. Instantly, everyone seemed so much more interesting than before—and my electric guitar solos grew to be even less standoffish. I suppose you could say, my F-you's were flying now.

BACK AT THE MANAGEMENT OFFICE, I had asked Joel to look out for me on a particular date. June 13th was coming up, and that was the Grand Masters Fiddle Championship in Nashville. They increased their prize money to $1,500 that year. Joel decided to conclude the Dregs run on the 12th at the Beacon Theater in Manhattan. I had no idea if the others were oblivious to the scheduling scheme, or maybe it was just a coincidence. But what a great way to end that run—headlining at the Beacon Theater, our most prestigious show on the road yet. I flew to Nashville in the morning, got there just in time to play my first round, made it to the second round and then won the Grand Masters for the third time, and broke another record for the most wins. A bunch of friends were there: Randy Howard came in 3rd, Texas Shorty came in 5th and Jeff Pritchard from Kansas came in 6th. I could play breakdowns at the top of my form, with literally no practice or preparation—months of loud electric violin all the way to the acoustic white fiddle overnight. At this point, I didn't even try to dress the part of any Texan cowboy fiddler to play this music—the power of *imagining* music and *transporting* myself to another place was already at my behest, at the fullest of my powers. I learned to *dream* myself there as a child musician and I could experience these things seemingly on a whim. Three times the National champion and three times the Grand Masters champion.

Nobody had done that kind of stuff before.

The Idaho Statesman by Tom Knappenberger, June 1982

"WEISER — Mark O'Connor is a competitor. Three grand national fiddling championships in the past three years attest to that.

But this year, he'll be hundreds of miles away when the top fiddlers compete at the National Oldtime Fiddler's Contest in Weiser—sidelined by a rule he inadvertently helped to create.

After the 20-year-old, who now calls Atlanta, Ga., home, won his fourth junior championship in a row five years ago, the city's fiddle committee responded by passing a rule that fiddlers must either move up a division or sit out a year if they win three consecutive division championships.

Unfortunately for O'Connor, there's no step up from the grand championship. There's little doubt, however, O'Connor is itching to compete again...

Although out of the main competition this year, O'Connor said he couldn't resist returning to Weiser, 'I came back to see my friends and to hear some music,' said the shy fiddler, who grew up in Mountlake Terrace, Wash.

One of the friends relaxing with O'Connor Wednesday was Benny Thomasson, a 73-year-old fiddling legend. O'Connor said he was 11 when he met Thomasson in Weiser and the Toledo, Wash., fiddle master 'showed me the tricks of the trade.'

'I showed him some things and he just took off,' Thomasson added.
Only a few of the best fiddlers, like O'Connor, earn a living at it.

'If you want to make it pro, you need to go outside the contest world,' O'Connor said. 'I'm not saying I had it hard; I've had it easy. But that's because I've worked at it all the time.'

Saturday, when his fellow fiddlers vie for the grand national championship in Weiser, O'Connor will be back in Atlanta playing with the Dixie Dregs, a band he joined in early 1981.

O'Connor said he likes the classical, rock, country and jazz numbers the band does because they offer variety. 'I hate to keep playing the same thing over.'"

RECEIVING MY NEW ITINERARY, I was excited to read over the details of our return to the illustrious Fox Theater. The Dregs were quite a well-known band in our hometown of Atlanta—we expected to fill the 4,000-seat hall this time. Things were looking up for the band, and the gigs were finally getting better. June 26th, a Saturday night—the band itinerary said our showtime was at 8 p.m. I was thrilled to play the Fox Theater again, we were booked there the first week I was in the band. What a magnificent place to be, let alone perform in.

I don't remember anything particularly remarkable about our performance, except there were scads of Dregs fans and friends in attendance.

Tom came down to see us. Steve Mastro and Jeff Pinkham were there. Bert from the guitar shop, my guys at the Emile Baran Violin Shop, they were all there. We got rid of the mannequin by then, thankfully. It was gone once we realized that "Crank It Up," was never going to be cranked up on very many radios. But I thought it was a good thing to get rid of our screwy, lifeless "lead singer." The Dregs ground game was building regardless of the squatty airplay. It was a great band, with dedicated audiences, and we sure put in some good performances lately—like the Beacon in NYC. Can't top that with a band like ours. Finally making a little more bread, too. A lot more at the Fox—$800 per man.

State University of NY at Albany, Feb, 26, 1982

"The most imaginative individual figure in Tuesday's show proved to be twenty year old fiddler Mark O'Connor, a three time Grand National Fiddling Champion. O'Connor was afforded extended solo space on [The Bash] and his duets with the virtuoso Morse were very well received. His inclusion [to the band] may have caused the relative commercial success of 'Unsung Heroes.' His handling of earlier Dregs material far surpasses that of the original. He spoke of his upcoming appearance with Merle Haggard for a PBS special focusing on the young musicians of America, to be aired in April."

Tucson Daily Citizen, Tucson, AZ - May 4, 1982

"The show closed with the traditional Dregs' combination of 'The Bash' (an electrically amplified version of 'The Wabash Cannonball') and another high-amp hoedown, 'Cruise Control.' But with O'Connor up there, it was a whole new show.

Lanky and long-haired, wearing green pants and a yellow T-shirt, the 20-year-old fiddler was absolutely magnetic. Though his manner is unassuming, his playing has the power to command.

O'Connor shows a remarkable understanding of his instrument as an electronic device. He plays it as a voice combining qualities of synthesizer and guitar.

As the Dregs worked through 'The Bash,' which everyone in the audience seemed to know line for line, you could feel anticipation building for the fiddle breakdown section at the end. As O'Connor ripped into it, the audience was on its feet, cheering in the same instant."

IT WAS JUST A FEW DAYS after the Fox when I got a call from Joel, our manager. He told me that he had some rather unsettling news;

"I am sorry to report to you that the Dregs have broken up, Mark."

I was shocked. Shocked out of my mind. No one from the band called me to explain what was happening, except for Joel, and he didn't have much to add. Shelly Banks, our new tour manager, and I got together to talk it over, but she really couldn't add anything to the story, other than she thought it was mostly about Steve. She wasn't that familiar with all the band personalities yet. Steve didn't call me to let me know what in the Hell was going on? It was Steve who had me move across the country 3,000 miles to play in his band.

My number was listed in the Atlanta phone book. One night in late July, about a month after the show at the Fox, I got a rather strange call from a Dregs fan;

"Is this Mark O'Connor of the Dregs?"

"Yes, but the Dregs are no longer," I replied.

I could tell the guy was calling from a noisy club of some kind, because I could hear some sort of distorted live music in the background.

"The Dregs are performing and you are not here! They're playing right now, Mark!" The guy said.

"Hold on a second. Where are you calling from?" I asked.

"North Carolina, Mark, where are you? They're playing now!"

"Please, slow down! I need you to tell me how many members of the Dregs are playing on stage?"

"Four: Steve, Andy, T, and Rod," the guy said.

I confirmed with him that there was no violinist on stage, but I felt like I was going to throw up all the same. I felt so utterly rejected and betrayed, after working so hard to learn a band's entire repertoire and to do it as well as anyone could—the many months I put in with half an arm...

All for one, and one for all on that reckless plane flight in New Hampshire came haunting back. So, after all this, the other band members tried to see what it was like without me—the problem child, the "Mr. Champion, Sir" mocking—just to see if they could get Steve re-interested in the band without me around. That is why no one called me to explain, they were ditching me while they worked on Steve.

Their quartet *experiment* lasted all but a couple of weeks, as it turned out. The band broke up for good after that. Nobody wanted to do that material without violin, so Steve threw in the towel. Cutting off all his long hair to become a commercial airline pilot, Steve provided that additional exclamation mark of departure. He was sick of it all. Quite an ending to this quintet, almost as thrilling as the end of my other Quintet.

I was dejected, demoralized—all of this threw me into a panic, knowing I had to find work as a musician on top of it, which for the first time in my own life, was very difficult. After those two bands, I didn't want to just sign up with some dumber-music country band. When I couldn't find much of anything I wanted to do, more depression came on with no outlet to perform on stage. Going from 60 to 0 was a mind trip as a young adult, my head was playing too many games with me. I began to hit the booze more so—the drug-taking increased. That debilitating head pain I got a few times around cigarette smoke… that began to be more persistent. The initial doctor visits in Atlanta provided no explanation for it. I didn't even want to think about Mom's condition and what was happening up in Seattle.

I heard from Joel that the others applied for welfare; the crew *and* the band. Steve evidently had applied for it in the beginning, but he made too much in royalty income to qualify. I could've figured as much. I told Joel that I didn't believe in welfare for myself. I had an able body, I could always swing a hammer like my Dad. I thought I needed more discipline in my life anyway. For a few months I thought about training to become a tennis pro. Far-fetched. For another few months, I thought about joining up with the armed services—not as far-fetched. I felt like I needed to go through some real boot camp, not Grisman's and Morse's musical boot camps anymore. I was done with those. My mind was active and wandering… out of control. Scary. I wanted to find a musical environment that might be more nourishing and less cut-throat for a change

I was still that struggling artist: an esoteric 20-year-old who had been hired to play in two of the greatest instrumental bands in the world, miles apart in musical style, instrumentation, heritage, and geography. I succeeded in replacing both founding members, but had absolutely nothing to show for it now.

EVENTUALLY, SOME OF OUR Dregs membership began to find their way forward. Steve Morse re-entered music full time. In a few years, he joined up with Steve Walsh and Kansas, before becoming a long-time member of the classic rock band Deep Purple. Within no time, Steve and I exchanged appearances on our individual solo recordings. Allen Sloan became both a medical doctor and played concertmaster for the Augusta Symphony where we eventually collaborated on one of my violin concertos. Rod Morgenstein got on the ground floor of a platinum-selling heavy metal band, Winger. Andy West left the music profession altogether to work in computer software. T Lavitz bounced around in several mid-level groups, even got hired by acts we had toured with, Little Feat and the Jefferson Starship, before tragically dying from a heroin overdose.

GOING THROUGH AN OLD STACK of mail—the pile had been sitting around for over a year, embarrassingly, some of those envelopes from fans even longer than that. I guess I had been preoccupied as a member of the Dregs for the last year-and-a-half with a non-stop schedule on the road. I had barely enough time to turn around. Until now. All kinds of time on my hands, these days. Never got back to any of them. Since I was out of work, maybe there was a musician contact in there I overlooked. Maybe some kind of offer to do something, other than sitting in with Mastro and Pinkham at local Atlanta bars in exchange for lines left for me on the back of toilets in bathroom stalls.

Flipping through old letters, one of them postmarked from over a year ago, said it was from Chet Atkins of Nashville. I finally read it, a very kind letter Chet Atkins had written. I'd never met the man besides that one time when I was 13 at the Grand Masters. It was very brief. But here, he was writing about listening to my guitar album, *Markology*. He writes that he's a "fan of my guitar-playing." Chet Atkins is inviting me to Nashville.

Nashville... So much had happened to me since I tried moving to Nashville as a young teenager. My mind was finally settling down some from the band breakup, and things began to clear away. I was having a different premonition for my music now. An abstraction really. I thought I just might be able to introduce my style of fiddle playing into *classical music*. I wasn't at all sure how that would happen yet, but I had some ideas, and *False Dawn* was the beginning of it—maybe a pathway. If it were to happen, I would need to *compose my way there*. I wasn't about to take classical violin lessons—working up the Mendelssohn violin concerto or something like that. I loved the music, but so many others could play it. Thousands could play it well. That just wasn't my path. But I did learn this much; both David Grisman and Steve Morse broke down walls for their own instruments in a unique fashion first and foremost. They were looking out for their mandolins and their electric guitars; everything else seemed to be a distant second to them. I wanted to look for scenarios where my composing and creativity was encouraged, and where I could feature the fiddle and put it out front.

But I did get a lot better as a player during these tenures, and I saw up close how top composers got their music prepared for performances and recordings. Boy, did I ever see that up close. The boot camp for musicians: Jump. *How high? Can I jump even higher for you? Is 4' 6" high enough— while riding a skateboard?*

I had more or less concluded that Nashville wasn't for me any longer. Out of a job, and broke, Shelly Banks had helped me send my resume out to several jazz-rock bands, but no one got back to me. I probably should've gotten back to him, though. Chet Atkins that is: "Mr. Guitar," they call him, the president of RCA Records, the producer of Elvis Presley. My God. Shelly agreed that it was the wrong man to snub for a year. Giggling over it a little, she said, "It's not too late, Mark."

"That's your ticket. It's been sitting there in this stack of mail right under your nose this whole time."

I took stock of what music gave me at this point in my young life. I could still win the big fiddle contests, but there wasn't enough of them to keep me busy, keep me going—plus I was growing bored of all that. Pinkham said to me, "Why don't you tour around the country as the national fiddle champion?" I could sense there was something else in the air.

Of all things, a young violinist from the esteemed Chicago Symphony called me for a violin lesson. Fox Fehling told me, "You are like a Mozart." She flew down to take one lesson from me and insisted on paying me $200 for it. "It's what a private lesson cost me at Juilliard, and you are worth every penny they are getting," she said. Fox was interested in my fiddling, creativity and improvisation, the use of the bow, my rhythm, and the various styles I could play in. It was quite flattering to hear about all this. She was playing one of my transcriptions of a fiddle tune during an orchestra break, when their conductor, maestro Georg Solti, walked by and asked,

"Who is the composer of this music?" He was intrigued by it. She said the transcription was from my first album, when I was 12.

Fox Fehling invited me to perform a concert of fiddle standards and swing classics with a few members of the Chicago Symphony. They called themselves the CSO Okies. Burl Lane, the orchestra's principal contra-bassoonist who doubled as the saxophone player in the group, told me that nearly the entire first violin section was in the audience for it.

In time to come, the Chicago Symphony Orchestra gave the world premiere of my "Double Violin Concerto" at their summer home in Ravinia. Classical violin virtuoso Nadja Salerno-Sonnenberg and I were the two violin soloists.

I started to teach Pinkham weekly fiddle lessons. Not for $200 or any-thing—more like $20. I began to formulate a lesson plan for beginners.

"Jeff, you gotta learn 'Boil 'em Cabbage Down' before anything else. That's what I did and it worked! It led me to everything."

"So, not practice 'Twinkle, Twinkle Little Star?'" Pinkham asked.

"No, skip it," I told him. "It's good as the alphabet song, but not for the violin. I don't like that Suzuki Method."

Eventually Shar Music released the O'Connor Method for violin.

Of course, I saw him on TV growing up—Chet Atkins that is. Had those guitar records he did with Jerry Reed. Yeah, I should've gotten back to him all right. Chet Atkins writes in his letter that he's inviting me to Nashville to meet with him at his office on Music Row. Even though I'm barely out of my teens, I've been around a little: "Mr. Guitar" didn't seem like he was just *playin'*. I wondered what this could mean for my music? For the fiddle as well as my guitar?

If fiddle contests were becoming uninteresting to me, would country fiddle hold my attention anymore? Or would *my own* version of country fiddle be the entire point of it? I was probably too different for Nashville anyway—too intense and probably too crazy to be playing country music or to work in recording sessions like I'd hoped to do when I was younger. I dressed like a rocker, too. That couldn't help me any. Feather earrings, one in each ear. Purple and yellow pants, sandals—long hair *way past the collar.* Even wore women's shirts—found them more interesting. I was not a chillin' laid-back hippie. Far from it. I was high-strung. I could be as tightly wound as Morse or Grisman.

I had no idea what Chet Atkins had in mind yet, but I could use another mentor, one who was nicer to me, hopefully. Maybe a bit more mellow. I wanted to know more about music, still I wanted to know more about *my* music. Like *DownBeat Magazine* wrote: I lived a whole lifetime in my first 20 years. But, the way I saw it, I still needed to grow—I had to put all of that kid stuff behind me, let go of the "child prodigy years." I wanted to forget I was ever 12 years old. Cast it all out. I needed to *outrun* my own childhood in music.

It was time to take charge of my own musical destiny. While the boss-men got what they needed from me—in order to help themselves—they showed me what it looks like to fight for your own art. Where my music led me next, would be of little consequence to them, now. On the other hand, the passion from my fiddle teachers was ceaseless. Benny Thomasson and Stephane Grappelli considered me their legacy. I wasn't entirely on my own—with both of them still around.

This is the power I learned as a young professional musician. No matter how much you think you know, you're never done learning something—just as a teenaged Marty Stuart told me when I was a little kid. I learned that even your fiercest competitors are your teachers, and that didn't stop at the fiddle contest's door. I called Mom and told her I was on my way up to Seattle to visit for a while, and I had an idea for us. It would require one last trip in our yellow Ford Econoline van, for old times' sake. Mom was at her happiest on the road—with her son and his fiddle *daring* the world. My sister Michelle said that she would go with us and help drive.

Within a couple of months, Mom would be gone. The final time she ever saw me perform was on that trip in the van. We rode together that September to Kerrville, Texas where I finally won the world mandolin championship. Parked at the top of the ravine, the back doors were open so she could enjoy the music, but when the awards ceremony took place something else happened. Mom made it down that rocky, dusty hill on her own strength and seated herself in the front row. One false step and she would have broken in half. When they called my name out for the 1st place trophy, I spotted her. At first, I thought I was seeing her ghost. Everything slowed down, like a film in slow motion. All I could do was stare at Mom with her genuine cheek-to-cheek Duchenne smile. She was making sure I would never outrun a childhood like mine.

DownBeat Magazine, June 1982

"O'Connor is quite candid about the changes he's gone through recently. 'A lot of stuff has happened to me during the past year and much of it is emotional,' he said. 'That's been the hardest part for me to conquer, but the music is a relief. When I do get to play it, on-stage, I realize this is my natural being, and although I know I'm missing a lot, like books and other things, I don't want to tamper with the natural expression of life that I'm doing right now. I want to keep doing this until I become successful in my mind. I'm not even sure whether that means the fact that many people know my name or that I'm financially well-off, and I don't know when I'll be satisfied or when I'll ever have enough. I don't think I'll ever have enough, but then again that's me talking when I'm 20 years old, before I'm burned out. Music is such a big art and it's everywhere and to go around the world and just record and play music would be the greatest. Right now I'm just happy to have had the opportunity to be a member of two of the best instrumental bands in the world.'"

INDEX

v

CPSIA information can be obtained
at www.ICGtesting.com
Printed in the USA
JSHW040339140223
37676JS00002B/2